# The Best American
# Travel Writing 2020

GUEST EDITORS OF
THE BEST AMERICAN TRAVEL WRITING

2000 BILL BRYSON
2001 PAUL THEROUX
2002 FRANCES MAYES
2003 IAN FRAZIER
2004 PICO IYER
2005 JAMAICA KINCAID
2006 TIM CAHILL
2007 SUSAN ORLEAN
2008 ANTHONY BOURDAIN
2009 SIMON WINCHESTER
2010 BILL BUFORD
2011 SLOANE CROSLEY
2012 WILLIAM T. VOLLMANN
2013 ELIZABETH GILBERT
2014 PAUL THEROUX
2015 ANDREW MCCARTHY
2016 BILL BRYSON
2017 LAUREN COLLINS
2018 CHERYL STRAYED
2019 ALEXANDRA FULLER
2020 ROBERT MACFARLANE

# The Best American Travel Writing™ 2020

Edited with an Introduction
by **Robert Macfarlane**

Jason Wilson, Series Editor

MARINER BOOKS

HOUGHTON MIFFLIN HARCOURT

BOSTON • NEW YORK   2020

hmhbooks.com

ISSN 1530-1516 (print)     ISSN 2537-4830 (e-book)
ISBN 978-0-358-36203-6 (print)     ISBN 978-0-358-36204-3 (e-book)

Printed in the United States of America
DOC 10 9 8 7 6 5 4 3 2 1

# Contents

# Foreword

BY THE TIME I finished my editorial work on this year's edition of Best American Travel Writing—about five weeks into my state's mandatory stay-at-home order—I'd had plenty of time to think about the future of the form. During the first few weeks of lockdown, I was invited on to a podcast with several other travel writers to discuss our predictions. With gloom and doom, I speculated about magazines suspending publication, compared this to how travel had "irrevocably" changed after 9/11, and declared that this was "the extinction event" for a certain type of travel publishing. To be honest, I had no more idea of what might happen than anyone else, and I still don't. But I held forth anyway, and I am aware that whatever I write here in the spring of 2020 may seem naive, hysterical, or wildly inaccurate by the fall, when the anthology is published, never mind a year or five from now.

Otherwise, I have whiled away the days in isolation thinking a lot about oddly divergent (and convergent) things: Iceland, Robert Byron's classic travel book *The Road to Oxiana,* and the pond across from my home in New Jersey—where an alligator, according to local legend, may or may not live.

My musings on Iceland were spurred, no doubt, by the fact that two of the most noteworthy pieces in this year's anthology deal with that country: Lacy Johnson's moving piece on "How to Mourn a Glacier" in this time of climate change, and Kyle Chayka's "My Own Private Iceland," about its current state of overtourism. In Chayka's piece, he argues for "inauthentic" travel, suggesting that "when a destination is deemed dead might be the best time to go there, as the most accurate reflection of our impure world" and declares that "the less authentic an experience was supposed to be in Iceland, the more fun I had and the more aware I was of the consequences of 21st century travel."

While an excellent, funny, and insightful meditation on the current state of travel, Chayka's piece also made me incredibly sad and yearning for an era of my own past, my own private Iceland of the late 1990s and early 2000s. I spent a lot of time in Iceland then, living for short periods in Reykjavík, and traveling the island extensively.

It would be misleading and disingenuous to call this pre-Instagram time "authentic," though when I first arrived there, lots of Icelanders still believed in elves, there was no gourmet coffee, and it was not uncommon to see Björk at a hot-dog stand or to catch her doing a late-night guest-DJ set. I remember being so taken by Icelandic moss—so prevalent and vivid, so many varieties and hues —that I foolishly smuggled a few samples back into the United States (pre-TSA) to try to grow in my yard. This feels like another lifetime.

Back then, when you traveled around the Icelandic countryside, you didn't need to book in advance for a hotel. Airbnb did not exist. In the summers, one of the cheapest places to stay was in the dorms of the secondary schools, emptied for vacation, which cost slightly less if you brought your own sheets and pillowcases. The tiny towns at the end of ice-blue fjords were pungent with the smell of fish factories, and, besides the working port, consisted only of a community geothermal swimming pool, a few shops, an Esso station that doubled as a bakery, café, and hot-dog stand, and a chain restaurant called Pizza 67 that specialized in "Hawaii" pizza, with pineapple and ham.

I once visited the Herring Era Museum in the northern village of Siglufjördur, dedicated to the booming early-20th-century herring industry, which eventually went bust from overfishing. I spent an afternoon there chatting with one of the museum docents, a young blonde woman dressed in a flannel shirt and big rubber boots, what the so-called herring girls wore during the boom when they spent all day packing salted fish into barrels. I was so taken by all the nostalgia that I enthusiastically accepted the Herring Girl's invitation to go hiking after her shift. We climbed to a waterfall high above the fjord, picked purple wildflowers, then swam in a hot spring.

She laughed hysterically when I asked if she believed in elves. As she removed her work costume and slid into the steaming water, she showed me her tattoo of Tupac Shakur and cursed being trapped in this tiny remote town. She wanted nothing more than to move to Reykjavík as soon as possible, dye her hair black, and find work in a fashion boutique or a cocktail bar. Chasing authenticity in travel has always been slippery—a Gordian knot, a nesting doll, an onion.

I've been thinking a lot about the strange travel books that British writers produced in the decades between the two world wars. A time of serious upheaval and disruption to travel—a complete breakdown of what had been the narrative of journeying. The great travel writing of that era, books such as D. H. Lawrence's *Sea and Sardinia,* Graham Greene's *Journey Without Maps,* or Rebecca West's *Black Lamb and Grey Falcon,* began to explore new forms. The itineraries, trips to Italy or Africa or the Balkans, were similar to previous generations', but the writers began employing modernist techniques borrowed from fiction and poetry: fragmentation, collage, juxtaposition, dialogue-driven scenes. This was a period when, as the critic Paul Fussell says, "writing travel books was not at all considered incompatible with a serious literary career."

One of the strangest books of this era is Robert Byron's *The Road to Oxiana.* "What *Ulysses* is to the novel between the wars and what *The Waste Land* is to poetry, *The Road to Oxiana* is to the travel book," said Fussell. Bruce Chatwin called it a "masterpiece." It's ostensibly a travelogue about Islamic architecture, charting a course across the Middle East, Afghanistan, and Iran. But the book quickly veers into a wild stew of diary entries, mini-essays and rants on politics and art history, twenty comic dialogues (almost playlets), news clippings, and fragmented notes. At some points, the book feels almost unhinged, and may or may not glide into fiction. Tom Bissell once described *The Road to Oxiana* as "reportage and analysis, travelogue and autobiography, fiction and nonfiction. It did not happen, but it did." It's no wonder that *The Road to Oxiana* was held up as a "sacred text" by writers like Chatwin as, during the 1980s, travel writing once again went through a revolution of form.

In the months that have passed since my pessimistic podcast appearance, I've had a change of heart about the future of travel writing. Of course it will survive, as it has before, even if the publishing models radically change. Travel writers, once again, will embrace new forms, experiment, borrow from other genres, and find novel approaches. Many people have also suggested that, once we're free from lockdown, more modest domestic or local travel, rather than exotic foreign adventures, will take center stage. They say narratives about home might become significant and popular. Perhaps.

When I think of local travel, I think of Hopkins Pond, a small body of water in the wooded park near my home in Haddonfield, New Jersey. The park is not very well maintained by the county, but on sunny days it's still beautiful. I often take long walks there around the edge of the pond, where I'll encounter a handful of people fishing, joggers, or families riding bikes. In most ways, it's a completely typical suburban recreational area.

Not far from Hopkins Pond is the place where the world's first complete dinosaur skeleton was discovered in 1858. A National Historic Site plaque marks the spot. They named it the Hadrosaurus, but in Haddonfield it now goes by the nickname Haddy. When they dug up Haddy's bones, the Victorian media of the era went into a frenzy with the discovery of a true-to-life monster, and journalists from all over the world came to Haddonfield. I've always loved this part of our town history.

A century and a half later there was another discovery, accompanied by a minor panic, when my neighbors and a local policeman spotted what they thought was an alligator swimming in the water of the lake. I very much welcomed the excitement of a large reptile living across the street in my neighborhood pond. I was hopeful that a little exotic danger and intrigue might find its way into what is normally a quiet town.

The alligator was estimated to be around four feet long, and when a police sergeant arrived on the scene, he saw the reptile feasting on a goose. For a few days, our woods were roped off with yellow tape, and TV news helicopters hovered overhead. A sign by my son's school read PLEASE JOIN OUR EFFORTS IN KEEPING OUR CHILDREN AWAY FROM THE AREA UNTIL IT IS SAFE. A guy from the Philadelphia Zoo was quoted in the newspaper as saying, "It's not going to go rampaging through neighborhoods, but I would not take my teacup poodle on a walk around that pond."

I had hoped our alligator in Hopkins Pond would take up permanent, mysterious residence, and that it might grow from four feet into a real monster. After all, right around the same time, in Los Angeles's Lake Machado, there were sightings of an elusive alligator named Reggie. By the time the city caught Reggie, he was over eight feet long. But Hopkins Pond was not Los Angeles. After those initial sightings in our pond, whatever reptile had been seen simply disappeared. A year went by without any sightings, then longer. The freezing winters surely would have killed an alligator, people said. After a few years, most people figured the story of the Hopkins Pond alligator was simply make-believe. The local police began characterizing the alligator sighting as "unfounded." About five years after our alligator sighting in Hopkins Pond, there was finally another, a few miles away in the Cooper River. This reptile, too, was said to be four feet long. It made me happy to think that our gator had perhaps survived the cold winters and made it to a larger body of water. They never caught the reptile in Cooper River, either. And no one ever saw it again.

It had been some time since I'd thought about our local reptiles, but during lockdown the only "travel" I'd really been doing was a daily walk around the pond. Early spring buds, ducks, our boring New Jersey, non-Icelandic moss. Of course, I was keeping my eyes peeled for any hints that our alligator still exists.

It occurred to me that I could write a travel article about the pond. And that's what I intended to do: to take some notes on my next walk, do some reportage. Then, a few days later, the governor of New Jersey shut down the parks. For the moment, the only travel essay I could write about Hopkins Pond would have to exist in the same nostalgic space as Iceland or Oxiana.

On my short-lived local nature walks, it struck me that Robert Macfarlane, who over the past decade has reinvented and reinvigorated nature writing (travel writing's close cousin), was the perfect person to have worked with as guest editor on this year's anthology. He's already thought deeply about challenging form in writing about place (and of moss).

In *The Old Ways*, Macfarlane insists that too often we only think of landscapes as affecting us when we are in them. "But," he writes, "there are also the landscapes we bear with us in absentia, those places that live on in memory long after they have withdrawn in actuality, and such places—retreated to most often when we are most remote from them—are among the most important landscapes we possess."

Being forced to stay at home in isolation might be the ultimate in so-called inauthentic travel. Yet it offers a frighteningly accurate reflection of our world and the consequences of journeying in it. Now that I sit with the nostalgia of the pre-pandemic places I once loved to visit, perhaps those landscapes I carry inside will become the only authenticity worth exploring.

The stories included here are, as always, selected from among dozens of pieces in dozens of diverse publications—from mainstream glossies to cutting-edge websites to Sunday newspaper travel sections to literary journals to niche magazines. I've done my best to be fair and representative, and in my opinion the best travel stories from 2019 were forwarded to Robert Macfarlane, who made our final selections. I'm grateful to Alicia Kennedy for her essential assistance with this year's collection, as well as to Jessica Vestuto and Nicole Angeloro at Houghton Mifflin Harcourt.

I now begin anew by reading the travel stories published in 2020. As I have for years, I am asking editors and writers to submit the best of whatever it is they define as travel writing—the wider the better. These submissions must be nonfiction, and published in the United States during the 2020 calendar year. They must not be reprints or excerpts from published books. They must include the author's name, date of publication, and publication name, and must be tear sheets, the complete publication, or a clear photocopy of the piece as it originally appeared. I must receive all submissions by January 1, 2021, in order to ensure full consideration for the next collection.

Further, publications that want to make certain their contributions will be considered for the next edition should make sure to include this anthology on their subscription list. Submissions or subscriptions should be sent to: Jason Wilson, Best American Travel Writing, 230 Kings Highway East, Suite 192, Haddonfield, NJ 08033.

JASON WILSON

# Introduction

I WRITE FROM A world in which travel has stopped. Around half of the planet's population is presently under lockdown. Apartment block doors are welded shut. Police set checkpoints on major roads. National borders have closed. We find ourselves trapped within concentric confinements: home, city, region, nation. During this state of exception, we shelter in place.

Place itself is changing around us, though. Cities, neighborhoods, and landscapes have become defamiliarized to the point of unrecognizability. Central Park is crammed with white tents—scores of marquees have sprung up almost overnight, like a riot of mushrooms after spring rain. From a distance, out of context, it looks like a medieval jousting tournament or a music festival. But it's a field hospital. This isn't a world's fair come to New York, it's a world war. California's highways are a location-scout's dream for a romantic road movie or a zombie apocalypse: scarcely a car in sight, the motels standing empty.

Not all the changes are grim. Blue spring skies can now be seen above Delhi, London, Wuhan: clear of contrail graffiti, the cauls of smog thinned almost to nothing. Birdsong is newly bright on the ear, unmasked by the absence of traffic noise. A friend calls from southwest London, where she lives under the Heathrow flight-path and wakes usually to the roar of the first planes. *I've never really heard the dawn chorus before! Is it always like this?* Yes, I say, I think it probably is. You live in a wildwood of a megacity, with a tree for almost every one of its nine million or so citizens . . .

Setting down these sentences, I've found myself flickering in and out of disbelief. They fall from the mind of a dystopian novelist, surely, not a travel writer. But no, these are the realities of the time. Even the cosmopolitan world-traveler—passport a collage of customs stamps and visa stickers—is suddenly grounded. Meanwhile the virus probes hairline cracks in global systems, finding most victims among the most vulnerable. If the long biopolitical history of pandemics has taught us one easily memorable but frequently forgotten thing, it is the falsity of oratorical generalizations about how disease does not discriminate. Inequality is a comorbidity. Environmental degradation and public health justice are inseparable. In New York, the COVID-19 death-distribution map echoes poverty and deprivation maps of the same districts. In Gaza, where there are 40 ICU beds and 56 ventilators for two million people who live in a permanent confinement, the virus will rip killingly through the population in coming weeks. These outcomes aren't indiscriminate tolls, they're tracings of power.

Travel has stopped, but writing, reading, and dreaming about travel have not—they've surged. Lockdown has triggered a greed for what cannot now be done as we restlessly pace our cages. People's bodies are anchored, so they journey in imagination and memory. We have all become versions of Xavier de Maistre, the 18th-century aristocrat, soldier, and author who wrote *Voyage autour de ma chambre* (Voyage Around My Room [1794]), when confined to his room in Turin for six weeks after being arrested for his part in a duel. "When I travel through my room, I rarely follow a straight line: I go from the table towards a picture hanging in a corner; from there, I set out obliquely towards the door . . ."

On Twitter and Instagram, millions ransack their image-archives to post photographs of where they have been, and where they will go when This Is All Over. New online communities have spontaneously self-generated, celebrating and documenting journeys no one can now make. A young Indian naturalist, Yuvan Aves, takes his Instagram followers on "guided walks" of the Chennai coastline each day, stopping at landmarks, documenting the birdlife and sea-life of the coast, the shells and cephalopods cast up in the wrack-line: all of this done from memory and pre-taken photographs. A British writer, Julian Hoffman, who lives in the Prespa Lakes region of southern Europe, where three national borders (Greece, Albania, North Macedonia) converge, has turned his social media feeds into unfolding natural-historical deep maps of his remarkable home-landscape.

I miss two things most in lockdown: my parents and the mountains. I live in Cambridgeshire, a region of Fens, a county so flat —as the old joke goes—that you could fax it. A county so flat (Bill Bryson's quip, this) that you can stand on a chair and see into Norfolk, the next-door county. There are two chalk hills a mile or so from my suburban home, which rise to the dizzying heights of 76 meters above sea level: that's as Alpine as it gets round here. So when lockdown began I decided to find a way to travel to the mountains without leaving home. I set up a book group on Twitter to read Nan Shepherd's slender masterpiece *The Living Mountain,* written in the 1940s—at another time of world crisis—but not published until 1977. Thousands of people from more than 30 countries joined the group, and over the course of three weeks we walked virtually together "into" both Shepherd's prose and the Cairngorm Mountains of northeast Scotland where it is set. As I write, we're still walking. Thousands of comments, replies, memories, photographs, and creative responses have been posted by the community. A nurse wrote to tell me that after coming back from 14-hour shifts in intensive care on a COVID ward she would log on to join the journey, finding it allowed her to escape temporarily from the horrors of the front line. Is this travel, and travel writing, though no one has moved anywhere? It is to me, for now at least.

I chose the pieces gathered in this anthology in February 2020, back in a former world. In those weeks, the novel coronavirus was —to most outside East Asia at least—a distant storm, squalling somewhere over southern China. We'd known such things before: SARS, MERS, H1N1. . . . It would be contained elsewhere, affect other lives. As we now know, what we experienced then as calmness was in fact the drawing back of the ocean that precedes the tsunami.

On what I recall as the last normal day—the last day before futures began to foreclose, the last day when you could go for hours without mentioning or even thinking of the virus—I traveled with my graduate students on a field trip to Orford Ness, one of the eeriest landscapes I know. The Ness, as it's usually called, is a 12-mile-long shingle spit off the coast of the county of Suffolk, in the east of England. For seven decades in the 20th century, it was used as a weapons testing site by British and American states: initially for "lethality and vulnerability" testing of conventional ballistics during World Wars I and II, and then for the "stress testing" of nuclear weapons, especially their detonators, during the Cold War. You get across to the Ness by boat, and though I've been there more than 20 times in the last 15 years, it still feels like a border crossing: from the chocolate-box English coastal village of Orford to the secret shadow-world of the Ness, where crumbling ferroconcrete laboratories stand as relics of a globalized geography of ultraviolence.

That day, my students and I jokingly referred to the field trip as a "journey to the Terminal Beach." Certainly it felt as if we had entered a short story by J. G. Ballard, or been signed up as extras in Andrei Tarkovsky's film *Stalker*. W. G. Sebald writes of Orford Ness in his masterpiece of "long-distance mental travel," *The Rings of Saturn* (1995), and evokes these slippages of time and space: "Where and in what time I truly was that day at Orfordness," says his narrator, "I cannot say, even now as I write these words." We returned from the Ness similarly disoriented—and woke up the next morning to a transformed world: lockdown preparations underway, stock-market graphs like falling Himalayan ridgelines, travelers desperately scrambling home from holidays and business trips.

So to read the pieces gathered in this volume now is to experience a peculiar kind of double vision: to be struck again by their individual excellence and by their diversity as a gathered group, but also to see many of them anew in light of the convulsions the world has undergone since my first encounter with them. Revisiting Heidi Julavits's "What I Learned in Avalanche School," for instance, I understood it in part as a prescient meditation on prescience: a long exploration of how to read and heed warning signs in order to foretell and thus forestall a possible future catastrophe. Kyle Chayka's "My Own Private Iceland" reads as uncannily premonitory of the forms of virtualized and disembodied travel that have proliferated under lockdown. Chayka—a Baudrillard for the 21st century, but far funnier—explores "overtourism" in Iceland. Much of that small country has become a version of what Don DeLillo parodied in *White Noise* (1984) as "the most photographed barn in America": a location whose self-generating layers of mediation have become its identity, smothering whatever "real" place might once have existed there. Much of what Chakya lovingly skewers here—the mass consumption and exhaustion of destinations, the prioritization of "engagement over originality"—is likely to be collapsed, at least temporarily, by coronavirus, even as the "simulations and the fictions" he describes are thickened by it.

I must stop. I run the risk of COVID-izing everything; a symptomatic side-effect of the pandemic. There was life before this virus and there will be life after, even if future global historians will divide 21st-century history into the eras of BC, DC, and AC: before coronavirus, during coronavirus, and after coronavirus. There are other crises burning on, crises that preceded this pandemic and that will outlast it, from the "slow violence"—in Rob Nixon's durable phrase—of climate change, to the everyday sufferings of migrants, refugees, and other immiserated groups. These crises are recognized in this collection too, and by diverse voices. I think here of Jackie Bryant's brief "Life, Death, and the Border Patrol," about kindness and distress on the Mexican-American border; Paul Salopek's dispatches from his epic walk in the footsteps of restless humanity; Lacy Johnson's profound discussion of what it might mean to "mourn a glacier," at a time when we are "witnessing geological time collapse on a human scale"; Mojgan Ghazirad's journey to Iran, recording and evoking the damage US sanctions have brought to everyday life there; Ken Budd asking hard questions about how best to do good far from home, when volunteering in a Kenyan orphanage; Emmanuel Iduma's experimental, Barthesian letter to a stranger; and Emily Raboteau's brilliant "Climate Signs," which may travel no farther in space than the five boroughs of New York, but is planetary in terms of its attempt "to grasp the effects of global warming on the place where we live."

Other themes and threads bind these pieces together, and one of them is lostness. This finds its strongest expression in Molly McCully Brown's extraordinary account of feeling "always lost," due in part to the oxygen deprivation she suffered at birth, which injured the neural structures that allow orientation. Brown cannot find her way alone to the banks of a river half a mile away from her home, despite having made the journey many times with help; she can't make a voyage to the end of her room without crashing into furniture. Reading her work reminded me of the etymology of the word "travel," from the Latin *trepalium,* meaning "a three-pronged instrument of torment." Despite or because of the challenges she faces, Brown is a compulsive traveler: "Constant motion camouflages the extent to which I'm alien even to myself." Her essay intertwines in arresting ways with Fred Bahnson's account of foot-stepping the American mystic Thomas Merton along the Californian coast, to his monastic retreat among "immense silent redwoods." Bahnson's own journey itself braids with Merton's, and provokes Bahnson to open his own heart to himself in surprising ways. The essay asks hard questions for hard times: "Can we redeem the desire to run *from* and turn it into a desire to run *toward*? If so, toward what?" and—Merton's, this—"What can we gain by sailing to the moon if we are not able to cross the abyss that separates us from ourselves?" I recalled that line when reading Yiyun Li's heartbreaking meditation on travel in the aftermath of her son's suicide. Her essay exists in that "abyss," even explores the possibility of making it a long-term dwelling-place. "I repeatedly found myself disoriented," she writes; like Brown, but for different reasons, Li discovers that finding herself has become near impossible.

"Perhaps all places—landlocked or surrounded by water—are islands," writes Li. In Welsh, "self-isolation" translates as *hunan ynysu,* meaning literally "self-islanding." We are all living on islands right now, waving across the water to one another in fear and love. At such moments literature realizes urgent new versions of its old powers: carrying hope, creating connections, transporting readers to other-worlds, and imagining alternative presents and alternative futures. The COVID-19 crisis has taken many things from us, but it has also reminded people about what they value most, and for many whom I know, writing—perhaps especially travel writing—has been a vital part of this reckoning.

Our word "quarantine" is from the early-modern Venetian term *quarantena,* meaning "40 days"; the length of time a ship needed to remain isolated before its crew and passengers would be allowed to disembark during the Black Death epidemics of the 14th and 15th centuries. An old practice, then, repurposed for a globalized contemporary world. What will travel look like by the time the coronavirus outbreak has been brought under control globally? What will it look like by the time people read this introduction for the first time, in November of 2020? One certain consequence will be the severe tightening of restrictions on freedoms of movement. Tough extra layers of bureaucracy will be introduced. Forehead scanners will join passport scanners at immigration controls.

Travelers will fear quarantine upon arrival in a foreign country, so will travel far less. The World Tourism Organization counted 1.4 billion international tourists in 2018, and predicted—before coronavirus—1.8 billion by 2030. That rise will not now happen, thankfully.

For travel writing, coronavirus will lead to a cinching of the curtilage. Those easefully epic journeys, when a travel desk might commission a writer to switch hemispheres for a week or a weekend, will diminish (desirably so, to my mind). Travel writing will tend toward the deep rather than the wide; new localisms and regionalisms will emerge, new forms of attention and description will be required, and encounters with difference and otherness will often occur a few dozen or hundred miles, rather than several thousand, from one's own home. Many travel writers will likely become—to borrow a phrase used of my friend Roger Deakin, whose classic book *Waterlog* (1999) involved him swimming *through* Britain, via its rivers, lakes, lochs, and streams—"explorers of the undiscovered country of the nearby."

In this respect, the coronavirus crisis might be seen to stand as the mirror-point to a crisis experienced by travel writing half a century ago, brought about then by the newly widespread availability of international air travel. In the course of the 1970s, flight became increasingly affordable, and globalization was starting to standardize even far-flung places. Tourism was just beginning its metamorphosis into, in Chayka's phrase, "not a localized phenomenon . . . but an omnipresent condition, like climate change or the internet." This posed complex challenges for what might be called Anglophone travel-writing's regrettable late-imperial mode, whereby the discovery of terra incognita was the default aim, and the heroic male adventurer the default protagonist. How was the "other" to be encountered when the world was so swiftly becoming self-similar? How was adventure to be performed upon such a crowded stage? In 1984 Susan Sontag famously diagnosed the problem as fatal to the form, declaring travel writing to have become a "literature of disappointment," unable—like the empires that had produced it—to come to terms with its dwindling domain and diminished responsibilities. Sontag was wrong, though. The crisis of territory didn't kill travel writing, it revolutionized it. Travel writing was in dire need of both decolonization and redirection, and the best writers rose to the challenge by seeking not originality of destination, but originality of form and sensitivity of encounter.

That earlier crisis was a function of travel's drastic expansion; the COVID crisis will result in travel's drastic contraction. In the past few locked-down weeks, as I make my voyages to the end of my small suburban garden and back, I have found myself thinking several times of Robin Wall Kimmerer's remarks in her beautiful book of (among many other things) microtravel, *Gathering Moss*. "Mosses and other small beings issue an invitation to dwell for a time right at the limits of ordinary perception," she writes there. "All it requires of us is attentiveness. Look in a certain way and a whole new world can be revealed." In the months and years ahead, we will all need to learn to become better at seeing moss.

ROBERT MACFARLANE

# The Best American
# Travel Writing 2020

# Rick Steves Wants to Set You Free

FROM *The New York Times Magazine*

RICK STEVES CAN tell you how to avoid having your pocket picked on the subway in Istanbul. He can tell you where to buy cookies from cloistered Spanish nuns on a hilltop in Andalusia. He can tell you approximately what percentage of Russia's gross domestic product comes from bribery. He can teach you the magic idiom that unlocks perfectly complementary gelato flavors in Florence ("What marries well?").

But Rick Steves does not know his way around New York City.

"In the Western Hemisphere," Steves told me one afternoon last March, "I am a terrible traveler."

We were, at that moment, very much inside the Western Hemisphere, 4,000 miles west of Rome, inching through Manhattan in a hired black car. Steves was in the middle of a grueling speaking tour of the United States: 21 cities in 34 days. New York was stop No. 17. He had just flown in from Pittsburgh, where he had spent less than 24 hours, and he would soon be off to Los Angeles, Denver, and Dallas. In his brief windows of downtime, Steves did not go out searching for quaint restaurants or architectural treasures. He sat alone in his hotel rooms, clacking away on his laptop, working on new projects. His whole world, for the time being, had been reduced to a concrete blur of airports, hotels, lecture halls, and media appearances.

In this town car, however, rolling through Midtown, Steves was brimming with delight. He was between a TV interview at the New York Stock Exchange and a podcast at CBS, and he seemed as enchanted by all the big-city bustle as the most wide-eyed tourist.

"Look at all the buildings!" he exclaimed. "There's so much energy! Man, oh, man!"

A woman crossed the street pushing two Yorkies in a stroller.

"How cute!" Steves shouted.

The town car crawled toward a shabby metal hulk spanning the East River.

"Wow!" Steves said. "Is that the Brooklyn Bridge?"

It was almost the opposite of the Brooklyn Bridge. The Brooklyn Bridge is one of the most recognizable structures in the world: a stretched stone cathedral. This was its unloved upriver cousin, a tangle of discolored metal, vibrating with cars, perpetually under construction. The driver told Steves that it was the Ed Koch Queensboro Bridge—or, as most New Yorkers still thought of it, the 59th Street Bridge.

This revelation only increased Steves's wonder.

"The Fifty-Ninth Street Bridge!" he said. "That's one of my favorite songs!"

With buoyant enthusiasm, Steves started to sing Simon and Garfunkel's classic 1966 tune "The 59th Street Bridge Song (Feelin' Groovy)," a skippy tune about slowing down and taking your time and enjoying yourself.

"Just — kickin' down the cobblestones," he sang.

The car hit traffic and lurched to a stop. Steves paused to scan the street outside. "Where are the cobblestones?" he asked. Then he refocused. He finished the song with a flourish: "Lookin' for fun and feelin'—GROOOVYYYYYY!"

There was a silence in the car.

"Can you imagine those two guys walking around right here?" Steves said. "Just feeling groovy? Gosh, that's cool."

Steves pulled out his phone and, for his online fans, recorded a video of himself singing "The 59th Street Bridge Song (Feelin' Groovy)."

"It's fun to be in New York City," he signed off. "Happy travels!"

There was another silence in the car, this one longer.

"You know," the driver said finally, "you're not very different than you are on your show."

This was correct. The driver was referring to Steves's long-running, widely syndicated, family-friendly public-television travel series *Rick Steves' Europe,* on which Steves is a joyful and jaunty host, all eager-beaver smiles and expressive head tilts. With a backpack

over one shoulder and a hand tucked into his pocket, Steves gushes
poetically about England's Lake District ("a lush land steeped in
a rich brew of history, culture, and nature"), and Erfurt, Germany
("this half-timbered medieval town with a shallow river gurgling
through its center"), and Istanbul ("this sprawling metropolis on
the Bosporus"), and Lisbon ("like San Francisco, but older and
grittier and less expensive"). He reclines jauntily atop the cliffs of
Dover and is vigorously scrubbed in a Turkish bath. The show has
aired now for nearly 20 years, and in that time, among travelers,
Steves has established himself as one of the legendary PBS super-
dorks—right there in the pantheon with Mr. Rogers, Bob Ross,
and Big Bird. Like them, Steves is a gentle soul who wants to help
you feel at home in the world. Like them, he seems miraculously
untouched by the need to look cool, which of course makes him
sneakily cool. To the aspiring traveler, Steves is as inspirational as
Julia Child once was to the aspiring home chef.

Eventually, Steves's busy New York day ended on the Upper East
Side, where he was scheduled to give a talk at a Barnes & Noble.
As we drove to the event, Steves confessed that he wasn't sure what
kind of crowd he would get. You never knew exactly where his
Rickniks (as the hard-core fans call themselves) would materialize en masse. Some Steves appearances were mobbed; others were
sparse. His appeal is slightly cultish. For every Ricknik out in the
world, a large contingent of average people have no idea who he is.

I was mildly skeptical about Steves's drawing power in New York.
It was hard to imagine a bunch of cynical, worldly, urban, polyglot,
multicultural East Coast sophisticates—people who probably vaca-
tioned at deconsecrated eco-hostels in Oman or Madagascar—getting excited about public television's reigning expert on Europe.

We arrived, however, to find the bookstore overflowing. A solid
wave of applause met Steves at the door. Fans had been pouring
in, the organizer told us, for two solid hours. People sat in the
aisles and stood in the back. Some wore T-shirts and hats bearing
the Rick Steves slogan: "Keep on Travelin'." The crowd's body heat
overwhelmed the building's climate control.

I noticed a group of hipster 20-somethings standing near the
back, and at first I assumed they had all come sarcastically. But
as Steves began to speak, they grinned and laughed with absolute earnestness. Everyone here was, apparently, a superfan. At
one point, Steves showed a slide of tourists swimming in a sunny

French river underneath a Roman aqueduct, and the whole crowd gasped. When he mentioned that his website featured a special video devoted to packing light for women, a woman in the crowd actually pumped her fist.

At the end of his talk, Steves offered to sign books—but not in the traditional way. There were too many people for a signing table, he said, and anyway, single-file lines were always inefficient. (This is one of his travel credos: avoid waiting in line.) Instead of sitting down, Steves walked out into the center of the room and invited everyone to open their books and surround him. He pulled out a Sharpie. And then he started to spin. Steves held out his pen and signed book after book after book, fluidly, on the move, smiling as the crowd pressed in. "We went to Portugal on our honeymoon," a man shouted. "How romantic!" Steves answered, still spinning. A woman asked him where to celebrate Christmas in Europe. Steves, in midrotation, still signing furiously, told her that he had made a whole special about precisely that question and that it was available free on his website. "Keep on travelin', Rick!" someone shouted. "Keep on travelin'!" Steves shouted back. As he spun, Steves thanked everyone and gave quick, off-the-cuff advice. In an astonishingly short time, he had signed every book. The people were satisfied. The crowd thinned. Steves finally came to a stop.

Rick Steves is absolutely American. He wears jeans every single day. He drinks frozen orange juice from a can. He likes his hash browns burned, his coffee extra hot. He dislikes most fancy restaurants; when he's on the road, he prefers to buy a foot-long Subway sandwich and split it between lunch and dinner. He has a great spontaneous honk of a laugh—it bursts out of him, when he is truly delighted, with the sharpness of a firecracker on the Fourth of July. Steves is so completely American that when you stop to really look at his name, you realize it's just the name Rick followed by the plural of Steve—that he is a one-man crowd of absolutely regular everyday American guys: one Rick, many Steves. Although Steves spends nearly half his life traveling, he insists, passionately, that he would never live anywhere but the United States—and you know when he says it that this is absolutely true. In fact, Steves still lives in the small Seattle suburb where he grew up, and every morning he walks to work on the same block, downtown, where his parents owned a piano store 50 years ago. On Sundays, Steves wears his jeans to church, where he plays the congas, with great arm-pumping spirit, in the inspirational soft-rock band that serenades the congregation before the service starts, and then he sits down and sings classic Lutheran hymns without even needing to refer to the hymnal. Although Steves has published many foreign-language phrase books, the only language he speaks fluently is English. He built his business in America, raised his kids in America, and gives frequent loving paeans to the glories of American life.

And yet: Rick Steves desperately wants you to leave America. The tiniest exposure to the outside world, he believes, will change your entire life. Travel, Steves likes to say, "wallops your ethnocentricity" and "carbonates your experience" and "rearranges your cultural furniture." Like sealed windows on a hot day, a nation's borders can be stultifying. Steves wants to crack them open, to let humanity's breezes circulate. The more rootedly American you are, the more Rick Steves wants this for you. If you have never had a passport, if you are afraid of the world, if your family would prefer to vacation exclusively at Walt Disney World, if you worry that foreigners are rude and predatory and prone to violence or at least that their food will give you diarrhea, then Steves wants you—especially you—to go to Europe. Then he wants you to go beyond. (For a majority of his audience, Steves says, "Europe is the wading pool for world exploration.") Perhaps, like him, you will need large headphones and half a tab of Ambien to properly relax on the flight, but Steves wants you to know that it will be worth it. He wants you to stand and make little moaning sounds on a cobblestone street the first time you taste authentic Italian gelato—flavors so pure they seem like the primordial essence of peach or melon or pistachio or rice distilled into molecules and stirred directly into your own molecules. He wants you to hike on a dirt path along a cliff over the almost-too-blue Mediterranean, with villages and vineyards spilling down the rugged mountains above you. He wants you to arrive at the Parthenon at dusk, just before it closes, when all the tour groups are loading back onto their cruise ships, so that you have the whole place to yourself and can stand there feeling like a private witness to the birth, and then the ruination, of Western civilization.

Steves wants you to go to Europe for as long as you can afford to, and he also wants to help you afford it. (Much of his guru energy is focused on cutting costs.) He wants you to go as many times as possible, and while you're there, he wants you to get way down deep into the culture, to eat with locals in the teeming markets, to make a sympathetic fool of yourself, to get entirely lost in your lack of America.

Out of this paradoxical desire—the enlightenment of Americans through their extraction from America—Steves has built his quirky travel empire. His guidebooks, which started as hand-typed and photocopied information packets for his scraggly 1970s tour groups, now dominate the American market; their distinctive blue-and-yellow spines brighten the travel sections of bookstores everywhere. Steves is less interested in reaching sophisticated travelers than he is in converting the uninitiated. ("There will be more rejoicing in heaven over one sinner who repents," the Bible tells us, "than over 99 righteous persons who do not need to repent.") Last year, his company led close to 30,000 paying customers on dozens of elaborate European itineraries. Steves teaches his followers everything from how to pack a toiletries kit to how to make themselves at home in a small hotel room to how to appreciate a religious tradition they may have been raised to despise. (In order to enjoy St. Peter's Basilica, Steves admits, he had to learn to "park my Protestant sword at the door.") He is a sort of spiritual travel agent for America's curious but hesitant middle classes. He is simultaneously goofy and dead serious; he can ping, in an instant, from golly-gee Pollyanna cheerfulness to deep critiques of the modern world. In a series of long, affectionate, candid conversations, Steves's colleagues described him to me using the words "sophomoric," "knucklehead," and "Santa Claus"—but also "juggernaut," "evangelical," and "revolutionary." Rick Steves wants us to travel because it's fun, yes, but also because he believes it might actually save the world.

I can testify, firsthand, to the power of Rick Steves. In 1998 he spoke at my college. Nothing about the encounter seemed promising. Our campus was a tiny outpost in a tiny town, and Steves delivered his talk not in some grand lecture hall but in a drab room in the basement of the student union. I was poor, shy, anxious, sheltered, repressed, and extremely pale. I was a particular kind of Pacific Northwest white guy—blind to myself and my place in the world. I had never really traveled; I was more comfortable on

Greyhound buses than on airplanes. Going to Europe seemed like something aristocrats did, like fox hunting or debutante balls.

My girlfriend dragged me to the talk. I had never even heard of Steves. He entered looking like the kind of guy who would bring an acoustic guitar to every single church picnic within a two-hour radius of his favorite Applebee's: large glasses, floppy hair, blue jeans, wholesome grin. But what he said over the next hour or so changed the rest of my life.

It's hard to describe how thoroughly energized Steves becomes in front of a crowd. He paces, gesticulates, and speaks very fast. He tells his favorite old jokes as if they were eternally new. ("Eet smells like zee feet of angels," the French cheesemonger always exclaims.) Onstage, he is a combination of preacher, comedian, salesman, life-hacker, professor, and inspirational speaker. Steves told us, that day, how to pack our entire lives into a single bag measuring 9 by 22 by 14 inches. ("It's enlightened to pack light," Steves insists. "It's a blessing to pack light.") He told us how to find excellent cheap hotels, how to survive on minimalist picnics in public parks, how to wash clothing in bathroom sinks, and how to make friends without sharing a language. Steves's signature book, *Europe Through the Back Door,* seemed less like a travel philosophy than a whole mode of being: scrappy, prepared, independent, extroverted. Europe's front door, he told us, was positioned to feed travelers directly into exploitation: overpriced cafés, trinket shops, long lines, corporate high-rise hotels. The back door, by contrast, led to revelations. He showed us impossibly enticing photos: cobblestone piazzas teeming with fruit stalls, quirky wooden hotels among wildflowers in the Alps, vast arsenals of multicolored cheese. He made travel seem less like a luxury than a necessary exploration of the self, a civic responsibility, a basic courtesy to your fellow humans. It seemed almost unreasonable *not* to go. Above all, Steves told us, do not be afraid. The people of the world are wonderful, and the planet we share is spectacular. But the only way to really understand that is to go and see it for yourself. So go.

My girlfriend and I left the room converts to the gospel of Rick Steves. We bought his book and highlighted it to near-meaninglessness. We started mapping itineraries, squirreling away money, asking relatives for donations. (In probably the worst phone call of my life, my rancher grandfather expressed shock and dismay

that I would ask him to support this meaningless overseas lark.)
Eventually, over many months, we scraped together just enough to
buy plane tickets and order minimalist Steves-approved supplies,
including a travel towel so thin and nonabsorbent that it seemed
to just push the moisture around your skin until you forgot you
were wet. We packed exactly as Steves taught us: T-shirts rolled into
space-saving noodles, just enough clothes to get us from one hotel
laundry session to the next. Then, for the first time in our lives, we
left North America.

One of Steves's strongest recommendations is to keep a journal. Mine was so corny that its cover actually said "A Traveler's
Notebook" over a picture of the Eiffel Tower. When I opened it
recently, the reality of that long-ago trip hissed out with fresh urgency. My 20-year-old self recorded everything. On our first day
in Europe, we bought imported Austrian apples with fat, heavy
English coins and saw a woman stumble on a staircase, breaking
an entire bag of newly bought china. We arrived at our first hostel,
the YMCA in Bath, to find a man urinating in the stairwell—so we
kept walking until we happened into a nearby churchyard, where
the gravestones were so old and thin they were almost translucent.
As we tried to make out the names of the dead, songbirds sang
strenuously in the trees all around us. This juxtaposition—old
death, new life—blew my jet-lagged American mind. "Already, after just one day in Bath," I wrote in my journal, "the world has
grown firmer. Reality fills its gaps."

That, more or less, was the theme of the trip. For six weeks, we
followed the Steves game plan. We shared squalid bunks with other
young travelers from Denmark, Australia, Canada, and Japan. In
the stately public parks of Paris, we ate rotisserie chickens with our
bare hands. One stifling afternoon at the Colosseum in Rome, we
watched a worker slam his ladder against the edge of an arch and
break off some ancient bricks. (He looked over at us, looked down
at the bricks, kicked dirt over them, and kept working.) We were
moved by Van Gogh, Picasso, and Gaudí, but unmoved by Ver-
sailles ("more vain than beautiful," I wrote), bullfighting ("more
brutal than artful") and Goya ("vague and blurry"). Once, I left my
underwear on a Mediterranean beach overnight and, since I could
not afford to lose a pair, had to go back and pick it up the next day,
in full view of all the sunbathers.

Wherever we went, Rick Steves was with us. In my journal, I

referred to him half-jokingly as our "worldly uncle and guiding light," and as we walked around, I annoyed my girlfriend by doing impressions of him. We seemed to have entered the world of his slides: the fruit markets and overnight trains, the sunny French river under the ancient Roman aqueduct. Sometimes our European hosts, with the quiet pride of someone who once met Elvis, told us stories about Steves. He was a gentleman, they said, a truly good man, and he always came in person to check out their hotels, and he never failed to ask them how their children were doing.

By the end of our trip, we were completely broke. We couldn't afford even a baguette on our last day in Paris. We flew home looking ragged, shaggy, weather-beaten, and exhausted.

But of course Steves was right: our lives were never the same. We were still young Americans, but we felt liberated and empowered, like true citizens of the world. The most important things we learned all had to do with home. As the English writer G. K. Chesterton once put it, in a quote I found printed in my corny old travel journal: "The whole object of travel is not to set foot on foreign land; it is at last to set foot on one's own country as a foreign land." After looking at a Roman stone wall topped by a Saxon stone wall topped by a medieval English wall next to a modern paved street, I began to see what a thin crust of national history the United States actually stands on. I began to realize how silly and narrow our notion of exceptionalism is—this impulse to consider ourselves somehow immune to the forces that shape the rest of the world. The environment I grew up in, with its malls and freeways, its fantasies of heroic individualism, began to seem unnatural. I started to sense how much reality exists elsewhere in the world—not just in a theoretical sense, in books and movies, but with the full urgent weight of the real. And not just in Europe but on every other continent, all the time, forever. I began to realize how much I still had to learn before I could pretend to understand anything. Not everyone needs Steves's help to get to this point. Some people get there themselves, or their communities help them. But I needed him, and I am eternally glad I was dragged that day to see him talk.

Steves answered his front door slightly distracted. I had come in the middle of his breakfast preparations. He was stirring a block of frozen orange juice into a pitcher of water. "Freshly squeezed from the can!" he quipped. This was April 2018, exactly 20 years after my first trip to Europe. I had come to see Steves in the most exotic place possible: his home. He lives just north of Seattle, in a town so rainy it has a free umbrella-share program. There is nothing particularly exotic about the house itself. It has beige carpeting, professionally trimmed shrubs, and a back deck with a hot tub. What was exotic was simply that Steves was there. He had just returned from his frenetic speaking tour of the United States and would be leaving almost immediately on his annual trip to Europe. For now, he was making breakfast: frozen blueberries, Kashi cereal, OJ. "I would eat this every day for the rest of my life if I could," he said.

But of course, he could not. Steves is gone too much, yo-yoing between the misty forests of the Pacific Northwest and the sun-baked cathedrals of Europe. Every year, no matter what else is going on, Steves spends at least four months practicing the kind of travel he has preached for 40-odd years: hauling his backpack up narrow staircases in cheap hotels, washing his clothes in sinks, improvising picnics.

He is now 63, and he could afford to retire many times over. But he doesn't have the metabolism for sitting around. Among his colleagues, Steves is a notorious workaholic. After grueling days of filming in Europe, he has been known to slip script revisions under the crew's doors at 2:00 a.m., and then to ask them, at breakfast, for their feedback. On long car rides, he sits in the back seat and types op-eds on his laptop. His relentless hands-on control of every aspect of his business is what has distinguished the Rick Steves brand.

It is also, obviously, exhausting—if not for Steves, then at least for the people around him. He has two children, now grown, and for much of their childhoods, Steves was gone. He was building his company, changing the world. For very long stretches, his wife was forced to be a single mother. (She and Steves divorced in 2010 after 25 years of marriage.) Every summer, when the family joined Steves in Europe, his pace hardly slackened: they would cover major cities in 48 hours, blitzing through huge museums back to back. The kids complained so much, on one trip, that Steves finally snapped—if they were so miserable, he said, they could just go sit in the hotel room all day and play video games. They remember this day as heaven. One year, while Steves was away, the children converted to Catholicism. His son, Andy Steves, eventually went into the family business: he now works as a tour guide and even published a European guidebook.

Steves is fully aware that his obsessive work ethic is unusual. He admits that he has regrets. But he cannot make himself stop. He has the fervor of the true evangelist: the more people he meets, the more cities he visits, the more lives he might change. At one point, as we talked, he pulled out the itinerary for his coming trip —from Sicily to Iceland, with no downtime whatsoever. Just looking at it made him giddy. I asked why he couldn't ease up slightly —maybe just spend two months in Europe, maybe just speak in 10 American cities.

"It's a strange thing," he said. "I get energy from it. It's like I'm breathing straight oxygen. What would I do if I stayed home? Not much. Nothing I would remember."

In his house, Steves offered up a little show-and-tell. He pointed out an antique silver cigarette lighter shaped like the Space Needle. He sat down at his baby grand piano and lost himself, for a few happy minutes, playing Scarlatti. He took me to a room filled with books and reached up to a very high shelf. "I don't show this to too many people," he said, "because they'll think I'm nuts." Steves pulled down a thick red binder, the contents of which were, indeed, pretty nutty. When Steves was 13, he decided, for no apparent reason, to conduct a deep statistical analysis of the 1968 Billboard pop charts. Every week, he would clip the rankings out of his local newspaper and, using a point system of his own devising, graph the top bands' success on sheets of gridded paper. The lines were multicolored and interwoven—it looked like the subway map of some fantastical foreign city. You could see, at a glance, the rising and falling fortunes of the Beatles (red) and Creedence Clearwater Revival (black) and Elvis Presley (dots and dashes). Steves kept this up for three years, taping together many pieces of graph paper, and in the end he summarized the data in an authoritative-looking table that he typed on the family typewriter. This is what was in that binder: a systematic breakdown of the most successful bands from 1968 to 1970, as determined by the objective statistics of an analytical adolescent weirdo. (The winners, of course, were the Beatles—1,739 points—followed by Creedence, Simon and Garfunkel, Neil Diamond.)

Steves laughed. It was ridiculous. But it was also a perfect window into his mind. Even at 13, a powerful energy was coiled inside

him—an unusual combination of obsession and precision, just
waiting for some worthwhile project to burst out in.

And that, coincidentally, was exactly when he found it: the
project of his life. In the summer of 1969, when Steves was 14,
his parents took him to Europe. They owned a business tuning
and importing pianos, and they wanted to see factories firsthand.
Steves approached this first trip abroad with the same meticulous
energy he brought to his Billboard graphs. As he traveled around
the continent, he recorded the essential data of his journey on
the backs of postcards: locations, activities, weather, expenses.
One day, Steves spent 40 cents on fishing gear. Another, he met a
79-year-old man who had witnessed the assassination of Archduke
Franz Ferdinand. To keep everything in order, Steves numbered
the postcards sequentially. He still has them all packed lovingly
into an old wooden box.

On that same formative trip, the Steves family visited relatives
in Norway. They happened to be there in July 1969, when Neil
Armstrong walked on the moon. "Ett lite skritt for et menneske,"
the television said, "ett stort sprang for menneskeheten." In that
moment, in that strange place, young Rick Steves felt the concept
of *menneskeheten*—mankind—at a depth he never would have been
able to access back home. Europe was a crash course in cultural
relativity. In a park in Oslo, he had an epiphany: the foreign humans around him, he realized, were leading existences every bit as
rich and full as his own. "Right there," he would write later, "my
14-year-old egocentric worldview took a huge hit." A life-changing
realization clicked into place. "This planet must be home to billions of equally lovable children of God."

That first trip set the course for everything that followed. When
Steves was 18, he went back to Europe without his parents. Soon,
life in America became a series of interludes between travel. He
taught piano to earn money, then stretched that money as far as
he possibly could, sleeping on church pews and park benches, in
empty barns and construction zones, from western Europe to Afghanistan. He turned his cheapness into a science. Instead of paying for a hotel room in a city, Steves would use his rail pass and
sleep on a train for the night—four hours out, four hours back.
He would stuff himself on free breakfast bread, then try to eat as
little as possible for the rest of the day. Naturally, he recorded all
this, and today he has an impressive archive of old travel journals.

Their pages preserve, in tiny handwriting, shadowy young dissidents in Moscow, diarrhea in Bulgaria, revolution in Nicaragua.

In his 20s, Steves brought his wide-roaming wisdom back to the United States. He started to supplement his piano teaching with travel seminars. His signature class, European Travel Cheap, ran for six hours. Steves could have talked longer than that, but it struck him as impractical for his students. In Europe he rented a nine-seat minibus and started to lead small tours. Eventually, his seminars and tour notes morphed into his books. The first edition of *Europe Through the Back Door,* published in 1980, was typed on a rented IBM Selectric. It had no ISBN and looked so amateurish that bookstores assumed it was an early review copy. "Anyone caught reprinting any material herein for any purpose whatsoever will be thanked profusely," it said. This was the birth of the Rick Steves empire.

Rick Steves both is and is not his TV persona. Off-screen, he allows himself to be much more explicitly political. He has the passion of the autodidact. Growing up, Steves led a relatively sheltered existence: he was a white, comfortable, middle-class baby boomer in a white, comfortable, middle-class pocket of America. Travel did for him what he promises it will do for everyone else: it put him in contact with other realities. He saw desperate poverty in Iran and became obsessed with economic injustice. He started searching for answers in books, scribbling notes in the margins of *Bread for the World,* by Arthur Simon, and *The Origins of Totalitarianism,* by Hannah Arendt. He studied the war industry and colonial exploitation. The first time Steves traveled to Central America, he came back so outraged that he wrote a fiery tract called "There's Blood on Your Banana," then flew to Washington and hand-delivered a copy to the office of every member of Congress.

In the early days, Steves injected political lessons into his European tours. Sometimes he would arrive in a city with no hotel reservations, just to make his privileged customers feel the anxiety of homelessness. In Munich, he would set up camp in an infamous hippie circus tent, among all the countercultural wanderers of Europe.

Today, Steves is more strategic. His most powerful tool, he realizes, is his broad appeal. He has an uncanny knack for making serious criticism feel gentle and friendly. Often he disguises cri-

tiques of America with a rhetorical move that I like to think of
as "USA! USA! USA! (But. . . .)" "I'm unapologetically proud to
be an American," he writes in the introduction to his book *Travel
as a Political Act.* "The happiest day of any trip is the day I come
home . . . But other nations have some pretty good ideas too."

That's when he hits his audience with legal prostitution, high
tax rates, and universal health care.

When I asked Steves about this strategy, he chuckled.

"It's not America-bashing," he said. "It's America-loving. I think
it's loving America to look at it critically. But you've got to set it
up. You've got to allay people's concerns that you're a communist.
So you explain to them: I'm a capitalist, I make a lot of money, I
employ a lot of people, I love the laws of supply and demand. It
seems kind of silly, but you've got to say that. Then, especially the
husbands who are dragged there by their wives, they go, 'I thought
he was a commie, but he's OK.' And then you don't need to be too
gentle. You can confront people with a different perspective, and
you'll get through."

Steves learned this strategy, he said, from his early days running
tours, living with the same people for weeks at a time. Survival
required being pleasant. People didn't want grating lectures about
America's shortcomings—even if that was sometimes his instinct.
Instead, he pointed out different perspectives with a smile. He became fluent in the needs of American tourists. "I know what their
buttons are," he said. "I know what their attention span is. I don't
want to just preach to the choir. I want to preach to organizations
that need to hear this, so I need to compromise a little bit so the
gatekeepers let it through to their world."

This balancing act has become increasingly difficult over the
past two decades, in a world of terrorism, war, nationalism, and
metastasizing partisanship. After the September 11 attacks, most
travel companies anticipated that the bottom was about to fall out
of the market. They canceled tours and cut back budgets. Steves,
however, remained defiantly optimistic. He promised his staff that
there would be no cuts, no layoffs, and no shift in message. He insisted that a world in crisis needed travel more, not less. Soon the
shock of September 11 turned into the Iraq War, which strained
the relationship between the United States and even its closest European allies, sending the travel industry deeper into its trough.
In his hometown, Steves caused a controversy when he walked

around removing rows of American flags that had been set up in support of the war. It was, he argued, an act of patriotism: the flag is meant to represent all Americans, not just war supporters. "I was shark-bait on Seattle's right-wing radio talk shows for several days," he wrote.

Lately, Steves concedes, his political message has begun to take over his teaching. In *Travel as a Political Act*, the familiar elements of his guidebooks—walking tours, museum guides, hotel reviews —are replaced by rabble-rousing cultural critique. Steves expresses deep admiration for Scandinavian-style social democracy and calls out many of America's faults: our addiction to cars and guns and mass incarceration; our deference to corporations; our long history of cultural imperialism ("one of the ugliest things one nation can do is write another nation's textbooks"). Some moments in the book verge on un-American. "Sometimes, when I'm frustrated with the impact of American foreign policy on the developing world," Steves writes, "I have this feeling that an impotent America is better for the world than an America whose power isn't always used for good."

Occasionally, despite his best efforts, Steves still ruffles feathers. Recent TV specials have covered Iran—"I believe if you're going to bomb a place," Steves has written, "you should know its people first"—and the rise of fascism in Europe. In a special about the Holy Land, Steves refers unapologetically to "Palestine" instead of "the West Bank" or "Palestinian territories"; some viewers were so outraged that they told Steves they were removing PBS from their wills. After one recent speech in the Deep South, event organizers refused to pay Steves—their conservative sponsors, he learned, considered his message a form of liberal propaganda.

In recent years Steves has become a happy warrior for an unlikely cause: the legalization of marijuana. He first tried the drug in Afghanistan, in the 1970s, in the name of cultural immersion, and he was fascinated by its effect on his mind. Today he is a board member of NORML, the National Organization for the Reform of Marijuana Laws, and a regular speaker at Hempfest. In his headquarters you will find a poster of the Mona Lisa holding a gargantuan spliff. In 2012 Steves campaigned hard for Washington State's successful legalization initiative, and since then he has barnstormed other states (Oregon, Maine, Vermont, and more) to make sure the civil liberties are properly passed around. On a

shelf in his living room, right there among all the European knick-
knacks, Steves displays a sizable bong.

Sometimes, fans urge Steves to run for office. When I asked him
if he would ever get into politics, he had an answer ready: "I already am." Good travel teaching, in his eyes, is inherently political.
To stay in a family-owned hotel in Bulgaria is to strengthen global
democracy; to pack light is to break the iron logic of consumerism;
to ride a train across Europe is to challenge the fossil-fuel industry. Travel, to Steves, is not some frivolous luxury—it is an engine
for improving humankind, for connecting people and removing
their prejudices, for knocking distant cultures together to make
unlikely sparks of joy and insight. Given that millions of people
have encountered the work of Steves over the last 40 years, on TV
or online or in his guidebooks, and that they have carried those
lessons to untold other millions of people, it is fair to say that his
life's work has had a real effect on the collective life of our planet.
When people tell Steves to stay out of politics, to stick to travel, he
can only laugh.

"It's flattering to think I could run for office," he admitted.
"And it would be exciting. But I think I'm accomplishing more
right now than I would in office, and I'm having more fun. I'm skiing with beautiful wax on my skis. When I want to do something,
I can do it."

Steves is deeply indifferent to creature comforts. When I visited
him, the back seat of his car was covered with a greenish slime,
practically disintegrating, because of a mysterious leak. He just
cracked the windows to try to dry it out. Steves prefers to spend
his money on his favorite causes. His activism can be quirky and
impulsive. In 2011, after hearing that his local symphony orches-
tra was struggling, he stepped in with a gift of $1 million, spread
over 10 years, to help keep it operating. (This, pointedly, was how
much money he would get back from President George W. Bush's
tax cut over a decade.) Last year, during a chat with one of the
national leaders of the Lutheran Church, Steves wondered how
much it would cost to send every single Lutheran congregation
in the United States a DVD of his recent TV special about Martin
Luther. It was something like $30,000; Steves happily wrote the
check. In the 1990s, working in partnership with the YWCA, he
started investing his retirement savings in local real estate in order

to house homeless mothers and their children. The plan was to take that money out of the banking system and let it do a few decades of social good, at which point Steves could sell the buildings to fund his retirement. Eventually he worked his way up to buying a whole 24-unit apartment complex—and then he donated it outright to the YWCA. The mothers, he said, needed it more than he would.

Steves is obsessed with the problem of poverty and amazed at our perpetual misunderstanding of it. "It's not just: You screwed up, so you're poor," he said. "There's a *structure* that keeps half of humanity poor. This needs to be talked about. I can do it, and I can get away with it." His next TV special, in production now, will investigate extreme poverty and hunger through two very different non-European countries: Guatemala and Ethiopia. In the meantime, all the royalties of his latest book—an updated edition of *Travel as a Political Act*—are being donated to Bread for the World, an organization that lobbies on behalf of hungry people. He is working on making his company's tours completely carbon-neutral.

"If I was trying to build a career on the speaking circuit—if I was struggling, and I needed these gigs—I would not talk about that stuff," he said. "I could just talk about light stuff, and everybody would love it. But I'm not working right now to do that. I'm not trying to get anywhere that I'm not already. I don't need to be anything I'm not. I'm sixty-three years old. I could retire now. But I'm ramping up."

Indeed, Steves's business has been booming. Once the travel market finally recovered, some years after September 11, Steves occupied a disproportionately big share of it—precisely because he had refused to scale back. By taking a principled stand, Steves flourished. Today, his chipper voice is reaching more Americans than ever. "Fear," as Steves likes to say, "is for people who don't get out very much."

One night, in his living room, Steves pulled out a plain black notebook. "Here's something you might find interesting," he said with his trademark cheer, and he flipped open to a random page and prepared to read aloud. I was familiar, by then, with Steves's deep archive of old travel journals, and so I settled in to listen to further adventures from 1975 Moscow or 1997 Paris. This, however, was something else entirely—a record of a very different kind of journey.

"Getting high," Steves read, "releases the human in me."

"Intelligence is a rubber band," he continued. "Getting high is stretching it."

I was sitting in the beige living room of America's foremost travel guru, underneath framed reproductions of popular European masterworks, and my mind was about to be well and truly blown. For the next 20 minutes, Steves would read me koans about the glories of being stoned.

"High is the present," he read.

"When you're high, you debate long and hard over whether to put on your sweater or turn up the heat."

This journal, Steves explained, contained what he called his "High Notes." For nearly 40 years, he had been writing in it exclusively after smoking marijuana. He would get baked, open up to somewhere in the middle, and jot down whatever he happened to be thinking—deep or shallow, silly or angry. There is no chronology; on every page, axioms from many different decades commingle. It is a lifelong treasury of Steves's stoner thoughts.

He continued to read.

"As soon as I stop mattering so much, I'll be happier."

"A baby doesn't know if the hanging is on the wall or if the wall is on the hanging."

"Make a rug with vacuum marks, so it always looks freshly vacuumed."

The entries covered an impressively wide territory. Some were little shreds of oracular poetry ("We all have a divine harness"), while others were dashed-off semiwitticisms ("Wolfgang von Bewildered") or bitter social critiques ("The spiritual cesspool of America—our shopping malls"). "They don't let you into heaven without calluses on your soul," he read at one point. "Suffer or weep." There were scraps of humorous dialogue ("'Nothing is wrong with an ego!' he bellowed") and sentences that would have made great bumper stickers on rusting VW buses: "I'd like to be quarantined from reality."

I found myself wondering, for the thousandth time: Who *does* this? What kind of mind not only thinks of such a project but actually follows through with it, decade after decade after decade? Who, for God's sake, is this disciplined when they're high?

As Steves read, he interrupted himself again and again with great shouting honks of laughter, and I cackled right along with him. Then, suddenly, with almost no transition, we would find ourselves deep in earnest conversation about the nature of true happiness or the dangers of ambition. And then we would suddenly be cackling again. We were, in other words, getting high on Steves's "High Notes."

He kept reading.

"I've been craning my mind to see you," he said.

"I feel like a hungry bird, but I won't eat any worm I don't like."

Steves showed me complex analytical graphs about true love and divorce rates, about the way music sounds when you're high versus sober, about the degrees of honesty possible with the various people in your life. ("Scale of Unconditional Regard," this last one was called.) One page of the journal had a strand of hair taped to it, labeled "split end." There was a drawing of a woman's breasts. And of course there were many, many more descriptions of getting high itself. "Getting high is like roasting an English muffin," Steves read. "You start out cold and doughy, and you toast it to a crisp brown, and just a little more and you get all black and burned."

At some point, he looked up from the journal. "To me," he said, "this is a precious thing. Because this is *me*."

He kept reading.

"Time spent socially is time spent at the expense of personal betterment," he said.

He shook his head. That's how he had thought when he was young. "That's my problem," he added ruefully. "I work all the time."

Then he kept reading.

"When I die," he read, "scatter me all over the budget hotels of Europe."

FRED BAHNSON

# On the Road with Thomas Merton

FROM *Emergence Magazine*

## I. Woods

ON THE FLIGHT from San Francisco to Eureka, he looked out the window and caught his first sight of them: redwoods.

Even from the air, the trees appeared enormous. To the north, Lassen Peak and Mount Shasta *rose like great silent Mexican gods, white and solemn.* When he looked down again, the trees were gone. Entire hillsides slashed into, ravaged, stripped.

Life seemed to be unraveling everywhere that year. The date was May 6, 1968. Vietnam was in full swing, and King had been assassinated just one month earlier. *Ever increasing frenzy, tension, explosiveness of this country,* he wrote in his journal.

Thomas Merton was perhaps the most important Christian mystic of the 20th century. For the past 26 years, he had lived as a Trappist monk at the Abbey of Gethsemani in Kentucky, and for the past 3 he had lived in a cinder-block hermitage in the woods. *I am accused of living in the woods like Thoreau instead of in the desert like St. John the Baptist,* he wrote to a friend. Whatever else can be said about Merton, and much has been said, one thing is certain: he was a monk who loved trees. *One might say I had decided to marry the silence of the forest,* he wrote. *The sweet dark warmth of the whole world will have to be my wife. Out of the heart of that dark warmth comes the secret that is heard only in silence . . . Perhaps I have an obligation to preserve the stillness, the silence, the poverty, the virginal point of pure nothingness which is at the center of all other loves.*

He had been searching for that center his whole life.

*Le point vierge,* he called it.

Now, in May 1968, he was beginning a three-week journey out West in search of a new hermitage site. He was on his way first to Redwoods Monastery in Whitethorn, California, then on to the Monastery of Christ in the Desert in Abiquiu, New Mexico. During a brief stop in San Francisco, he would spend the night at City Lights Books, talking poetry late into the night with Beat poet and City Lights cofounder Lawrence Ferlinghetti. This monk who wed the silence of the forest was also a gregarious lover of people, which is exactly why he needed to flee their presence. He yearned for the kind of deep solitude where he could shed his public persona and live for God alone. Perhaps he would find it among the California redwoods, along the Lost Coast, or in New Mexico's Chama River Canyon.

Before the flight, he sat at the airport bar in San Francisco and drank two daiquiris. *Impression of relaxation,* he wrote. Ever the wide-awake monk, he couldn't even enjoy a decent buzz, only the distanced *impression* of such, yet even in the airport bar, he was recovering something of himself that had long been lost.

On the flight into Eureka, he jotted down notes for talks he would give to the nuns at Redwoods Monastery, a young abbey nestled among trees that were already saplings by the time Jesus was born. He copied dense philosophical quotes by Hegel, Unamuno, and Sartre, but in his journal such abstract quotes soon gave way to the language of direct encounter, as if once his hand touched redwood bark, those erstwhile forests of philosophical thought quickly lost stature, dwarfed by comparison.

When he stepped off the plane in Eureka, Sister Leslie complimented him on his beret. They bought a couple cans of beer and hit the road, driving south along the Eel River. From his view in the passenger seat, he took in the passing world. *Everything from the big ferns at the base of the trees, the dense undergrowth, the long enormous shafts towering endlessly in shadow penetrated here and there by light. . . . The worshipful cold spring light on the sandbanks of Eel River, the immense silent redwoods.*

*Like a cathedral,* he wrote.

On a Wednesday evening in late May, 50 years later, I step into the cathedral of trees surrounding Redwoods Monastery and enter the ongoing stream of silence.

I'm following the itinerary Merton described in his journal from that 1968 western journey, posthumously published as *Woods, Shore, Desert.* "It's one of the world's truly interesting journals," Annie Dillard wrote of the book. Merton's photographs from that journey, a selection of which appear in *Woods, Shore, Desert,* depict the surf crashing on Big Sur, a clump of ferns beneath a redwood, a beach empty of all but driftwood and fog. After 26 years of the inward journey, Merton was finding a new bearing in the American landscape itself. *I dream every night of the West,* he wrote upon his return.

I was curious why he made the journey at all. For years he had longed to live in a hermitage in the woods on the grounds at Gethsemani Abbey, until finally his abbot granted his request. What more was he still seeking?

What am I seeking? Here at the beginning of my journey following Merton's steps, I wonder why, even in the midst of a flourishing family life, I still feel pulled toward silence and solitude, or why I can't seem to shake this spiritual restlessness that has driven me most of my life, a propulsive desire to seek out the horizon. I feel those same yearnings in Merton's writings. But my connection to him goes deeper still.

Merton was an orphan. His mother died when he was 6, his father when he was 16. His parents' deaths marked him in profound ways, but in his autobiography, *The Seven Storey Mountain,* the most harrowing scenes from his childhood occur during the three years he spent at a French boarding school. Thomas was 11 when he was sent to the school. Once there, he pleaded in vain with his father to let him come home. For the next three years, Lycée Ingres, a place full of "some diabolical spirit of cruelty and viciousness and obscenity and blasphemy and envy and hatred that banded [the children] together against all goodness and against one another," became his home. When young Thomas lay awake at night "in the huge dark dormitory," he knew for the first time in his life "the pangs of desolation and emptiness and abandonment."

When I was 10 years old, one year shy of Merton's age when he went to boarding school, my parents sent me to a place with diabolical spirits of its own. They moved our family to Nigeria so they could volunteer as medical missionaries, and I was sent to a mission boarding school. For the next three years, I lived in a dorm with 20 other children and a pair of adult caretakers who gave us food and gave us shelter but did not give us love. Neglect crept through the halls of our dorm each night and entered our rooms, looking to devour any exposed piece of our young hearts, so the trick was to keep them hidden. I came to know those pangs of desolation and emptiness of which Merton spoke. Years later when I discovered his writings, I knew that I was not alone. I had joined the camaraderie of the abandoned.

I arrive at the abbey in time for compline, the last service of the day. As the nuns chant the Psalms, I look around the church and take my bearings. In place of pews, wooden benches stand along three walls together with a selection of *zafus* and *zabutons*. The monastery is Catholic, yet a Zen-like aesthetic is everywhere present, perhaps most pronounced in the center of the chapel, which remains empty. Into that center the day's last light pours from clerestory windows high up in the ceiling. Along the chapel's fourth wall, floor-to-ceiling windows reveal a single redwood tree beyond, a four-leader trunk whose girth must be close to 30 feet. On the concrete floor, a series of long cracks run the length of the building. Redwood roots, I learn from one of the sisters, pushing upward. The trees are lifting the entire monastery off the ground.

The sisters of Redwoods Abbey are Trappists, also known as Cistercians of the Strict Observance, a worldwide Catholic monastic order of men and women who follow the Rule of Saint Benedict and the Cistercian reforms of the 11th century. Those reforms brought a return to simplicity, contemplative prayer, and silence. At a time when Christianity was taking a centuries-long detour into logic and rationalism, Cistercian monks were turning their attention inward, to the heart, where Jesus said we would find the kingdom of God.

The sisters chant the Psalms here in this chapel and in between chants they listen. Words are spoken or sung, but they are borrowed from silence and to silence they return. "The monastic journey is learning how to listen," Sister Kathy, the abbess, tells me one day during my visit. "I don't think we ever stop learning how to listen." I experience it many times over the next five days—standing inside a circle of ancient redwoods across the Mattole River, sitting on a beach at nearby Needle Rock—but I find it first here among the sisters in their chapel of wood, steel, and concrete upheld by the roots of trees: a deep, welcoming silence.

Saint Ephraim the Syrian, a fourth-century monk, said to his brothers, "Good speech is silver, but silence is pure gold."

After compline, Sister Karen, a nun from Bolivia, shows me to the guesthouse and assigns me the same room where Merton stayed. It looks unchanged since 1968. Cinder-block walls, a single bed, worn carpet, a desk and chair. I throw my bags down and walk to the patio, where I sit and watch the silent show unfolding out in the meadow. Two wild turkeys strut and preen. Beyond them a lone whitethorn bush stands in full bloom, its blossoms as white as the sisters' cowls. When the fog settles, obscuring the remaining daylight, I turn in.

Unable to sleep, I sit at what I think of as Merton's desk, a stack of his books in front of me, and reflect on why I've come.

As I confront the lingering feelings of exile and loneliness from my childhood, I find myself pining after what I call the geographical cure. Much more than simply an urge to travel, the geographical cure is the belief that whatever problems I'm facing at the moment will magically disappear if only I change zip codes for a day, a month, a lifetime. My awareness that the geographical cure is not a cure but an escapist fantasy makes it no less powerful an influence on my daily life.

So many of us are looking for escape routes these days: from depressing news cycles, from yet another school shooting, from climate change. Most days, though, my escapist fantasies are avoidance strategies for those mundane responsibilities of adult life. Still, I wonder: In our imaginative flights from reality, is there some original impulse that is worthy and true? Can we redeem the desire to run *from* and turn it into a desire to run *toward*? If so, toward what? I pick up my copy of Merton's essay "From Pilgrimage to Crusade" and read the opening paragraph:

> Man instinctively regards himself as a wanderer and wayfarer, and it is second nature for him to go on pilgrimage in search of a privileged and holy place, a center and source of indefectible life. This hope is built into his psychology, and whether he acts it out or simply dreams it, his heart seeks to return to a mythical source, a place of "origin," the "home" where the ancestors came from, the mountain where the ancient fathers were in direct communication with heaven, the place of the creation of the world, paradise itself, with its sacred tree of life.

Merton's essay describes two forking paths in the spiritual life, the choice between pilgrimage and its warped image, the crusade. But on another level we can see Merton working out his own restless desire for pilgrimage, why he felt unsettled at Gethsemani Abbey, why he needed to go in search of his own "center and source of indefectible life." Did he really need to leave the monastery to find that center? Or was he, too, a victim of the geographical cure? Who were his models to help him discern the difference?

As I sit at Merton's desk in the guesthouse of Redwoods Abbey, I want to believe that what brings me here is more than escapist fantasy. I find hope in Merton's search, for it means that even a man who spent nearly three decades chipping away at his ego through prayer and stillness and contemplation was still a restless wanderer. Our yearning for paradise and its sacred tree of life may be part of our glorious human inheritance, but to help that yearning find shape and substance in our daily lives, we need guides.

Merton consciously sought out his own guides, most of whom had been dead for hundreds of years. "There are people one meets in books or in life whom one does not merely observe, meet, or know," Merton wrote in *Conjectures of a Guilty Bystander*. "A deep resonance of one's entire being is immediately set up with the entire being of the other . . . Heart speaks to heart in the wholeness of the language of music; true friendship is a kind of singing."

The early music that moved him most he found in Blake, Meister Eckhart, Ruysbroeck, Coomaraswamy, Dante, and he followed that melody line as it led him in later years to Sufism, Taoism, Zen, the Bhagavad Gita. But in the months leading up to his western journey in May 1968, the strongest singing came from the 17th-century Japanese poet Matsuo Bashō. Six months before Merton would depart for California, he read *The Narrow Road to the Deep North*, a series of travel sketches describing the pilgrimage Bashō undertook late in his life, a journey on foot over hundreds of miles. Opening himself to the elements, the aging poet carried little more than hat, staff, and satchel. Upon reading Bashō's travel sketches, Merton wrote in his journal that he was *completely shattered by them. One of the most beautiful books I have ever read in my life . . . Seldom have I found a book to which I responded so totally.*

When I came across this line in Merton's journals, I felt as though I'd found the interpretive key to his journey. I immediately reread Bashō, hoping to find clues as to what Merton found so moving. "Days and months are travelers of eternity," Bashō wrote. Like those who spend their lives traveling, he had "been tempted for a long time by the cloud-moving wind—filled with a strong desire to wander." Bashō is a connoisseur of simple pleasures found on a mountain pass or in one of the hermitages he encounters, or on the beach at Suma: "The scene excelled in loneliness and isolation at that season."

Bashō walked north with no purpose other than his own unfulfilled longings: to see the full moon rise over the mountains of the Kashima Shrine, to see the pine tree of Aneha and the bridge of Odae, or to inhabit a scene like the one he describes in this haiku:

Tell me the loneliness
Of this deserted mountain,
The aged farmer
Digging wild potatoes.

I believe that what most drew Merton's affection, more than any individual passage in Bashō, was the man himself, this aging poet who walked hundreds of miles through his native Japan in an act of self-abandonment. Like Merton, Bashō was a famous writer who, late in life, had wearied of his fame and who, after a lifetime of giving his words to others, needed to place himself before the Unsayable. Merton loved Bashō for the same reason he loved Russian icons or paleolithic cave paintings: they were all examples of *pure seeing*. In the final years leading up to his western journey, this desire for direct awareness became an increasing preoccupation for Merton. He was seeking bedrock. The undistilled center of our being in God. The pure drop.

At a castle ruins in the village of Ichikawa, Bashō wrote: "I felt as if I were in the presence of the ancients themselves." He left those ruins and took a small boat to see the islands of Matsushima, which appeared to him "like parents caressing their children or walking with them arm in arm . . . My pen strove in vain to equal this superb creation of divine artifice."

Such is the power of literary influence. For much of our lives, the world spins past at too great a speed for us to notice, but sometimes we find a thread. We trace it back. Time and distance fall away. Suddenly we feel as if we are in the presence of the ancients themselves; we stand beside Merton as he stands beside Bashō on a deserted mountain in 17th-century Japan, all of us watching an aged farmer digging his wild potatoes. We feel the loneliness of that scene, yet we are not alone. We partake together. Heart speaks to heart across the centuries. This is the divine artifice at work and we strive to equal it: with our pens, with our lives.

At dawn it's still raining. I awake to a chill in the air. I dress quickly, then realize I've slept through lauds and need not hurry. A brief stroll across the meadow, still shrouded in mist, brings me to the monastery. How pleasant on such a cold morning to find in the abbey kitchen a pot of hot coffee, cream from a local dairy, a mug, and a plate of oatmeal cookies, all of it left for me by one of the sisters. Monastic austerity, it seems, does not preclude cookies before breakfast.

I join the sisters for Mass, and afterward Sister Kathy invites me to sit and chat over more coffee and cookies. Sister Kathy arrived at the monastery in the early '70s, driving a green Triumph Spitfire convertible. When I ask what drew her to the monastic life, she tells me of a certain experience she had as a child, which she marks as the beginning of her spiritual quest. When she was six, her appendix ruptured. She nearly died. After two weeks in the hospital, Kathy arrived home. It was Easter Sunday, and while her large Italian family bustled around her, she remembers sitting in a chair, feet dangling over the edge, watching a single ray of sunlight spill through the window and illumine the space beneath her feet. Adults and siblings kept talking, oblivious to what she was sensing. In that moment she dropped beneath the noise and discovered God waiting for her. Here, she felt, was the life beyond life.

"That sounds like *le point vierge*," I say.

"That phrase in Merton's writings means a lot to me," Kathy says. I ask her to elaborate. "The virginal point. It means pure, untouched, like the old-growth redwoods. He's talking about an old-growth forest of the soul. It's a profound metaphor for the spiritual life."

I first discovered the phrase in Merton's book *Conjectures of a Guilty Bystander*, where he wrote:

> At the center of our being is a point of nothingness which is untouched by sin and by illusion, a point of pure truth, a point or spark which belongs entirely to God, which is never at our disposal, from which God disposes of our lives, which is inaccessible to the fantasies of our own

mind or the brutalities of our own will. This little point of nothingness and of *absolute poverty* is the pure glory of God in us.

Merton helped me articulate a belief I'd long suspected, that the core of our being is not rotten, as my Protestant upbringing had insisted, but is a place of untouched beauty and wholeness reserved for God alone, a place beyond ego that no evil can touch.

Merton borrowed the phrase *le point vierge* from Sufi scholar Louis Massignon, who borrowed the idea from the ninth-century Sufi Mansur al-Hallaj. As al-Hallaj wrote, "Our hearts, in their secrecy, are a virgin alone, where no dreamer's dream penetrates —the heart where the presence of the Lord penetrates, there to be conceived." As Kathy explains it, the idea is also deeply embedded in Cistercian tradition. Among Cistercians, you won't find anyone banging on about original sin. Against the myth of "total depravity"—that small-minded theology invented by Calvinists in the 16th century to which an unfortunate number of American Protestants still cling—Cistercian anthropology is essentially positive. Which doesn't imply a naive attitude about human nature. Cistercians know of our innate propensity for self-delusion, which they speak of as "woundedness." When we act out of our woundedness, we inflict collateral damage: on ourselves, on others, on the earth. Yet Cistercians believe that beyond the reach of our woundedness there remains a place in the depths of our being reserved for God alone.

Sister Kathy leans forward, her eyes ablaze. "We are stamped —*stamped*—with the image and likeness of God," she says. "We are loved by the One who loved us first."

Over the next several days, I fall into the rhythms of Cistercian life: prayer, silence, long walks in the forest. The meals—delicious vegetarian fare featuring local organic produce—are eaten in silence. Most communal work is also performed in silence so as to allow more time for prayer and contemplation. I spend much of my days here wandering through the redwoods. One morning I cross paths with Sister Veronique. Dressed in scarf, sweater, denim dress, and a pair of old leather hiking boots, she's off on her morning walk, and I ask if I can join her.

It's a lovely morning. The fog is lifting, and by the time we stroll over the Mattole River, the sun is coming down through the redwoods. Sister Veronique, age 85, was one of the first nuns here at Redwoods Monastery, and perhaps because of her community's isolation and the Cistercian practice of silence, her accent retains a lovely Flemish burl. She rolls her *r*'s, says "Very *huud*" to express approval, and speaks with much care and deliberation, occasionally stopping to take my arm and looking me in the eye. I sense that I'm in the presence of what early Christian monastics called an "amma," a spiritual mentor whom pilgrims would seek for a word of counsel.

Sister Veronique leads me through a small wooden gate, then we walk down a narrow footpath in silence. We enter the cathedral: a stand of old-growth redwoods. Sister Veronique often comes here to pray. When she arrived here from Belgium, she told me, the redwoods prevented her from praying. She had to climb a hill near the monastery to get above them, and it was only on the hill that her heart would open to God as it had when surrounded by the wide skies of Belgium. In those early years she was depressed. Reading Hermann Hesse's novel *Siddhartha* helped, but what helped most was poetry: Isaiah and Rabindranath Tagore. When Thomas Merton visited, he gave her his copy of *The Tagore Reader*. But her dawning realization that God was always and everywhere present came most from watching the moon. The recent full moon was hidden for three days, Sister Veronique tells me. Just because she couldn't see it didn't mean it wasn't there, exerting its gravitational pull on her and on every other thing on earth. So it is with God. Always there, exerting a pull on us, but not always felt.

Before we leave the redwood grove that morning, I ask Veronique about my own prayer life. I tell her of my struggles as a father of three young boys, how difficult it is to find time for silence and prayer, how I continue to search for that center of stillness and repose that seems beyond the reach of whatever emptiness I happen to be experiencing. Sister Veronique stops, takes hold of my arm, and looks me in the eye. "You have a beautiful life, hmm?"

It comes out of nowhere, less admonishment than reminder.

I already have everything I need to begin.

One evening that week, Sister Veronique approaches me after vespers and presents me with a gift: a bottle of Belgian Westmalle Trappist Ale—a Tripel, no less. "Belgian beer is the best," she says, winking at me. I try to convince her to join me but she won't hear of it, so I return to Merton's room back at the guesthouse and raise a glass in her honor. A toast to Sister Veronique, my "desert mother," who dispenses not only wisdom but also the finest of ales.


## II. Shore

On the Mendocino coast, Thomas Merton sat on a grassy bench halfway between Needle Rock and Bear Harbor. Farther north toward Shelter Cove he saw *a manufactory of clouds where the wind piles up smoky moisture along the steep flanks of the mountains. Their tops are completely hidden.*

It was probably raining back in the Mattole Valley at Redwoods Abbey, he thought. On Sunday one of the Flemish nuns danced barefoot in the choir. He was struck by the beauty of these sisters, both Flemish and American. The affection was mutual. When he told them he wanted to ask his abbot's permission to spend Lent in the abandoned house at Needle Rock, one of the sisters told him they would all fight one another for the chance to bring him supplies.

Bear Harbor he liked better than Needle Rock. More isolated. At Bear Harbor wild irises and calla lilies grew wild among the ferns. Perhaps he could set up a trailer and live here in this hollow, surrounded by ancient Lombardy poplars, green firs, wild foxgloves.

He jotted down a line from Theophane the Recluse: *Not to run from one thought to the next, but to give each one time to settle in the heart.*

Eight crows wheeled in the sky overhead, casting their shadows on the bare hillside. He read the Astavakra Gita on reincarnation, looked out over the Pacific, and wrote: *Reincarnation or not, I am as tired of talking and writing as if I had done it for centuries. Now it is the time to listen at length to this Asian ocean.* In the fall he would cross this Asian ocean on a different pilgrimage, one that would be his last.

Before he left, he photographed Needle Rock. *The great* Yang-Yin *of sea rock mist, diffused light and half hidden mountain . . . an interior landscape, yet there. In other words, what is written within me is there. "Thou art that."*


One afternoon, one of the sisters kindly packs me a picnic dinner and I set off for Needle Rock. As she sees me off in the parking lot,

Sister Kathy looks at my economy-size two-wheel-drive rental car, with its pathetic clearance, smiles, and says, "Boy, you really came prepared, didn't you?"

The dirt road down to Needle Rock is even worse than she described: steep, heavily rutted, hairpin turns. I'm not sure I will make it back up. On the final curve down to the coast I come upon a herd of Roosevelt elk, perhaps a hundred or more grazing on a broad, grassy bench.

I pull into a small parking lot in front of Needle Rock cabin. Except for two other cars, the place appears deserted. Before I'm even out of the vehicle, a woman approaches. It's Carla, the campground host. Carla introduces herself and immediately begins to answer questions I have not yet asked, a voluminous outpouring of trivia relayed in that way of campsite hosts everywhere who love the place they're in. The coast is disappearing five feet a year, Carla says matter-of-factly. The cliffs are soft and they're falling into the sea, so it's best not to walk too close. She says this by way of warning, for my own good, because she can tell by my poor choice of vehicles that I'm in need of such advice, and perhaps I am. I nod absently through Carla's lecture, catching about every third word, until I hear "one of the most seismically active places in the world." I ask her to repeat.

Yes, she says, and points past Needle Rock toward a headland in the distance: the Mendocino Triple Junction. She explains how, just off the coast, three tectonic plates—the Gorda, the North American, and the Pacific—collide in a single point. A convergence of tectonic forces.

I walk north along a wide, grassy bench above the coast, a cool breeze on my face. Uphill to my right I pass the elk herd. Below to my left big rollers crash against the cliffs, coaxing the land back into the sea. Everything in bloom reaches my nose: wild mustard, bush lupine, wild iris, and the hypnotic perfume of calla lilies. I walk down a steep trail to Jones Beach and take off my shoes, the small, black pebbles warm on my toes. Around a bend I discover a flat-rock outcrop, the perfect perch on which to sit and watch the surf.

The ocean has long been the great symbol of mystical union with God. With the vast Pacific before me, I recall the story Merton told of the early Irish monks who took that metaphor literally, becoming pilgrims on the open sea.

*

They were called *peregrini*.

Inspired by Abraham, the archetypal pilgrim who left his home in Ur and traveled to the land God would show him, the Irish monks of the sixth and seventh centuries adopted the practice of *peregrinatio*, "going forth into strange countries."

The *peregrini* set off alone or in small groups in tiny coracles made of willow and animal hide, abandoning themselves to the winds and currents of the North Atlantic. Most never returned. This exercise in ascetic homelessness was practiced by men like Saint Columba, a sixth-century monk who founded a monastery on the island of Iona, and Saint Brendan the Navigator, thought by some to have reached North American shores long before the Vikings. As Merton wrote in his essay "From Pilgrimage to Crusade," the *peregrini* set out not in order to visit a sacred shrine but to seek solitude and exile. If the *peregrinus* had a goal, it was to find his "place of resurrection"—a specific place where he might live out his remaining days in prayer and solitude. This was not simply wandering for its own sake, Merton wrote: "It was a journey to a mysterious, unknown, but divinely appointed place, which was to be the place of the monk's ultimate meeting with God."

We moderns find it difficult to grasp the enormity of such an undertaking. Given how frequently we travel, we barely notice the existential threshold crossed upon leaving home. The *peregrini* remind us that we go on pilgrimage not to consume experience, but to be consumed. To feel again the porous borders between our inner and outer lives. If our rational age has obscured what Seamus Heaney called "a marvelous or magical view of the world," pilgrimage helps us find it again.

Whether we think the oceangoing *peregrini* merely quaint or even deranged, Merton was at pains to show them as utterly sane. The historical and literary records, he wrote, show that such journeys were not simply the acting out of unsatisfied romantic notions or psychic obsessions. The *peregrinatio* was a result of the "profound relationship with an inner experience of *continuity* between the natural and the supernatural, between the sacred and the profane . . . a continuity in both time and in space."

We can feel here a strong undercurrent of Merton's own leanings. This description of the *peregrinus* could be read as his own spiritual dossier: "His vocation was to mystery and growth, to liberty and abandonment to God, in self-commitment to the apparent irrationality of the winds and seas, in witness to the wisdom of God the Father and Lord of the elements . . . The deepest and most mysterious potentialities of the physical and bodily world, potentialities essentially sacred, demanded to be worked out on a spiritual and human level."

The tide laps at the base of my rocky perch at Jones Beach. I should think about getting back. Here on the California coast, I've begun to feel the geographical cure giving way to something more durable. A longing for God that is vast, oceanic, yet as close to me as the waves beneath my feet. A feeling of presence that paradoxically comes when I feel most alone.

Was this *le point vierge,* the virginal point of pure nothingness that Merton found at the center of all other loves?

Perhaps this is our place of resurrection, not a fixed point but a longing, a portable question endlessly posed and endlessly answered whenever we go in search of God. A tectonic convergence of our desire for God and God's desire for us, all of it mediated through that fickle, insatiable organ of perception that will travel to the ends of the earth to find what it craves, though it needn't travel further than the next breath: the human heart.

On my final evening at Redwoods Abbey, I decide to give something back to the sisters. I want to honor their hospitality and pay homage to Amma Veronique's singular gift.

Which is to say, I make a beer run.

When I roll into dinner that evening, twelve-pack of Belgian ales under each arm, Sister Kathy shakes her head in mock disapproval. It doesn't take much sweet talk to convince her to give her abbatial permission. The party that ensues is lively by Cistercian standards, which means that the sisters drink one beer each, I drink two, and the normally silent meal gradually gives way to furtive titters, then whispered exchanges, then full-blown table conversation.

These women, most of them in the final third of their lives, have been on pilgrimage without ever leaving the monastery, yet what sights they have seen, what depths they have plumbed in their search for the life beyond life. The first pilgrimages may have been a search for the mountain where the ancient fathers were in direct communication with heaven, as Merton wrote, but here at

Redwoods Abbey I've found the ancient *mothers,* and their communication with heaven occurs deep in a stand of old-growth redwoods. I am honored to have been admitted into their presence.

"We had a *huud* connection," Sister Veronique tells me at our
parting, "a very *huud* connection." The following day I will get into
my rental car and drive south to San Francisco, where I will buy a
copy of Hermann Hesse's *Siddhartha* at City Lights Books, catch a
plane for Albuquerque, and make the two-hour drive to the Monastery of Christ in the Desert. Before I go, Sister Veronique cradles
her belly with both hands and says, "Hold on to what you have and
let it flower."


## III. Desert

Driving that May of 1968 on the road to Christ in the Desert, a
new Benedictine monastery in the Chama River Canyon of northern New Mexico, Merton was *bombarded by impressions.* Snow up
high in the Sangre de Cristo Mountains, and then a *marvelous long
line of snowless, arid mountains, clean long shapes stretching for miles under pure light. Mesas, full rivers, cottonwoods, sagebrush, high red cliffs,
piñon pines. Most impressed of all by the miles of emptiness.*

After leaving the highway, he drove 13 miles down a rutted dirt
road and arrived at the remote monastery, a place of *perfect silence.*
Inside the adobe church he marveled at the images of Santos as
*serious as painted desert birds.* He spent the next several days hiking
alone in the canyon. Small pine, cedar, a gang of gray jays, the
cold, muddy Chama River—his eyes were hungry for all of it. He
could use up rolls of film on nothing but the rocks along the canyon walls. *The whole canyon replete with emptiness.*

One day he lunched with Georgia O'Keeffe. He photographed
Pedernal, the mesa dominating the skyline and one of O'Keeffe's
great subjects, and asked her what one sees from the top. O'Keeffe
said, "You see the whole world."

Each morning he read René Daumal's *Mount Analogue,* which
he declared a very fine book. "The gateway to the invisible must be
visible," wrote Daumal.

Whether Merton sought God here in this desert canyon or
along the desolate Mendocino coast or in the deep hush of the
redwoods, he began to suspect that his search for the perfect her-

mitage was a chimera. *The country which is nowhere is the real home.* His real home was *le point vierge,* the place in himself reserved only for God. *Perhaps I have an obligation to preserve the stillness, the silence, the poverty, the virginal point of pure nothingness which is at the center of all other loves.*

Though it has since flourished in every part of the world, Christian monasticism began in a desert.

The founder of Christian monasticism was Saint Anthony the Great. In the third century, Saint Anthony left his life in the city and went to live and pray in solitude in the wilderness of Egypt. Others soon followed his example. Within two centuries, so many men and women had fled to monasteries that chroniclers from that period report that the desert had become a city.

The Monastery of Christ in the Desert is no monastic metropolis, I discover when I arrive for a three-day retreat, but it has grown much since Merton's visit 50 years ago. Surrounded by the deep silence of the Chama River Canyon, the monastery feels like part eco-commune, part African or Asian village. The immediately striking thing about the place is that most of the monks here are from the Global South.

Prior Benedict, the jovial right-hand man of the abbot, gives me the full tour. In front of the dormitories, he introduces me to a novice from Zambia mowing the lawn. In a side office, I meet a monk from Kenya studying ESL. In the kitchen, we bump into a Filipino monk in his 80s who was once a literature professor in Manila. He taught the metaphysical poets. Prior Benedict asks me who I think is his favorite. George Herbert? "No," the Filipino monk says, laughing, as if the answer were obvious. "John Donne!" I learn that a number of the monks have advanced degrees. Prior Benedict has a PhD in medieval intellectual history. He is also an immigration attorney. For all the foreign brothers needing visas and green cards, Prior Benedict is their man. As we stroll through the grounds, he lists offhandedly the home countries of the brothers we pass: Laos, Cambodia, Vietnam, Zambia, Congo, Philippines . . . 16 or 17 nationalities in all.

The monks live off the grid. They plant vegetable gardens. Grow peonies. Build straw-bale buildings and put up solar panels to power them (theirs is the oldest and largest private solar array in New Mexico). They grow hops for their own Abbey Brewing

Company. For exercise they ride horses or run trails or hike in the Chama Canyon or play volleyball—"full contact," Prior Benedict says with a wry grin—using team names like Chastity and Stability. They study and read and play music and daily gather in the chapter room to confess their faults before one another—thereby preventing the buildup of that destroyer of intentional communities and families and marriages the world over, resentment—but mostly what they do is pray: eight services a day, more than four hours of prayer, every day of the year.

If Redwoods Abbey was a temple of stillness, the sisters embodying Rilke's dictum that solitudes should "protect and border and greet each other," then Christ in the Desert is by comparison a beehive. If you want solitude here, I realize, you have to hike for it.

I ask Prior Benedict for recommendations on that score. He points to several trails behind the monastery. His favorite, though, is a hike to some distant Anasazi ruins on the canyon rim across the river. Normally he would take me, but he is leaving the next day for Costa Rica. I'm happy to go on my own, I venture. But the hike is dangerous and steep—a full-day affair—and he cannot grant me his permission without a guide. "Ah well," he says, "good reason for you to return." We stand for a moment looking across the Chama River at the canyon rim. I picture myself climbing up to the mesa and walking in that ancient landscape, alone with God in the vast emptiness of the desert.

"You don't choose to live in the desert," Brother Chrysostom tells me. "You are *called* to live in the desert."

Brother Chrysostom's call came three years ago, on a three-month pilgrimage on Spain's Camino de Santiago de Compostela. His life was already quasi-monastic—he attended daily Mass, prayed the canonical hours—yet something pulled him toward a deeper commitment. He decided to walk the Camino as a way to discern his vocation. About halfway through the pilgrimage he heard an inner voice saying, "John, I want you there." When he got home he put his affairs in order, returned to Christ in the Desert, and took the name Chrysostom, the golden-tongued fifth-century saint.

There are many parallels between Brother Chrysostom's life and Thomas Merton's. Both men lived a full life before becoming monks: traveled the world, had rich social lives, were men of letters (although Brother Chrysostom is reluctant to speak of his accomplishments, I learn that he has degrees from MIT, Johns Hopkins, and Wharton, plus a doctorate in political science). When I tell him I'm following in Merton's steps, he says, "Thomas Merton is my imaginary neighbor." Brother Chrysostom lives in cell 8, right next door to where Merton stayed, in cell 6. He is the same age Merton was when he died: 53. "Merton loved this place, and I know he wanted to be here," he says. "Now I'm part of the continuation of his story."

Whatever their mother tongue or place of origin, the monks here feel a certain camaraderie with Merton. To Brother Jerome, a 36-year-old monk from Zambia, Merton was an ordinary monk who, by immersing himself in prayer, became extraordinary. "He shared the fruits of his contemplation with the rest of the world, and we try to do the same. We nourish ourselves individually with God, then we share it with the world." People like Merton are guides. Jerome quotes an old Zambian proverb: "The one who has crossed the river knows the story of the river." Merton crossed the river of prayer. He was a human being like us, Brother Jerome says, and he gives us courage to make the journey.

Over the next three days, I speak with different monks about their experience crossing that river. Brother Leander, a quiet 92-year-old monk from Scotland with a cloudy right eye, takes to calling me "dear brother" and "laddie." He sees prayer as central to the monastic life. "If we were just a jolly bunch of farmers and ecologists, well . . ." His voice trails off, his right hand waving the thought away. He quotes Karl Rahner, a famous midcentury Catholic theologian. The Christian of the future, Rahner said 50 years ago, will either be a mystic or cease to exist. Brother Leander looks hard at me with his good eye. "And what is mysticism? The experience of God in the interior of one's being. I always liked Hermann Hesse's definition of a mystic: a poet without verses, a painter without a brush, a musician without notes." I tell Brother Leander that I pray the Jesus Prayer, a kind of mantra used by the early desert monks. "Yes, laddie, and you must pray the prayer not only with your lips or your mind but with your heart."

Brother Isidore became a monk after fleeing war in Congo. He has seen much suffering and death, yet he possesses a deep calm and joy. "Contemplative life is the heart of the church," he says, and that involves a commitment to silence. "Most of the time we have a lot to tell God. We must learn to be silent before God who made us."

As I talk with these monks, each of them grows animated. They speak of God as one speaks of a dear friend, a family member, a lover. But as they make clear, such connection with God doesn't come without struggle. The desert in the biblical tradition may be a place of stillness, contemplation, and deep encounter with God, but it is also a place of temptation, despair, and madness.

It was a collective madness that befell European Christianity in the medieval years when Christians gave up wandering in search of God and turned their search toward wealth and power.

By the 12th century, the peaceful and defenseless *peregrinatio* of the Irish monks had been replaced by the violence of the Crusades. When knights, kings, and priests attempted to liberate the land of Abraham through force, Merton wrote, they implanted within the European psyche an insidious pattern of conquest that would repeat itself many times over the coming centuries. The promised land, paradise, the place of resurrection—such metaphors for the spiritual journey became actual places that needed to be conquered through violence and preserved through politics, and those who inhabited those places became barriers between the European pilgrim and his god. At that point, Merton wrote, Christian life took on an embattled, martial character. The colonizers of the Renaissance were capable of the horrors they inflicted on native peoples precisely because they were alienated from themselves: "History would show the fatality and doom that would attend on the external pilgrimage with no interior spiritual integration, a divisive and disintegrated wandering, without understanding and without the fulfillment of any humble inner quest. In such pilgrimage no blessing is found within, and so the outward journey is cursed with alienation."

By the time Europeans set foot in North America, the pilgrim mentality and crusader mentality had finally fused, creating a singular and disastrous form of alienation that resulted in the conquest of indigenous peoples. As Merton wrote: "Centuries of ardent, unconscious desire for the Lost Island had established a kind of right to paradise once it was found. It never occurred to the sixteenth-century Spaniard or Englishman to doubt for a moment that the new world was entirely and rightly his. It had been promised and given to him by God. It was the end of centuries of pilgrimage."

"There is no lost island merely for the individual," Merton concluded in his essay on pilgrimage. "We are all pieces of the paradise isle." In no time is that more true than now, in this age when our paradise isle is threatened at every turn. Perhaps the meaning of pilgrimage now in this age of climate change and species loss is that the fruits of our inner life in God cannot remain ours alone; they must be shared for the sake of all life. The portal to the invisible must be visible.

"What can we gain by sailing to the moon if we are not able to cross the abyss that separates us from ourselves?" Merton asked. "This is the most important of all voyages of discovery, and without it all the rest are not only useless but disastrous." To update Merton's question: What can we gain by fixing climate change or ending poverty or terraforming Mars if we remain alienated from ourselves? How to cross that abyss?

Brother Leander: You must let the prayer descend to your heart, laddie!

Brother Isidore: Let us be silent before God who made us.

Brother Jerome: You learn to talk to silence, and silence answers in silence.

On my last full day at the Monastery of Christ in the Desert, I decide to climb up to the canyon rim in search of the Anasazi ruins. I want to approach with as much humility as I can that holy place where silence answers in silence. Prior Benedict might disapprove of my solo mission, but by now he is in Costa Rica, and after all, I have taken no vow of obedience.

I pack light: running shoes, shorts, T-shirt, two liters of water, and some desert rations—a boiled egg, a few dates. Before I can begin climbing I first need to cross the cold, muddy Chama. *The one who has crossed the river knows the story of the river.* Down along the river bottom I wade through milkweed stalks looking for a way across, until I discover under a willow tree a battered, leaky rowboat. Like the *peregrini* of old, I launch my coracle into the swift, dark waters. The current is strong. I have to row diagonally across, working the oars with all my strength so as not to be swept downstream. Midway across the river I feel something tingle deep in my spine, that mixture of fear and wonder that accompanies any such journey: I am traveling alone; no one knows where I am going; I might not return.

The cliff face above appears impregnable save for one slot. I aim for that. The climb takes me up a steep arroyo choked with ocotillo, white sage, and juniper. On a cliff to my right I notice strange markings. Petroglyphs? I can't be certain, for the rock face lies hidden in morning shadow. Within an hour of climbing, I near the slot and find my first cairn. Beside the cairn are signs of life: a pile of coyote scat drying in the sun, a lone cactus in bloom. This seems to be the way.

Once reaching the canyon rim I see another cairn, but a bit farther on when I top a small rise at the rim's edge there is no trail, only a broad, juniper-choked mesa stretching away to the west. For the next hour I move outward in concentric semicircles trying to find the path. By now it's late morning. The sun is fierce. Most of my water is gone. I find a few more scattered cairns, but they don't lead anywhere—or rather, they lead me in circles. For another two hours I wander around increasingly uncertain of where I am. I know how to go back, but I don't know the way forward.

In the shade of a juniper tree I sit down, confused. A breeze picks up. My sweat dries, my skin prickles. Perhaps because I feel so alone in this desert, I think of the others on my journey who've confronted this same emptiness. Bashō. The *peregrini*. Sister Veronique, Sister Kathy. Brother Isidore, Brother Chrysostom, Brother Jerome. And Merton. I've had many trustworthy guides on this descent to the heart, but here in the desert I have no guide, and perhaps for now I no longer need one. Sister Veronique said I should hold on to what I have and let it flower. What I have, rooted in me since childhood, are these unresolved feelings of exile, loneliness, neglect. What if I make those my offering? When you've been stripped of all but your indissoluble self, what core remains?

This is the work: to take these feelings of loneliness and exile and bring them into the furnace of the heart, where emotional abandonment becomes mystical abandonment.

Sitting in this tiny patch of shade, surrounded by white sage and ocotillo, I bring these thoughts into prayer. Normally my prayers are a dull litany of requests and complaints, the hypes and gripes of a lukewarm spiritual life, but here on the edge of this vast mesa, I feel those petitions giving way to something more compelling, an opening into a more spacious country. An uncomplicated resting in God, who seems to have no other agenda than to welcome me into this place of silence and mercy and at-oneness. A feeling of Presence that is so much more than the breeze on my face or the sweat evaporating on my skin.

I never find the Anasazi ruins. Just as well that I don't. After a time, I swallow the last of my water, stretch my stiff legs, and retrace my steps back to the last cairn along the canyon rim. I can see far below on the river's edge a small, damaged vessel, waiting to ferry me home.

## Coda

Let us see him once more. He's driving south along the Eel River under trees as old as the faith he follows. Soon he will be back home in Kentucky, watching the small hardwoods fill with new growth and wondering if they are even real trees, so much are his thoughts filled with redwoods. *Who can see such trees and bear to be away from them? I must go back. It is not right that I should die under lesser trees.* Six months from now, in Bangkok, after speaking to an international gathering of monastics, he will return to his room for a bath, reach for a fan, and receive the accidental electric shock that will end his life. His body will be placed on a transport plane carrying the bodies of American soldiers killed that week in Vietnam and then returned to Gethsemani, with its lesser trees, where it will be waked, prayed over with Psalms, wrapped in a monastic habit, and planted in the earth beneath cedars and oaks and sycamores that I will walk under 50 years later. But now, driving south along the Eel River, he is still innocent of what's to come. His journey has only begun. As we see him there in the passenger seat, spinning down Highway 101, we need not tax ourselves with forethought of grief, for here in this ongoing moment, there is only *the worshipful cold spring light on the sandbanks of Eel River, the immense silent redwoods.* The light leads him onward to his place of resurrection, he knows not where.

# If You Are Permanently Lost

FROM *The Paris Review*

I NEVER HAVE ANY idea where I am. I lived my whole childhood in the purple foothills of the same five-square-mile town and I still couldn't tell you whether you turn left or right on the single thru-way to get to the grade school or the grocery store, or how to find the houses of any of my childhood friends. I can't tell you how to find the conspicuously modern angles of the apartment building in the small Mississippi town where I lived for three years in graduate school, or even easily direct you from my old house in Austin to the bright little bar where I wrote much of my first book. I never know how far I am from the airport or the highway. I can't read a map effectively, and even though it's less than half a mile from my current apartment in London, I couldn't get to the Thames without the artificial voice on my cell phone—set to an Australian accent so its omnipresence is less tiresome—calling out *Turn left* every 250 feet. Half the time, to remember which way is left, I have to imagine for an instant that I am picking up a pen.

Even on a much smaller scale, space makes no sense to me. I walk all the way around the perimeter of a room to reach a door that's immediately to my right, and I set my glass down half an inch from the edge of the table with such frequency that anyone who knows me well gets used to nudging it back again and again over the course of an evening in this small, choreographed two-step. As a girl, I put my shoes on the wrong feet so reliably that my parents directed me just to behave in defiance of my inclinations: if I thought a sneaker should go on one foot, put it on the other. This is a strategy I still use sometimes: if I'm certain an office is to the right out of the elevator, I go left down the hall. I'm almost always wrong about the layout of the world.

I come, after a while, to recognize landmarks—pale-blue awning of the nearest dry cleaner's, wrought iron railing along the railroad bridge, surprise of a green-painted storefront among all the brick—which is how I learn, eventually, to navigate some frequent paths of travel, but no collection of spaces, no matter how habitually I move through them, ever knits into any kind of coherent map inside my head. I'll be wandering in the city convinced I'm miles away from anywhere I've ever been, and then turn a corner to see the shapes of my own block rising up as if transplanted, their familiarity more unsettling than encountering something new, proof I lack a homing instinct of any kind.

There's a neurological explanation for at least some of this. The ability to process information about distance, angles, and direction—to reason, essentially, about the physical expanse around you—is called spatial cognition, and the oxygen deprivation at birth that caused my cerebral palsy resulted in some injury to the neural structures that make this kind of reasoning possible; it's as if there's a blown fuse in the wiring of my brain. Lights from down the hall provide a little glow, but the chamber is permanently dim.

Even beyond the oxygen deprivation, though, it turns out that, in young children, spatial cognition begins to develop concurrently with what professionals term "independent locomotion": the ability to get around under your own steam. Essentially, you gain the capacity to map the world as you begin to move intentionally through it, the brain wiring in sync with what the body does. I never wiggled or crawled effectively, my muscles too spastic and stiff, and I didn't learn to walk until I was four, which is too late for typical cognitive progress to occur. There's an allotted developmental window for the needed synchronicity to come to pass, and if it doesn't, it's impossible to perfectly correct the disjunction. With attention, you can create some new neural pathways, alternate routes to comprehending space, but you can't retrace the steps you should have taken.

My terrible sense of direction is a long-running joke among family and friends, who know better than to trust my baseless assurances that I'm positive we're heading the right way this time, and for a long time my lack of spatial awareness mostly felt like an inconvenience, minor in comparison with my difficulty walking, or my chronic pain. But I've been thinking, lately, about home and navigation: what it means to be perennially dislocated, what it means when space, no matter how you try to fathom it, refuses to coalesce into a place you know.

Displaced from their breeding pools, marbled newts can find their way back home only when certain stars are visible; they spend whole days paused with their bellies pressed to the ground, waiting for the sun to set, the clouds to clear. Homing pigeons' compass mechanisms rely on the sun, but when it's dark or clouded over they can feel the earth's magnetic field. Iron particles collected in their beaks will always tug them toward true north. Honeybees navigate by polarized light, give directions to one another relative to the position of the sun. Bats and cave swiftlets and porpoises map intricate and perfect distances from echoes. And even some mollusks, base and faceless, are thought to hold a topographic memory of the land, finding their way via familiar contours, the rises and gullies they remember how to fit inside. All these bodies that know home somewhere inside them.

It isn't at all that I don't get attached to landscapes: the exact color of the clay in the mountains where I was raised, part rust, part something redder; the miles and miles of cool blue flat driving through a Mississippi January morning; the wildness of California palm trees in the winter. There's a scent of Virginia magnolia, dusk-sweet and too much, that I can call up instantly, and my favorite sound is the particular loud, humid crack of a weirdly rainless southern thunderstorm, come out of nowhere and then gone again. But you could put me down on the land I love most in the world and I would still be lost inside it: the familiar made alien and unsteady by my inability to fuse its fragments into a whole.

I have lived in six different cities and towns in the past 10 years, and now two foreign countries in the past six months. Without really meaning to, I've made a life composed almost entirely of leaving and arrival, a life where it's reasonable to never know my way around. *I'm new,* I say, or, *I'm about to go,* or, *I don't live here, I'm just visiting.* I think: *This isn't my real life.*

At a medical library in London, I stand in front of a photographic print of the human brain and spinal column strung with nerves, magnified to many times its size. Hung there on the wall, huge and in black and white, it looks more than anything like a tangle of netting and driftwood and rope, like a raft someone assembled swiftly, in a panic, trying to survive a storm. I keep thinking of the last stanza of that Adrienne Rich poem "Song": of the rowboat she conjures, grounded on the shore in the wintertime, and how she writes that it knows itself. Knows it is comprised not of "ice nor mud nor winter light / but wood, with a gift for burning."

If there's any territory I should know well, it's the country of my own body. So much of my life has been devoted to attending to its margins and features: its tenuous center of gravity; the tense curl of my hamstrings and heel cords; the banks of calluses along the perimeters of my feet, hardened from years of walking on my toes with my feet listing stubbornly to one side; the thickets of scarring behind my knees and at my ankles; the fading ridgeline where they sliced me open at the spine. I've had so many cartographers and architects: doctors' appointments and surgeries designed to know and map my body, alter its geography, to make it more habitable. It, at least, should be comprehensible: place instead of merely space.

But here there is a double alienation. Because the world refuses to grow knowable and navigable, because my brain cannot compose a cogent map, my body is rendered new to me each time I try to move through space. Each turned corner is an uncharted expanse I have no idea how I will traverse or respond to. And because my body itself has been reshaped so many times, both through the intentional, artificial manipulations of surgery and by its own ongoing and present disintegration, I can't truly know or trust its geography either. The tectonic plates of who I am are always shifting. My friend Susannah has also had a great deal of surgery, her own profound erosions. This heavy grief, finally shared with another person, yielded a nearly instant bond between us. We both know there's no returning to the beginning, no knowing who you've always been, no going home again. But we also know that there's no staying where you are: that the moment that your body sutures together into a whole and steady place you know, something will give way and you'll be changed to mere parts again.

Sometimes I think I've made myself into a constant traveler as a defense mechanism. On a practical level, it's a bad strategy: to compound with still more newness the permanent unfamiliarity my brain and body engender, evolving practical obstacles in every

unmappable place. But in another way it makes a kind of sense. I'd
rather be a stranger, transitory and alone, because of something
I decided than as a consequence of something in me, some lack
that proves again and again just how damaged an animal I am.
Constant motion camouflages the extent to which I'm alien even
to myself.

Again and again I return to Rich's rowboat, beached on the cold
shore. I think: *I don't know where or what I am*. But then I consider
how, in laying out a litany of what that rowboat knows it's not,
Rich transfigures it again and again in the course of a single line:
*boat* to *ice* to *mud* to *winter light* and finally to *wood*, raw material
whose most miraculous property is its ability to burn, break down,
change. How it's a gift to alchemize to something else.

In the world of a poem, it's an advantage to be inescapably a
stranger, an explorer. The task is so often to render the familiar
changed and charged and new, or to chart a path through constantly evolving territory, thick with shifting shadows. The woman
in Rich's "Song" drives continually onward, leaves behind so many
towns she might have stopped and made a life in, but the poem
itself holds all those possible lives at once. The fragment is rendered its own small, self-contained place, its capacity for continual
transformation a gift of metaphor, music, and line.

To work your way forward when you are permanently lost means,
yes, to be exhausted and adrift, a stranger in a strange land. But,
as a writer, it also means living in a state of endless discovery. The
world unfurls itself anew each day with *dawn's first cold breath on the
city*. You reencounter what you are: lonely like a body with a gift
for burning.

# Life, Death, and the Border Patrol

FROM *Sierra*

WE'VE BEEN HIKING for a half hour when we see the SUV driving across the sand in our direction. We are not surprised that we've been seen. Our group of 12 hikers is the tallest thing around that isn't a cactus.

The SUV pulls up alongside us. "What are you doing?" says the Border Patrol officer inside.

"Hi, sir," says one of the volunteers leading us. "We're just a group of friends on a day hike."

"What's with the water jugs?" says the officer. Each of us is carrying a gallon of water. Some are carrying two. "You wouldn't be doing anything special with those, would you?"

"It's ninety-seven degrees, sir," says our group leader.

The officer smiles, but it's not friendly. He doesn't believe us. But we're on public land. There's not much he can do, for now.

He asks to see our identification. We open our packs and begin digging. Before we can pull out our IDs, he abruptly speeds away, kicking up a plume of dust that leaves us all coughing. "Hope you guys have a nice day," he shouts sarcastically.

We start walking again, slipping in the soft sand.

When I met up with the Border Angels this morning, we separated into groups according to hiking ability. I joined the most experienced group. I recently spent a month hiking the Camino de Santiago across Spain. But walking with no trail is brutal. A few hikers have already turned back.

Border Angels is a nonprofit, run by volunteers, that has provided legal aid and education to immigrants in San Diego since the 1980s. For the past two decades, it has also left caches of water in the Sonoran Desert for migrants crossing it. Last year, at least 283 people died trying to cross the borderlands between the United States and Mexico, mostly from dehydration. The actual number of deaths could be higher—not all bodies are discovered or reported to the Border Patrol.

We reach a wall that is more like a pile of boulders and begin to scramble up. More hikers turn back. Many first-timers don't ever return, one of the guides tells me. The ones who don't quit aren't necessarily the most athletic but have the strongest belief in what they're doing. I wasn't expecting this to be like the Camino, but it feels like a pilgrimage. Everyone wants to tell you why they're here.

Soon, we're inside a canyon. Signs of human activity are everywhere—empty water jugs, a shelter made of a tarp stretched across two boulders. It's difficult to say how recently people have been here. The sound of distant gunshots ricochets off the walls. BLM land is a popular spot for day-trippers to drink and shoot guns, but the sound makes everyone tense. We boulder our way through, leaving water jugs and bags filled with food, clothing, and emergency supplies as we go.

If the Border Patrol find these supplies after we leave, they might destroy them. But migrants and asylum seekers try to cross over on terrain where the Border Patrol can't drive. It's likely they'll find these supplies, at a time when the food and water could mean the difference between life and death.

As people set down their jugs, some write messages on them. I think for a minute and then write "Bienvenidos."

We reach the top of the canyon. In the distance, I can see the watchtowers and the white surveillance blimps flown by the Border Patrol. I can see the campers who are shooting guns and the distant glitter of the Salton Sea. I can see a smudge in the distance that must be a city in Baja California. There is no fence at this point, which sits at the junction between the United States and Mexico. It's impossible to tell where one ends and the other begins.

KEN BUDD

# The Volunteer's Dilemma

FROM *The Washington Post Magazine*

I SMILE AT A round-cheeked, two-year-old girl, sitting in the lap of Kim Martin, a *mzungu*—white person—like me. We are at the Calvary Zion Children's Home in Kenya; the girl is one of 41 children, from infants to university students, who live here. Her Zion brothers and sisters share many bonds, but one life experience is central: tragedy. Several years ago, one newborn was found in a trash dump, his umbilical cord still attached. Another was abandoned at Nakumatt, the Kenyan equivalent of Walmart. Others lost their parents and had no family members who could accept the hardship of raising another child.

Days after this girl was born, she was abandoned by her mother on a beach. Two local women saw the newborn in the sand, lying amid limp, washed-up seaweed. Luckily, they found her before high tide. The government children's department brought her here, to Calvary Zion, in Bamburi, outside Mombasa.

The girl's braided hair is tied in a ponytail; her dress is a bright and buoyant pink. We sit in the shade as friends of the home set up tents and prepare for today's party to celebrate Calvary Zion's 20th anniversary. Some of the older girls are laughing and fixing their hair. The older boys seem to be wondering about lunch. Kim's husband, Howard—they run a bed-and-breakfast in England —entertains a 12-year-old boy by showing videos on his phone of Howard's beloved Everton soccer team. The boy smiles and nods at Howard's play-by-play. When he was 5, the boy was abandoned in a telephone booth by his mother.

The three of us, along with two other foreign supporters—Susan Peattie, a Scot who created a nonprofit to support the home, and a fellow Scottish supporter, Liz Brown—have been placed in the shade, partly because of the heat. December in Kenya is like July in Washington, DC, hot and humid, only without the ubiquitous air-conditioning.

Soon, we're greeted by the home's founder, Jane Karigo, who smiles and embraces me. "Ahhhhhh," she says, laughing. "Long ago. Long ago."

I last saw her in 2009, when I volunteered at Calvary Zion for two weeks with my wife. I'm not a religious person, but the born-again Jane, now in her 60s, exudes a joy that I rarely associate with the devout. With her short, thick build and boisterous laugh —a laugh that makes *me* laugh—she reminds me of the Buddha, though as a Christian she would be dismayed by the comparison.

"You need to look more Kenyan," she says, and hands us each a gift: a traditional African dashiki shirt. We soon look like an Earth, Wind & Fire tribute band, and by making us more African, we of course look more white. Yet somehow that seems appropriate. I'm not sure I should be here—and I was reluctant to come back. Ten years ago, I volunteered at Calvary Zion because I wanted to do a tiny bit of good in the world, and we've continued to make a modest annual donation to the home. But volunteering at an orphanage is now often seen as an international sin.

For years, volunteer vacations, as they were then known, attracted little scrutiny. People would use their vacation time to serve others, both at home and abroad, and see a foreign place in a different way. Now better known as voluntourism, global volunteering is frequently criticized as privileged, unqualified First Worlders —many with a "white-savior complex"—traipsing around developing countries, posing for selfies and doing more harm than good.

Volunteering at orphanages, or "orphanage tourism," to use its occasional, unfortunate name, has received particularly intense condemnation. The criticism began roughly 10 years ago, following reports that orphanages in Cambodia were holding "orphans" —many of whom had at least one parent—to attract donors and volunteers. Today, some organizations no longer place volunteers in orphanages. Author J. K. Rowling is an outspoken critic, telling a BBC radio program in 2018 that volunteers "are driving a system that we know from eighty sound years of research irreparably harms children." Children are frequently abused and neglected, according to Georgette Mulheir, CEO of Lumos, a nongovernmental organization founded by Rowling to end the institutionalization of children. But they are told "to smile and sing and tell the volunteers they love them, otherwise they'll be beaten or locked up or they won't get food," Mulheir said in an interview with the *Telegraph* newspaper. A story from an Australian news site called orphanage tourism "slavery hidden in plain sight."

My experience at Calvary Zion has been profoundly different from those descriptions. And yet the more I read the negative stories, the more I wondered: By supporting Calvary Zion, was I propping up a damaging system? By trying to help these kids, was I hurting them? Jane says that God told her to create the home. What if God was wrong?

From the outside, Calvary Zion looks like a fortress. Razor wire stretches across an imposing 10-by-15-foot metal entry gate. Concrete walls, roughly 8 feet high, lined with electric wire, surround nearly five acres, with thick trees looming above. If not for the words on the gate — CALVARY ZION CHILDREN'S HOME — A HOME OF SIGNS AND WONDERS — it could be mistaken for a government compound or a drug lord's estate.

Susan Peattie's nonprofit raised money for the electric fencing and other security after the home was attacked by thieves in 2014. Six men armed with machetes and guns stole cell phones and roughly 100,000 Kenyan shillings — about $1,000 — from Jane's house. Jane told the thieves she would pray for them. A thug smacked her in the face. The children hid under their beds, though one girl was chased outside and hid in the dark behind banana trees.

It's hard for me to imagine the fear of that night, because Calvary Zion feels like a sanctuary from the often-dangerous world outside. As we bumped over pocked rural roads in a tuk-tuk (a small three-wheeled taxi) to visit the home, we passed the wood remnants of squatters' shacks, destroyed by police. Trash dumps frequently form on street corners, fields, and roadsides; skinny cows nose through flies and debris. But Calvary Zion is bucolic. Jane and the kids grow their own crops: bananas, tomatoes, mangoes, spinach, and corn (the electric fence prevents monkeys from stealing food). A well provides water. Cows munch lazily on hay; newborn piglets suckle their mothers' teats. Three of the home's goats gave their lives for the 20th-anniversary feast.

Jane and the kids moved here several months before the attack. A German couple, Tanja Fischer and Rainer Frank, raised money for the land and two houses; Tom Greaves, a former volunteer from England, raised money to finish construction of one of the houses by swimming the English Channel in 2017.

When I volunteered with Calvary Zion in 2009, it was a far different scene. Back then, 40-plus kids lived in a cramped three-bedroom house, sometimes sleeping two and three to a bed. The small enclosed "yard" was concrete; the house had no running water, and each day someone would drive roughly 20 miles to fill barrels with water for bathing, cooking, washing dishes, filling toilets, and scrubbing clothes.

I had arrived in Kenya after volunteering in five countries, wanting to live a life that matters. My dad, the best man I've ever known, had died after a sudden heart attack. I had turned 40, and my wife and I didn't have kids. I was struggling not only with the loss of my father, but with accepting I would never be a father myself. When an opportunity arose through my job to volunteer in New Orleans after Hurricane Katrina, I jumped on it. That led to volunteer excursions at an elementary school in Costa Rica, a special-needs school in China, and a scientific project in Ecuador, as well as a variety of work in the West Bank.

Midlife crisis? I suppose. I'm not crazy about the term. It was a search for meaning, and travel is a way to do that. It pulls you from your comfort zone. And I had begun toying with an idea: If I can't have children of my own, maybe, in some microscopic way, I can help someone else's child. "Success," my father once told me, "comes from helping others succeed."

My search for purpose may seem like a First World quest, but Jane experienced something similar. When she married her husband, John, in 1977, he didn't want her to work. "I felt so bad because I was used to working," says Jane, who had been a dressmaker and then a receptionist for Air India. "My parents were not happy, because they had educated me. I had gone to college. Working was very good for me. And now I am somebody's wife. And from that day, I stay as a housewife."

In 1983 Jane was born again. She soon became involved with

Aglow International, an organization of Christian women. She was named chair of the Mombasa chapter in 1991 and began traveling to other towns. "I see children suffering," she says. "I see children crying. Sometimes it is in the slums or the streets. I say, 'Whose children are these?' They are orphans. God started preaching to me about these children. And I organize for a group to visit the children in the slums. We used to go, fifteen women, we give them food, we take clothes, we talk to them about Jesus, and the love of God. But when I come home, I don't have any peace. I was crying. And my husband is worried. 'You are going to get yourself sick. What can you do? You cannot care for all of those children.'"

When you sleep, Jane tells me, God can talk to you. And one night she heard the voice of God. And God said to her: *You have been crying for the children. What are you doing about them?*

Jane sat up from her bed.

*These are the children,* God said.

"Which children?" Jane asked.

She looked around. She didn't know where she was, but it's like she was watching a screen. "I see children," she tells me now. "Crying. Very hungry. Very abused."

And she said to God, "What do you want me to do?"

*I want you to take them in for me.*

"And I said, 'Me, God? Me?' It is like a film, I'm seeing the film. And I say, 'God, what's all this about?'"

*Take them in for me,* God said.

Her husband was angry when she shared God's vision. They had four children of their own. "He said, 'How would you feed them? What are they going to eat?' And I said, I don't know. But I am *going* to do it. And he said, 'I don't understand.' He was afraid."

She told her skeptical friends at Aglow International that she was starting a children's home, and to understand how the homes work, she decided, yes, to volunteer. Six women joined her. And when her training was done, God told her to find a house. Through small donations raised by Jane and her friends, they somehow covered the 18,000-shilling deposit and the 9,000-shillings-a-month rent. Next they began collecting supplies, from beds to kitchen utensils.

In 1999, after the home was approved by the government children's department, the agency contacted her: A five-year-old girl had been abandoned. They asked Jane to take her. "Her name is Asia," says Jane. "I say, no. I need the grace of God. So from today your name is Grace." She soon received two other children, and two more arrived three months later. "Everybody, my family, my friends, they are praying for me," says Jane. "It is like they are thinking, 'This is madness.'"

In November 2018 two charities, Forget Me Not of Australia and UK-based Lumos, led a call to eliminate orphanages. Of the approximately eight million children living in orphanages worldwide, 80 percent are not orphans, the two organizations reported, but rather victims of child trafficking, frequently to support voluntourism. Catholic Relief Services (CRS) says as many as 90 percent of children in orphanages have at least one parent.

"The internet has made it very easy for unscrupulous orphanages to attract volunteers and donors, and for volunteers to continue raising funds through blog posts and Facebook pages—often with the ubiquitous orphan in a selfie," wrote Tina Rosenberg, cofounder of the Solutions Journalism Network, which supports reporting on social problems, in a two-part October 2018 opinion piece for the *New York Times*.

CRS has launched a campaign titled Changing the Way We Care, with the goal of "keeping children in families instead of orphanages." CRS and other organizations maintain that care in orphanages can lead to mood and attachment disorders; stunted social, emotional, and cognitive development; and increased risk of abuse and neglect. According to Forget Me Not and Lumos, young adults raised in institutions are 10 times as likely to fall into sex work as their peers, and 500 times as likely to take their own lives.

Organizations such as Projects Abroad have stopped sending short-term volunteers to children's homes. In March 2018 the Australian government launched a campaign to discourage its citizens from engaging in short-term, unskilled volunteering in orphanages.

And children's homes such as Calvary Zion may be vanishing in countries like Kenya. In 2018 Disability Rights International released a report based on visits to 21 Kenyan orphanages, which "documented severe neglect, physical and sexual abuse and torture." The Kenyan government has also reviewed children's homes, and in 2014 President Uhuru Kenyatta banned the registration of new orphanages. Roughly a month and a half before my recent visit to Kenya, the Nairobi-based *Daily Nation* focused on changing attitudes. Children may receive food, shelter, and clothing, said Ukur Yatani, the nation's labor and social protection secretary, but "there is the other bigger challenge of sociopsychological support that is required, which can only be found within the family or the society." It is unlikely, he added, that the government will ever register new orphanages.

When my wife and I volunteered in 2009, I was already worried that our short visit would contribute to a cycle of abandonment for the children. Our local contact reassured us, though, that the kids were used to volunteers, and that Jane and the home's three house mothers were a stable presence in their lives. She thought the presence of volunteers was useful because the children received individual attention. And when we were there, we rarely saw the kids. They were at school. It was usually just us, the three house mothers, and the infants.

We did whatever work the mothers requested, from washing dishes to slicing vegetables. We also did jobs they didn't have time for. I washed all of the windows, and we sorted and organized mounds of clothing donations. In the afternoons, we would walk some of the younger kids home from school. Once all of the little ones were there, the quiet house was suddenly like *Lord of the Flies* —kids were running, yelling, laughing, fighting. We would help some with homework and play with others. But we were also a welcome novelty for the mothers. The three women worked hard jobs, and we were a break in their exhausting routines. They would ask us about America, we would ask them about Kenya.

When I ask Jane and John—who, despite his initial reluctance, has supported Jane and the home since he retired in 2000—if they've seen fraudulent children's homes in Kenya, they tell us about a home that had financial sponsors but diverted much of the money, as well as supplies. "The home was closed five times," Jane says. "And each time they start again." (Six of the children were sent to Calvary Zion.) When the home's leader knew that sponsors were coming, according to Jane and John, he would gather local children to pretend that they lived there. "When you come you see *so* many children," says John.

Calvary Zion, of course, is not immune to difficulties. But Jane has worked to build a loving, stable environment. She has created small family units for the kids, a mix of ages and genders, so they have older and younger siblings (each group also has a house mother). When she started the home, she created an advisory board that includes a physician, a teacher, a pastor, and a social worker. They offer support and host fundraisers. At the 20th-anniversary party, the number of local supporters is large.

For much of that afternoon, the party resembles a revival, as one by one pastors grip a microphone and shout their lessons for life.

"The second half of your life is about your legacy!" one pastor shouts.

"Amen," attendees reply from the shade of tents.

"True prosperity is not money in a bank account!"

*Amen.*

"When your life is over, what will people say about you?"

*Amen.*

"Strength is not what you can lift, but how long you can lift it!"

*Amen.*

Jane sits, nodding her head, smiling, offering a quiet "Amen" as a baby lies asleep in her arms.

Grace, Calvary Zion's first child, is breastfeeding her baby girl in her apartment. The place is small but stylish, with furniture—shelves, sofa, chairs, rugs—all in matching black and white. Her flat-screen TV shows *Silver Linings Playbook*, making Bradley Cooper the first American I've seen since I arrived.

Grace, now 26, has been interested in fashion since she was a little girl, and as a teenager, she sold magazines and beauty products to pay for college. On our walk to her building, Susan and Liz and I stopped at her small, open-front clothing store in town, La Grace House of Fashion.

When the baby falls asleep, Grace makes us masala tea. A ceiling fan hovers above, but it's not turned on, and I'm wiping my forehead with a small towel, trying to pretend that I'm not sweating through my shirt. Grace seems comfortable despite wearing a long floral dress and a colorful head wrap.

I ask about her experiences growing up in an orphanage. When critics slam global volunteers, they rarely ask locals what *they* think. They accuse volunteers of being paternalistic neocolonialists, but isn't assuming that you know what's best for others also, well, colonialistic?

Grace says she learned how to raise a child from her time at Calvary Zion, since the older kids help care for the younger ones.

"What was Jane like as a mom?" I ask. "Was she tough?"

"She's not tough," she says, smiling.

"Really? I wouldn't want to mess with her."

"Jane is a God-fearing woman, and so she likes you to be a God-fearing person," says Grace. "She doesn't like children who are disobedient. She wants you to be respectful. She wants to bring up children with the right morals."

Susan tells a story of how some of the older boys were watching TV and told one of the house mothers to make them tea. Jane walked in the room, unplugged the TV, carried it out, and told them, "Make your own tea."

"Jane is caring as a mom, and she is strict," says Grace. "She doesn't like 'cheeky cheeky.' She doesn't like someone to lie to her. But she is forgiving."

I ask what was good about living there. Grace says she's close with the boys and girls at the home. "We help each other," she says. And she was thankful when they moved to the more-spacious home. "Because the children have a big field, they can play," she says. "At the old house the children are really squeezed."

I ask her what was difficult. She thinks for a moment.

"You know, Mama Jane cannot love everyone. We are so many."

"So it's hard to get individual attention."

"Yeah."

Her comment makes me think about one of the boys who lives with Jane. At the party, I didn't recognize most of the kids from when I volunteered. They were 10 years older. But I instantly recognized this boy. He was two the last time I saw him. His mother, Jane says, had discarded him behind a bush and was jailed for abandoning the child. When he arrived, one of the house mothers said, he didn't know how to eat: he would lie there with his mouth open.

Back in 2009 he would frequently approach me in his wobbly, baby-walk way, wanting to be held. And I would think, *How can you say no to this child?* So I would walk with him in the concrete yard, and he would point at things and say his one word, *Ahh-dahh.*

At the anniversary party, I didn't speak to him. If I were him, I'd find it strange if some white guy from another country suddenly approached like a long-lost friend. But I watched him. He joined

a group to sing "The Lord Is on My Side," and he was the first
back to his seat when the song was over. Mainly he squirmed in his
chair, sweating in the sun, looking bored and shy in a preteen way.
But he laughed during a dance competition and wolfed down goat
and potatoes and watermelon with the other boys. Susan said she
watched him playing soccer and thought he had emerged from his
shell. He does OK in school, she said. Not at the top, not at the
bottom. But when you've had such a terrible start to life, average
might be heartening.

For children like him, Jane offers love, not judgment. One
young man is albino, and in many African countries, including Kenya, albinos are hunted and killed. People believe they have supernatural powers and that their body parts bring wealth, power, and
good health. Jane never questioned the risks of accepting him.
He's a teenager now but cannot leave the home by himself—it's
too dangerous. To Jane, he is a child of God and a child of Calvary
Zion. And to the children, he is simply their brother.

Inside Jane's house, the children are singing for Belgians. The
foreigners have brought soccer jerseys from their hometown and
food supplies, including boxes and bags of rice, sugar, flour, and
powdered milk. The children sing a church hymn for their guests.

The donations are a lovely gesture—people throughout their
village raised money for the supplies. And yet the scene makes
me uncomfortable. It is an orphanage cliché: the African children
performing for their white benefactors. A mustachioed gentleman
requests a photo of the kids in their light-blue jerseys. They stand
in rows on the front steps as if posing for a class picture.

The man studies the image on the back of his camera and then
introduces himself. A blonde woman, who appears to be his wife,
holds a baby. We chat, and I ask about their time in Kenya. He tells
me they were on safari, and I think: *He's taking pictures of orphans
the same way he snapped pictures of giraffes.* But I'm sure I did the
same when I first volunteered. They want to help, he says, but he
is realistic. "You can give a little bit, but you can't change Kenya,"
he says. "Kenya is Kenya."

Susan and I discuss the Belgians one night as we drink Tusker,
the local beer, at our hotel. Susan, too, is a white benefactor,
and she arguably saved the home. Susan works internationally as
a teacher, from Guatemala to Japan, and while in Kenya, some

friends had given her money to donate to a good cause. She happened upon Calvary Zion. Susan calls it serendipity, Jane calls it God's will. But when Susan arrived, the home was struggling. She created the Calvary Zion Children's Home Support Trust, which raises money and finds sponsors for the kids.

"The bottom line is we need money and food," Susan says. She has mentioned to Jane that the performances are probably uncomfortable for the older kids. "But Jane," she says, "may see it as a necessary evil, because we've kind of got to give people what they want." And the gifts are meaningful. The donations of rice and flour will last for weeks.

When Susan and Liz and I visited Grace—a strong-minded, independent woman and not someone, I suspect, who feels the need to flatter the Scottish aunts she's known since childhood—I asked what she liked best about living at Calvary Zion. Her answer surprised us. "I was happy when visitors come," she said. "Because when visitors come you feel loved. You know you're not alone. There are people caring outside."

A day or so before I leave Kenya, a dead body washes on shore near my hotel. The bleached, bloated corpse floats on the ocean waves like a raft, arms outstretched, until slowly reaching sand. The popular theory is that the man was a sailor who fell overboard, but the body is a reminder: for many people, life is hard here. Skinny men walk the beach selling trinkets. The area is well-known for its "beach boys" and women looking for hookups. We see several old European men with young Kenyan women, and vice versa. Some, presumably, are prostitutes. Others get what they can. Free meals, free drinks, a night out.

Jane is determined to save the children from this type of life. When I was here before, I saw children living on the streets in Mombasa and thought that whatever the disadvantages of life at Calvary Zion, the children are sheltered; they are fed, protected, and loved. They go to school and church. They have strong adult role models. They are expected not only to be good citizens, but to be successful. One recent high school graduate is studying to be an auto mechanic. Another is studying electrical engineering. Their older brother started medical school in April. Others, like Grace, have gone to college and started businesses.

The children are sponsored by Kenyans and by Westerners,

some of whom are here for the 20th anniversary. When my wife and I first volunteered, Jane told me that this is how God provides: the volunteers are guided here by God. "*You* are a vessel," she said.

Over the past several years, I have wrestled with that idea. By serving as a tiny but steady vessel for Calvary Zion, by attempting to forge some good from my childless life, am I supporting the children? Or am I supporting an outdated Dickensian system? No child should live in an orphanage. I know that. And yet after returning here, I know that I will be back, and that I will continue to support Jane and Calvary Zion. The way I see it, I'm helping a friend and her kids who deserve whatever support they receive. I believe in Jane's work. And I believe in her exceedingly large family. Jane, I've come to realize, doesn't think she's running an orphanage. "This is a home," she tells me. "When they are married, they come home to see Mama Jane and Papa John. Because God has given us these children."

Unlike Jane, I doubt that God exists, but she makes me think that maybe there's . . . something. Something unexplainable. Something unseen that's loving and bright. Too often, the supposedly religious shout their showy faith yet ignore the suffering of others. Jane will talk endlessly of God's love and grace, but it is more than words.

There is both love and pain at Calvary Zion, and the two are intertwined, like the razor wire twisting upon the home's front gate. And there are other things here too: hope and pride and strength. Jane has instilled these qualities in her children. I understand the evidence against orphanages, but seeing her work up close—and seeing the lives she's changed—makes it impossible to turn away.

The afternoon of the event, we listen as some of the teenage girls recite a poem:

> Mother, father.
> Where are you today?
> If only you could see me.
> I am beautiful.

# My Own Private Iceland

FROM *Vox*

THERE'S A PLACE in Iceland where you can see the northern lights any time of year, regardless of the weather. You don't have to ride a snowmobile into the mountains or rent a glass-roofed igloo. You don't even need a winter jacket.

Leaning back in my recliner, I gaze upward at the ethereal reds, greens, and blues arcing across the sky, wavering like alien signals, an extraterrestrial message that we don't know how to decode. I'm struck by their closeness. The bands of color appear right above me, like I could reach out and pass my hand through them.

These northern lights are glowing at 1:00 p.m. on an 8K resolution screen inside a well-heated IMAX planetarium at Perlan, a natural history museum set on a hill above downtown Reykjavík. Every hour on the hour the planetarium plays *Áróra,* a 22-minute-long documentary with footage of the lights taken from all over Iceland. The screen's pixel density is so high that it runs up against the limits of what the human eye can perceive. The digital image might be clearer than reality. It's definitely more convenient. All you need is a $20 ticket.

Places like Perlan—magnets for visitors and secondary representations of the country's natural charms—are increasingly a necessity for Iceland, which in recent years has become synonymous with the term "overtourism." Overtourism is what happens to a place when an avalanche of tourists "changes the quality of life for people who actually live there," says Andrew Sheivachman, an editor at the travel website Skift, whose 2016 report about Iceland established the term. In other words, Sheivachman says, "a place becomes mainstream." Iceland has about 300,000 residents, but it received more than 2.3 million overnight visitors last year. Tourists have flooded the island, crashing their camper vans in the wilderness, pooping in the streets of Reykjavík, and eroding the scenic canyon Fjaðrárgljúfur, where Justin Bieber shot a music video in 2015, forcing it to close temporarily. No wonder the museum is safer.

Overtourism also comes with a kind of stigma signified by that word "mainstream." A reputation for excessive crowds means the tastemaking travel elite actually start avoiding a place, like a too-popular restaurant. "The early-adopter travelers are already onto the next cool, cheap, relatively intact place," Sheivachman says. Since the Skift article, the term has been widely applied to places like Barcelona, Venice, and Tulum to suggest that no one who's in the know would want to go there anymore.

Such is the case with Iceland. From 2013 to 2017 the country saw tourist numbers rising more than 20 percent annually, but in 2018 and for projections into the near future, it looks more like 5 percent. There's a sense that the tourists took all the Instagrams of waterfalls and glaciers they wanted and then left, leaving the Icelandic economy vulnerable. In 2017, 42 percent of the country's export revenue was tourism, meaning that Iceland's biggest product, larger than its fishing and aluminum industries, is itself. There are both too many tourists and not enough; Wow Air, one of the major conduits of Icelandic tourism, declared bankruptcy in March after an unsustainable expansion.

While traveling in Iceland this spring to talk to Icelanders about the boom and subsequent slowdown, however, I began to doubt the concept of overtourism itself. The stigma of overtourism is contingent on the sense that a place without as many tourists is more real, more authentic, than it is with them. It poses tourists as foreign entities to a place in the same way that viruses are foreign to the human body. From the visitor's side, overtourism is also a subjective concern based on a feeling: it's the point at which your personal narrative of unique experience is broken, the point at which there are too many people—like yourself—who don't belong in a place.

There are more tourists now than ever before: the World Tourism Organization counted 1.4 billion international tourists in

2018 and predicts 1.8 billion by 2030. In terms of creating new tourists, developing countries are growing the fastest. Even the Icelandic "collapse," as Bloomberg described it, seems to be more of a pause; Wow Air plans to relaunch late this year. If fully one-fifth of humanity are traveling away from home, then how foreign are tourists, after all? Tourism is not a localized phenomenon that we encounter in crowded piazzas and then leave but an omnipresent condition, like climate change or the internet, that we inhabit all the time. Maybe we need to accept it.

Watching *Áróra* in Perlan's theater, I sit in the dark surrounded by empty seats while a disembodied female narrator with an Icelandic accent explains how the various colors of the northern lights come from the vibrations of different atmospheric gases hit by electrons. It strikes me that it doesn't matter that I'm not seeing the actual northern lights; the season ended just before my arrival anyway. I am here in Iceland—surely that makes it a little more real than seeing it in New York? And besides, I'm not damaging any glaciers or emitting gas fumes. In the era of overtourism, the digital display isn't just responsible. It's authentic.

Iceland might be the modern symbol of overtourism, but it was hardly the first or only victim of tourists. The tradition of the Grand Tour started around the 17th century: British nobility would take a spin around the classical sites of the European continent after university, before settling down. Hordes of young men traipsed through Italy, returning with oil portraits of themselves amid castles or ruins to document the journey for their friends back home. In a journal published in 1766, the Scottish author Tobias Smollett complained of carriages packed with travelers on the Tour route: You "run the risk of being stifled among very indifferent company." In Rome, Smollett also observed his compatriots acting badly:

> A number of raw boys, whom Britain seemed to have poured forth on purpose to bring her national character into contempt: ignorant, petulant, rash, and profligate without any knowledge or experience of their own.

It's an 18th-century description of overtourism that's still applicable today. But now the scale is vast and extreme, a hyperobject of loutishness enabled by cheap flights and social media. Tourists seem to be ruining tourism everywhere. Geographical places have been reduced to disposable trends.

Over the past year, headlines have presented a litany of the absurd ways that we're wrecking the places we attempt to appreciate. Indonesia's Komodo Island considered closing because people keep stealing the lizards; Greece's Santorini posted signs asking visiting Instagrammers to stop trespassing on scenic rooftops; selfie-takers ruined fields of tulips in the Netherlands as well as California's poppy superbloom; and Peru instituted timed tickets to Machu Picchu to stop the archaeological site from being trampled into nonexistence.

The crowds can even cause a kind of overtourism rage. Last year, two visitors beat each other up trying to take photos at Rome's Trevi Fountain and local protestors stormed a tourist bus in Barcelona, agitating against the invasion of the city by travelers. Venice, the most tragic victim of overtourism, recently instituted a new entrance tax to compensate for the damage the sinking city suffers; each visitor requires a daily fee of €3 to €10, depending on the expected traffic.

The pace of tourism fads also seems to have accelerated. One year the popular place to go is Berlin, the next it's Iceland, then Lisbon, Bali, Mexico City, Dubrovnik, or Athens. Suddenly everyone is Instagramming from the same place, reproducing the same cliché images. In part, the speed is because of media, both print and digital. Travel and lifestyle magazines have long sold the dream of the next hot destination, from *Condé Nast Traveler* and *Travel + Leisure* to *GQ, Vogue,* and *Monocle.* The *New York Times's* "36 Hours in . . ." and "52 Places to Go" series instantly become #goals. Guides published by *Eater* (also owned by Vox Media), Goop, and the content farm Culture Trip occupy online search results.

These tips expire quickly in the age of overtourism; you have to follow them while the spots are still semi-obscure in order to cash in your cultural capital—before they're pictured on Tinder profiles above the words "Travel is my life." Tourism is competitive. "The places where the magazine editors go, they're quick to turn them into something, then quick to declare them over," says Colin James Nagy, head of strategy at the agency Fred & Farid and a travel tastemaker himself. "In Tulum, that happened in five years." *New York* magazine declared the Mexican beach town "dead" in

February 2019. Nagy suggests instead Denmark's Faroe Islands, Todos Santos in Mexico, and Dakar, Senegal, as up-and-comers. No doubt they'll be deemed dead soon, too.

The ephemeral trendiness—travel as fast fashion—is part of a structural change in the tourism industry, according to Stanislav Ivanov, professor of tourism economics at Bulgaria's Varna University of Management. Centuries ago, Grand Tour trips would take up to three years; you could stay in Rome for six to eight weeks alone. In the 20th century, traditional travel agents and tour operators offered prepackaged trips that encouraged a sense of loyalty to particular places or hospitality brands, which tourists would return to repeatedly. There was less variety and more consistency. But since the 2000s, any traveler can easily use an "online travel agency," or OTA, like Expedia or Booking.com and visit a new place every holiday. "People are collecting destinations," Ivanov says. "Loyalty is not toward the hotels or destinations but toward the distributors."

Plug in your travel dates and an OTA will serve you a long list of possible flights from various carriers, plus bonus car and hotel rentals and activity suggestions. OTAs were once cheaper and considerably smoother than direct booking; many companies have since upgraded their digital services, but the preference for OTAs remains. In the end, the service is less personalized and more automated.

Operating at a massive scale with call centers full of staff who may not know much about a traveler's destination, OTAs end up serving the same itineraries over and over, according to Skarphéðinn Berg Steinarsson, the director-general of the Icelandic Tourism Board and a vehement critic of the digital platforms. They create what he calls a "top 10" list effect, reducing a country or city to a series of boxes to check off. OTAs "don't give a damn about what's really happening" in a place, Steinarsson says. "They are just shoveling out packages."

The problem is particularly acute in Iceland because so much of its tourism is routed through packaged bus trips; charting your own route with a rental car is both more expensive and more forbidding due to the weather, terrain, and not-insignificant chance of, say, getting stuck in a river. So visitors are most likely to succumb to convenience and take a spin around the Golden Circle, a 190-mile loop through the southern uplands that features the

geysers, waterfalls, and rocky cliffs that everyone posts on Instagram or Facebook—the same spots that are sustaining the most
damage. "If you go to Iceland, you have to do that list. 'Go onto
our site, it's on the front screen, just take out your credit card, pay,
get it over with, and start enjoying,'" Steinarsson says. "How deep
do you have to dig before you start seeing places that would really
be something special?"

Where we go and how we get there are increasingly influenced
by a series of digital platforms—not just big OTAs, but Airbnb,
Yelp, and Instagram—that prioritize engagement over originality.
Overtourism is a consequence, not a cause. The more often a particular destination or package proves successful, the more users a
site's algorithm will drive to it, intensifying the problem by pushing travelers to have the same experiences as one another on a
single beaten track around the globe, updated and optimized in
real time. When one spot gets too crowded and its novelty used up,
the next is slotted into its place.

For my trip, I decide to take the path of least resistance, relying on
OTAs and recommendation sites to tell me exactly what to do—a
tourist experience as well as an experience of tourism. It is indeed
frictionless. I book an apartment in downtown Reykjavík through
Airbnb and day-trips through Arctic Adventures, a local OTA. I
buy tickets for a tour of *Game of Thrones* shooting locations and a
day-long Golden Circle trip that hits all the main spectacles. Every
activity seems to be rated 4.5 stars out of 5 or above. Weeks before
my Icelandair flight, I'm algorithmically bombarded on YouTube
by hypnotic pre-roll ads for the northern lights.

On the plane, I'm forced to watch a three-minute trailer for
Iceland before I can even access the entertainment system. The
flight map shows me why the country is such a tourism target. The
frozen ovoid island is like a period in a chain of ellipses linking
North America to the United Kingdom, Europe, and Scandinavia,
making it a perfect stopover point. Iceland has no native inhabit-
ants; in a sense, everyone has been a tourist since Norwegian and
Swedish Viking sailors started accidentally landing there in the
ninth century and settled when they found out the summer wasn't
so bad. Anything that exists on the island is a result of its visitors,
making it difficult to determine where the "real" Iceland ends and
where tourism begins.

Almost every flight passes through Keflavik Airport outside Reykjavík, by far the largest city, which functions like a fire hose, spitting out tourists. Icelandair has been offering free layovers through Keflavik since 1955 but only began marketing them aggressively in 1996 as it added destinations in North America, branding the country as a quick drop-in. The 2000s brought marketing campaigns including one with the euphemistic slogan "Fancy a dirty weekend in Iceland?" showing a photo of a couple with geothermal-bath mud on their faces.

In 2008 the financial crisis sunk Iceland's previously expensive currency, which was terrible for Icelanders but great for tourism — the income from added visitors sped up economic recovery. "People were flocking there because it has a very high standard of living, it's very beautiful, and now you could get it for one-third of the price," Michael Raucheisen, Icelandair's US-based communications manager for North America, tells me. Raucheisen, who flew Icelandair with his German father as a child, has worked at the company for two decades. "Nineteen years ago, people had no idea where Iceland was," he says. "They thought Icelandair was an air-conditioning company."

Iceland is also located on the Mid-Atlantic Ridge, the crack between the North American and Eurasian tectonic plates, making it one of the most volcanic spots on earth. Beginning in the early 1900s, Icelanders harnessed this energy as geothermal and hydropower for heat and electricity, making it much more comfortable than in chilly centuries past. Ninety-nine percent of the primary energy use in Iceland now comes from local renewable sources. The countryside is dotted with natural hot springs and futuristic power plants, all gently leaking steam. The place is a planetary Juul. (Reykjavík's name, given in 874, means "smoke cove.")

A volcano was in fact the biggest spark for the tourism boom. In April 2010 Eyjafjallajökull erupted, grounding more European flights than at any time since World War II, though in Iceland its impact was limited to the evacuation of a few farms and about 800 people. The eruption put maps and videos of Iceland on prime-time TV news around the world, which amounted to free advertising. "Even during the volcano, the rest of Iceland was clean and beautiful. It was like, 'Oh, it's there, I didn't know that,'" says Inga Hlín Pálsdóttir, the cheerful director of the tourism initiative Visit Iceland. The eruption happened, by chance, just as Pálsdóttir was helping to launch the country's biggest tourism marketing push yet. "It was basically crisis communication," she says. Several weeks of her life blurred together, but the campaign succeeded.

Iceland became a year-round destination, not just the warm months. Summer had been peak season; now, more tourists come for winter and the "shoulder seasons" between peak and off-peak, thanks in part to marketing campaigns highlighting the northern lights, festivals, and outdoor activities. American tourists gradually surpassed the German and French groups that traditionally came for long hiking trips. Tourists from Asia are now the fastest-growing demographic.

My first stop after Keflavik is the Blue Lagoon, a short, sparsely filled bus ride away. It's recognizable from photos: a luminous pool of bright-blue water, like an aqueous latte, set amid jagged black volcanic rocks. But rather than the idyllic natural hot spring it resembles on Instagram, it's actually a kind of giant artificial bathtub filled with wastewater from a nearby geothermal power plant. The Svartsengi power plant opened in 1976 and its superheated liquid and steam bubbled up through the surrounding lava field; one psoriasis patient bathed in it and saw an improvement and thus a business began.

Blue Lagoon built a cement-bottomed pool that spreads out in a faux-organic layout and a clutch of modernist spa buildings. In 2017 the site accommodated 1.2 million visitors who buy timed entrance tickets and pay extra for bathrobes and drinks at the lagoon's float-up bar. "Can you imagine how many people have sex in it?" the Icelandic politician Birgitta Jónsdóttir later asks me. The 240°C water that gets pumped from deep underground is so mineral-heavy, however, that no bacteria can survive, even after it gets cooled down to bathing temperature for visitors to soak in.

I get a wristband for locker access and cash-free payments, then make my way through the bustling locker rooms. Guards in all-black uniforms yell at guests for not showering nude and scrubbing down according to Icelandic hygiene, helpfully illustrated by explicit diagrams. The hot water is a fast cure for my jet lag but the lagoon feels like a crowded hot tub. The first thing I notice after I get a plastic goblet of prosecco and smear my face with some local silica—filtered out of seawater by precipitation and served up in a bucket—is just how international the crowd is. An Indian family snaps selfies, holding each other's drinks. A German man asks me to take a photo of his friend and send it to him, maybe because I had followed the advice of travel blogs and squeezed my phone into a nerdy waterproof bag strung around my neck. I hear as much Chinese as English.

An American man floating by declaims to his friends, "Can you imagine if we built a concept like this in Las Vegas?" And that's exactly what the Blue Lagoon is: a concept, a playground-Iceland that can be consumed at will, something packaged and branded as representative of the place despite its artificiality. (One TripAdvisor review deems it "expensive and fake.")

The rest of the resort follows the same logic. When I begin feeling like a wobbly sous-vide egg I wade out of the water, shower again, and go inside for my reservation at Lava, an upscale restaurant where one wall is polished lava-rock and two others are floor-to-ceiling glass. Guests in the same white robes as mine dot the tables like hospital patients in a waiting room. I order the $50 two-course set menu that features local lamb. It tastes transcendentally gamey and like nowhere else on earth, literally, because Icelandic sheep were first brought to the island 1,000 years ago and left alone to evolve in uniquely delicious ways.

The condition of overtourism pressures places to become commodities in the global marketplace the same way we warp our lifestyles to attract Instagram likes. "You have to compete as a brand," Pálsdóttir tells me. Countries and cities must constantly perform their identities in order to maintain the flow of tourists.

Icelandic tourism is a paradox. Visitors might outnumber locals, but the place must take care to preserve the brand of lonely natural grandeur that has become its product, offered up like a dish of roast lamb belly. The maintenance of this image is its own kind of artificiality. Fun fact: if an Icelandic horse ever leaves the island, it isn't allowed to come back.

My Reykjavík Airbnb was listed on the website as a penthouse, but that's not hard to achieve when few buildings are more than three stories tall. It's polished and pleasantly anonymous without lacking personality entirely; above the TV there's a giant photo print of the Brooklyn Bridge. From the balcony on one side I can see the white specter of Snæfellsjökull, a glacier-capped stratovolcano,

across the chilled blue of Faxa Bay. On the other is downtown
Reykjavík, like an overgrown ski town, with the skeletons of new
hotels and high-rise glassy condos under construction on the out-
skirts.

Though Airbnb initially helped the growth of Icelandic tourism by housing visitors while development was only in planning,
the government instituted a new regulation in January 2017 limiting most short-term rentals to 90 days a year; more than that and
the owners need special certification. My place clearly falls into
the latter category, since the owner rents out the building's two
penthouse apartments full-time and lives in a unit below them.
The apartment is on a quieter stretch of the main shopping strip,
Laugavegur, sprinkled with storefronts selling outdoor gear, souvenir puffin dolls, and Viking kitsch. It's easy to tell tourists apart
from the locals because they wear brightly colored Gore-Tex coats
despite the relative warmth, and wander aimlessly, unsure of where
they're going. When I go out I try to wear a casual jacket and carry
a tote bag instead of a backpack, wanting, illogically, to be dis-
guised.

These days, Reykjavík is full of the kinds of signifiers that mark
an "authentic" travel experience, at least according to the influ-
encer set: artisanal coffee shops like Reykjavík Roasters, locavore
restaurants like Skál, and shops with names like Nomad.store selling minimalist coffee-table books and scented candles. None of
these things are bad, necessarily, but they're also not particularly
local to Iceland in the first place. Unlike Paris, for example, where
the centuries-old urban culture is what attracts visitors, Reykjavík
developed in tandem with tourism.

"I grew up in the city center and I remember the streets used to
be empty. It was a small fraction of the cafés and restaurants you
have now," says Karen María Jónsdóttir, at the time the director of
Visit Reykjavík, the marketing office for the city. We're sitting in
the Coocoo's Nest, a homey farm-to-table bar-slash-restaurant in
the harbor neighborhood, where old fishermen's supply sheds are
being turned into boutiques and food halls in a familiar flavor of
industrial gentrification. We drink two fashionably nonalcoholic
lemonade cocktails at the wood bar. Icelanders used to only go
out on the weekends and shop at outlet malls outside the city;
now things are open all week long. "You need a certain mass of
people to [sustain] a selection of good restaurants and services for

everybody," Jónsdóttir says. "We all want the services but then we complain about the people using them."

Gunnar Jóhannesson, a professor at the University of Iceland who studies tourism, tells me about a recent survey: the closer to the center of Reykjavík, the more positive locals are in their perception of tourists. We need to "rehumanize tourists and tourism," Jóhannesson says. "It's important to stop thinking about tourism as the other and realize that we are also tourists. Tourism is part of our society." (After all, whenever Icelanders leave their small island, they're tourists too: according to data sent to me by Visit Iceland, 83 percent of Icelanders traveled abroad for vacation in 2018.) There's a "standardization" that follows global travel, the professor says, a wave of generically luxurious cafés, hotels, and food halls. "Maybe it's a bit comforting. It shows that people like the same things."

Perhaps the problem isn't the actual tourists but the way that some people—international entrepreneurs and developers in particular—profit from the tourism industry while others don't. In other words, extractive capitalism is at fault, causing gentrification and displacement. "When tourism grows out of proportion, when it starts to be based on and motivated by international capital but not the community's values, then we might have a problem," Jóhannesson says. "I don't think it has gotten to that point in Iceland, but it easily can get there." Of course, it's easier to say that on an island with plenty of extant empty space than at a Barcelona market so crowded with people Instagramming produce that residents can't actually shop there.

Whether the balance has already tipped in favor of capital depends on who you ask. One evening I open Yelp and search the city for natural-wine bars, which are the latest international hipster shibboleth and the 2010s update to Thomas Friedman's Golden Arches theory of peace-via-globalization: instead of McDonald's, no two countries with natural-wine bars will ever go to war with each other. I head to Port 9, down the alleyway of a residential complex. It's a faux-industrial space with raw cement walls, hanging pendant lamps, and plush green-velvet banquettes, like every other cool bar. A piece by minimalist composer Steve Reich is playing. Wine connoisseurship is itself a recent import in Iceland; the country had a form of alcohol prohibition from 1915 to 1989, and beer is far more popular.

Sitting at the bar are two young men swirling glasses with the bartender. They are both musicians and graduate students in the whimsical, long-term manner enabled by Nordic socialism. They both recently moved back from Berlin, nostalgic for the Icelandic summer and nature in general. Markus Sigur Bjornsson is wiry and wry, dressed in streetwear, while Thorsteinn Eyfjord is taller, neck-scarved and more formal in manner. We discuss the state of the country over a funky Italian red pulled from under the bar. Bjornsson says he might not have ever left his home if it weren't for exposure to tourists showing him that an outside world existed (Iceland is 93 percent Icelandic; the second-largest demographic is Polish at 3 percent). "The tourism bubble, in twenty years we can look back and think, OK, this did more positive than negative to our society," he says. In fact, as Elvar Orri Hreinsson, a research analyst at the Bank of Iceland, tells me, Iceland is more financially secure now than it used to be, even with the slowdown: the economy is more diversified, the central bank holds a large currency reserve, and foreign investors are more interested than ever.

Eyfjord is more pessimistic. Like most millennials, he feels a looming generational burden. If the bubble bursts, "we will have to take the blame and build up society again," he says. But he has a plan. Without tourists, there will be a lot of empty hotels and Air-bnbs. "I hope there will come a wave of squatting and the young people and artists will take over." The spaces could be turned into affordable housing, art studios, and startup offices. "Then at least I can live alone without having to have help from my parents."

The rise of isolationist nationalism might slow it, and climate change, accelerated by every plane flight, will change its targets, but as a global growth industry tourism doesn't seem likely to stop. We can't return to a time when overtourism didn't exist, and the desire to do so is as problematic as the concept of overtourism it-self: there's prejudice at work when wealthy, white Westerners have been tourists, if not colonizers, for centuries, but now that the rest of the world is joining in, it's cast as excessive. Rather, the task left to us is to imagine a post-overtourism world in which we can all participate in and benefit from the human flow.

I meet Birgitta Jónsdóttir, the 52-year-old former Icelandic Parliamentarian and onetime friend of Julian Assange, in a Fleetwood Mac–soundtracked hostel café that she suggests near her apartment in a quieter area east of downtown. Across the street, chil-

dren bounce on a trampoline. As the former face of Iceland's Pi-
rate Party, a loose, global coalition of digital-freedom activists that
was the most popular political party in the country between 2015
and 2016, Jónsdóttir is something of a celebrity. Icelandic style
is usually sober; she has purple-tinged eyelashes, iridescent nails,
dyed-blonde hair, and a set of chunky, biomorphic rings, a contrast
to her anonymous black winter jacket.

While in Parliament, she tried to pass a bill that would tax new
hotels and direct the funds toward Reykjavík itself but was stymied
"because people in the countryside wanted their share of it," she
says. The funding would fight what she calls the "Disneyfication"
of Reykjavík as well as help safeguard the area's natural sites. "A
lot of places I hold sacred in nature, places I would go to get some
energy, there are so many people, so noisy, so disrespectful to the
space they're in, that I don't go there anymore. I just get very upset," she says. "You do not become sympathetic to other people's
cultures just tracking through it like a horde of oxen."

She thinks we might need a different kind of tourism altogether.
Rather than her old favorite spots that are now overrun, these days
Jónsdóttir prefers exploring her own backyard garden, a choice
that's both quieter and less damaging. She plants potatoes, like
her family did in the village where she grew up. "I have a different experience every day because of the weather and the way the
plants grow," she says. "Look at the crisis we're in with our planet.
It's time that people go on trips in their own area and say goodbye
to the diversity that is there."

There's a blank-slate quality to Iceland, extending to the freshness
of the air itself. The place has spun stories around itself since the
Vikings wrote down their sagas, tales of family lineages and heroic
deeds, in the 12th century—some of which went on to inspire a
novelist named George R. R. Martin. The landscape has had many
things projected upon it. "There are different layers to the fantasy of Iceland," the Icelandic novelist Andri Magnason tells me
over dinner at Snaps, an old-school French bistro beloved by locals
down the street from Hallgrímskirkja, the wave-like, expressionist
church that is one of Reykjavík's best-known symbols. "The sagas
are one layer, *Game of Thrones* is another layer, maybe the economy
is another."

The fantasy can be the attraction. Early one morning I climb onto a coach bus familiar from childhood field trips for an eight-hour tour of *Game of Thrones* shooting locations. In the front of the bus sits our bearded guide, Theo Hansson, who is wearing a Night's Watch outfit complete with faux-fur cape, drinking horn on his belt loop (I watch him fill it with coffee), and two actual swords, his long hair tied back with a bandanna. Hansson explains that he worked as an extra on the show in various seasons playing a Watchman, an undead wight, and a wildling, braving thin costumes, recalcitrant horses, and very bad weather. Hansson speaks in a deep growl that's half Hound rumble and half Littlefinger hiss; I assume it's a put-on until he later speaks on the phone the same way, his voice shot from a day of narration. A Reykjavík native, in Hansson's off-time he is an academic studying Viking history at the University of Iceland.

"I really, really hate tourists," Hansson growls with feeling. "But you guys aren't tourists. You're *Game of Thrones* enthusiasts." The tour happens the day after the finale of the television show, which I had stayed up very late Iceland time to watch, using a proxy to access American HBO. I'm the only one in the group to have done so, and so no one else is massively disappointed yet. I'm jealous.

On the bus are two-dozen other tourists, mostly American, including John and Marsha, an older couple from Buffalo, New York. They booked a free stopover through an OTA when it popped up as an option on their flights back home from Copenhagen, following a long cruise. "We never even thought of Iceland. I couldn't even spell 'Reykjavík,'" Marsha tells me. But it turned out their neighbor had just visited and loved it, then a woman they met on the Copenhagen flight suggested this specific tour. Marsha says she wishes they had planned to stay for a day longer.

Hansson swears a lot, tells repeated ex-girlfriend jokes, and puns incessantly. He's had the gig since 2016. "This used to be a normal tour, then it became an R-rated tour," he says. His humor has offended some groups, especially Germans, but his boss has been on the tour and loved it. In between anecdotes, we make our stops, like Thingvellir, where Vikings established Iceland's first parliamentary government, the Althing, in the 10th century, in a ravine-ridden field where the earth is actively splitting apart. It's also where *Game of Thrones* shot the Bloody Gate, an elaborate tiered guardhouse outside of the Eyrie castle, in season four. Hansson holds up laminated screenshots from the show that he printed out himself so that we can see the precise camera angle and observe that reality conforms to the image, except, of course, for the missing CGI gate. We ooh and aah.

Westeros is not a real place. Even the northern parts of the show were shot between Iceland, Scotland, and Ireland, then spliced together as if they were contiguous. But we are tourists of the fiction regardless. Hansson brings us to Þjóðveldisbærinn Stöng, a replica of a Viking-era farm on a hilltop, where the show shot a Wildling raid. Hansson was in the scene; his job was to chase down a six-year-old child. "I just kept stabbing her again and again and again. It was marvelous," he says. Then he selects a volunteer from the audience and proceeds to demonstrate the stage-stabbing technique.

I drift away from the group and lean up against the grassy sod that covers the entire structure of the farmhouse to insulate it from the weather and cold. It starts to rain, but the grass shields me just enough so that I can look out into the gray mist over the surreal landscape, which stretches and pitches into hills and valleys like a skate park for giants. I feel briefly connected to some universal sentiment: the authentic dreariness of the Vikings and the *Game of Thrones* villagers alike.

My Golden Circle tour is more prosaic. I climb aboard another bus, this time filled with a group of quiet Norwegians and a single American family with two rambunctious kids; I'm the only solo traveler. Emil, the tour guide, has an affectless storytelling style, like a podcast of Wikipedia entries, much less appealing than Hansson's profane patter. Whenever we stop, he seems more interested in talking to our otherwise silent driver, whose name he says is Gummy Bear, than explaining anything. On the itinerary is Thingvellir again, sans CGI; Geysir, the much-photographed clutch of geysers on a hillside; Gullfoss, an iconic waterfall; and the Secret Lagoon, a not-so-secret geothermal spring whose ironic slogan is "We Kept It Unique for You."

Geysir actually refers to the single Great Geyser, but that one only erupts around earthquakes. The star of the show is Strokkur (Icelandic for "churn"), which explodes every 10 minutes or so, causing a great gasp from the assembled visitors. Rings of tourists face backward and lean over the boiling-hot water in order to take possibly fatal selfies. Footprints mark a trodden path in the muddy hill that winds around each pool.

More than a natural wonder, it's now something of a highway

rest-stop, grandiose in its attempt to cater to tourists. On the other side of the road from the geysers is a sprawling visitor center, featuring a huge store selling clothing from the brand Geysir, one of Iceland's most recognizable fashion labels, named after the place itself. The food court offers pizza as well as fish-and-chips ready-made under heat lamps. Next door is a newly developed spa hotel, geyser-themed. Compared to the infrastructure, the waterworks themselves seem even smaller and less remarkable. I recall Markus Bjornsson, the student in the wine bar: "If you've seen one geyser, you've seen them all."

Gullfoss—Golden Falls—is a mammoth crack in the earth through which runs 140 cubic meters of water per second. The gathered force is like a nuclear bomb but all the time. There were attempts to turn the falls into a hydroelectric power plant, but the story goes that the daughter of one of the farmers who own the land mounted a charismatic protest and saved it. Now there's a beaten trail with staircases and handrails along the lip of the canyon where we could look down and take photos. Patches of grass that draw even closer to the edge are blocked off with signs. ("If you fall over, it's impossible to find you, you're just gone," Skarphéðinn Berg Steinarsson of the ITB tells me.) We stand with our phones in front of our faces, the surging water too massive to consider as reality, as anything other than a picture that we can save to show friends later, shorn of its existential dread. I think of Don DeLillo's description of "the most photographed barn in America" in his novel *White Noise:* "No one sees the barn."

In the face of overtourism, I want to make an argument for the inauthentic. Not just the spots flooded with tourists but the simulations and the fictions, the ways that the world of tourism supersedes reality and becomes its own space. It is made up of the digital northern lights on an 8K movie screen, the manmade turquoise geothermal baths, and the computer renderings of high-budget television shows overlaid on the earth. I don't regret any of these activities; in fact, the less authentic an experience was supposed to be in Iceland, the more fun I had and the more aware I was of the consequences of 21st-century travel.

This is not to discount the charm of hiking an empty mountain or the very real damage that tourists cause, disrupting lives and often intensifying local inequality. But maybe by reclaiming these experiences, or destigmatizing them, we can also begin regaining our agency over the rampant commodification of places and people. We can travel to see what exists instead of wishing for some mythical untouched state, the dream of a place prepared perfectly for visitors and yet empty of them. Instead of trying to "live like a local," as Airbnb commands, we can just be tourists. When a destination is deemed dead might be the best time to go there, as the most accurate reflection of our impure world.

Back at my Airbnb, I call Theo Hansson to see what he thought of the end of *Game of Thrones*. He was, like me, dissatisfied. "I'm very glad I was not a part of the last season. It would have soured everything," he says. He doesn't expect his gig to last forever. In 2016 "I was doing groups of forty or fifty people to a hundred people. It's gotten a lot less," he tells me in a low, hoarse rumble. "I'm expecting maybe two years more of this. The engine is going to fade." *Game of Thrones* will drift away like the other narratives, maybe faster than slower.

Hansson's other sideline, making use of his academic background, is being a Viking reenactor. He's in a group of 200 people, not just born-and-bred Icelanders, who train in sword fighting, archery, and crafts. They camp out for a week at a time, wearing period-correct clothing and sleeping in Viking tents based on archaeological discoveries. They fight, cook food over open fires, and get very drunk.

This is what refreshes him, participating in the illusion of another life, which is the same thing that we're always seeking when we travel: to get outside of ourselves and imagine new possibilities, however unlikely or unreal they are. Iceland remains ideal for this purpose. "It's what fantasies are made of," Hansson says. "This untamed wild, this alien landscape, this vastness."

# Revisiting My Grandfather's Garden

FROM *Longreads*

IN A CUL-DE-SAC, I hear the purring of a gas stove and the popping of boiling tomato juice bubbles on the surface of a cauldron. The tomato paste aroma saturates the air. It's August and it's high time for making pastes and jams in Tehran. My grandmother kept us busy this time of the year. "Let's put those little feet into work," she used to say to my sister and me as she emptied buckets of vine tomatoes into deep basins. We removed our socks, rubbed the bathing brush on our feet, and rinsed until the last cluster of soap bubbles vanished into the drain. She watched our brushing ceremony and inspected our feet for any specks of dirt. When she was satisfied with the whiteness of our soles, she hoisted us into the basins. We jumped up and down and stamped the tomatoes to extract the juice. Vine tomatoes squished and screamed under our feet. Their plum, tender and succulent, painted our legs. She boiled the juice and the ambrosial aroma of the boiling tomatoes wafted in the garden. The thickening tomato juice boiled over the sides of the hot cauldron, smearing the tiles of the terrace. When my grandmother removed the gas stove, a striking corona of fiery red drops of paste remained on the tiles. I thought those red coronas were the reason they named my grandparents' street the Sun Street.

How I wish I could enter that garden one more time to see those fiery rings. In 2018 I plan a return trip. But my mother tells me—before I go back—that the Sun Street is closed to the public. Nobody knows what has happened to that house since the Islamic government took it from us.

## The Imam Airport

I hurry down the zigzag path that leads to the gate. I proceed to the passport checkpoint. Only one flight has landed at Imam Khomeini Airport tonight and that flight is the Lufthansa 600. There is hardly a queue in front of me. I have never seen the airport this empty before. The border patrol officer asks for my documentation and I slide my Iranian passport under the bulletproof glass of the border inspection kiosk. I try to adjust the scarf I've thrown on my head in the plane. The fear of getting arrested for not observing the obligatory hijab still nests in me. It strikes again as I land in Iran. The young officer has beard stubble and wears an olive shirt that bears the golden-thread insignia of the word "Allah" on his right chest. His eyes are surrounded by heliotrope hollows. He looks tired and disengaged, and doesn't bother to raise his eyes to look at the one who claims to be the holder of the passport. He doesn't say welcome to Iran.

Baggage claim is located on the ground level, below the arrivals. Escalators carry the passengers between the two levels. I step on the emerging steps and peek at the scant, welcoming crowd that stands behind a tall glass wall that separates the baggage carousels from the rest of the waiting area. People are waiting for their loved ones to appear from the sky and descend on to the ground. There are at most 50 people, unlike many years ago, when I was a young teenager who stood behind the glass wall, impatiently waiting for my aunt to arrive from America. I could hardly reach the glass wall back then, since it was covered, inch by inch, with bodies of the individuals who carried bouquets of flowers and waved their hands in the air with the sight of their passengers. No one is waiting for me tonight. It is more than two decades since my parents and my siblings left Iran for different parts of the world.

I park a baggage cart beside the only carousel that is wheeling around with a screech. Luggage on the belt appears dirty and soiled. Someone stoops to look more closely at a suitcase, another person pulls a large black bag from the rotating surface. Everyone looks old—mostly parents of Iranian students who live abroad. No one seems to be a tourist on this flight.

As soon as I walk out of the arrivals sliding door, a gush of soot-filled, dry air blows into my face. I smell the half-burnt gasoline in the air, the familiar, welcoming scent of gray, polluted Tehran. The drivers rush toward me. They offer the cost of transportation in tomans, every one trying to beat the other driver. A young van driver nears my luggage and offers the cheapest price. I go with him. When I convert Iranian tomans to American dollars, the cost is negligible.

He asks where I'm heading and I give my parents' address. He combs his hair with his fingers and ignites the engine. He stares at me in the rearview mirror as soon as I tell him I'm coming from America. "What has brought you from heaven to this hell, beautiful lady?" I wonder what sort of beauty he traces in my exhausted, puffy face. Maybe he assumes I am an angel descending from heavens of America. Maybe he finds the vivid scarf I am wearing liberating from the lead-color load of this city. On the stereo he plays an old song from Mahasti, a famous prerevolutionary singer, stored on his flash drive. I have listened to this song many times before. I am surprised—with so many younger-generation artists to choose from, he is still listening to a prerevolutionary singer in his car. Is he, like many Iranians, trying to cling to the glory of the past? We pass the golden dome of the mausoleum housing the late Ayatollah Khomeini—founder and spiritual leader of the Islamic Republic. With its four illuminating minarets, the structure shines like a jewel in the desert at night. "They've named this area the Sun City," the driver says, and points to the urban structure facing my right. "They've built five-star hotels, guest suites, a children's amusement park, a book fair, and even a university." I remember the parched land that used to be here, when I last traveled from the airport to Tehran. The driver laments the broken economy of the land, the depreciation of the Iranian currency and the sense of insecurity people feel every day. He asks if I enjoy living in America in the Trump era. I realize this is going to be the main question people will ask me during my stay in Tehran. I just smile and don't elaborate. The flight has been too long and I am too tired for a serious discussion with a stranger.

We reach my parents' apartment in the high mountains of Alborz. I pull off the sheets covering the furniture, draw back the lacy curtains that blind the guest bedroom, and open the window facing the backyard. The cold breeze of the August night embraces my cheeks. Here, in northern Tehran, the chillness of the night is still awakening. The honeysuckles have pawed and clung to the neighbors' wall. The bone-white cement on the wall is now brushed with vivid green. A scant number of yellow flowers still hang from the vines. I remember the days I impatiently waited for the young white flowers to ripen and change color, becoming golden yellow, in my grandfather's garden. He had revealed their secret to me. If I pinched the yellow flower and pulled out the thin, inner string, a pearl-drop of honey nectar awaited me at the end. I thought I was the only girl in the world who knew the secret of the honeysuckle flowers.

## The Abdul Azim Shrine — The Parrot Garden

I hire a Snapp, the Iranian version of an Uber, to take me to Abdul Azim Shrine, where my grandfather is buried. A mature woman drives the car. This is the first time I have a female driver in Tehran. She is wearing a light hijab, most of her hair peeking out from beneath her cherry-red shawl. I notice her painted, curved nails as she touches her mobile screen, which is facing her on a stand. She knows the roads well and uses the Waze app to avoid Tehran's heavy traffic. It is so entertaining to observe the app's voice speaking the long-forgotten words in formal Farsi. We descend from the high mountains of Alborz and drive to Rey prairie, where the cemetery is located. As we get close, the tar-filled, compressed buildings of Tehran give way to vegetable farms. The young workers shade their faces with straw hats as they pluck mint leaves or uproot basil. Scattered elm and poplar trees stand at the corners, remnants of crowded rows of trees that flanked the farms.

The hymns from the minarets of the Abdul Azim shrine are music to my ears. It is Friday and soon there will be noon prayers there. I enter from the eastern gate and rush to get to the Parrot Garden, where my grandfather is buried. Inside the chambers, the shrine keepers are spreading the fine Persian carpets on the marbled floor, for the prayer. A little girl with a cute floral chador bumps into me while chasing after her sister. She looks at me and smiles as an apology. Her blushed cheeks are budding out of her chador. I remember the time I came to the shrine with my grandfather and my sister, roughly at her age, a nearly identical floral chador engulfing me. I tugged the rubber band sewn into the chador's sides around my ears, so that it wouldn't slip from my head. It was fun to wear those colorful chadors, a ritual for visiting the shrine, and a reminder of the time before the Iranian Revolution when hijab-wearing was not a rigid, compulsory obligation forced on women by the Islamic government. I wore it then ceremonially, with childhood gaiety as we ran and played in the chambers of Abdul Azim.

I leave the shrine and pace into the garden. I wonder why they have named the cemetery adjacent to the shrine the Parrot Garden. Maybe the garden, before being turned into a cemetery, was full of green parrots living on the elm trees, like the heaven's garden described in old Persian texts. Parrots are silent to the aliens according to those texts, but if they're tamed, they can reveal secrets of the universe to their companions. Maybe the parrots were telling the secrets of the dead in the original garden. But now, with the scant elm trees remaining in the corners, and the burning sun scorching the gravestones, the Parrot Garden is nothing but a wistful name.

I find my grandfather's grave, a flat granite stone at the eastern corner of the cemetery where many respectful businessmen from Tehran's bazaar are buried. He owned a glaziery in the bazaar, and made many mirror artworks in his workshop. I fetch some water from the ablution pool and wash the hot stone with my hand. The epitaph emerges letter by letter: HERE, THE RESTING PLACE OF A RESPECTFUL HAJJ PILGRIM, A BELOVED FATHER AND HUSBAND. I lost this man 20 years ago. The man who shaped my childhood imagination with his stories, and all these 20 years that have passed, I have visited him only a couple of times. His stories—the tales he'd kept in his heart to unveil for my sister and me on the hot summer nights, when we all slept under the canopy in the front terrace of his house, gazing at the bright, shining stars of Tehran.

The Rey Traditional Bazaar, beside the shrine in southern Tehran, brims with people. They go to restaurants after the Friday prayer, where two skewers of kebab are served with fresh batches of mint on oven-baked, whole wheat naans. The mouthwatering smell of grilled kebabs fills the bazaar at noon. My mother never trusted those restaurants, and every time we came here with my grandfather, he only bought naans with two bowls of yogurt for us. My sister and I loved the Reyhan Restaurant, for it lacked the luxurious ambiance of the places we normally dined, and the servers

liked us and treated us like little princesses coming from another
world. Men wore chapeau hats and tied red, checkered handker-
chiefs around their necks, made morsels of wrapped kebabs in
small pieces of naan and ate them with their hands, quite an unusual scene in a house of kebab in northern Tehran.

In Rey Bazaar I search for the jewelry shops. Rows of rings with
flowers, butterflies, or hearts are on display in the vitrines of the
shops. Golden bangles glitter on models' hands, their nails long.
They are perfect for little girls, dangling on their soft wrists as
they dance. We used to treasure the bangles like trophies we'd
found on a victorious journey to a faraway, unfamiliar land. I step
into one of the jewelry shops. The guy at the counter asks me if I
need help and I ask for the tray of rings on display. "Those are for
little girls, khanum," he says. I nod and pick a blue butterfly with
golden dots. I roll it onto my pinky, the only finger it fits. I recall
being here with my grandfather. I'd asked, "Agha Joon, will you
buy this for me?" He smiled and patted my floral chador, which
covered my curly hair. "Of course," he said, "You can buy two. Let
them be pairs."

## The Sun Street

I take the metro to Monirieh Square to get to central Tehran,
where I spent most of my childhood in my grandparents' neighborhood. Even though my mother told me the area is now closed
to the public, I need to see it for myself. As soon as the escalator
reaches the ground level, a shallow pool appears at the center of
the square. A plaster statue of a young boy sits on a wooden deck,
wishfully staring at the pool and waiting for fish to come and take
the bait. I have never seen this statue before. It is far from the
photograph I've carried in my mind from years ago and certainly,
this tender young boy longing for a little fish is different from the
bloody symbols of martyrs that used to be in every square in Tehran after the Islamic Revolution in 1979.

It's midmorning and the heat of an August day is not yet in full
effect. I walk toward the north on Vali-Asr Street. The chinar trees
flank the wide street and their broad leaves offer a pleasant, cool
shade to pedestrians. One of the oldest streets in Tehran, Vali-Asr
starts in the South, at Tehran's railway station, and stretches all

the way to the mountainous North. The railway station was built in 1927 by Reza Shah, the founder of the Pahlavi dynasty, the last monarchy before the Revolution. The street connects the important squares of Tehran, and many historical events have occurred on its pavement. Based on the calculation on Google Maps, there is a 15-minute walk from Monirieh Square to the Sun Street. I pass the sport shops that are abundant at this part of the street. The shops are not busy, due to the economic crisis that happened a month ago, the value of the Iranian toman falling to one-fifth of its previous value in its exchange rate with the American dollar. Where a dollar once bought 3,000 tomans, it can now buy 15,000. Very few customers enter the shops. People gaze at the astronomical prices attached to the Sketchers and Nikes, and pass. I am surprised to see the sport shops still presenting the American brands in the stores.

I pass the Sepah intersection where the Marble Palace is located. The intersection is busy and cars honk at each other nonstop. The palace was built by Reza Shah and he resided there with his family until he was forced to abdicate the throne in September 1941. After Reza Shah, his son, Mohammad Reza, came into power, and all his three marriage ceremonies took place in this palace. With its delicately tiled dome and white marble walls, the Marble Palace once shone like a sublime coral castle in the green sea of surrounding gardens. But now, the pristine white walls have turned gray, after years of soot and lead precipitating on them. The magnificent lion-and-sword emblem of the Pahlavi dynasty engraved on the arched gate has been replaced by a neon-green banner that has turned dirty and dark, reading, THE MUSEUM OF THE HOLY KORAN. There is a narrow, tunnel-like detour beyond the gate to the museum, but the palace is closed to the public. The Guardian Council of the Islamic Republic holds its regular meetings inside the edifice.

I walk alongside the barbed-wired, monumental walls of the Marble Palace toward the Sun Street. The northern side of the street is closed to passersby by iron chains, and two police officers are guarding the entrance. I hope I can schmooze my way in just for a quick visit. I approach the older officer and ask him if I can pass.

"Why do you want to go in?" he asks.

"My grandparents' house used to be here," I say. "I want to see it after many years."

"No one can pass unless they are a government official," he says.

"I don't live in Iran," I say. "I'm coming from overseas." He smiles and shakes his head.

"You can get to the other end of the Sun Street if you walk back to the Marble Palace," he says. "You may want to keep your good memories."

I have come all the way from Washington, DC, to Tehran, after so many years, to see this patch of earth, and to revisit the past I've been writing about for the last two and a half years. In my memories, I roam around the Sun Street, searching every corner of the house where I lived my childhood dreams. I reach the other end of the street, where pedestrians are allowed to walk, to get to their homes. The sidewalks are still narrow like before. The chinar trees have grown tall and thick, their seaweed-green leaves turning yellow in the last days of August. The houses are still attached like 30 years ago, but many new, contemporary homes are plugged in between. I pause beside a wide window that faces the street. It is guarded by wrought iron bars. Tendrils of black ivy climb them, their heart-shape leaves facing the sky. I had passed those iron tendrils hundreds of times on sunny days, when I rode my bicycle up and down this street.

Ripe figs wink at me from above a brick wall opposing the window. I cross the street and search the sidewalk for sticky stains of fallen fruit. Squished figs have polka-dotted the mosaic tiles of the sidewalk. I am reminded of the tree in my grandfather's garden. He loved gardening and asked my sister and me to help him with the garden work. He slanted the short ladder toward the fig tree and gave each of us a basket to stand under the tree with while he picked the ripened figs and threw them down to us. Sometimes the broad leaves landed on our heads like little doll umbrellas as he pulled the boughs to pluck the fruit. If a fig fell down by mistake, we raced to snatch it from the ground. We played a game to see whose basket filled up first. My grandfather listened to our ravings and tried to distribute them equally. I see my grandfather between the leaves. He whispers the old fable of Man and the Fig Tree in my ears. The Mythical Tree, the one that covers Man and his mate with its leaves. The Oath Tree, the one about which Allah makes a vow, regarding its yield. I wish I could traipse the other end of the street, and enter the heavenly garden that nurtured the fig tree.

## Tehran's Grand Bazaar—The Crystal Store

The day I plan to go to Tehran's Grand Bazaar it's cloudy. Rain is a rare incident in Iran nowadays, and the country is suffering from years of drought. A few drops fall on my cheeks as I get out of the taxi. The indelible perfume of earth disperses as the drops mix with dust on the ground. It heralds the end of the sweltering summer and enunciates the advent of Mehr, the first month of fall in the Persian calendar. People express joy on the streets, as if pearls are descending from the sky. When was the last time it rained in Tehran?

The vaulted entrance of the bazaar absorbs the buyers like a giant horseshoe magnet. A few porters have parked their trollies beside the entrance to carry people's merchandise. Colorful shawls twirl around the hangers when the mild current drifts from the roofed bazaar. I don't remember the last time I came here. Decades have passed since I visited this part of Tehran. With the economic crisis and the United States sanctions, I see fewer buyers. The bazaar is not as busy as always. The dried-fruit stores are colorful and full of life. Mounds of spices, dried herbs, and ground flower petals are on display in huge buckets. Some of them have a notice beside the price card. The notice tells customers what medicinal benefits each herb possesses. My grandmother loved rose petals. She sprinkled the tiny pink particles over the early harvest of fava beans in the spring. She believed the petals prevented stomachache from the beans. The salesman mixes seven different spices for me. Sumac powder snows on the crushed cumin in the plastic bag. He pours the turmeric on top and hands the layered spice bag to me. He comments that his spice recipe can be added to any stew or curry. "Take it with you to America," he says. "It will work like magic."

The beauty of curved shapes draws me to the china stores. The narrow paths of the bazaar in that section shine from the light reflected off the white china on display. There are many young girls accompanying their mothers in this area. It's a tradition in

Iran that a bride's family provides the chinaware to the newlyweds. In one crystal store, fashionable Czech crystals glitter on mirrored shelves. The parallel mirrors increase the images of the crystals to infinity. A 24-karat-gold ring embellishes the new crystals' rims. The shop boy polishes the golden rim of a fruit bowl with a damp towel and hands it to a young girl whose soft braided hair is showing beneath her white scarf. She has delicately lined her eyes with black kohl, making them look larger in her face. The boat-shaped fruit bowl sails in the air and lands on the girl's lap. The hull glitters during the sail as if a thousand mirrors are worked on the outer surface. I remember the conversation I had once with my grandfather, when he was working on the edges of a mirror artwork. I'd asked, "Agha Joon, can I cut this mirror in half?" He shook his head.

"No! You'll cut your hands."

"But how come you don't?"

He showed his hands to me. Scars marked his palms and the back of his hands. "I did. But I learned with time not to cut myself."

The girl smiles and asks for the price. The boat-shaped crystal is expensive, about a month's salary for a city worker. But she wants the whole set, and her mother haggles over the price.

I buy a small water bowl and exit the crystal store. Will I ever learn not to cut myself? Will I be able to spare my heart while dissecting memories of the past? Can I avoid cutting open the old wound from losing our home? Will I ever stop brooding for the home we were forced to surrender to the Islamic government? With time, my grandfather says, and all the sage in the world. And isn't it true that—one way or another—we will all lose the home that embeds our childhood memories? That the loss of home is the inevitable fate of us all, as we age and part from the place where we were born? Maybe my agony for the old fig tree originates from my ache for the lost Eden, for the void Garden, the vanished Abode, the forgotten Land. Or for the old fable of the invisible bond between the mythical tree and me. Maybe—like what the guard said at the gate of the Sun Street—I should not pry open the bleeding wounds of the past. Maybe I should just try to keep my good old memories.

## To the Follower of Cheikh Bamba Whom I Met in Dakar

FROM *Off Assignment*

YOU HAD INSISTED that I look at the postcard until the Cheikh revealed himself to me. I write you to tell you of how, once I returned home, and looked as you encouraged, F., who died recently, came into focus.

I met you when I arrived in Dakar from Lagos, and you invited me to your house. After our conversation, you handed me a postcard with a photograph of a man whose image I had seen on my drive into the city from the airport. The man's image was reproduced on drawings, lithographs, murals, glass paintings, almanacs, and postcards. It showed up on walls, windshields, doors, T-shirts, pendants: on any surface against which belief could be affirmed. I have set the postcard above my desk. I look at it intermittently as I write to you. The photograph is of Cheikh Amadou Bamba, a Sufi mystic, and you consider yourself his follower. "I am a Muslim only because of him," you told me.

F. was a preacher in the Presbyterian Church of Nigeria, and before that an itinerant evangelist for the Scripture Union, a nondenominational Christian organization. I knew him all my life. The Cheikh, as you taught me, told the people of Senegal that as black people they could be good Muslims. He produced a prodigious amount of tracts on the Quran, ritual, work, and the pacifist struggle against the French. He became so highly regarded that the colonial government sent him on exile.

Studying the gravitas of the Cheikh on the postcard you gave

me, I was reminded of F., of one Sunday while we sang the closing hymn—decked in his cassocks, which had become extrawhite
from the light that streamed into the chapel, as if to foreshadow
a transfiguration. Both men, evoking saintliness, swirl together in
my mind's eye. In writing of one, I slip into writing of the other.

How is it that in looking at the photograph of Cheikh Bamba,
I became *aware* of F.—his death? From its Germanic and Old English roots, "awareness" infers watchfulness and vigilance. The state
of being aware—like the potency of a presence in the dark. Once I
looked at the image as you advised, I began to attend to the image
on the postcard, to keep watch. I couldn't have kept watch *over* it—
what audacity could I have mustered to cast a supervisory net over
a culture I entered into as a stranger, one who has never been a
Muslim, or Sufi? In taking note of the presence in the photograph,
becoming curious about it, I offset an inner alarm, that of grief.

When, later, mindful of F. in his cassock, I considered the possibility of inhabiting the Cheikh's photograph myself. I returned
to Dakar. I wore a similar dress as the Cheikh, posed in front of a
similar shack. I mimicked his gravitas, and asked a photographer
to record my pose.

I am attracted by the Cheikh's poise, a semblance of grace. I
like his brilliant white. I like the shadow that falls aslant, and the
little heap of fine sand near his feet. I like the 9-shape that his
turban forms. I like what might seem like missing hands, and the
hint of a leg. You had explained that the missing leg was symbolic
of a man straddling two worlds. I like that many before me have
looked so devotedly at this photograph that I seem to have learned
to venerate secondhand, like a little boy who sees a painting and is
convinced all bearded men carry invisible halos.

In order to return to Dakar, I convinced a cultural magazine to
commission me to write about the Cheikh. We agreed I would be
paid upfront, to enable financial security while I conducted interviews with Islamic scholars and Mourides. The money never came,
and I floundered. I did conduct interviews, relying on translators,
on chance English words that fell through the cracks of French.
But all the writing I did in those four weeks, about the Cheikh, was
—believe me and excuse my duplicity—writing about wanting and
failing to write about F. It was as if I intended to refract the light
from his cassock through the saintliness of the Cheikh.

I remember that when you gave me the postcard, you encour-

aged me to write about the Cheikh, even though, you warned, "a
lot has been written." I was reminded of Roland Barthes in the last
week of his life. He had just completed his lectures, "La Prépara-
tion du roman," and he had announced that he wanted to write
a novel—one he will never write—copying out a sketch for it day
after day. The sketch comes to eight pages in his slender, sparse
handwriting: he has given lectures for two years about the novel
he wants to write and it comes to eight skeletal pages. When the
subject is vast and vague, a writer traces the outline of the indis-
cernible.

In fact, the book by Barthes I should think about is his *Mourning
Diary*, fragments written for over two years after his mother died.
And Barthes, like me, is unable to talk about his bereavement without the anxiety of not knowing how to properly talk about it, as he
writes in one of the entries: "I don't want to talk about it, for fear
of making literature out of it—or without being sure of not doing
so—although as a matter of fact literature originates within these
truths."

Of all the miracles attributed to the Cheikh, none is more fa-
bled than one performed aboard the ship deporting him from
Senegal to Gabon in 1895, where he would begin his seven-year
exile. Kept from praying, he broke free from his chains and cast a
prayer mat on the surface of the sea. Then climbed down the ship
to affirm his submission. Once he was done he rolled up the mat
and returned amidships. During the annual pilgrimage to Touba,
the city he founded in Senegal, pilgrims honor this miracle one
prayer out of a day's five, by turning their backs to Mecca, facing
the sea. Cheikh Bamba had also authored an estimated 20,000
mystical verses in Arabic. "My writings are my true miracles," he
wrote.

Writing as a miracle.

In Dakar you told me I must make a pilgrimage to Touba to
grasp the extent of his worldview, his spin on Islam, but also to ask
God for anything. I was unable to go to Touba, even when I visited
your country a second time. When you go on pilgrimage this year,
would you pray for me? I am in need of a miracle, to write about F.

LACY M. JOHNSON

# How to Mourn a Glacier

FROM *The New Yorker*

ALONG THE WESTERN edge of Iceland's central-highland pla-
teau, in the far east of the Borgarfjörður district, the Kaldidalur,
or "cold valley," stretches 25 miles between two barren volcanic
ridges: the Prestahnúkur system to the east and the Ok volcano
to the west. These volcanoes form part of the Mid-Atlantic Ridge,
the longest mountain range in the world, which runs under the
ocean from Antarctica to the Arctic and into the Siberian Sea. On
the valley's eastern slope, massive glaciers push dolerite boulders
down the mountainsides with their shining blue snouts. The western slope rises slowly toward the summit of Ok, a low shield volcano shrouded in mist.

Although nearly every mountain, stream, and valley in Iceland has a name and a history, Ok isn't particularly famous. No
path brings tourists to its summit, and those who travel the one-
lane gravel road through the valley floor typically take no note
of Okjökull—meaning "Ok's glacier"—which spanned 16 square
kilometers at its largest, at the end of the 19th century. By 1978 it
had shrunk to 3 square kilometers. In 2014 Iceland's leading glaciologist, Oddur Sigurðsson, hiked to Ok's summit to discover only a
small patch of slushy gray ice in the shadow of the volcano's crater.
Okjökull could no longer be classified as a glacier, Sigurðsson announced to the scientific community. It had become "dead ice."

In August I joined about 100 scientists, activists, dignitaries,
farmers, politicians, journalists, and children, as they gathered at
the base of Ok to mourn the lost glacier. The day began cold and
gray; a cover of low clouds threatened rain. "The climate crisis is

already here," Iceland's prime minister, Katrín Jakobsdóttir, told the crowd. "It is not just this glacier that has disappeared. We see the heat waves in Europe. We see floods. We see droughts." Film crews pointed their cameras, while the wind whipped Jakobsdóttir's hair and the paper on which she had written her remarks. "The time has come not for words, not necessarily for declarations, but for action," she said.

Her message was echoed by Mary Robinson, the former president of Ireland and former UN high commissioner for human rights, and by Kumi Naidoo, the secretary-general of Amnesty International, who assured us that the planet would be fine. But, if we sustain our current trajectory, he continued, humans would be gone. Naidoo passed the microphone to the writer and former Icelandic presidential candidate Andri Snær Magnason, who gripped it with both gloved hands. "Some of the students who are here today are twenty years old," he said, his voice shaking. "You may live to be a healthy ninety-year-old, and at that time you might have a favorite young person—a great-grandchild, maybe—who is the age you are now. When that person is a healthy ninety-year-old, the year will be 2160, and this event today will be in the order of direct memory from you to your grandchild in the future."

Magnason, who wore black glasses, a black stocking cap, and waterproof pants, had written the text for a memorial plaque that was to be installed at the top of the volcano, at the site of the former glacier. Like his speech, the plaque was meant, he said, to connect us to "the intimate time of the future." He asked us to turn toward the mountain. I followed the crowd away from the road and up Ok's slope. Behind us, the volcanoes darkened with rain.

When Sigurðsson first announced Okjökull's death, it was reported with little fanfare. A brief program aired on public television, and one short, four-line story appeared in an English-language newspaper. Around that time, two American anthropologists, Cymene Howe and Dominic Boyer—my colleagues at Rice University —began conducting fieldwork on the social impacts of the climate crisis in Iceland. The story about the death of Okjökull caught their attention, they told me, because Ok (pronounced "auk") "was not OK." Photographs of the melting ice cap showed the caldera in the shape of an O; inside the crater, a black rock jutting from the ice, looked like a C. One Icelander they spoke to pointed out that

"Oc" is the spelling of Ok in medieval Icelandic. The mountain, they said, seemed to be writing its own name.

Howe and Boyer began making a documentary about the glacier. Working with a team of Icelanders, they filmed interviews with farmers and artists who lived near the volcano, and with scientists, politicians, folklorists, writers, professors, tourists, and religious leaders. When asked how they felt about the death of Okjökull, some people shrugged and said that they were sad. Others admitted that they were hearing its name for the first time. Sigurðsson, the glaciologist, insisted to Howe and Boyer that, even though Okjökull was the smallest named glacier in Iceland, its death was a major loss. "It should not feel like just brushing something off your coat," he told them. Children learn the name of Okjökull in their earliest geography lessons; they see its name printed on nearly every Icelandic map. "A good friend has left us," Sigurðsson said.

After the documentary premiered, in 2018, Howe and Boyer sought a sense of closure. They settled on the idea of installing the memorial plaque and asked Magnason to write the text. It was a difficult prompt, Magnason told me: only a handful of people might ever climb the mountain, and fewer still would happen to stumble across the plaque. The other challenge was how to evoke, in words, the linkage between glaciers and memory. "The oldest Icelandic texts are a thousand years old," Magnason said—around the same age as the ice in the country's oldest glaciers. "In all that time, the earth has been quite stable, but the earth will have changed more in the next two hundred years than in the last thousand years." The plaque, cast in copper, would need to cohere for a reader two centuries from now, he explained, while also enshrining a specific moment of urgency.

Magnason decided to address his imagined audience directly. A LETTER TO THE FUTURE, the plaque reads in both Icelandic and English. OK IS THE FIRST ICELANDIC GLACIER TO LOSE ITS STATUS AS A GLACIER. IN THE NEXT 200 YEARS, ALL OUR GLACIERS ARE EXPECTED TO FOLLOW THE SAME PATH. THIS MONUMENT IS TO ACKNOWLEDGE THAT WE KNOW WHAT IS HAPPENING AND WHAT NEEDS TO BE DONE. ONLY YOU KNOW IF WE DID IT. As Howe, Boyer, and Magnason planned the ceremony, the first public photographs of the plaque were released and went viral. Soon they began hearing from people all over Europe, Asia, and North America—scientists, journalists, even the prime minister of Iceland—who wanted to be part of the funeral for the dead glacier at the top of the world.

If we say something has died, can we also say it once lived? A few days before the memorial ceremony for Okjökull, I met Sigurðsson for coffee on an uncommonly sunny morning in Reykjavík, hoping to learn more about why he had chosen to frame the loss of the glacier as a death. For a glaciologist, Sigurðsson has amassed an unusual degree of celebrity. His phone rang several times as we talked, and he admitted that he was not used to the attention. He was looking forward to a trip with his wife, the next week, to celebrate their anniversary.

Sigurðsson brightened when I asked him about glaciers. "They are enormously interesting as a natural phenomenon," he said. Partly his passion was aesthetic—"They just *shine*," he said—but he was also interested in why they surge suddenly and without explanation. When I asked him directly if glaciers were living, he hesitated. Things that grow and move, we tend to consider animate, he said, even if we resist the idea that every animate thing has a soul. A healthy glacier grows each winter more than it melts each summer; moves on the ground under its own weight; and is at least partially covered with a thick, fur-like layer of snow. Glaciers also move on their insides, especially in Iceland, where the glaciers are made of temperate ice, which exists right at the melting point. This sets them apart from the Greenland and Antarctic ice sheets, which are frozen and older by hundreds of thousands of years.

In Iceland, Sigurðsson said, the oldest ice was born more than 1,000 years ago, before the Little Ice Age, on the north side of Vatnajökull, the largest glacier in the country. Vatnajökull is roughly the area of Delaware and Rhode Island combined, and stands almost as tall as the Empire State Building. Okjökull, by comparison, was small and young when it died; ice covered the mountaintop for only a few centuries. Sigurðsson knows this because he had counted the glacier's rings, which were formed by dust each year —not unlike the rings on a tree. The rings contained a sort of memory—a record of pollen clouds, volcanic eruptions, world wars, and nuclear meltdowns. When a glacier melts, Sigurðsson explained, its memory disappears.

Having "memory" is just one of the many ways scientists refer to glaciers in terms that make them seem alive. They also "crawl" and have "toes"; when they break off at the ablation edge, they are said to have "calved." They are born and die—the latter at increasing rates, especially during "the great thaw" of the past 20 years. When Sigurðsson conducted a glacier inventory in the early 2000s, he found more than 300 glaciers in Iceland; a repeat inventory, in 2017, revealed that 56 had disappeared. Many of them were small glaciers in the highlands, which had spent their lives almost entirely unseen. "Most of them didn't even have names," he told me. "But we have been working with local people to name every glacier so that they will not go unbaptized." Now, he intends to complete their death certificates and bring a stack of them to meetings. The next to go, he thinks, will be Hofsjökull, to the east.

It is unusual for a glaciologist to fill out a death certificate, but something concrete, like a piece of paper or a plaque, helps to make clear that the loss is irreversible. The last ice age began in the Pleistocene and ended 10,000 years ago, when Iceland was covered in a massive ice sheet thousands of feet thick. The planet has warmed, cooled, and warmed again since then; ice has advanced and retreated, and this movement has carved the mountains and valleys that we claim as our own. But, in the past several years alone, we have witnessed not only an acceleration of the great thaw but also the sudden bleaching of the coral reefs, the rapid spread of the Sahara desert, continuous sea-level rise, the warming of the oceans, and record-breaking hurricanes each season and every year. This is one of the most distressing things about being alive today: we are witnessing geologic time collapse on a human scale.

Climbing Ok, we scrambled for hours over dolerite boulders, pitted lava rocks, patches of thick moss, and the small streams that trickled down the volcano to the lake below. We paused for lunch before the final leg of the hike, and Magnason instructed us to approach the caldera with reverence and humility. Elsewhere in Iceland, he explained, climbing to the summit of a mountain in silence and without looking back is said to grant the hiker three wishes. Wishes are sometimes too grand to be of use, Howe added, but it can be useful to imagine the future we hope to see.

As we walked the last few hundred feet, I realized that we lack metaphors for comprehending the future, much less the scale of the disaster that it has in store for us. Then the mountainside leveled, and the sight of the crater purged all thoughts from my head. The ice was gray, lifeless, uncanny. Guðmundur Ingi Guð-brandsson, Iceland's minister of the environment, stood on the boulder that had been chosen as the site of the memorial. Children surrounded him with protest signs, demanding that their political leaders, their parents, and their teachers do more. "When I grew up as a little boy not very far away from here, my grandmother taught me the names of all the mountains we could see on the horizon, and the names of the four glaciers," Guðbrandsson said. "When I visit my parents today on their farm, I can see only three." The windchill had dropped below freezing, and the crowd huddled together for warmth. Sigurðsson read a list of vital statistics from Okjökull's death certificate. "The age of this glacier was about three hundred years," he said. "Its death was caused by excessive summer heat. Nothing was done to save it."

Howe and Boyer asked the children to come to the front of the crowd. "We need to understand our relationship to the world in ways we haven't had to in the past," Howe said. "We need to be able to imagine a new future." There was a moment of silence as the children pushed the plaque into place. The day had cleared a little, and I could see across the Kaldidalur to the glaciers on the opposite peaks. Below them, in the valley's deepest crevice, a meltwater lake was forming, already so blue and deep.

# Such Perfection

FROM *The Believer*

NO ONE ELSE is paying attention. The train approaches the station at Varenna Esino. It is a small, regional train, headed north from Milan, its passengers whiling away the boredom of their daily commutes. A young man across the aisle gazes at the floor. A woman swaps her heels for a pair of sandals and reads.

But I struggle to keep my composure. The mountains have slowly been gathering themselves up, out of the fields and above the rooftops. They are now so high and so close to the train. Without warning, the lake is upon us. I notice first a change in the light. The sun breaks freely on the water, drawing sharp silver lines along lapping waves. In the changing light, the faces of strangers on the train look new. I see now a faint scar on the young man's temple, and the woman reading the book is younger than I'd first thought. Her mouth appears bisected, half in shade, half illuminated. Her lipstick is red in shadow, magenta in the light.

I once heard that every painting is a solution to the problem of how to best carve light, but it is only at that moment that I finally understand what that could mean. My way of looking shifts. Every painting I'll see from now on will bring with it, if gently, the memory of being on this train, watching the lake spread out before me, the light changing all I'd been observing. The moment is educative; it retrains my eye, refines my perceptual discernment. I see dust particles dancing, a static laid upon the scene. The passengers look lit as if by soft spotlights. I see their bodies plainly, the curves under their clothes, where their skin is smooth, their sweat, the whites of their eyes. The woman with the brilliant lipstick glances up from her book, tilts her chin to the window. The young man with the scar no longer looks so bored. He watches the lake with clear longing, as if he wished to strip himself bare and dive in. The sun penetrates our train car and I feel it, a heat on my body, and I know that the passengers can now see more of me too. The train ducks behind a grove of trees, and shadowed patterns of leaves grow across our laps. I hold my breath. I've never seen light carved so beautifully.

The night before I left for Italy for a vacation alone, I had dinner in Brooklyn with a man whom I'd been skeptical of for years. We have many friends in common and so I'd run into him at parties and housewarmings. Each time, I left unsure whether I liked him. He was indifferent to me, which was not unusual and did not offend me. He didn't owe me his attention, nor had I expected we'd be friends just because we knew the same people. I myself was indifferent to most people I met and resented any implication that I should be nicer or more socially gracious than I felt inclined to be.

The quality of his indifference intrigued me, though. At parties, he would sometimes answer my questions tersely and then walk away with no concern, it seemed, for a guise of reciprocal politesse. Once, at a dinner hosted in a friend's Williamsburg loft, I made a game of seeing how many questions I could ask before he'd ask me one in return. It was a one-sided game played for my own satisfaction, and it was, perhaps, ungenerous of me to play it. But I was feeling ungenerous. I asked him where he grew up, did he have siblings, where had he traveled, did he like living in Williamsburg. I got to 36 questions, 15 of which were follow-ups based on his answers, all of which he answered while looking mostly at his phone. As I asked the 37th, he got a text about another party, and left.

I disliked this man and found it exhilarating to be so near someone who projected a radical social freedom. I wanted to be as free, but was trained to keep such feelings as small as possible. But the exhilaration came mostly from the possibility that I'd met someone who did not look at me, at my body, and feel obligated to handle me with pitying care.

And so I invited the indifferent man to have dinner with me, certain he'd say no, and that he'd say it just like that—*No!*—instead of speaking to me from behind a mask of muffled sympathies. But to my surprise, he agreed. The night before I left for Italy, we met at a Chinese restaurant.

Toward the end of the meal, the subject of a mutual friend and that friend's new girlfriend came up. I'd been told by others that this mutual friend's new girlfriend was the most beautiful woman in Brooklyn. I said this to the indifferent man, and he shrugged and showed me pictures of the woman, our mutual friend's new girlfriend, on his phone, and she was, as advertised, quite beautiful. I was struck by how accurately I'd imagined her without any prior, concrete description. Her body fell within a familiar range. She was tall, but not so tall she might emasculate, and thin, but with soft weight in the necessary places. I found myself wishing I could touch this woman's hair. It was long, auburn, and had a wild quality to it. The unruliness of her hair granted her a specificity that made the spectator believe she did not evoke just the general concept of beauty, but rather a particular, a singular, instance of it. She was young, white, symmetrical, able-bodied. A million times I'd seen this body shape and variations on this same face and been told, and sometimes agreed, that it was beautiful.

My own body exists outside of this range. I was born with a rare congenital disorder called sacral agenesis, which means that my sacrum, the part of the spine that connects the spinal column to the hips, failed to form. My body is visually marked by difference. I'm much shorter than the average adult woman. My legs from the knees down and my feet are underdeveloped and disproportionate to the rest of my body. My spine is curved, which makes my back arch forward. I have hip dysplasia, which means the ball-and-socket joints in my hips are malformed. This is painful. I walk by rolling my hips, which gives me a distinctive side-to-side gait. If I wear my hair in a long ponytail, it whips back and forth like a pendulum. I walk slowly. I'm slow on stairs. A significant amount of my daily energy is spent managing chronic pain, specifically in my hips and along my spine.

Looking at the picture on the indifferent man's phone, I'd wondered, not for the first time, what my life would have been like had I been born with this woman's hair and face and body. The recurrent thought is that I could have had anything I wanted.

I asked the indifferent man why he had pictures of our mutual friend's new girlfriend. He said he'd dated her, too, just a few months before she got together with our friend.

"How long did you date her?" I asked.

He shrugged. "A few months."

"And what happened?"

"I wasn't all that attracted to her," he said.

"But don't you think she's beautiful?"

He shrugged again, then told me stories about being at bars with male friends who were able to pick out 5 or 6 or 10 women who were attractive to them, but whom he, the indifferent man, would not even consider.

"A ten in the eyes of most men will be a six to me. The girls our friends will date are all, like, a three for me," he said. I sensed a reluctant pride. He needed a really beautiful woman, a supernaturally beautiful woman, he explained. He leaned in to make me his conspirator.

"This may be more than you want to know," he said, "but if a woman is not, like, model-beautiful, I can't even keep up an erection when I'm with her."

I had multiple feelings collide. I was disgusted by what he was saying, but I wanted him to keep talking. It was clear he could confess all this to me because I was not visible on the same plane as these other women—the 3s, the 6s, the 10s. I saw that my body barred me from his realm of possible women. The feeling brought with it a strange relief, as if I'd been looking in a distorted mirror and someone had just replaced it with a normal one. What he reflected back wasn't kind, but it was clear. This is how men see me. The indifferent man offered no excuses or apologies.

"Really, it's a curse," he continued. "I'd like to be able to date more women. But it's not like you can control these things."

"Can't you?" I said.

"Of course not," he said, looking at me in disbelief.

I thought to leave the bar. Instead I said, "What you are describing is so superficial."

"I know where it comes from," he said. "I know I'm controlled by media and advertising and what they deem the norm in terms of beauty, blah, blah, but I can't help that. I can't be at fault for being a product of my environment."

"But can you control it? Or adjust your thinking? If you are aware of the external forces influencing it?"

"How?"

He said this with such finality. It was a challenge. A light flashed outside, stippling his face into garish shadows. Did I really believe, he was asking me, that we could rewire ourselves; that we could use our intellect to unlearn our cultural training? To unsee what we've been taught to recognize as beauty? I felt unsure. His gaze was convincing. I wondered why he'd agreed to this dinner. I was likely the least physically attractive woman whose full name he knew. Were we here to make sure I knew exactly that?

"Does experience eventually alter the immediate effect of beauty?" I asked.

"No," he said.

"But haven't you met someone," I asked him, my voice rising, "who seemed very beautiful at first, but who was, I don't know, boring, and so you lost interest? Haven't you gained interest in a woman you'd initially too quickly overlooked?"

He shook his head. He'd grown tired of the conversation.

"This is all embedded in us from birth! You can't undo it. What we're told is beautiful becomes the truth."

The ideal of Western beauty begins with a lost sculpture. It is the form of a man, cast in bronze; in his left hand he holds aloft a phantom spear. He steps forward, torso torqued, his weight on his right leg, his left at ease. The *Doryphoros*, "the Spear Bearer," was the masterpiece of Polyclitus, a beloved sculptor in fifth-century BCE Athens.

"Such perfection in proportion," wrote the physician Galen of the sculpture nearly 600 years later, "comes about via an exact commensurability of all the body's parts to one another: of finger to finger and of these to the hand and wrist, of these to the forearm, of the forearm to the upper arm; of the equivalent parts of the leg; and of everything to everything else."

In the *Canon,* a companion treatise, Polyclitus detailed the exact measurements of each part of the body as well as the necessary proportional relationship between the parts and the whole of the form. Both the treatise and the original sculpture are lost, although there exist—in various stages of deterioration and imperfection—Roman copies remade in marble. The most famous copy was pulled from the ashes of Pompeii.

These perfect proportions were, for the Greeks and later for the artists of the Italian Renaissance, the true, objective measurement of human beauty. Beauty was not a subjective, individual experience, but rather a property that could be evaluated mathematically.

But our proportions did not reveal merely something as superficial as pleasing physical beauty. Plato believed that proportionality in the body was evidence of a divine architecture, the same that could be found in the intricate order of the natural world around us. A beautiful body conveyed an innate, divine harmony—the godly awe of many disparate parts functioning together in perfect relation to a whole. It was more than what made us beautiful—it was what made us virtuous, aligned with our ideal forms.

"Measure and proportion are everywhere identified with beauty and virtue," Plato wrote. "Beauty, proportion, and truth . . . considered as one."

Just as falsehoods threatened truth, disorder threatened beauty.

"Ugliness," warned Plutarch, "is immediately ready to come into being if only one chance element is omitted or inserted out of place."

My disability: sacral agenesis, born without a sacrum, the bone that connects the spine to the pelvis. *Agenesis,* from the Greek, means "a lack or failure to generate." My missing sacrum, my omitted element.

Two days after my dinner at the Chinese restaurant, I stand at the edge of Lake Como in awe. Rays of golden light, sliced up by palm fronds, hang suspended in the air. I look for a long time, my suitcase at my feet, watching the trees and glittering lake beyond the trees and the ring of mountains beyond the lake.

My hotel is a 20-minute walk from the station. I pass through the small town square and see people seated outside, drinking wine and watching a group of musicians play on the steps of San Giorgio, the medieval church. The scent of rosemary and brine permeates the air. If only someone would beckon to me, hand me a glass, and pull out a chair, I could abandon my walk, my suitcase, and join them.

There is a specific ache in my right hip that has steadily become more painful over the past year. As I walk through the square and up a hill toward my hotel, the ache focuses into a thin blade wedged into my hip joint. The muscles in my back and along my spine bear what feels like a thousand small rips.

The driveway up to the hotel is steep. I inch up it sidewise, one foot shuffling beside the other. Halfway up, I lose my grip on my suitcase and it rolls on its wheels a few feet before toppling over and skidding to a stop. I am glad no one was around to see me, their gaze relaying back to me my perceived helplessness. But I'm not helpless; I'm struggling. People don't always recognize the difference.

The hotel is a former monastery built into the side of a steep mountain. Reaching my room requires a ride in two rickety funiculars. It is dark now. The lake has disappeared, but I can still see the twinkling lights of Varenna below. In my room, I open the balcony doors and voices drift in. I want to be with people, but my physical pain commands the moment. The sound of laughter echoes in the valley. I stand above, separated from it. For so long, I'd told myself not to travel—better to stay home than move closer to something beautiful that excluded me.

I think about the indifferent man and how he'd spoken to me. Sitting across from me in the restaurant, he'd held the posture of someone waiting for a timer to expire. He probably didn't enjoy being seen out with me, lest someone mistake us for a couple. Or perhaps that had been the motivation behind agreeing to dinner. I'd heard from male friends that they had better luck with women when they were seen with me. I was an excellent prop. Their close association with me, some sad cripple, made them seem like sensitive, good-hearted men. A past girlfriend of a male friend had once pulled me aside at a party to tell me that my friendship with her boyfriend was what had drawn her to him in the first place. She'd said, "It was nice to know that he could care about any kind of woman."

The indifferent man had spoken about beauty and ugliness in objective terms. The absence of beauty took tangible, measurable effect: it robbed him of his erection. Whereas the presence of beauty could be enough to inspire in him love and devotion. He'd said all this calmly and without judgment.

The indifferent man had been paternal at times, as if he were merely doling out life's hard facts to prepare me for a cruel world. He wasn't the first, though, to offer this twisted version of tough love. That honor belongs to Jim. Jim and I were in a close circle of high school friends. We dyed our hair pink or purple or orange, wore studded belts and bracelets, had face piercings and hand-made stick-and-poke tattoos—on my left forearm is a permanent reminder of this era: a faded, shaky image of the character Harold from Hal Ashby's film *Harold and Maude* that my friend Jon, after a few beers, drew freehand using a razor blade and india ink. In the film, Harold—young, disillusioned, misunderstood—falls in love with eighty-year-old Maude. Their romance is strange, specific, joyful, socially unsanctioned. I identified with both characters. Like Harold, I was disillusioned and misunderstood. Like Maude, I was regarded as a socially inappropriate object of romantic desire.

Romance was for me an incongruent concept. I wanted it, but the world treated me as though I was disqualified from it. I would listen to other kids my age talk about attraction in terms of a sliding scale—someone could be sexy or not, or sort of sexy, or not sexy before but kinda getting more sexy all of a sudden.

My disability kept me, in the eyes of others, off that scale altogether, like an animal or a child. I saw people cringe when I referenced a crush or joined my girlfriends in lusting after a celebrity. I made people uncomfortable.

But Jim knew me well and cared for me, it seemed. The shortest boy in our friend group, he liked to stand near me because it made him feel tall. He took swing-dancing lessons and taught me moves. I was the one he could lift the highest and with the greatest ease, swinging me through his legs, flipping me around his arm. Afterward, he'd always hug me tightly and kiss my cheek.

When it came time for the homecoming dance, everyone in our friend circle began to pair up. I didn't have a date and Jim didn't, either. It seemed obvious, for purposes of group unity, that Jim and I would agree to go together. But it was also well-known that I had a crush on Jim. When the subject came up, Jim would look at me expectantly. My girlfriends would ask me at the end of each day, "Has he asked you yet? Has he asked you?" And each day, I'd say, "Not yet."

At night, I'd imagine the moment when Jim would lift me into the air and spin me around and kiss my cheek and ask me to be his date. All the angst I'd curated as a teen dissolved into romantic cliché. I, like everyone else, wanted to be chosen. As the dance grew closer, I became anxious. Our friends had started to make plans for the dance, and I wasn't part of them. Finally, my girlfriends urged me to stop waiting and just ask Jim to be my date.

I asked him in the library of our school. We were studying together for an upcoming geometry test, when finally he closed his notebook and smiled.

"I feel like," he said, teasing me, "there might be something you want to talk to me about."

I told him yes, there was, and I said simply that I wanted to go to the homecoming dance with him and would he take me.

"Of course," he said. "I'd love to." Relief flooded me to the point of dizziness. "But," he continued, "there's something very important I need to talk to you about first."

He proceeded to tell me that our female friends had been pressuring him for weeks to ask me to the dance, not wanting me to feel left out.

"They love you," he said, "but they pity you, and their pity won't help you in the world." I can, to this day, recall the exact, even tone in his voice, his syrupy smile. He reached across the table and took my hand. "I'll go to the dance with you as your friend," he said. "And that's fine. But before we go, I need to tell you something important, and I tell you this as your friend. I want to protect you. You can't go around asking people on dates. Men like me will always feel pressured to say yes when they want to say no, and then all you've done is put us in a bad position. We have to either sacrifice our happiness or reject you, and that just makes us feel bad. I feel bad now having to say all this." He smiled a wincing smile. It was clear to me that he saw my crush as a cute delusion and what he needed to tell me was a painful but loving fact.

He continued, "Maybe no one told you, though, and I'm the one to tell you. It's just the truth. No man will want to date you unless he, too, is desperate or ugly."

I never much cared for the Greek concept of beauty, nor did I agree that it was a virtue on par with truth or justice. I'd always preferred Hume's notion that beauty was not a set of external properties, but rather that it existed in the contemplative mind.

"Each mind perceives a different beauty. One person may even perceive deformity, where another is sensible of beauty." Hume argues that some people are better judges of beauty than others. He calls them the ideal critics. And this is a better theory for me, a woman with a body that could never be mistaken for symmetrical or orderly.

In contemporary aesthetic scholarship, the Greeks' objective evaluations of beauty are often regarded as wrong, outdated—or, worse, uncool. But as I lay there in Varenna listening to the sound of the lake's gentle waves coming to shore, I wondered if I'd rejected the possibility of divine, objective beauty simply because I was excluded from it. Being excluded from a theory doesn't make it incorrect.

The next morning, I walk along the edge of the lake. The beauty of Lake Como is so massive and all-consuming that it accosts me. I turn a corner and cringe. I curse. The beauty of the lake is absolute, resounding. Birds sing, waves lap, the air smells of fir and jasmine. The sun shines, but it is not too hot; the wind blows, but it is not too cold. There is something restorative, palliative, in the air. I can walk farther; the twinge in my hip that I'd felt worsening for so many months is gone. I can sleep more, eat less, drink less, hear better. I take off my glasses and can see a great distance.

I'm easily seasick, but I want to see the other villages sprinkled around the lake. With fear, I buy a ticket for the ferry and stay on it for hours, taking in the grandeur of the mansions perched along the shore, the old churches, the verdant mountains. I feel not so much as a twinge of nausea. I take the boat to Bellagio, where the English during the Victorian era flocked to recover from tuberculosis. To be here, to witness the lake, seems suddenly the most logical prescription for any ailment.

I sit on the shore, eating pizza and then gelato. The sun sets. I watch the palms at the edges of the water. I think of the scholar Elaine Scarry's writings on the beauty of palm trees. In her book *On Beauty and Being Just,* she argues that there are two common points of error in our perceptions of beauty. The first, which she refers to as "the error of overcrediting," occurs when we recognize that something we'd formerly thought beautiful no longer is. The second comes when we realize we've withheld the attribution of beauty from an object that has rightfully deserved it all along.

"For example," she writes, "I had ruled out palm trees as objects of beauty and then one day discovered I had made a mistake." This latter error, "the error of undercrediting," is the more serious, as it is evidence of our "failed generosity."

Scarry recounts a moment when she is on a balcony watching the leaves of the palm tree move—they are "lustrously in love with air and light." Her perception shifts; a mistake is corrected. "The vividness of the palm states the acuity with which I feel the error, a kind of dread conveyed by the words 'How many?' How many other errors lie like broken plates or flowers on the floor of my mind?"

Night comes and still Scarry is on her balcony watching the palm tree, witnessing the missed beauty. "Under the moonlight, my palm tree waves and sprays needles of black, silver, and white; hundreds of shimmering lines circle and play and stay in perfect parallel."

When men in my life had found me sexually alluring, they would often describe it as a shock, an unforeseen surprise, like they'd found an old coat with a $20 bill in the pocket. The word "actually" was commonly employed: "You're actually attractive." A stranger once stopped me on the street and said, "I'm not sure what you have going on here with"—he pointed down the length of my body—"this. But I actually think you're pretty." He asked for my number, which I declined to provide. This was not the response he'd expected, and so he followed me for a few steps. "No, no," he said, diagnosing the problem. "I actually want to take you on a date. I'm actually being serious."

A man had fucked me once and afterward said, "Wow, you feel just like an actual woman."

Elaine Scarry wonders how she's missed the beauty of the palm and decides it is because she'd held in her mind some sort of palm tree composite, maybe made of television images, bad drawings, blow-up plastic palms at party stores, and that composite was ugly. It becomes beautiful only when the individual, specific elements line up, when the light is just right. It isn't palms but *this* palm that corrects her error. It's the singular instance of one palm. She looks up from under a canopy of palm leaves and sees an owl sleeping. By weaving its plumage with the palm's leaves, the owl is able to suspend itself midair to sleep as if still in flight. *Beautiful,* she thinks. So now it is not just the particular palm that convinces her. It's a set of particulars. This palm, this minute, the coolness of the spot where she stood, looking up. The noticing of the owl.

The next day, I go to Villa Monastero and walk through the great gardens there. The brochure tells me that several species of rare plants are able to flourish on the steep slopes of the botanical gardens in Varenna, and among them are certain varieties of palms. African and American palms, Chilean wine palms, European fan palms, Mexican blue palms. With Elaine Scarry in mind, I find myself very attuned to the beauty of these trees, especially the Mexican palm, whose blue-gray fronds shimmer and stir, its thin fringe waving in movie light. The whole scene is beautiful to the point of looking manufactured. When I look out over the water to the painted mountains, I feel certain the scene will flicker and reveal a green screen. The brochure explains that the Mexican blue palm is somewhat rare, able to flourish around Lake Como due to the exceptional climate, which is mild year-round.

I hike into the mountains. The path I take is so steep that at times I get down on all fours and use the rocks to drag myself up, like a mountain goat. At the summit is yet another monastery. I climb its turrets and look out at paradise below. This is what the poet Longfellow was looking at when he wrote, *I ask myself, Is this a dream? / Will it all vanish into air? / Is there a land of such supreme / And perfect beauty anywhere?*

Beyond the monastery I find myself surrounded by trees. Ahead, two older women, grocery bags in hand, are cursing in Italian at a bush. I hear a rustling. A third, much deeper voice emerges, laughing, and the rustling speeds up. The women curse louder, and the deep voice laughs louder. I approach the scene. There, in the bushes, a man is masturbating. His pants are around his ankles, and his thin penis sits gently in his palm. It has a gray and waterlogged look, like it's been submerged in the lake for days. He makes kissing sounds at the women, but when I pass into view he freezes. He looks at me for a moment, then pulls up his pants. He glances down at my shriveled legs, visible below the hem of my dress.

"Mi dispiace," he says. (I'm sorry.) "Dio ti benedica, signora." (May God bless you.)

Of Lake Como, Longfellow wrote, . . . *but ye have left / Your beauty with me, a serene accord / Of forms and colours, passive, yet endowed / In their submissiveness with power as sweet / And gracious, almost might I dare to say, / As virtue is, or goodness . . .*

\*

A few months after the homecoming dance, Jim tried to kiss me.

He said, "I was wrong before. Something has changed. And I like you."

Before, Jim had spoken to me as if beauty were an unalterable fact, but now suddenly my beauty was discernible, visible if only in the right light.

"What changed?" I asked him.

"You grew on me; you made me laugh enough times that I started to want to be around you more; you are smarter than my last girl."

I remember the pang of pride I felt when Jim said this. I remember how it motivated me, like a dog wanting to please its owner, to prove my worth to him over and again.

Jim's perceptual shift, not what he said in the library, is the worst part of this story. It embedded a damaging idea in me, one I'd recognize deeply when I read Scarry years later: beauty is a matter of particulars aligning correctly. My body put me in a bracketed, undercredited sense of beauty. But if I could get the particulars to line up just right, I could be re-seen, discovered like the palm tree is discovered. In order to be accepted as a whole person deserving of the whole range of human desires, I had to be extraordinary in all other aspects. My worth as a woman wasn't apparent otherwise.

In this new light, I started to see my work, my intellect, my skills, my moments of humor or goodness, not as valuable in themselves, but as ways of easing the impact of my ugliness. If only I could pile up enough good qualities, they could obscure my unacceptable body.

"The correction," Scarry writes, "the alteration in perception, is so palpable that it is as though the perception itself (rather than its object) lies rotting the brain . . . The perception has undergone a radical alteration—it breaks apart . . . or disintegrates . . ."

Philosophically, Hume and Scarry provide richer views of beauty than the Greeks do with their conception of mathematical perfection. But accepting the argument that beauty is malleable came, for me, at a cost. The Platonian view rejected me cleanly, but Hume and Scarry left a door ajar, and I've spent a lifetime trying to contort my form to see if I can pass through it.

\*

I sit in the town square and eat my final meal in Varenna. Church bells clang, echoing strangely out across the lake, colliding with the mountain walls, playing a mangled melody. The bells are chaotic, sharp, abrasive.

I watch the sun disappear. I will it to set slowly so that I may linger over this perceptual moment, to somehow swallow it up and keep with me forever this view of the lake, the mountains, the flowers, the palms. The next morning, my last, I sleep too late, miss the sunrise.

As the train rattles away from Lake Como, I close my eyes and see myself naked at the edge of the indifferent man's bed. I hear him tell me what he sees: that I am too ugly to fuck. It isn't my fault or his, merely a fact, impossible to undo. I imagine him saying it without intended cruelty. It is a regrettable truth, a door firmly shut. This is what I really want. Not his sex, but the intimacy of his decree, not masked in sympathy. I want to see his bare face. I imagine how beautiful it would be to hear someone speaking plainly and without subtext to me.

Later, I'm back in Brooklyn, chatting idly with an Italian barista in a café near my house. I mention that I've just returned from Italy. She asks me where I went. I tell her Rome, Venice, Lake Como, Milan.

"Ah, so a first time to Italy."

I blush. How quickly I've revealed myself as one of the uninitiated.

I ask her about Lake Como, saying how I'd found it so beautiful, so hard to leave. She shrugs.

"It's nice for the tourists," she says. "But I'm accustomed to that view and prefer others."

And just like that, the lake I'd beheld is gone.

# What I Learned in Avalanche School

FROM *The New York Times Magazine*

THE PARTY OF eight set out to ski the southern slope of Microdot Peak, located in Alaska's Hatcher Pass, on the morning of March 1, 2003. All were experienced skiers. Some had spent more than 100 days in the backcountry that winter. They were familiar with the properties and behavior of snowpack. They'd refined their safety assessment and prediction skills, sometimes through negative outcomes. A few had triggered and survived avalanches. One had witnessed an avalanche fatality.

The southern slope of Microdot averages an angle of 35 degrees. Avalanches are most prevalent on slopes with angles of 30 to 45 degrees. When the skiers began their ascent, the sky was blue, and the winds were calm. The week before, four feet of snow fell on Hatcher Pass during a storm that, given the wind direction, covered Microdot's southern slope with an additional burden of blown snow. Snow and wind create "slabs," which in turn create weakness in the snowpack. When subjected to stress—like the stress that a skier, carving over the surface, might exert—rapid shape-shifting can occur. A slab can detach from the stable snowpack beneath it and career downhill like a runaway tectonic plate that transforms, within milliseconds, into a many-ton, half-frozen wave, subsuming whatever is in front of or on top of it, before instantaneously seizing, when it settles, into a substance resembling cement.

Midway up the slope, the eight skiers paused to dig a pit in the snow. They discovered the existence of storm slabs and wind slabs, confirming the "considerable to high" avalanche danger determined by the local rangers. They continued their ascent.

Solar radiation and rapidly increasing temperatures cause melting and weaken the snowpack's top layer. Beautiful weather causes skiers to disregard warning signs, or take risks beyond their comfort zone. Once the skiers reached the summit of Microdot, they descended the southern slope one at a time. Four reached the bottom safely. The fifth triggered a slab avalanche that carried him 700 feet over a rock ledge, partly burying him and two others.

My Level 1 avalanche course started early on the fifth day of 2019. So far there had been zero avalanche fatalities and one partial burial in the Eastern Sierra, the mountains visible through the windows of the storefront where we met. Ten men and three women, including me, sat in folding chairs around a C-shaped arrangement of collapsible tables. Because the temperature inside was around 55 degrees, most people wore hats and high-tech layers—some form-fitting and bright, others worn to a black sheen and multiply patched—and held travel coffee mugs between their hands. The room's broody, slightly misanthropic mood fit the occasion: over the next three days, we'd be learning how not to be buried alive.

The instructor, an amiably intense man in his 30s named Ryan, asked us to introduce ourselves and answer the question Why am I here? ("Why am I here?" we'd soon learn, is the question backcountry skiers must repeatedly ask themselves as they encounter new pitches with new conditions.) Most people lived on the West Coast and had summited famous peaks. A pair of men in their 20s were members of a locally itinerant rock-climbing community that truck-camped during the winter in a place called the Pit. People, on the whole, were here for two reasons: half the room wanted to become less scared of avalanches; the other half wanted to become more.

I was here for neither reason. I don't often ski avalanche terrain. I don't venture into areas unpatrolled by ski-resort crews that, in the middle of the night and after dawn, drop hand charges onto "loaded" slopes or shoot rounds from a 105-millimeter howitzer, forcing the mountain to shed its menace before people line up at the lifts. I pretended, when it was my turn, to be part of the "wanted to become less scared" group, because my real reasons weren't reasons so much as prompts. But had I stated them, there were two.

One: Because I had been an indiscriminately fearful child—and, despite repeated exposure to "considerable to high" dangers over many decades, that child failed to be eradicated and replaced by someone braver—the act of preparing for every type of unknown, even one I'm unlikely to encounter, began as a coping mechanism and evolved over the years into a passion. Preparing for hypothetical terrible events (a terrorist attack involving high-speed elevators in a Vegas hotel; the dismasting of a sailboat while rounding Cape Horn) provides a creative high to which I've become addicted. Acrobatic feats of problem-solving and projection make the future elongate and then bend back around the present. Time becomes spherical and exudes the deep glow of cogent busyness. Possibly as a result of—or as forecast by—this beloved hobby, I became a novelist; I've reconfigured this oft-pathologized "catastrophic/paranoid/neurotic" tendency as a peril of my trade. Out of professional necessity, I obsessively engage in outcome empathy.

"Prepare for the worst," the avalanche course manual advised, "and know what to do."

Two: among the deaths I do not wish, being buried alive is the one I do not wish the most. Edgar Allan Poe published a story called "The Premature Burial" in 1844. (Poe most likely suffered from taphophobia—technically the fear of being mistaken for dead and then sealed in a coffin and buried in a grave—but I imagine he'd be equally inspired by the live-burial potential of avalanches.) After listing a number of horrors, including plagues, earthquakes, and massacres, Poe's narrator asserts: "To be buried while alive is, beyond question, the most terrific of these extremes which has ever fallen to the lot of mere mortality."

Learning how not to be buried alive, however, turned out to be a little bit boring. Ryan opened a snowpack PowerPoint while we took notes about storm slabs and wind slabs and persistent slabs, all of which sounded like subcategorical psychiatric disorders from the *DSM*.

When Ryan shifted the conversation to "avalanche problems," we perked up, maybe because the term would seem provocatively redundant, the avalanche itself being the primary problem. But no. Ninety percent of human-avalanche encounters, Ryan said, are triggered by humans, making *humans* the primary avalanche problem. Nature doesn't kill people with avalanches. People kill people with avalanches.

Then Ryan revealed a second twist: By entering the storefront two hours earlier, by taking an avalanche-safety course, we had statistically increased our chances of being killed in an avalanche. We were more likely to die now than we were at 8:00 a.m.

The room absorbed this information. It felt like being in a movie in which you thought you were at a normal dinner party, but just by showing up, you'd implicitly agreed to fight the other guests to the death.

The problem—the primary human problem—is that people are susceptible, prideful, bullheaded, egotistic, dumbstruck, and lazy. Add to this doomed slurry a little avalanche training (or what used to qualify as avalanche training, and its focus on analyzing snowpack), and people make terrible decisions with greater frequency and confidence.

I already knew about the human problem, because I did some of the recommended reading before class, including "The Human Factor 2.0," a seminal 2016 article about avalanche education published in *Powder* magazine and written by David Page (who also happens to be an ex-boyfriend from long ago). Page's article tracks the shift in avalanche education away from snow-pit forensics and toward human forensics, a change in large part attributable to Ian McCammon, an engineer and avalanche researcher. McCammon dryly states the learning-death paradox in his 2004 paper "Heuristic Traps in Recreational Avalanche Accidents: Evidence and Implications": "The blatancy of the hazard in avalanche accidents would be understandable if most victims had little understanding of avalanches. Unfortunately, this does not seem to be the case."

In class, Ryan identified McCammon's six decision-making or "heuristic" traps. (Per McCammon: "Most of the time, the consistency heuristic is reliable, but it becomes a trap when our desire to be consistent overrules critical new information about an impending hazard.") The traps that interested me most, because they were traps against which I was typically guarded—and so was happy to have them validated as specieswide frailties rather than personal quirks—were Familiarity (failing to remain vigilant when faced with the known), Social Facilitation (everybody's doing it, so it must be OK) and Expert Halo (the experts must know what they're doing, and so it's safe to unquestioningly follow them).

The others are Consistency (or "commitment"—every moment you don't turn around for home, it becomes harder to do so), Scarcity (powder fever), and Acceptance (peer pressure). The broad solution, Ryan said, to avoiding all heuristic traps is group decision-making, constant communication, and the regular practice of emotional vulnerability.

McCammon's findings, and Ryan's curiously detached and uneasy way of talking about emotional vulnerability, confirmed my working theory: The curriculum of preparedness, no matter the cataclysm, isn't only about the concrete knowledge and skills a person must acquire to survive. Often these curriculums make legible human contradiction and weakness.

We broke for lunch. When we returned and sat in our seats and waited for Ryan to emerge from the back office, I looked around and did some math. Seventy percent of our student body fell into the demographic that, according to Ryan, was most likely to die in an avalanche: male, late 20s, intermediate-to-expert experience level, some formal avalanche training.

A man at the end of the table asked the class if anyone had seen the 2014 movie *Force Majeure*. I was the only person who had. Another man asked what the movie was about. I didn't say it was about the ongoing shame and denial experienced by a husband who abandoned his wife and children during an avalanche scare. I didn't say, "Much like this course so far, it's a referendum on masculinity." All-female groups, Ryan told us before lunch, make better decisions in risky situations than all-male groups or mixed-gender groups. When asked why women became less smart in the company of men, Ryan speculated that "women, around men, feel uncomfortable speaking up." I did not say, and not because I was uncomfortable speaking up, that in my experience as a midlevel skier who had more than once been taken up slopes I could not descend—for example, a deep-powdered backcountry slope under which lurked many cliffs, that two male friends, insanely enough (in retrospect), insisted I could ski—I do and did speak up, often repeatedly. I was just never heard.

The wilderness-death or near-death "case study" is a literary genre unto itself. Not unlike an Austen novel—in which, among other things, readers of the time could learn, via the characters' calculations and miscalculations, how to navigate the treacherous early-19th-century social terrain—the wilderness case study allows readers to learn from others' (sometimes mortal) mistakes. The American Avalanche Association, based in Bozeman, Montana, publishes semiregular compendiums of human-avalanche encounters called *The Snowy Torrents*. I own the second and the latest issues (subtitled, in turn, *Avalanche Accidents in the United States, 1967–1971* and *Avalanche Accidents in the United States, 1996–2004*). While written for educational purposes, the case studies don't lack for narrative flair. "Sally Chambers had just picked herself up from a fall when she heard someone say, 'Oh, no!' She turned around just in time to see a wall of snow descending upon her." The methodology is both causal and objectively speculative. The analysis breaks into five sections: weather conditions, accident summary, rescue, avalanche data, comments.

Ryan might have used a synopsis of *Force Majeure* as an in-class case study, because shame and denial inhibit the reporting of human-triggered avalanches, which subsequently reinforces a culture of silence and impedes the sharing and disseminating of instructive stories in which the main characters do not choose wisely. Instead, during the second half of class, Ryan distributed a case-study synopsis about a party of experienced skiers on Microdot. (He didn't use a case study from the latest *Snowy Torrents*, intuiting, perhaps, that many in our course had already scrutinized it cover to cover.) We divided into smaller groups to discuss what "stood out" in terms of the party's preparation, safety, teamwork. The incident was notable less for the body count (zero) and more for how, even though several members of the eight-person party had previously triggered avalanches and even, in one case, witnessed a fatality, they had ignored the many obvious dangers, suggesting that these skiers had become dazzled by their own expertise, falsely brightened by luck.

The case study didn't include—as the case studies in *The Snowy Torrents* don't include—the psychological factors that led these skiers to continue when the signs against it were so compelling. Here's where my skill set came in handy. Here's why all avalanche courses should include at least one novelist. In my head, I imagined the real "avalanche problems" on Microdot.

Skier 1, an avalanche survivor, hadn't slept well for weeks because his business, which he hadn't run scrupulously, was being audited by the IRS. Skier 2, a past witness to an avalanche fatality, was dating Skier 3, who had recently expressed doubts about their long-term compatibility prospects, and so Skier 2, though worried by the ranger report, said nothing when Skier 3 insisted they keep climbing. Skier 4, a tech executive, learned over the years that she could gain the respect of her male coworkers by behaving in a cavalier manner, and so, wanting the same respect and acceptance from her male skiing friends, she employed this strategy on mountains too. Skier 5 wanted to appear "committed to the plan" to Skier 6, creator of a successful series of life-coaching videos for aspiring CEOs, and for whom Skier 5, an unemployed filmmaker, hoped to work. Skier 7, also an avalanche survivor, had lost his father, a Libertarian, to bone cancer in January, and his father's final admonition was, "never cave to the mediocrity of groupthink," which Skier 7 took to mean that caution equals cowardice. The sun was temptingly warm. The sky was temptingly blue. A wolverine crossed their path. Skier 8, a folklore scholar, said that wolverines, in Finland, signaled safe travel.

We'd never know, of course. But Ryan encouraged us to be empathetic, because empathy helps us learn, and judgment does not (the Microdot case study warns, "This story underscores the fact that all humans are capable of making poor decisions"), which I believe to be superficially true, though it strikes me as a conclusion drawn from data sourced from the Bible, not actual data. Regardless, we didn't judge, if only because we were going into the mountains for the next two days and, based on whatever biblical or superstitious story math we did in our heads, we didn't want to curse our outcomes. As we packed up our notebooks and travel mugs, however, I wondered why these case studies were called accidents. To call these deaths and burials accidents implicitly perpetuated the idea that the randomness of nature was the killer, not the shortsightedness, cowardice, or hubris of people. It acquitted the subject and the object of the action: "Damage was done." In the interests of vulnerability, growth, shame-reduction, and clear communication, *The Snowy Torrents* might revise their subtitle: *Timeless United States Avalanche Mistakes.*

Bad winter weather in the Sierra is nothing like bad winter weather in the Northeast, where I'm from. Snow falls so quickly in the Sierra that you can barely keep up while shoveling it. If you've never seen snow like this—and I hadn't, not until I moved to California in my 20s—you might realize, upon first experiencing it, that you never understood why the Donner party couldn't just walk out of the mountains when winter hit.

As always, before starting the course, I enthusiastically prepared for the worst. Preparing for the worst, when you're not on an avalanche course, can earn you the label "catastrophist." To some, ceaselessly scanning a plain day for big and little dooms is a highly optional and neurotic activity. David Page, who lives in the nearby mountains and who met me for dinner the night before the course began, told me that he prefers to call otherwise-pathologized attentiveness "heightened situational awareness."

I preferred this term, too.

Because I knew how quickly the weather in the Sierra could turn, I reserved a four-wheel-drive car weeks in advance. Right before my flight, I called the rental agency to confirm that my car would have four-wheel drive. When I arrived, and was given the keys to a vehicle, I checked with the lot attendant before putting my bags in the trunk: Does this car have four-wheel drive? He said he didn't think it did. I returned to the desk. The clerk apologized for the error. On my way back to the lot, the same attendant said, "Oh, you'll be really happy, that's a good four-wheel-drive car."

Avoiding the Expert Halo Trap is my most innate gift. I never let somebody, or a fleet of somebodys, reassure me that a persistent and inexplicable irregularity should be ignored, just because they say it should. I suspected my car didn't have four-wheel drive soon after I left the rental lot. But I was late to meet a friend for a drink (Consistency Trap), and as I'd already pointedly asked two people at the rental agency, I was too embarrassed to return and ask them, are you really, really sure (Acceptance Trap).

Because it was more convenient and less awkward to do so, I let it go.

But now, looking at the weather report, I reengaged my skepticism. (Though my hotel would receive no more than a dusting over the next day, in the mountains—a distance of only 42 miles —it would snow five feet.) I was desperate to conserve my analytical resources for the mountain, but I didn't want to commit the confirmation-bias error we learned about the day before. When testing snow, Ryan said, you should never look for proof of stability. With stability the goal, you're testing for permission to do what you want to do. Instead, you should test the snow for proof of instability. You should look and look and look until you find it.

The first, second, and third looks online suggested the rental car had four-wheel drive. I kept searching for instability. I finally found it.

Because my two-wheel-drive car wouldn't make it past the chain patrol, stationed on the highway midway between the valley and the mountains, I caught a ride with a 20-something man from Los Angeles. He was giving a ride to another 20-something man. I asked them personal questions from the back seat, because we were supposed to be vulnerable with one another and practice our communication skills, but all conversational paths quickly led us back to the day's sobering avalanche advisory. "BOTTOM LINE: CONSIDERABLE avalanche danger will exist throughout the day."

At 8:00 a.m. we met Ryan and a second instructor, Mike, at a trailhead and performed a gear check. One student—a trauma medic who had amputated the black, dead fingers and toes of avalanche survivors, and who confessed to being claustrophobic —took me aside. The avalanche report, he said, really concerned him. Most accidents happen when the avalanche danger is "considerable." (There are five danger ratings: low, moderate, considerable, high, and extreme.) Oddly, when the avalanche danger is "high," fewer people are killed, because people on high-danger days are certain about their uncertainty. "Considerable" danger, on the other hand, requires that people deal with their uncertainty about their uncertainty; on a "bluebird day" with clear sky and fresh powder, the two uncertainties can conveniently cancel each other out. The survivor of a 2013 avalanche in the Yukon, when asked about her group's decision-making process, said: "For me, the word 'considerable' was not dangerous. I don't know why. You just 'consider' it."

At this particular moment, however, I was less scared of avalanches and more worried about a pop quiz. Obviously we were being tested about the six heuristics! We should speak up and veto the trip!

Nobody said anything. Instead we huddled in a low-wattage sun patch near the parking lot and resisted the wind that noisily whipped the snow around, making it impossible to hear Ryan and Mike's lecture about avalanche beacons. We practiced strapping

the beacons like a gun in a chest holster under our jackets. We
practiced turning them from "transmit" to "receive" mode, which,
because the dial was finicky, required that we remove our gloves.
Every second of skin exposure registered to the brain as a stupid
and optional risk, and so we learned firsthand how skiers commonly commit the puzzling oversight of wearing an avalanche beacon yet failing to turn it on.

Then we practiced finding fake buried people on a low-angle
slope. Mike hid a plywood board and a beacon two feet below the
surface. He yelled, "Avalanche!" and we switched our beacons to
"receive mode." We held our beacons to the snow like metal detec-
tors, but because we were mildly freaking out, the straightforward
(in class) "grid method" failed to ruler the slope into manageable
patches of unknowability. Before digging, we tried to locate the
"body" with our probe, but poking down through the snow—soft,
hard, soft, hard—it was impossible to tell plywood from depth
hoar, a layer of crunchy, large-grained snow.

"In a real situation," Mike reassured us, "you'll feel a squish."

We paused to talk about what was happening, somewhere beneath our feet, to our pretend friend or pretend partner or pretend child. Unless a victim is with others, and those others brought
shovels and probes, which give them 10 minutes to dig the victim
out (after which the chance of survival declines by 80 percent), the
victim probably wants death to happen as quickly as possible. The
victim does not want to be one of the unlucky 2 percent who die
of hypothermia over the course of hours, rather than of trauma
instantly (25 percent of deaths) or of asphyxiation within roughly
15 to 45 minutes (75 percent of deaths). Unless the victim is buried at the surface (unlikely, as the average depth of burial in the
United States is almost four feet), the chance of escaping, without
help, is basically nil. The snow, as it slides, heats up and becomes
wetter. When it stops, it freezes instantly. If a victim is caught inside the churn when this happens, they're effectively sealed inside
an ice coffin. Instead of fighting, a victim could take a tip from
the survivor of the Yukon avalanche: "I tried just to relax a little
bit," she said in *Rescue at Cherry Bowl*, a video posted on Avalanche
Canada as part of its online education. "I was actually OK with dying—I was happy with the life I lived."

But how to learn any of these skills via actual experience when
the stakes are so high? A climbing friend—he camped, for a while,

in the Pit—once complained to me about the hypocrisy of the mountaineer's version of *The Snowy Torrents,* called *Accidents in North American Climbing,* and what he identified as its "moralizing" tone. One case study, for example, cited "exceeding abilities" as a reason for a climber's death. "How are you supposed to learn if you don't push yourself?" my friend asked. "The people writing these reports have been doing that their entire lives."

It was a conundrum. In many nonavalanche-terrain scenarios, if a person falls into a heuristic trap, the outcome isn't death. Most people, on a daily basis, engage in what Mike called "kind learning." Kind learning allows a person to make mistakes. "Wicked learning" does not. (An avalanche course, assuming no mistakes are made along the way, is kind learning about wicked learning.) A kind learner, for example, because she had written a novel, could believe that she understood how books were written (Familiarity Trap) and so, enthused by a new project, obsessively storm ahead for years (Consistency Trap), and refuse, because of the shame involved, to reassess when doubt threatened (Acceptance Trap) before realizing the excursion was ill fated. Time is killed, and a bit of ego, but nobody tends to perish while learning how to better write a book, or build a boat, or smoke a brisket. Because my life wasn't typically on the line, I'd become an enthusiastic, mistakes-based learner. I tried to make mistakes. I learned best by messing up, sometimes badly, even expensively, but never mortally. I could figure out what went wrong and better prepare the next time, even if that preparation included "make more mistakes" as one of the necessary steps.

The snow and wind intensified, the sky dimming to near-dusk levels. By 1:00 p.m., the day felt over. Yet we still had to dig a pit. One to two feet of snow had fallen since we had arrived. The lee slopes were loaded. Nonetheless, we lined up behind Mike and snowshoed or skinned to just below 9,000 feet. ("Skinning"—the act of ascending a mountain on skis—refers to the removable, sticky strips of nylon and mohair, stretched and affixed to the skis' underside to prevent backsliding, called "skins," because they were originally made from animal hides.) Forty-mile-per-hour gusts knocked us around. Nobody seemed particularly happy, not even a guy who climbed Mount St. Helens earlier that winter. He looked dazed and hypothermic. Mike's mustache froze.

We dropped our packs on a 23-degree-angle slope (7 degrees

below the optimal avalanche angle) and started to dig. If a person tried to create, in material form, a pause, it would look like a snow pit. Its negative space is square, and only after Mike shaved the walls to perfect 90-degree angles did it start to look like a mass grave that could easily fit us all. Mike scuffed the wall with a plastic card, and we listened to the sound of round snow versus faceted snow. (The sound of snow is crucial. A sign that an invisible weak layer has collapsed beneath you, meaning the layer on which you are skiing is no longer attached to the mountain, is an audible *whumpf.*) We punched the snow. Then with four fingers we pushed. Then with one finger. We noted the resistance variation between the layers.

Then I stopped paying attention. I watched the spumes of snow spiraling upward from the nearest peak. A giant shard of marble and granite loomed a thousand feet above us, looking like the prow of an ocean liner emerging from the fog. We could have been weathering the sea during a hurricane or blinded by a sandstorm in a frigid desert. The material substance of our isolation —frozen water, salt water, sand—ceased to matter, save how it dictated our survival strategy, and thus our thinking, if we could actually think and refuse to be hypnotized, as I was, by the sumptuous terror and beauty.

I sat on the floor of the snow pit, where it was 10 degrees warmer. Because I was either dying or about to die of hypothermia, I found myself falling into a Nostalgia Trap—not yet coined by McCammon, but a human factor nonetheless—wherein a person is tempted by the bluebird days of the past, and the sense of loss she feels for the person she might have been, had she been, from the start, a different person. Snow pits are no longer the primary focus of avalanche-training courses, in part because human beings are the more erratic variable but also because of a phenomenon called "spatial variability," meaning that a snow pit provides information only about itself and says nothing about the stability a person might find in a different snow pit, dug two feet away in any direction. Snow pits are self-reliant loners. But snow pits are useful because they insert, into a day where Scarcity Traps abound, a moment of reflection. You can stop and listen and touch and appreciate that you are fully alive, but depending on your choices, by the end of the day, you might not be.

*

For the third and final class, I hitched a ride again with my two 20-something friends. We'd gone out to dinner the night before and by now were pretty chummy. Neither of them, however, was interested in the game I proposed over tacos: Which of our two instructors, Ryan or Mike, was more likely to die someday in an avalanche?

The 20-somethings found death speculation macabre. I countered that analyzing "experts" was essential practice. We'd be in situations, in the future, in which we'd have to psychologically sum people up, deciding which ones to trust with our lives.

We met Ryan and Mike in the atrium of a failing mall. We sat on a pair of abandoned couches around an abandoned coffee table and read the online daily avalanche advisory, which predicted "avalanche problems" that would produce slides both "very large" and "likely."

"BOTTOM LINE: HIGH avalanche danger exists this morning where 1–2ft of new snow fell overnight accompanied by the most EXTREME SW winds of the season."

We unfolded our maps to plan our day, but the danger was so prevalent that there was practically nowhere safe to go. Ryan said that we'd be fine if we stuck to the few low-angle slopes. We'd need to constantly assess and reassess the conditions as we ascended, however, and "relentlessly think about the consequences." We'd need to regularly ask ourselves whenever we encountered a new pitch: Why am I here?

The claustrophobic ER doctor who yesterday was scared of dying was eager to get outside, despite the advisory's being drastically worse. One day of survival, and he had either learned what he had come here to learn—how to safely, and without being pointlessly terrified, travel through avalanche terrain—or he'd experienced the first of many instances of another human frailty we'd learned about, called "normalization of deviance."

I felt a snag of dread but talked myself out of it. (I was traveling with Mike, who I had decided was less likely to die in an avalanche than Ryan.) I was being neurotic, not highly situationally aware. Mike and Ryan were both certified. They had both skied this terrain hundreds of times. I considered ways in which a heuristic trap could actually *help* in a situation like this, how a trap could promote prudence and sagacity. Because of the Acceptance Trap—the desire not to be seen as a fool by others—neither Ryan nor Mike would want to kill his students on an avalanche-survival course.

We divided into two groups. I didn't have a lot of experience on backcountry skis, and confessed as much to Mike. I offered to snowshoe, but Mike reassured me that I'd be fine on skis, and besides, everyone else was on skis (two men had "splitboards"—a snowboard that splits in half to create two skis for climbing); he also implied that on snowshoes, I would be unhappy and slow, and I would hinder where the group could go. I told him again—because I didn't want to re-create past experiences in which, despite my detailed and increasingly exaggerated descriptions of my inabilities, a man took me up a mountain I could not, without risking injury or a total loss of affection for him, get down—that I was essentially a beginner. Mike again reassured me: I'd be fine.

We attached our skins and followed a gradual incline along a ridge. It was a bluebird day for sure. Warm, sunny, an abundance of new powder. Along the way, Mike quizzed us. We found a vertical crack in the snow layers on a low-angle slope. Mike said, "What do I think about this slope?" I said, "That you should not go over it." He said, "Well, I'm about to."

We hung out at the top of a dome and then headed back down and then again up. We kept among the trees to reduce our risk of becoming buried in a slide starting above us (trees can act like the teeth of a comb, thinning an avalanche into weaker rivulets). We took turns cutting track through many-feet-deep snow. At one point, the claustrophobic ER doctor disappeared to his waist in a wind hole.

Just after lunch we found what, in some respects, we'd traveled to see: an avalanche. Mike estimated it to be eight hours old. We stood 25 feet downhill from the toe (the edge of the debris field) and discussed the conditions that created the slide, like the slope's angle. I asked Mike why none of us were scared. I definitely wasn't. The absence of fear was a peculiar sensation, akin to coolly scrutinizing my own amputated hand. He said that the slab had already slid, and that if there were to be another, which there wouldn't be—based on the wind direction, the slope hadn't reloaded—it wouldn't reach us; also, he was familiar with this area, and knew we weren't in any danger. Still, we were breaking a few rules. We had stopped directly in the avalanche's "run-out" path. We were relying on familiarity as an indicator of safety. In neither case did I think Mike made a poor decision. But our avalanche autopsy left me wondering: When is a trap a trap, and when is it wisdom?

As we continued to ascend steeper and steeper terrain, I started to get nervous. Skinning up mountains requires endurance. Getting down them requires skill. We climbed all the way to the base of the formerly storm-enveloped granite-and-marble shard, its crags and facets now sharply highlighted by the sun. We detached our skins and flipped our bindings so that our uphill skis became downhill ones. The two splitboarders connected their two halves to make a single plank. Mike warned, as we paused at the top of the slope, "these are gnarly conditions." The snow, after hours of absorbing solar radiation, had thickened to what one student referred to as "elephant snot." A two-foot layer of sticky, dense snow lay atop a few more feet of loose, grainy hoar. Unless we moved quickly over the surface, our skis would punch through the top layer, which would then trap us up to our thighs. Our turns had to be fast and tight, near the trees, because it wasn't safe to carve more widely into the open.

Mike was right. It was gnarly. Half the students, myself obviously included, wiped out over and over again. The scene was deemed by another student "a yard sale." The pair on splitboards abandoned verticality and instead rode their splitboards through the trees like sleds.

And then, what we planned in the failing mall would happen, did: we survived. We sat between the twin ruts of a Sno-Cat trail and debriefed. Had we planned well, or were we just lucky? Mike asked if we would have done anything differently. We said we wouldn't have. He said, contemplatively, "I might have better taken into account people's skill levels." Then we dispersed.

I returned my skis at the rental store and met a local friend at her house, an A-frame with a giant triangular window, beyond which 6 feet of wind-sculpted snow obscured what, in spring, became a porch. Now snow wasn't a substance I could trigger and so kill myself. Now it was a refrigerator for our beer. My friend and I drank and laughed. I hadn't done any laughing over the last three days, while my classmates and I pretended our loved ones were asphyxiating beneath our skis. At around 8:00 p.m., one of the 20-somethings texted me a newspaper article posted that afternoon. The headline read: "Colorado's First Avalanche Death of 2019 Came During an Advanced Avalanche-Safety Course on Red Mountain Pass."

I clicked on the article. Earlier that day, six avalanche students were caught in the slide they had triggered. Five lived. The avalanche danger was considerable-to-high. No further analysis was available.

On the first day of class, Ryan made it clear that we were not eliminating risk—we were "managing" it. If we wanted not to die in an avalanche, that goal was easily accomplished. "The simplest way to mitigate avalanche hazard," the course's manual advised, "is to avoid avalanche terrain altogether." But "risk" to some is "just another day" to others. Risk, in the backcountry, is an occupational hazard, no different from the risk assumed by astronauts or explorers, save that backcountry skiing, for most practitioners, isn't a career; their risk-taking isn't considered noble or newsworthy (unless they die doing it), and it has no greater ambition save to make a single person happy. When people are together, their individual risk thresholds become destabilized, and some assume a degree of risk that, alone, they never would. But there is never no risk. Death is statistical, not eradicable. When I was pregnant, I was told my chance of having a child with Down syndrome was 1 in 400. My father-in-law, a mathematician, called my risk "functional zero."

Functional zero is zero, but—to the imagination, at least—it is also not zero, just like the fear of being buried alive is both 100 percent irrational and also not. Within those narrow gaps (between irrational and rational, functional zero and zero), creative ingenuity—not just neuroses—can thrive. The pursuit of joy, even if that joy begins as fear and takes the form of preparation against an irrational outcome, is a death wish, maybe. Or it's a life wish. Or there's no difference. Texture, at a minimum, better distinguishes days spent this way, and that texture becomes the record of the idiosyncrasies of an individual's mind. Were it not for the irrational fear of being buried alive, George Washington wouldn't have requested his corpse be kept on his deathbed for three days, or Schopenhauer on his for five. Poe wouldn't have written "The Premature Burial," not to mention "Berenice," "The Fall of the House of Usher," "The Cask of Amontillado," and "The Black Cat." John G. Krichbaum, in 1882, wouldn't have invented his Device for Indicating Life in Buried Persons, which involved a coffin fitted with a pipe extending to the surface, and Albert Fearnaught (truly, his name) wouldn't have invented a "grave signal" in which a rope around a buried person's wrist, if tugged, released a flag above the plot. Alfred Nobel wouldn't have written a will that stipulated, first, that his money be used to create an eponymous prize, and ultimately that his veins be opened and drained, after which he would be cremated. No one would have founded or joined the London Association for the Prevention of Premature Burial. I wouldn't have taken a course to learn to survive a danger I would rarely encounter.

I stepped into the drift to grab another beer. The wind had picked up. A clump of snow shook loose from a tree bough and barely missed my head. Had anyone in my class died that day, I wondered whose deaths would have been seen as the most pointless by outsiders, and thus the most harshly judged. Probably mine. I was the only person with no actual business being there. "This story underscores the fact that all humans are capable of making poor decisions." But I hoped that if I had been buried and, if luck were on my side, asphyxiated within minutes, people who knew me would understand: by learning to do something I didn't love, I was doing what I loved.

I slid the porch door shut. The snow against the glass gave me a cross-sectional view of its layers. The house was a snow pit, but a warmer one, with booze. From my apartment windows back home, I'd learned to read pedestrians, and their outfits, as a way to gauge the weather. Here I read the snow. It was buried time. The layers told me what had happened since the winter began. Events like storms, and cold nights followed by warm days, were stabilized in material form, until a person, crossing the surface, released them.

# Glow

FROM *The New Yorker*

ON JANUARY 31, 1913, King Haakon VII of Norway went to the University of Oslo to hear a lecture by the physicist Kristian Birkeland, who believed that he had unlocked the secrets of the aurora borealis, also known as the northern lights. Birkeland planned to demonstrate his theory with the aid of a specially constructed device: a brass-plated magnetic sphere, called a terrella, suspended inside a vacuum chamber with glass sides and an electrode on one end. When the electrode was heated, it would shoot cathode rays across the chamber toward the sphere. If all went well, the rays would interact with the sphere's magnetic field, producing eerie flashes of light that replicated, in miniature, the aurora borealis.

As Birkeland's biographer Lucy Jago tells it, the lecture was a triumph. The contraption didn't electrocute anybody or implode in splinters of flying glass, as earlier models had tended to do, and obligingly produced a diminutive version of the aurora's luminous flux, dazzling the king. Word spread, and a Nobel Prize was widely predicted, yet England's Royal Society—at the time the arbiter of scientific fact—was unimpressed, and treated Birkeland as an amateur with a hopelessly inadequate grasp of theoretical physics. He died in 1917, and it wasn't until the 1960s that satellite data proved his hypothesis to be correct. The lights are caused by high-velocity solar particles—the "solar wind," as it came to be called —interacting with the earth's magnetic field and atmosphere.

Birkeland remains underappreciated, but his imprint can be felt in the mixture of engineering wizardry and primal enchantment that is fueling a touristic boom in countries where the north-

ern lights appear. As I discovered on a trip to the Arctic in February, the glow of an aurora is sometimes difficult to perceive with
the naked eye, and travelers often must engage in a form of tech-
nologically enhanced rapture.

The best chances of seeing the lights are in the elliptical area
known as the Auroral Oval, which is centered on geomagnetic
north. The earth's magnetic field becomes almost perpendicular
to its surface here, drawing the solar particles into the atmosphere.
Much of Siberia falls within the zone, but I decided to visit northern Scandinavia, where the art of maintaining extreme comfort
in the face of extreme cold seemed likely to be more advanced.
Among the region's more tempting accommodations are the glass-
igloo hotels of Finland, where you can simply lie back and watch
the show in bed.

I stayed at a newish igloo hotel, the Aurora Village, near the
town of Ivalo, in the far north of the country. It sounded more appealing than the much Instagrammed original, in Kakslauttanen,
having fewer igloos and no Santa's Home on the compound. I
arrived late, exhausted from the knock-on effects of a canceled
flight. The hotel's 28 Aurora Cabins, set around a large reindeer
paddock, looked like quaint log huts from the front, with 20 inches
of moonlit snow on the eaves. Inside, the rustic gave way to the futuristic. A glass-paneled dome loomed over the north-facing end
of a single room, with luxe bedding and a complimentary drinks
tray arranged below, like the furnishings of a tastefully debauched
starship. Slipping under a reindeer-fur coverlet, I found myself facing the first conundrum of northern-lights tourism, which is that
the more comfortable your viewing situation the more likely you
are to be insensate when the lights appear. I was eager to see them,
naturally, but not obsessed. I had a whole week, and, from what I'd
read, at the time of my visit there were good odds for a display on
most nights. With this comforting thought, I fell asleep.

You can be woken in the middle of the night if you wish—and
there are apps that will rouse you at the right moment—but you
can't do anything about cloudy skies or daylight. (The phenomenon that produces the lights can occur at any hour.) For the tourist, the question arises: What do you do when there's no prospect
of seeing the lights, which is much of the time? The answer is activities, although "safari" is the perversely tropical term of choice:
you can go on a reindeer safari, a husky safari, an ice-fishing safari,

a snowmobile safari, a king-crab safari. I talked to the activities manager at the Aurora Village, Abraham Montes, over breakfast in the resort's dining hall—a conical structure made of spruce planks—and it became clear that his job had as much to do with managing expectations as activities. "The first thing people ask is 'What time does the aurora begin?'" he told me. He was exaggerating, but only a bit; in recent years, he acknowledged, tourists have become increasingly fixated on the goal of catching a brilliant display. Montes hedged against their disappointment by recommending at least one activity a day. In addition to the safaris, you could visit a sauna, or go on a cultural excursion called the Authentic Sámi Experience, in which native Laplanders welcome guests into a *lávvu,* a tepee-like shelter, and sing traditional songs around a fire.

I joined an ice-fishing safari that Montes was leading. We climbed into a covered sled with portholes, and zipped out onto a frozen river nearby. A cutting wind blew across the ice, and I was glad of the day that I'd spent in New Jersey malls, buying advanced thermal gear. With me was a German couple, who seemed serious about the fishing, and a Malaysian family, with a young daughter, who'd come to Finland because the lights were on their bucket list —a term that has gone global. Montes showed us how to drill holes with an auger, and baited our hooks with plastic worms. (He'd planned to use real ones, but they had frozen during the night.) The fishing rods seemed absurdly short and bendy, like something that you might use to win a prize at an amusement park. We squatted at our holes, dipping and raising as instructed. The flat landscape around us was more built up than I'd expected this far north, but pleasant enough under the fresh snow, with the wide sky showing different pinks and yellows every time you looked at it. Now and then, dogsleds carrying tourists hurtled by; each time, we laboriously took off our mittens and glove liners and rummaged for our phones, in order to take photographs.

I asked Montes what role social media had played in northern-lights tourism, and he gave an exasperated laugh. The Ivalo hotel was constantly being approached by YouTubers and Instagram influencers who offered publicity in return for free accommodations. "It's hard to calculate the benefits, but they post pictures, and it's good for us to have people know there are glass igloos beyond Kakslauttanen, so sometimes we say yes," he said. "We just had two of them staying, with five hundred thousand followers each. They wanted free rooms—free *everything*." He mentioned a 2012 BuzzFeed article on the Kakslauttanen igloos, citing it as a pivotal event in the aurora industry. It was published on the eve of a "solar maximum," a high point in the 11-year cycle of solar activity, and many people who visited the Arctic soon afterward were treated to glorious displays. The article also coincided with Instagram's drift from cats and food to landscapes and natural phenomena. "The image of those igloos was suddenly everywhere," Montes said. We were nearing the low point in the solar cycle now, he noted, though he assured me that the lights could still be thrilling, adding, "You just have to be lucky."

The Germans were looking a little frustrated by their ice hole, and I got the feeling that we weren't presenting much of a threat to the pike and grayling allegedly massing below us. Nobody caught anything. We headed back to the hotel, where I ate a bowl of spaghetti with a reindeer Bolognese sauce. I returned outside for a happy few hours of cross-country skiing. That evening, the forecast apps suggested that I had a less than 20 percent chance of seeing an aurora. It didn't seem worth mounting a vigil, and once again I fell guiltily, expensively asleep.

Something woke me at three. Groggy and myopic, I caught a promising green blur overhead and grabbed my glasses. The color of an aurora depends on which atmospheric gases are being pelted by solar particles. Oxygen emits a greenish hue and, occasionally, red; nitrogen emits violet and blue. In this case, the green turned out to be emitted by a light on the thermostat—its glow was reflected in the glass dome. Nevertheless, the sky had cleared, and the stars glittered promisingly above the snow-gloved spruce trees. I stared up for a while. Gazing at the sky at 3:00 a.m., however, in the hope of being granted a vision of dancing emerald lights, is an activity that quickly starts to feel absurd, even delusional, and I soon passed out again. In the morning, I learned that I hadn't missed anything.

Over the years, I've sampled some extravagant framings of natural wonders: a helicopter ride into the Grand Canyon; orcas seen from a hydrofoil in Puget Sound. I have some puritanical distrust of good things being handed to one on a plate, but I can't pretend that I haven't enjoyed these adventures. In those cases, the fun was partly about comfort, but it was also about the feeling of accelerated gratification. My igloo was extremely comfortable, but it lacked that crucial element of being able to speed things along. You need just as much patience in a glass igloo as you do in a motel.

I went a bit farther north, to the vast frozen lake of Inari, where the lack of light pollution supposedly raises the chances of seeing the lights. Here, as everywhere, my hotel was packed: tour buses and SUVs lined the parking lot. Guests in puffer jackets were riding fatbikes on the ice. Inside, at the buffet, they piled plates with sautéed reindeer and lingonberries. The "Activities Book" at the front desk offered the usual excursions, along with a Lappish Dinner featuring "a real Sámi person." I signed up for Aurora Camp, which promised warm drinks "while waiting for the sky to show its magic." I liked the confidence of the description; it made the magic sound more like a scheduled event than like a mere hope. *Fiat lux.*

At eight o'clock, a dozen other campers and I were issued stiff blue-and-black snowsuits that turned us into identical Lego people. A snowmobile towed us across the lake in a train of open sleds. Once we were on the other side, a guide lit a fire, draping reindeer hides over logs for us to sit on, and hung a kettle to boil. The simplicity of the arrangement appealed to my sense of how these things ought to be conducted, and even though there was thick cloud cover, I felt optimistic. We had two and a half hours to kill, and the weather, as we reminded one another at regular intervals, was unpredictable in these parts.

Most of the people in our group were Chinese, on vacation for the Chinese New Year. But I also heard Italian voices, and the genteel tones of Home Counties English. Those came from a British couple, recent retirees from Surrey who were checking things off their bucket list. A safari in Zambia would follow the northern lights. They'd been in Inari for four nights, and had seen a faint glow one evening, after being roused by the hotel's Aurora Alert. It hadn't impressed them. "*Definitely* not worth being woken up for," they said. They talked about the disparity between photographs of the aurora borealis and what you can actually see, making some technical point that I didn't take in at the time, and grumbled, "They ought to tell you about this." I asked them if they regretted coming. Not at all, they said. They had enjoyed the activities and appreciated the differentness of the place: the Finnish tundra is another world from Surrey. "It's like in Africa, where you know you might not see anything but you just enjoy the whole experience," they said.

Our guide, young but practiced in the art of distracting cold tourists, poured hot berry juice and discoursed on Arctic matters. He told us the average number of hairs on a square centimeter of a reindeer's back—1,700—and explained the logic behind the Kp index, a tool for predicting auroras. The index, in use since 1939, measures disturbances in the earth's magnetic field, with stronger disturbances indicating higher chances of seeing an aurora.

A smudge of light appeared to the west, and we looked at our guide hopefully, but he shook his head: it was just snowmobile headlights reflected by clouds. Someone asked him what it felt like to see a truly powerful display, and he replied that it was "a spiritual experience." I pressed him on this. "Well, it's about community," he said. "One person's wonder communicates itself to the rest of the group, and you get this flow of emotion." It seemed like a good answer. It certainly accounted for a vague feeling I'd had in my glass igloo, which was that even if I did see the lights there'd be something sad and incomplete about not having anyone with me to share the experience. I'd been with an old friend when I helicoptered into the Grand Canyon. My son was with me for the orcas in Puget Sound.

The sky showed no sign of clearing, and the Kp-index reading had plummeted. Meanwhile, the temperature had fallen to –10°F, which turned every gust of wind into a scouring assault. People were pulling up balaclavas and stamping their feet. No surprises occurred overhead, but an earthly one did: a woman suddenly slipped her arm through mine and began murmuring in my ear in Italian. I looked at her, and she gave a shriek: she'd mistaken me, in my snowsuit, for her husband. Peals of unnerving laughter broke from her as we sledded back across the lake. The incident gave concreteness to the dim sense of cosmic disfavor beginning to take hold in me. The nature of these wonder-chasing trips is that your success rate sooner or later gets entangled with your feelings about what you deserve. I had four more nights, so there was no cause for serious alarm, but I'd started entertaining irrational thoughts all the same. Was I unworthy in some way? Could I be harboring attitudes unconducive to the granting of heavenly visions?

A couple of incidents the next day deepened this mood. I was on my way to Tromsø, in Norway. To get there without making an extended southern detour to Oslo, I had to take a three-hour taxi ride from Inari to the Norwegian village of Lakselv, which has an airport. As we drove northwest, the landscape and the sky merged into a white haze, with only the dark-etched undersides of branches to distinguish one realm from the other. It was beautiful in an unearthly way, as if the world had become a silver nitrate photograph of itself. Road signs grew fewer and farther between, with Sámi place-names appearing under the Finnish. The road was covered with packed snow and the driver was going fast. On a long, straight, desolate stretch, we came over a rise and saw five reindeer galloping straight toward us. The driver cursed in English: "Shit." I braced myself, felt a slam, and saw one of the animals thrown into the air. It had antlers, and, as the previous night's guide had informed us, a deer that still had them in late winter was female, and probably pregnant. We backed up and found it lying, dead, in the snow. The taxi was dented but drivable, and after reporting the accident we continued on our way, both of us badly shaken.

We arrived at the airport at 11:00 a.m. I got out of the taxi and approached the automatic door, but it didn't open. I turned to call back my driver, but he'd sped off into the frozen wilderness. I shouted and banged on the airport windows, but nobody was inside. A stuffed reindeer, harnessed to a sleigh, stared at me through the plate glass of the empty departure lounge. Under the circumstances, it was impossible not to read judgment in its blank expression.

Nordic folklore tends to view the northern lights as a not entirely benign phenomenon. Sámi mythology, in particular, invests them with highly equivocal powers. They can predict the weather, but they can also whisk people away. You can attract them by whistling, but you do so at your peril. As I stood on the airport curb, wondering what to do, it struck me that the aurora industry was a kind of elaborate whistling for the lights, with all the folly and hubris that this entailed. It sold itself as a romance with nature at its most magical, but it was premised on a comprehensive battle *against* nature. Its imagery of cozy warmth and gliding ease had been concocted in defiance of a lethally dangerous environment where you were entirely dependent on protections devised by other humans. It seemed to me that I was now being shown what happened when those systems malfunctioned. I felt scared and stupid. I was a fool about to freeze to death in pursuit of a high-end tourist fad.

Eventually, I flagged down a passing car, whose driver promised to make a call on my behalf, and after a long 20 minutes an airport worker appeared and opened the doors. He laughed at my story, telling me that I'd arrived far too early for my afternoon flight. Two hours later, just before takeoff, other passengers began strolling in—blasé locals in T-shirts and sneakers.

Tromsø is a compact, gleaming city set dramatically on two sides of a sound, with an old quarter of timber buildings, a thriving fishing industry, and the world's northernmost university. I ate quantities of smoked and pickled fish, and visited the Polar Museum, with its baleful dioramas of trapped foxes and hunters clubbing baby seals. I took a dogsled safari, and guided Siberian huskies on a wobbly but exhilarating 10-mile dash, by moonlight, across stunning upland fells. In every one of Tromsø's hotel lobbies, screens glowed with images of the lights.

I'd been advised to try looking for them from the water, and went out in a catamaran. The city sparkled on either side of the boat as the skipper and I cruised down the sound, but the sky was solid cloud, and we soon gave up craning our necks and chatted about the aurora craze instead. Everyone seems to have a different origin story. The skipper attributed the boom to a 2008 BBC show on the lights, featuring Joanna Lumley. As he put it, "There was before Joanna Lumley, and there was after."

Six million people had watched the *Absolutely Fabulous* star diffuse English poshness into the Arctic mists as she traveled northward through Norway. The sites she visited were soon struggling with sudden popularity. (Google the Lofoten Islands, an archipelago south of Tromsø, and you'll learn more than you wanted to know about their insufficient number of public toilets.) Lumley was as unlucky as I was until she came to Tromsø, where her guide and photographer, Kjetil Skogli, finally delivered the goods. In the show's orgasmic climax, the actress lies on her back in the snow as the sky explodes in jets of green.

I met with Skogli in Tromsø. He is a slight, unassuming man in his 50s, with an impish way of deflecting questions about his post-Lumley celebrity clients (Brian May, of Queen, is among them). Skogli grew up in a small village where elders spoke the Sámi language and children hid from the lights, fearing cosmic abduction. An evening outing with a photographer friend in the fall of 2003 coincided with a series of unusually intense solar storms, and the spectacle awakened Skogli to the lights' glory. "Mostly, you just see green," he told me. "But you saw all the other colors that night. The snow was colored red." He was also awakened to the lights' commercial potential. "The northern lights wasn't a product at that time," he recalled. "But they're one of the purest wonders of the world." Moreover, the lights have the advantage of not being affected by global warming. As Skogli put it, "We can't do *anything* to spoil them!"

He set up a photography-tour company that pioneered the idea of the Aurora Chase: you're driven around for six or more hours in pursuit of favorable conditions for viewing the lights. Every fjord and fell has its own microclimate, and so in theory there's always a chance of finding clear skies somewhere. After the Lumley film aired, Skogli created a four-day Lumley Route and, as other Scandinavians got into the aurora-chasing business, he began working with local landowners to set up "base stations" for the tourist traffic that had spread across the region. "It's not good to see fifty or sixty coaches parked on the side of a road," he said. "There've been some very close accidents."

We discussed why the aurora often looks so much better in photographs. He explained that a camera on a tripod, set for a five-second exposure, takes in far more light than the human eye does when it looks at something, and consequently it produces a more vivid image. A camera can turn even relatively weak displays into dramatic pictures—and these images can then be subjected to digital enhancements. Posted online, the pictures are automatically sharpened by the high-contrast settings of most social-media platforms, and further boosted by the backlit screens of our devices. Cumulatively, these improvements have encouraged unrealistic expectations. "It's a shame," Skogli said. "You have a responsibility to show the truth." He has tried to open a discussion on the subject within the tourism industry, without success. In a rare departure from diplomatic geniality, he dismissed most Instagram photos of the lights as junk—"digitally colorized files to produce likes."

Thinking that I might win over the aurora gods by trying something more primitive than my other accommodations, I'd signed up for a night with a Finnish company that takes you out to a "wilderness camp" and leaves you alone until morning. That night had come around, and I was slightly regretting my plan. I had no idea what to expect, but various scenarios had begun filling the void, mostly turning on the idea of abandonment and slow death. It didn't help that the tour-company driver had a penchant for morbid tales. There was the story of his grandfather, who had died of a heart attack while herding reindeer and had been left in a tarp on the roadside, where his son recognized the boots sticking out. There was the whale that starved in a fjord, whose corpse had to be towed out to sea and exploded. Then, there were the two snowmobilers who'd recently disappeared after going off-piste. "They say the cold gives you a gentle death," the driver observed.

We crossed the border and entered the village of Kilpisjärvi, in western Finland. I climbed into a sled, and my amiable and capable guide, Jussi Rauhala, used a snowmobile to tow me to the camp, two and a half miles across the frozen surface of Lake Kilpisjärvi. At the midpoint of the journey, he stopped and got off the snowmobile, to see how I was doing. "The ice is fifteen percent thinner than usual this year," he remarked, in halting but studious English. "But for a snowmobile it should be fine."

We rounded a promontory with scrubby birches doubled over by snow, and came to a dark hut, raised up on sled runners, on the ice. An outhouse stood off to the side. It was cozy inside the hut, with a banged-together quality that I liked, though spending the night there still seemed disconcerting. Jussi turned on a propane heater, which blasted ferocious heat at wooden furnishings a few feet away. He attached several spare cannisters of fuel to the heater. "Just in case they run out," he explained. "But they won't." The door had been fitted extra tight, to prevent it from being blown open by the wind, and you had to give it a mighty kick to get out. The possibility of being unable to tug the door back open was enough to rule out any thought of a solitary nocturnal visit to the outhouse. Jussi, possibly noting my anxiousness, pointed to a transparent section of roof above the bed, and told me that it was made of riot-shield plastic. I tried to look reassured.

We walked about 30 feet to the shore of the lake, and set up a fire. Jussi assembled a camera tripod. The Kp numbers were promising, and a pool of clear sky had opened among the clouds, with the Big Dipper brightly visible. Jussi programmed his camera to take a long-exposure photograph every few minutes; after a while, he checked the monitor and saw a faint green glow. At first, I couldn't see anything in the sky, but after a minute what had looked like an oblique bar of cloud began turning a dim grayish green. It was tremendously exciting. The camera then began registering bands of red—although they weren't visible to the naked eye, they signaled that there was a strong solar wind. The bar in the sky grew brighter, but a terrestrial wind had also risen, driving thick clouds straight toward it. A tense couple of minutes followed, in which we seemed to be watching an elemental standoff between darkness and light. For a few moments, the green bar was surrounded by tinges of violet: the effect of atmospheric nitrogen complementing that of the green-glowing oxygen. But the clouds kept moving implacably forward, and, crushingly, the bar began to fade.

I could now say truthfully that I'd seen the northern lights, and I was happy, though my happiness had more to do with relief— mission accomplished—than with joy. It had been a very minor spillage of the green grail. The camera kept seeing it for a while, and Jussi was able to take some photographs of me posed against it with a thumbs-up and a grin—a triumphant bucket-list warrior. It's hard to gauge the documentary status of such images. Do they memorialize my evening, or the camera's? The question goes to the heart of what I was beginning to think of as the second conundrum of northern-lights tourism: its seemingly inextricable incorporation of digital technology into human sensory experience.

It was time for Jussi to leave. He gave me a basket of food and a Nokia phone for emergencies. He told me that his cousin would pick me up at eight in the morning, "if he wakes up." He paused, then added, "He has never *not* woken up. But, just in case he does not wake up, you can call me." I laughed, hoping that this was just Finnish humor, and watched him disappear into the darkness. Snow was falling. I battened down the hatches and got into bed. On the other side of the riot-shield roof, the clouds grew thicker.

I wondered if I'd have it in me to rise to the occasion if I did see a major display. When an industry is focused so determinedly on the commodity of wonderment, it spurs thoughts of resistance—at least, it does in me. Moreover, my knowledge that the lights were merely an effect of physical forces—and not, say, the souls of still-born babies, or reflections of the armor of the Valkyries—would surely limit my capacity to be awestruck.

I slept fitfully, trying to ignore the sounds of cracking ice that I kept hearing, and was possibly imagining. In the morning, congratulating myself on not having used the emergency phone, I breakfasted on cloudberry doughnuts and homemade dried reindeer. At eight o'clock sharp, Jussi's cousin picked me up.

For my final evening in Tromsø, I'd booked a seat on an Aurora Chase. At the appointed hour, I joined the crowds heading down to the waterfront, where the chase vehicles picked up passengers. I heard a coach driver mutter, "Not the best weather outlook to-night." The prospect of spending the next six hours driving around with little hope of seeing the lights was deeply unenticing. I was about to bail on the adventure when a burly Norseman barked out my name from his roster. I meekly boarded his sleek black van.

We headed southeast, toward Finland. The Norseman, whose name was Halfdan, kept up a jovial patter as we sped past frozen fjordscapes. I'd already learned most of what he talked about: aurora factoids, camera-settings advice, Kp numbers. The sense of déjà vu became terrifyingly complete when I heard the driver mutter "Shit" and saw a moose planted, like a thatched cottage, on the road ahead of us. At the last moment, it decamped over the guardrail, and our lunatic chase continued.

An hour into Finland, we pulled off the main road and parked. Using his phone, Halfdan had gathered data indicating that the spot was auspicious. I disembarked, with 15 companions, into the freezing night. Tripods were set up, a fire was built. I chatted with the driver, who told me that there were now 140 chase companies operating out of Tromsø, many of them without proper permits or insurance. Every hotel was at capacity. He mentioned that he had a day job, manufacturing fishing equipment, and I wondered how this might affect his night-driving skills.

A second bus, twice the size of ours, pulled into the parking area. I had become highly suspicious of all the apps and meteorological charts that were being consulted, but this time my skepticism was misplaced. A crack appeared in the clouds directly above us. It widened, showing a sprinkling of stars and then the entire Big Dipper. There was a stirring among the photographers: their cameras had started detecting things. After a moment, an oblique greenish bar like the one I'd seen the night before became visible. It grew brighter and denser, then contracted into an oval of emerald light. People chattered excitedly. I was about to warn them not to get too carried away when a streak of brilliant green shot out of the oval, at high speed, and zoomed over our tipped-back heads, corkscrewing across the sky. I almost toppled over while following its trajectory. The green light formed several tentacles, which twisted and writhed together and looped in circles. Astonishment was proclaimed in a half-dozen languages. The circles dropped needles of piercing brightness that traveled, in tandem, around the sky, as if tracing the undulations of a celestial shower curtain.

There is something at once mind-blowing and unassimilable about the phenomenon. The aurora borealis is, in Karl Ove Knausgaard's phrase, "immensely foreign," and it puts you into a kind of panic in which you want to simultaneously observe it, describe it, rejoice in it, interpret it, and record it. Nothing you've learned or read about the subject—scientific, folkloric, touristic—seems remotely adequate or even relevant to the experience. You develop the overwhelming impression that some cryptic but staggeringly powerful intelligence is staging a performance expressly for you, even as you remind yourself that this can't be the case. Surprisingly intense emotions grip you. I remembered something that Kjetil Skogli told me about one of his expeditions: an English guy, overcome by the display, dropped to his knees and proposed to his girlfriend.

Back in the bus, the photographers among the group compared images. I'd attempted to take some snapshots on my phone, but they were terrible. I was relieved to discover that Halfdan had taken nice pictures of each of us, including one of me with the stunned look of a nonbeliever witnessing a miracle. He promised that he would post them online in a day or two. We would then scatter these glowing pixels around the world, bringing our part in this drama of pain and pleasure, of eye and camera, of reality and illusion, to its inevitable close.

# To Hold Oneself Together

FROM *T: The New York Times Style Magazine*

"THE ÅLAND ISLANDS —where?" It was the first question my friends asked when I told them of my plan to travel there. "An archipelago in the Baltic Sea," I would say, "between Sweden and Finland." But that didn't quite seem to explain the place. "There are more than sixty-seven hundred islands there, and around sixty-five of them are inhabitable." Then their interest would be piqued: "How did you find it?"

The same question was also asked by the Ålanders I met. "I found it on the map," I said. What better way to discover a new place than to rotate a globe—these days digitally—and to set one's heart on an unfamiliar or unheard-of destination? (In 2018, 93 million American citizens traveled abroad. The same year, a total of 520 of them stayed on Åland.)

The archipelago is far geographically from my home in Princeton, New Jersey, though I was also searching for a different kind of distance. Two summers ago, I lost a teenage son to suicide. Two seasons ago, I was next to my father when the doctors took him off life support. "The only thing grief has taught me," Emerson wrote in 1844, in "Experience," after the death of his young son, "is to know how shallow it is. That, like all the rest, plays about the surface, and never introduces me into the reality . . . An innavigable sea washes with silent waves between us and the things we aim at and converse with. Grief too will make us idealists."

In the past 18 months, I have reread *Hamlet* many times, written in the years after the death of Shakespeare's son. I have listened to the compositions of Smetana and Dvorak, in which they mourned the deaths of their children. But Emerson's words, which are less accessible, made me wonder if his mind had traveled further. I was not unrealistic enough to expect grief to vanish on a trip, but I wanted to see if it could shed some light on Emerson's thinking.

The ferry ride from Stockholm to the port of Mariehamn (on the archipelago's largest island, Mainland Åland)—the town is the capital of the Åland Islands and is in fact its only town—takes about five hours. It was a sunny day in late June. The sea was a vivid ultramarine. The sky, streaked with wisps of unmoving cloud, was only a shade lighter. Red cottages lined the coast, white ferries traveled between islands, seabirds congregated on skerries. Such images, which one can describe with only stock language, are available on the internet. What is the difference between beauty preserved as still image and beauty experienced in person, in time?

At first, the question seems easy to answer: journeying through that landscape is a fuller experience. Is that so, though? When I look at the photos taken on the trip, I often have an acute reaction—the land and the sea have become part of my memory now. But no one can stare at a photo or a postcard for five hours. Soon one's mind drifts elsewhere—to hopes and distresses, regrets and anticipations, joys and despairs, to the lives of the departed and the cold fact that they no longer are here. These feelings and thoughts grant us an interior landscape, which, like the memory of a ferry ride, we experience, but often fleetingly.

On that June morning, however, I watched the sea and the sky, the islands and the boats, my mind void of any thought about the past, and incapable of forming a language for the future remembrance. Is it possible, I wonder, that one can fully experience something only on what Emerson calls "the surface"?

Åland is a Swedish-speaking autonomous region of Finland and consists of 16 municipalities. The island population is close to 30,000; around 12,000 live in Mariehamn. The smallest municipality, Sottunga, had 91 residents in 2018.

On the afternoon of my arrival in Mariehamn, I had tea with Karin Erlandsson, a local writer and journalist. We went to the shore, a five-minute walk from the town center, where she laid a picnic on a blanket.

I had imagined the beach to be austere, but it was golden and sandy. Children—some not yet able to walk steadily—ran in and out of the water. The summer before, Karin said, the sea had been especially warm. From there our talk turned to climate change, felt vividly on Åland—in the rising water temperature, which has created algae problems; in the more extreme storms, one of which, the previous winter, blew away the upper half of Karin's holiday cottage.

We discussed Brexit, the refugee situation (Åland admitted three families in 2017), teenage angst (a survey shows that the youths on Åland are not as happy as their peers on mainland Finland), and local news (Karin translated some headlines of that day for me: "A Man Is Convicted to Two Years in Prison for Many Crimes"; "Driver Had to Steer Down in the Ditch to Avoid a Collision with a Roe Deer").

Later, I went to the Åland Museum in Mariehamn, which houses the Cultural History Museum of Åland and the Åland Islands Art Museum. Early settlement began with the arrival of the nomads in the Stone Age, who hunted for seals and birds, and fished. Farming began in the Bronze Age, and by the Middle Ages, Åland was part of Sweden. Over the successive centuries, its strategic position in the Baltic led to the military presence of the Germans, the Russians, the French, and the British. In 1856 Åland was demilitarized, a fact of which the islanders are proud. Prior to the war between Russia and Sweden in 1809, Finland and Åland had been part of the Kingdom of Sweden. After the Russian Revolution in 1917, the archipelago sought to reunite with Sweden, but Finland, a unified entity with the Åland Islands under Russian rule, demanded its independence and refused to forsake Åland. In 1921 the League of Nations stepped in to broker a deal granting Finland sovereignty over the islands, provided the country guaranteed Ålanders an independent system of self-government. Today, 87 percent of the Åland population speak Swedish.

"We Ålanders are confident. We live on islands. It's all water around us. An island is always the center of the world," Karin said, laughing. "But we understand life on an island. Sometimes the weather is bad and the ferries do not stop. You can feel trapped. Or you can say, 'Ah well, it's just nature.'"

Water is everywhere. Drive any direction from Mariehamn for five minutes—or better, ride a bicycle—and you will come to an inlet, a cove, a patch of rocky or sandy beach. There is no briny fragrance: the Baltic Sea, fed by freshwater runoff from the surrounding land, has very little salinity. It's noticeably calm: the water's ebb and flow are no more than ripples. On a clear day, the sun, which in the summer doesn't set until 11:00 at night, seems to shine forever onto the rocks at the shallow bottom along the coastline.

Yet it is a deceptive calm, just as the white night—that perpetual dusk or dawn during the few hours when the sun is not in the sky—is an illusion of some sort as well, giving one a false sense of . . . what? Hope? Productivity? Unlimited possibilities? A summer visitor, I would not see the falling leaves in the autumn, the long darkness in the winter, the raging storms, or the iced-over Baltic that looks solid enough to cross on skates but that only experienced locals understand how to navigate.

On a sunny morning, I rented a bicycle for a solo trip. My destination was Järsö, an island less than seven miles south of Mariehamn. I marked on the map the islands I would pass: Granholm, Styrsö, Rödgrund, Nåtö, all connected by bridges. Åland is a perfect place for cyclists. Even as I cycled on the highway, the cars were infrequent, the sea breeze abundant.

Outside Mariehamn, I instantly became lost. I missed the turn onto the highway and rode onto a tree-lined path that cut through a village. On both sides were horse paddocks, houses with blooming gardens, boats moored along the inlets. A red-and-yellow maypole from the midsummer celebration stood among the green trees. This could have been a fairy-tale village, though I observed a few properties with emergency generators—a reminder of the power outages that will occur during winter's more extreme storms.

I stopped at what I thought was the first bridge on the route. On one side of the bridge was open water, and not far beyond were a few islands, with trees and cottages and more moored boats. On the other side was marshland, above which a wooden bridge, marked PRIVATE, led to a house hidden by the trees. I checked the map; it seemed as though I had already passed a few islands. I repeatedly found myself disoriented—on Åland, sometimes the departure from one island and the arrival on another is less perceptible than one hopes.

A couple of islands later, I arrived at Nåtö. According to the guidebook, there was a nature reserve. I got off the bike and in no time was lost again. I walked up a lane that led to a small inlet, around which several houses and their boats rested undisturbed. Is there a house without a boat on Åland? Islands give one the illusion of being isolated when needed: bridges and boats provide the freedom to come and go.

At the end of the lane, three adults and two teenagers were working with scythes and forks—making hay, which I had read about in novels but had never seen with my own eyes. I was especially interested in the two boys, no older than 18, unhurriedly gathering the cut grass on their forks.

One of the men directed me to the nature reserve, where I was the only hiker. I have always loved solitude, but without the crowdedness of human interactions—on a city street, in the virtual world—my aloneness felt no more than a neutral existence. Halfway into the woods, there was a grove of hazelnut trees. Their perfect geometric arrangement formed a green, winding tunnel. Wild orchids, mosses and lichen, unseen birds chirruping, a coastal meadow with soft grass carpeting the slight descent to the waterfront—all these sights were pleasant, but I experienced them with a sense of distance.

Beyond the meadow, the sky and the water, both intensely blue, met at the horizon, where there was another unseen island. There, too, might be another woodland and another coastal meadow like this, and there, too, a solitary traveler could be looking at the sky and the water—but this thought only touched me as superficially as did the tip of a tree branch I passed beneath.

On that day, and on the subsequent days, on foot, on bicycles, or taking a ferry to another island, I was baffled by the unexpected gap between what I had *expected* to feel and what I *did* feel. Here was a place my older son would never see. Here were the stories I could never share with him: of harvesting wheat in the summer heat when I was in the first grade; of bicycling to school in one of Beijing's infamous sandstorms (I was a middle schooler, arriving with my face covered with sand, mud clinging to my eyelashes—I never would have imagined that one day I would be riding a bicycle for pleasure); of marching for weeks in the mountains when I was in the Chinese army (the hiking reminded me of those long days of walking). These memories seemed all the more definitive while I was on the islands of Åland.

*

On another sunny day, I started early for Föglö, a group of islands in the southern archipelago. Föglö made world news in recent years: A 19th-century schooner was discovered to have been
wrecked off the islands. In 2010 divers salvaged 168 bottles of the
world's oldest champagne from the cargo. Preserved for 170 years
at 160 feet underwater, it was still of good quality.

The ferry ride, which took around 45 minutes, was the quintessential experience of journeying across an archipelago, the
routes well marked by buoys, poles, and lighthouses. Green islands
loomed on the horizon in every direction, and nearer, white sail-
boats lingered. Once in a while, a mute swan came as though out
of nowhere. So still, so impeccable in its posture, it looked like a
marble sculpture—but no marble sculpture could move with such
ease.

From Föglö terminal, I drove to all the islands crossable by
bridges, stopping each time when I reached the sea. On both sides
of the roads were cow pastures and barns, potato fields and or-
chards, the sights of prosperous farm life.

When I reached the very eastern end of Föglö, there was a public beach, empty but for a hammock, a shower shed, a picnic table
and two benches. Had there been a palm tree or two, it would
have looked like one of those hidden beaches on Kauai, Hawaii,
where my children and my father had once disturbed a tiny crab
while digging a sand castle. The beaches on Kauai had been full of
tourists then, and we had been a different family.

What does contentment mean when life is full of the unexpected and the unwanted? That day, nearly hypnotized by the sea,
the islands, the white sails, the sun that moved imperceptibly in
the sky, I asked myself this question. Part of my life is what I have
striven to make it be: I emigrated to America, I built a family, I became a writer. Part of my life has wounded me. I have experienced
joy and darkness, I have learned suffering and willfulness, but I
have never known discontentment or contentment. I had not even
thought about those words until I was on Åland.

The etymology of the words—"contentment," "contented"
—comes from Latin, *continere:* "to hold together, to hold in." It
strikes me that when people write congratulatory messages, their
wishes are for happiness, and in condolence letters, people mention peace as an alternative to grief. In any of life's moments, contentment seems a lesser state: How many of us would wish that a

friend or a beloved have a life of contentment, or a life free of discontentment? How many of us would make that the ambition of our own lives?

It is my habit, before visiting a place, to read a few novels set there. And when I returned from Föglö, I opened *Ice,* Ulla-Lena Lundberg's 2012 novel (translated in 2016 by Thomas Teal) set in the post–World War II era of Åland, and reread some favorite passages.

*Ice* is a novel of Åland, but the place it depicts, one far from the center of a nation or the world, also feels near to George Eliot's Middlemarch, Thomas Hardy's Wessex, Shen Congwen's Phoenix in Southwest China, John McGahern's Leitrim, Ireland, and Marilynne Robinson's Gilead, Iowa. History, politics, and religion do not manifest themselves as headlines or dramas; rather, they are woven into the tapestry of everyday life. Perhaps all places—landlocked or surrounded by water—are islands.

Toward the end of *Ice,* Sanna, a young girl who just lost her father in a drowning accident, is saying farewell to her favorite guardian, a teenager named Cecilia, before moving away permanently.

> Sanna is frighteningly wise and sensible. She doesn't ask even once if she can go with Cecilia a little farther. Nor does she beg Cecilia to stay. She doesn't say she's scared to walk home alone. Dusk comes quickly in August, and now they both have to go. She dries her eyes with the sleeves of her sweater and starts to run. Cecilia walks out onto the bridge and stops and looks around. Sanna is so little and slim that she quickly disappears among the junipers and shadows. The path is empty, as if she had never existed.

There is no way for Sanna to leave her own life: "She's in it all the time, and she's afraid." This is the same for many—most—of us. Perhaps contentment has nothing to do with what kind of life one has: harsh or easy, painful or joyful, profound or superficial. Perhaps true contentment—to hold oneself together, to hold everything in—is simply an agreement to be in life, to be in it *all the time.* True contentment does not make one an idealist.

The sense of contentment continued through another day of island hopping to Töftö, Vårdö, and Alören; on a visit to Kastelholm, a medieval castle surrounded by fjordlike bays; on my daily walk by the waterfront near midnight, after the last ray of sunshine vanished.

Karin, the journalist I had met on the first day, had grown up in Finland, in the Swedish-speaking region, and moved to Åland for her husband. Åland, she said, would be her home forever. A young woman at the car rental told me that she had moved with her parents from Finland to Åland when she was two. Åland's population has been steadily increasing in the past 50 years, and, more and more, it's because people born outside Åland have moved here. The majority are from Sweden and Finland; some are from other Scandinavian and Baltic countries; some are South American, Asian, and African immigrants.

I learned all this, along with many other facts about Åland, by writing to Katrin Sjögren, Åland's prime minister. "Her phone number and her address are listed in the telephone book," Karin had told me.

Upon returning home to Princeton, I have spent a lot of time studying the statistics about Åland. Weather, water supply, population, housing, incomes and assets, social welfare, trade, hunting and fishing, records of important life events—births, deaths, marriages, divorces, immigration, emigration—all fascinate me. Who were Åland's 46 Jehovah's Witnesses in 2017? The four suicides in 2016, all male—who were they? What happened to the 123 seals hunted in 2015, and the 179 elks? The 300 women employed in "sea transport enterprises" in 2016—how many of them were mothers, and how many of them worked on long-distance cruise ships, absent from their children's daily lives?

As a visitor, I could skim on the surface of the place, but these human stories, which I will never get to know, remind me of another Emerson line that I've often thought of: "Gladly we would anchor, but the anchorage is quicksand."

Is contentment, I wonder, an urge to make quicksand our anchorage, or, rather, an invention of buoyancy?

Toward the end of the trip, my melancholy caught up with me. This time, I was cycling north to Eckerö, a little over 18 miles from Mariehamn.

The landscape—unlike that of the ride south to Järsö, where the trees and the flowers and the village road made a perfect storybook setting—felt bleaker. It was July, but already the woods—birches, firs, and pines—were becoming autumnal, the tall branches naked at places, the bodies of downed trees strewn around in others. The sky, leaden with clouds, seemed ominous. Long uphill rides exhausted me. As I pushed my bike on foot, I studied the Icelandic horses, the cows and their calves, the flock of sheep huddling under the trees along the road, all at ease. Is this what Emerson called reality? Grief did not bring me closer to it, nor did it insert a distance in between.

When I arrived in Eckerö, an Elvis look-alike on a sign made me pause. GRACELAND, HOME OF ÅLAND ELVIS was written underneath. A few minutes later, I came to the waterfront, where an old fishing harbor lay beneath an overcast sky. Aged boathouses —rusty red, grayish brown, wooden panels peeled off—cast their shadows in the water. There was no boat and no fisherman; the harbor could be called peaceful or desolate. But these were only adjectives; the harbor itself did not dwell upon its peacefulness or desolation.

"Life only avails, not the having lived"—perhaps the fishing harbor would provide a good footnote to Emerson's observation. Or my trip to Åland. I went there neither to evade old memories nor to make new ones. It did teach me the meaning of contentment, which has nothing to do with holding onto. When we hold onto something—a moment, a memory—the loss is imminent, if not already permanent. But when we hold together and hold in—we are talking about life that avails, life not lived.

One day near the end of my stay, I asked the hotel receptionist to translate a newspaper story for me. It was July 4. "From apple orchard to Big Apple," read the caption beneath a photo of a young woman sitting in an orchard, with a giant red apple suspended above her head like a hot-air balloon. The woman, the receptionist explained, used to work on an Åland apple orchard and would be going to work as a law clerk in New York City in the fall—from one island to another.

On the day of my arrival, Karin laughed when I said I had chosen to visit Åland. "Why didn't you pick an exotic place?" she said. "A tropical island, for instance."

There is nothing exotic about Åland, though before leaving, I did wonder about coming back, and how I would spend my next holiday here. Perhaps I would hike to all the islands, or I could train myself to become a better cyclist and traverse them that way. Perhaps I could even dream of being a more adventurous traveler.

But it's equally possible that it may be a long time before I return, when the contents of my life are further shifted.

JEFF MacGREGOR

# The Last of the Great American Hobos

FROM *Smithsonian*

THERE'S A KIND of late-summer midwestern sunset, maybe you've seen one, so beautiful and so strange it's dislocating. From end to end the whole sky goes rose pink, and a giant sun hovers out there like a live coal over the corn. For a while, nothing moves. Not that sun, not the moon, not the stars. Time stops. It's dusk in farm country, coming up on twilight, but there's something of eternity in it.

Not long ago out in Britt, Iowa, they were watching that big sun hang behind the grain elevators while the orange light from the campfire flickered up in the hobo jungle. This is by the railroad tracks off Diagonal Street, just over from the cemetery and a couple of blocks down Main Avenue from the center of town. And after dinner, once the pots and pans are washed and stacked, the hobos will sit and smoke and sing a few choruses of what sounds like "Hobo's Lullaby." Not far away, at the foot of the boxcar, in the Sinner's Camp, they'll tell stories and drink beer in the lengthening shadows.

Maybe 50 hobos in the jungle this year, and an equal number of hobo hobbyists and hobo historians and hobos-at-heart. Connecticut Shorty and Jeff the Czech, Minnesota Jim and Mystic Will, Slim Tim and Jumpoff John, Sassy and Crash and Sunrise, Dutch and Half Track and IoWeGian, Tuck the King and Queen Minnesota Jewel, Gypsy Moon and 4 Winds and Honeypot Heather, Ricardo and K-Bar and New York Maggie Malone. Across from the boxcar are the outdoor kitchen and the equipment shed and the little pavilion with the picnic tables. The big fire sits at the center of it all, and the whole jungle, maybe an acre, is ringed by tents and cars and vans and little motor homes. Almost no one rides the freight to get here anymore. Way harder to catch out since 9/11 and harder still for an aging hopper. Jumping a train is still a dangerous act of sometimes desperate athleticism. Even in the firelight it's an inventory of faded tattoos and gray ponytails, of vivid misremembrance and missing teeth, of crutches and sunburn and spotless denim, of balky hips and whiskey breath and nicotine stains. But there are children and grandchildren running around here, too, and a few young hobos, gutter punks and dirty kids, and tourists and fans and citizens. There's even a group of students down from South Dakota State University. The whole place hums to life as day drains into darkness.

Every hobo has a moniker, a nickname grounded in habit or origin or appearance, like Redbird or Frisco Jack or Bookworm. Not every hobo wants to share his or her real name with the straights and the Square Johns, of which, with my notebook and recorder and wingtip shoes, I am decidedly one. (My hobo name is Seersucker. I wish I were kidding.) A few, the ones trying to outrun something, won't even talk to me.

So monikers it is. As an editorial matter, know that I spoke to these folks and they spoke to me, that my bosses know what's what and that these interviews were accurately recorded and transcribed, and that for the purposes of this story I respect every hobo's right to anonymity.

In a society of citizen-consumers, to have nothing, to own nothing, by choice, might be the most radical politics of all. And it's worth mentioning here that not every homeless person is a hobo. And as the hobo fades from the American scene—except as a visual or literary cliché—there's more and more confusion on the matter. A hobo is homeless by choice. Even then, not every hobo is completely homeless. Most these days have a semipermanent address somewhere for the winter. Especially the older hoppers.

Hobo slang can be intuitive, or impenetrable, but it's always colorful. For example, the "jungle" is just the communal hobo camp, usually near the railroad yard. Your "bindle" is your bedroll. Your "poke" is your wallet. "Hundred on a plate" is a can of beans, and the jungle kitchen is run by the "Crumb Boss." The "bulls" are the railroad police. "Flyers" and "hotshots" and "redballs" are all fast freights. "Catching out" means hopping the train. To die is to "catch the westbound." And understand this, above all else: A "hobo" is an itinerant worker; someone who travels and finds work. A "tramp" travels, but mostly does not work. A "bum" neither travels nor works.

And of course the whole thing runs on talk, endless talk. Because talk's free; because even if you give away everything you own, or they take away everything you have, you still have your stories. And every story here begins as the same story.

Why I left home.

*I did a lot of hitchhiking right after high school. And one time my brother was out hitchhiking in California, and some tramps got a hold of him and told him ride the trains instead of hitchhiking, and so he rode trains. They came back, and that was in 1973. They were talking in a bar about riding out to see Evel Knievel jump the Snake River Canyon, and I started to listening to it, and I worked seasonal and stuff. I had some freedom there. I was in. And so my older brother . . . There was eleven of us gone out of St. Cloud and hopping freights, and I fell in love with it right away. I mean, I like hitchhiking because you get to meet a lot of different people, but the freight-train riding was like the freedom, you know?*—**Ricardo**

*I first left home when I was sixteen, just to see the country and get out on my own for a while to see if I could do it. And I did.*—**Minnesota Jim**

*My father was a hobo, born in 1898 in Frog Level, North Carolina. Ran away from home when he was twelve or thirteen, rode freights for about seventeen years. He's a wonderful storyteller, musician, singer. He was always the one to tuck me in bed at night. He would say, "Two songs, one story. You get to choose one song, and I'll choose one." I always chose "Cocaine Jubilee," because he learned it out in the opium dens and it was a funny song. Then he would sing one, and he'd tell me one of his adventure stories.*

*I remember when he'd leave every night, I'd think, "I can't wait until I'm old enough to do that." I started hitchhiking right out of high school and eventually was a student at Indiana University. I had the honor of doing a directed writing course which I could choose the professor. He said, "You need to choose a good topic." And I chose hobos, and I said, "Because I grew up with it."*—**Gypsy Moon**

*When I was a really young kid, I lived in a neighborhood in Houston close to a big train yard. It's had a hobo jungle there for a long, long time. I had a buddy*

*named Dusty, and me and Dusty used to sneak out there in the field and watch*
*the hobos. We used to watch guys get on and off the trains all the time, so we kind*
*of knew how it all worked.*

*Dusty and I did catch a train, to Galveston. We just got on the train in the*
*dark. We got down there, and we're like, "We're sixty miles from home, how are*
*we going to get back?"*

*Maybe half an hour later, there was a train going the other way, rolling*
*real slow. We saw empties. We caught a train going the other way, and by sheer*
*luck, it went right back to the same place we were at. We were just really lucky.*
*—K-Bar*

Britt is a small town in north-central Iowa. Maybe 2,000 souls.
Tidy lawns and houses. A handful of shops and restaurants. A few
vacant storefronts. Nice library and municipal building, and the
police station used to be the dentist's office. Dan Cummings, the
chief at the time, just brought in a new popcorn maker he's pretty
happy with for the jail.

Twenty-five minutes east is Clear Lake, where Buddy Holly's
plane went down; 25 minutes west is Algona, where the motels are
—and the McDonald's and the Hormel pepperoni plant and the
factory where they make Snap-on tool boxes; 10 minutes north is
the Crystal Lake Wind Farm and its long horizon of bright white
turbines, and 15 minutes past that is the Winnebago factory over
in Forest City. Everything else this time of year is corn; corn to the
distant edges of the world, corn and more corn, and the kind of
immaculate farms for which Iowa is known.

The train tracks run east-west through Britt. There's been a railroad in and out of here since about 1870. First hobo probably
rode through not long after. Used to be a Chicago, Milwaukee &
St. Paul line; then the Iowa, Chicago & Eastern. Now it's the Dakota, Minnesota & Eastern Railroad. Mainly freight lines, carrying
mostly grain.

We're all here for the 118th National Hobo Convention.

Along with the County Fair and the Draft Horse Show, the
Hobo Convention is the biggest thing on the Britt calendar.

*From what I have gathered over the years growing up in Britt, it started in 1900,*
*where two businessmen had heard about this convention happening in Chicago,*
*and they thought, "Why don't we go out there and see what it's about, and maybe*
*that's something we could bring to Britt, bring people into Britt, and business."*
*—Amy Boekelman, president, Britt Hobo Days Association*

*My favorite part is starting the week before, there's a lot of hobos in town, and I try and go down to the jungle almost every night up until like Wednesday and Thursday when we get really busy on the festival. But it's those nights in the jungle just talking that are some of the best. You hear the old stories, everyone's reminiscing. A lot of them will share stories of riding with some of those steam-era hobos who used to come to Britt and aren't here anymore, so it's finding that common connection and they're so welcoming to people from the community and they love sharing their stories. To me, that's what it's all about, and I've formed some great relationships with several of them now. —Ryan Arndorfer, mayor, Britt, Iowa*

There's a carnival midway on Main, and concerts and dancing on the bandstand, and the selection of the new Hobo King and Queen, and their coronation and the big mulligan stew feed in the park, and the car show and the Hobo Museum is open and the Hobo Art Gallery too, and there's Mary Jo's Hobo House café, and the Hobo Omelet Breakfast Fund-Raiser and the Vagabond Craft Show, and the Four Winds Ceremony and the Toilet Bowl Races and the ice cream social. But the greatest of these, by far, is the parade.

Everyone in town is either in the parade or watching the parade, or in it then watching it, or watching it then running around to get back in it. Entire high school classes come home to sit on a bale and ride a flatbed pulled by a tractor. Turns out the hobo convention is a reunion for the whole town. The Iowa State Fair starts the day before, so everyone comes home.

The hobos have come here every year since 1900.

The history of the hobo is the history of modern America. Starts right after the Civil War and the building of America's great railroads. There had always been a small floating population of agrarian workers, but they were limited by geography and technology. They were regional. Local. Language historians and etymologists aren't sure, but the word "hobo" may come from this original population of farmworkers: "hoe boys."

The railroads change all that. After the war there's an expanding displaced population available to ride—and help build—a transportation network running from coast to coast. As this is happening, America is industrializing too, and the need for a mobile workforce, willing, adaptable, and relatively inexpensive to transport, becomes evident. The hobo.

By the late 19th century, the heart of Hobohemia was the main drag in Chicago, where train lines radiated out into every corner of America. It was easy to find work there in the slaughterhouses to make a buck before you caught out again; easy to go west and build a dam or go east and take a job in a new steel mill. So for decades it was America's hobo home. The Hobo Code was written there in 1894, an outline of ethical hobo practice and communal etiquette. Based in mutualism and self-respect, it remains every hobo's founding document, a simple and forthright set of instructions to live by. The same year, Coxey's Army of the unemployed makes its protest march on Washington.

The country is growing in booms and busts, and transient work like lumbering and mining and seasonal fruit picking are moving west into parts of the country without much population, so the hobo follows. And in the same way coffeehouses were indispensable to the American Revolution, railroads and hobos become an integral part of the modern US labor movement, especially in the Pacific Northwest.

The Industrial Workers of the World, its members known as the Wobblies, is founded in Chicago in 1905. Its radical labor politics and spirit are then widely and passionately distributed by rail, by hobos coming and going around the country, like an injection into the national bloodstream. One of the founders of the American Civil Liberties Union, Roger Baldwin, was an IWW hobo. But the greatest of these, and most famous, was Joe Hill. A martyr to corporate violence and the solidarity of labor, he remains America's best-known hobo.

Hobos came and went on the huge historic construction and infrastructure projects of the American West, and ridership rose and fell with the national economy. A surge of young men after World War I, another in the Great Depression. For decades fruit tramps are hauled west by rail, picking the produce that would soon ship east by boxcar at a premium price. That symbiosis held until trucks took over so much of the nation's shipping.

When the veterans came home from World War II, they bought cars or motorcycles and rubber-tramped. Fewer and fewer depended on the railroad. Populations of employable Americans filled in almost every corner of the map. Eventually that mobile surplus labor force became less necessary to the national economy.

Even the old art forms, like the hobo nickel and the wooden cigar box carving, were slowly being lost.

The transition from steam to diesel marks the beginning of the end for the Great Age of the Hobo, and the numbers have been declining ever since. After 9/11 it becomes so hard to hop a freight that only a few hardcore hobos remain.

There's a team of archaeologists exploring a hobo jungle at a dig in rural Pennsylvania. It's easy to feel like the hobo has already passed into history. From the Hobo Code to "The Hobo Code" episode of *Mad Men* in about 113 years.

To have been a hobo—or a tramp or a bum—is a pretty loosely held title, hard to pin down biographically. You'll see lists in books and online of famous hobos. I suspect plenty of the names reflect a long summer's walk rather than a life on the rails, or a sentence fragment in a press release to help sell an album. They were scenery bums. Still, Supreme Court Justice William O. Douglas is thought to have hoboed his way across country to attend law school. Writers James Michener and Louis L'Amour and Jack London, and billionaire oilman H. L. Hunt, all went on the bum. The best description of Jack Dempsey, hobo and heavyweight champion of the world, was written by Jim Murray, one of the greatest sportswriters who ever lived:

"Whenever I hear the name Jack Dempsey, I think of an America that is one big roaring camp of miners, drifters, bunkhouse hands, con men, hard cases, men who lived by their fists and their shooting irons and by the cards they drew."

By the end of the 19th century, all that steam-engine tramping and rail riding and the romance of what lies past the horizon begins to appear as a subgenre of our national literature. Bret Harte's "My Friend the Tramp," a short story from 1877, is an early exploration of the interpersonal politics and impossibly high price of radical individualism. Jack London gathers his own hobo stories first as a series of magazine pieces, then as a mashup of fiction and nonfiction, in 1907's *The Road*. Vachel Lindsay and Robert Frost are early poets of the form, and Frost's "The Death of the Hired Man" may be our most wrenching depiction of leaving home and returning home, of itinerant work and our obligations to one another:

Home is the place where, when you have to go there,
They have to take you in.


By 1930, when John Dos Passos writes *The 42nd Parallel*, the
first novel of his towering USA Trilogy, the hobo is no longer just
a foil or a cautionary tale, but the protagonist, often driven away
from home and into the world by injustice. As we see again in
John Steinbeck, and *The Grapes of Wrath*, the hobo, the landless,
the migrant, becomes a Christ. That impulse travels all the way up
the line to Jack Kerouac and the Beats.

By then there was plenty of social science writing about hobos
too, the most famous being *The Hobo: The Sociology of the Homeless
Man*, by Nels Anderson, 1923. In the years since, hundreds of
other books and studies and dissertations have drawn on its initial
research. And once every ten years or so, another writer hops a
freight and writes a book about it.

Hobos have been stock characters in the movies since the days
of the hand-cranked nickelodeon. Charlie Chaplin took the American hobo global. His Little Tramp is the bittersweet flip side of
radical labor politics and industrial/agrarian alienation. Always
broke but never broken, his struggles were everyone's. By cam-
ouflaging it as comedy, he presented us then—and presents us
still—the tragedy of modernity. Every hobo is a commentary on
capitalism.

There's the hobo played for laughs again in director Preston
Sturges's *Sullivan's Travels,* and Gary Cooper in Frank Capra's *Meet
John Doe,* but the summit of the early Hollywood hobo form might
be William Wellman's *Wild Boys of the Road* from 1933. Meant to
discourage Depression-era runaways and warn young Americans
about the risks of vagrancy and the hobo jungle, it had the opposite effect, and was so thrilling it became a kind of recruiting
instrument. The postwar American hobo, the TV hobo—Red Skel-
ton as Freddie the Freeloader, or Emmett Kelly as Ringling Brothers' sad circus clown—had the unintended effect of reducing the
hobo to a punch line. (You see this in how those well-meaning
SDSU students costume themselves. It's a baggy-pants vaudeville
with a five o'clock greasepaint shadow.) The 1970s delivered *Em-
peror of the North Pole* and *Bound for Glory*, two of the best, and last,
movies of the genre.

*Bound for Glory* is the story of singer-songwriter Woody Guthrie, and that's where the mythology of the American hobo will likely live forever, in music.

Go back to the American folk songs of the 1880s and '90s and you'll hear the beginnings of what became the IWW's *Little Red Songbook*. In it, you'll find the roots of everything and everyone from Woody Guthrie to Pete Seeger to Bob Dylan, Phil Ochs and Arlo Guthrie and John Prine, Steve Earle and Bruce Springsteen. One of this country's 20th-century greats, modernist composer Harry Partch, was a hobo.

There are events in Britt all week, beginning, ceremonially anyway, with the lighting of the jungle campfire, in which the hobos call down the blessings and benedictions of the Four Winds. This they do in the breezeless summer heat, and the next few days will be spent walking back and forth from the jungle to the midway and the park and the museum. Most of the 'bos come back here to eat at mealtime, and Hawk, the Crumb Boss, sees to it that everyone gets three squares a day. There's always coffee, too, and he makes sure everyone drinks a lot of water: "Gotta hydrate, man." Everyone drops what they can in the kitty to pay for it all.

Over at the Hobo Art Gallery, they've unveiled the portrait of Tuck and Minnesota Jewel, last year's king and queen. The walls are lined with these paintings of past royalty, including legends like Iowa Blackie and Bo Grump. The portraits are all painted by Leanne Marlow Castillo, a local artist of skill and renown. She is 85. "I did it all on my own. I was asked to restart an art show. I started painting them, and I painted six the first year, eight the second year.

I'm still around."

Across the street at the Hobo Museum—the old Chief movie theater—they've got case after case of memorabilia donated by the hobos themselves going back generations. There's a good PBS documentary running on a loop down in the little screening area. During Hobo Days, the mayor himself works at the counter.

Start Saturday in the little park by the gazebo, but start early —the big pots of mulligan stew went on the boil long before sunrise. This year's crew is made up of a dozen local homeschool athletes, sleepy-eyed and still yawning, every one of them stirring half a dozen giant, steaming cauldrons with what look like canoe paddles. The recipe is simple, which is roughly true to the origin

of the dish: whatever the hobos had went into the pot. This morning it's a ground pork stew with plenty of potatoes and carrots and
cabbage, rice and barley, onions and chili powder in a tomato-
paste base. By 11:00 in the morning there's a line to get it by the
cup.

Up in the gazebo, there's a radio broadcast of the parade, and
it goes out over the PA and everybody within a few blocks can hear
it. That's pretty much everyone in Britt. The old-timers set up their
lawn chairs on the sidewalk, and lots of folks from out of town
stand lining the streets and spooning up free stew.

The parade snakes a long S-shape through town, doubling back
on itself. It'll take more than an hour for every car and float and
motorcycle to pass wherever it is you're sitting or standing. Which
is OK, because they're all throwing candy at you. It's a pre-Hallow-
een chance for the kids—and some of the quicker adults—to load
up on sweets. I was out front of the fire station for most of it, and
caught licorice whips and bits and pieces of conversations as they
went past.

"I remember when this was bigger . . ."

". . . when these men were heroes . . ."

". . . real hobos like Steam Train Maury . . ."

"Did you see that old Plymouth?," which is a question asked by a
guy driving an old Pontiac. There are scores of old cars and trucks,
vintage and not, some of them carrying politicians, like the mayor,
others carrying signs for politicians, VOTE FOR SCHLEUSNER FOR
SUPERVISOR, and one carrying a cardboard cutout of the pope.
Those SDSU students, here doing research for their own homecoming Hobo Day, are out in their tin lizzie, waving and honking
and having fun. There's a 1946 Farmall tractor pulling the class of
1998, and there's the class of 1978, and the class of '93; there are
floats from the churches ("Here come the Methodists," says the
man to my right, to no one in particular) and from the seed companies, THE FUTURE OF FARMING AT WORK reads the sign; and
the golf cart advertising the local lunch counter, and then the class
of '88 and the class of '68 and an old man in a tall straw hat astride
a horse, then the Knights of Columbus and the polka band on the
flatbed sponsored by the veterinarian. The local co-op, the local
college, and the local veterans group go by, as Lee Greenwood's
"Proud to Be an American" shakes the trees, and the hobos pass

by on their trailer, holding signs like THE DUTCHMAN FOR KING, and IoWeGian walking next to the giant chicken from the local bank alongside a nice 1968 Camaro.

Then it's time to elect a new king and queen. The little park is packed shoulder to shoulder.

To get things started, hobo Luther the Jet sings what sounds like the second verse of "The Star-Spangled Banner." Luther is rumored to have a PhD in French literature and a faculty chair somewhere, but is notorious for slipping away at these gatherings and does so before I can get to him. In any case, it's time for the speeches. Every candidate for king and for queen has a minute or two to state their case. At the end of the speeches, the audience votes by applause and the judges crown the victors.

The odds-on favorite for king this year is Slim Tim.

"Hi. I'm Slim Tim. My dad Connecticut Slim was crown prince of the Hobos for life. My two sisters Connecticut Shorty and New York Maggie were queens of the Hobo. If you elect me, I will promote Britt Hobo history. I also will help to make the old State Bank into a hotel, which Britt really needs. So more people can stay in Britt and know what a great stay it is. No matter who you vote for, I hope it's me, but I will always be a promoter of Britt and the Hobos because I love them both, so be happy and have fun. Thank you."

There is a round of polite applause.

Then the dark horse, the Dutchman, who no one gives much of a chance.

"First, I'd like to say to the good people of Britt I surely appreciate your hospitality, and the real fine sit-down you've put on. This is very special. I'm touched. Really. Second, I'd like to say that I've been on the road since 1968. That's fifty years of riding trains and wandering places, chasing disasters.

"Everything I've owned, and everything I want in life, fits in this house [points to his knapsack], right in my pack. Anything that doesn't fit in my pack, I can't carry with me. I don't want it. I can't have it. It all gets left behind. It makes me a different kind of person. It's given me something special in life. I'm not attached to anything. I wander with the winds. I know that a lot of people wish they could do the same.

"It's a hard life in a lot of ways. It probably shouldn't be romanticized the way that it is. You get yourselves out there, and it's cold, wet, and the steel is hard. It's very dangerous. There are people out there that aren't very nice. But I wouldn't trade it for anything. It takes a lot. I'm a man of few words.

"So, I think that's about all I need to say. Only that . . . one last thing, I got fifteen states of dirt on me, and these pants are brand-new."

The crowd goes pretty crazy.

Half Track's daughter Crash is running for queen.

"When I decided to run for queen, I had no idea what my speech was going to be, so I decided to speak from the heart. Now, I grew up with the hobos, they came to my house. They even took me on my first ride, all the way to Long Island, New York. That was very exciting, but they've been a family to me, and so has Britt. Britt has been an escape since I was a child. I know I missed a few years, but I'm back, I've got my kid this year. And I would love, really love to show the people out there, the world, what the wealth that the hobo family and that the town of Britt shows, because this is one of the best places. I've never felt more welcomed or accepted than anywhere I've ever been. Thank you."

The final-question music from *Jeopardy!* plays while a selection committee officially confirms the audience choice.

Dutch and Crash both look surprised and sheepish, but happy, in their robes and crowns. Ecce Hobo.

It is a fair accounting of the day to say there were 2,500 attendees—and 2,500 participants. The crowd disperses up and down Main Avenue after the coronation, and you see Queen Lump, a former winner, walking slow, and Minnesota Jim, and the sun's hot in the street and the smell of fried dough and midway grease is thick in the heat, and the music and the clatter from the rides are loud and by the end of the day that Hobo Omelet breakfast might raise $2,500 or more, they tell me.

The carnies are all parked in their campers over on East Center Street, just up the block from the Toilet Bowl Races—a timed, point-to-point-to-point event involving teams of three pushing toilet bowls on wheels, the rapid consumption of popular snacks, a great deal of toilet paper, and many teeny-weeny toilet trophies. Whatever it is you're imagining it to be is no worse than whatever I might write about it actually being.

*Our kids grew up here and they've been in the hobo jungles all the years. My daughter has one of the Steam Train Maury walking sticks from way back when. So our kids are now grown and they come back to Britt with their kids. And now we babysit the kids while they do a little bit more of the activities. I've lived here forty-three years. It's a tradition that I hope will always stay alive.* —**Sally Birdman**

Best scene of the week was certainly this: Tuck and Jewel, as the outgoing King and Queen of Hobos, have a "photo op" up by the library. Which means they're sitting on a park bench across from the museum, and you can walk up to them and ask to sit for a picture. This they do, graciously, and every couple of minutes a citizen snaps a selfie, or gets a portrait made with royalty. There's small talk and handshakes and thank-yous and the whole thing is as unremarkable as it sounds.

Folks come and go, but one man hovers a few feet away for a while and watches it all with interest. He looks a little like Tuck, especially around the eyes, about the same age, but rounder, without the hollows in his cheeks. Cautiously, he steps forward.

"Do you remember me?" he asks. "I'm your brother."

They haven't seen each other for 30 years.

Tuck stands and says nothing and takes the man in his arms and everyone around the bench dissolves into tears. They hold each other a long time.

The lights on the rides are coming on, and the last thing I see on the midway is a happy kid, maybe nine years old, running past us with a souvenir dreamcatcher as big as a manhole cover.

The Dutchman's blue eyes are bright even in the half dark of the boxcar. He is lean and windburned, red-cheeked and gray-bearded. Sixty now, he's been on the road 50 years. His father chased him out of the house. He was always in Dutch back then, and the name stuck. He's smart and forthright and there is no menace to him, but the clarity of his purpose and the rigor of his personal philosophy can be unnerving to the citizens and the straights. When he's not catching out, he's catching work as an electrician. As you read this, he's as likely to be in California as he is in Indiana. Or riding the porch of a grainer anywhere in between.

In passing you'll hear that "Dutch owns the boxcar," and it won't

matter if they mean this literally or figuratively. The boxcar is a fix-
ture in the Britt jungle, permanent. Long off the main line and set
here years ago, it is a meeting place and a memorial, an antique
keepsake and a hideout. Dutch sits with his gear at the north end
of the car. Everything he owns fits in a knapsack. Heaviest thing he
carries are his memories. Folks come and go, talking. The Dutchman is a focused listener. Intense, even at rest. As often as not,
he's up there with the younger 'bos, the newer riders, answering
questions and giving tips. (For insight into this next generation of
gutter punks and crusties and dirty kids, the postmodern hobos,
search out the stunning photography of Mike Brodie.)

Dutch is one of the motive forces of the 'Bo-lympics, an 80-proof
skills and athletic competition among newly minted hobos. And
now he's the king. He even did a TV interview up in the boxcar
this year.

"You ain't free until your backpack's full and your pockets are
empty," he says.

Every culture has its seekers and its pilgrims, its mystic beggars
and holy wanderers, its ascetic prophets and barefoot madmen,
its itinerant poets and singers. Buddha and Moses and Jesus all
went on the bum for a while too, don't forget. And some of this
metaphysical shine rubs off on the hobo, who may or may not be
looking for enlightenment. Those holy men want you to get rid of
things to free yourself from wanting. To give away everything is to
pass out of this world, or into heaven, untroubled. A point made
one way or another at hobo church on Sunday morning by the
fire. But then why is every hobo song so sad?

Tuck and his brother are huddled up on a couple of patio chairs
near the pavilion. "We never thought you were dead," his brother
tells him, "but we always wondered where you were."

The Evergreen Cemetery in Britt is bigger than you expect and
this morning it's all sunshine and fine blue sky. There's Tuck and
Jewel with their walking sticks and there's Redbird and Skinny and
Slim, and George and Indiana Hobo and Connecticut Tootsie.
We're all here to say a ceremonial goodbye.

There's something profound in all this, in the week, something
ancient and right and good, of townspeople taking in the stranger,
the poor and the lost and the hurt, of the Samaritan, of Moses and
Buddha and Abraham. Five thousand years of wandering and it

turns out the real wilderness is inside us. Hats off and heads bent, the Square Johns and the tramps and the hobos, the citizens and the bulls take each other's hands, and all at once you see it, the community and the humanity and the love.

But the Dutchman's right, too. Don't romanticize it. Empty your pockets. Empty your heart. There's only what you carry on your back. There's whatever you're chasing and whatever's chasing you. Maybe there's some grace to be won in the burdens you bear, or in your swiftness, but at moments like this it feels like the price of your freedom is an unimaginable loneliness.

They call the roll, and Half Track reads the names, of those who caught the westbound, those gone before us, friends, strangers, the loved and unloved, the not yet forgiven and the not yet forgotten, not yet, and everyone closes their eyes to pray and the cicadas lathe the trees and the heat rises and the honor guard steps forward in a stiff-legged line of flags and rifles, older men mostly, from the VFW and the Legion hall, all American belly and grim solemnity, jackets too tight and ramrod straight with duty and country and for a moment the whole thing rides a thin line between comedy and tragedy and then they play taps and you realize you've been crying for a long time. Because here we are.

Home at last.

BEN MAUK

# The Trillion-Dollar Nowhere

FROM *The New York Times Magazine*

THE EURASIAN POLE of Inaccessibility is a striking name for an absence. It is the point farthest from a sea or ocean on the planet. Located in China just east of the border with Kazakhstan, the pole gets you a good distance from harbors and coastlines—at least 1,550 miles in any direction—into an expanse of white steppe and blue-beige mountain that is among the least populated places on earth. Here, among some of the last surviving pastoral nomads in Central Asia, nestled between two branches of the Tian Shan range on the edge of Kazakhstan, the largest infrastructure project in the history of the world is growing.

About 80 miles from the Pole of Inaccessibility, just across the border in Kazakhstan, is a village called Khorgos. It has spent most of its existence on the obscure periphery of international affairs, and its official population is just 908. But over the last few years, it has become an important node of the global economy. It is part of an initiative known informally as the new Silk Road, a China-led effort to build a vast cephalopodic network of highways, railroads, and overseas shipping routes, supported by hundreds of new plants, pipelines, and company towns in dozens of countries. Ultimately, the Belt and Road Initiative, or BRI, as the project is more formally known, will link China's coastal factories and rising consumer class with Central, Southeast, and South Asia; with the Gulf States and the Middle East; with Africa; and with Russia and all of Europe, all by way of a lattice of land and sea routes whose collective ambition boggles the mind.

Khorgos is a flagship project of this work in progress, an international shipping hub and free-trade zone that its promoters say is poised to become the next Dubai. Thanks to its location at the junction of the world's soon-to-be-largest national economy and its largest landlocked country, Khorgos has become an unlikely harbinger of the interconnected planet: a zone fully enclosed by the logic of globalization, where goods flow freely across sovereign borders, following corridors designed to locate every human being on the planet within a totalizing network of producers and consumers, buyers and sellers.

Such victories of the global and industrial over the local, isolated, and rural are heralded as the inevitable future—if there is to be a future—of our species. What would that future look like? Whom would it benefit? What would it cost? To find out, last July I caught a sleeper train from Almaty, Kazakhstan's largest city, to the Chinese border, where I woke up in a train yard surrounded by desert.

Khorgos is one of a cluster of villages encircling a former trading post of the ancient world called Zharkent. From Zharkent, I hoped to arrange a ride to the border. Frescoes of camel caravans flanked the entrance gate on Silk Road Avenue. In a central square stood a rainbow-colored mosque with the sweeping eaves of a Chinese pagoda and an inscription in Uighur enjoining visitors not to forget their past. Next to the mosque was the warren of chopped-up shipping containers that serves as Zharkent's central market. Taxi drivers hung unhopefully around the watermelon stands.

Among the drivers was a farmer named Nunur, who had come to Kazakhstan from China in 1962, when he was a young boy and Kazakhstan was a Soviet Socialist Republic. That year, more than 60,000 Chinese Uighurs and Kazakhs escaped to the Soviet Union, crossing with Soviet passports they received from the consulate in Xinjiang and with the apparent cooperation of Chinese border guards. Nunur remembered his parents walking him over red hills at night toward the checkpoint at Khorgos. "They opened the border and let us go into Soviet territory," he recalled. There were rumors that his relatives who stayed behind were imprisoned or killed. (Nunur, fearing trouble from the authorities, asked that I use only his first name.) His parents, who had raised wheat in China, found work on a collective farm. His mother became a cook while his father learned to drive tractors and Nunur to repair them. He became an expert mechanic. "I'm a master without a diploma," he said.

I asked Nunur to drive me to a place near the border where we could take in the booming hub of Khorgos at a glance. On the way, we passed his cornfields, apportioned to him after the breakup of the collective farm. Even as Kazakhstan modernized following its 1991 independence, growing rich by regional standards from the sale of oil and outfitting a new capital city with glossy architectural marvels, the eastern border with China remained sparsely developed, its economy dominated by livestock and grain production. Nunur said his village still had no indoor plumbing, and as we left his fields we passed some of the ruins of centralized planning the Soviets left behind: a former winery, a shuttered milk plant.

China's plans are significantly more ambitious, and they reach far beyond eastern Kazakhstan. The "belt" of the BRI refers to the Silk Road Economic Belt, a tangle of rail and highway routes currently vining their way untidily across the continent from eastern China to Scandinavia. The "road" is the Maritime Silk Road, a shipping lane that will connect Quanzhou to Venice, with prospective stops along the way in Malaysia, Ethiopia, and Egypt. To date, at least 68 countries, accounting for nearly two-thirds of the planet's total population, have signed on to bilateral projects partly funded by China's policy banks and other state-owned enterprises. Chinese firms are building or investing in new highways and coal-fired power plants in Pakistan, ports in Greece and Sri Lanka, gas and oil pipelines in Central Asia, an industrial city in Oman, and a $6 billion railway project in Laos, which in 2017 had a GDP of less than $17 billion. China's port holdings stretch from Myanmar to Israel and from Mauritius to Belgium. It has spent an estimated $200 billion on BRI projects so far, mostly in Asia, and has implied it will spend a total of $1 trillion on hundreds of projects around the world in the coming years, dwarfing the Marshall Plan by roughly an order of magnitude. When the investments from all the participating countries are combined, the estimated cost rises to $8 trillion.

The BRI is so big and multifarious that describing it can feel like trying to narrate the weather conditions of the entire planet. Some individual components span hundreds of miles and are themselves dauntingly complex and international, like the $68 billion China-Pakistan Economic Corridor, or the stalled and scandal-mired

Bangladesh-China-India-Myanmar Corridor. Taken as a whole, the BRI is unfathomable. But I had heard that, at Khorgos, a pioneering outpost, I could get closer than anywhere else to appreciating the scope of its aspirations.

Nunur drove me through his village to an overlook within view of a border sentry post, a few miles from the spot where he crossed into Kazakhstan almost six decades before. We parked near a small rock-crushing plant above a valley of bright-green cornfields. Beyond the fields, through a blue haze, I could see this improbable new crossroads of the global economy.

The Chinese side of the border was easiest to spot. Since 2014, an instant city of 100,000 people, also called Khorgos (sometimes spelled Horgos), has appeared; its dark high-rises glittered in the sun. The Kazakh side of the border was less impressive from afar, but I knew it now hosted a first-of-its-kind free-trade zone, opened on territory shared with China. Behind a copse of cypress trees, I could also make out the gantry cranes of the new dry port—an inland shipping-and-logistics hub for freight trains—that began operating in 2015 and could soon be the largest port of its kind in the world. Adjacent to the dry port was a nascent railroad company town, and other plots nearby were cleared for factories and warehouses to be staffed by some of the future residents of the city of 100,000 that, if all goes as planned, will soon rise to match the one across the border.

The manager of the plant wandered over. He asked whether we wanted to get through the checkpoint, beyond which was the last village in Kazakhstan and, beyond that, China.

We got back in the car and pulled up to two guards who stood at the gate, rifles slung over their shoulders. They looked young and bored. The manager shouted the name of one of them, who walked shyly up to the passenger-side window. It seemed as if everyone in town knew everyone else.

"Give me some sunflower seeds," the manager said. The guard pulled a bag from his pocket and poured seeds into the manager's cupped hand until it overflowed. The manager explained that we wanted to see China. The guard shrugged and raised the boom gate.

Two miles beyond the checkpoint, across a valley of farmland, a tangerine ridge signaled the start of China's largest territory, Xinjiang Uighur Autonomous Region. The border was somewhere in the valley beneath us. If we kept going, we would arrive at the Chinese sentry post we could just make out at the top of a train of switchbacks. We didn't test it, however. In recent years, the Chinese government has erected the most advanced police state in the world in Xinjiang, targeting the region's Turkic Muslims, especially its Uighur ethnic group, who make up about half the region's population. As part of what Chinese Communist Party literature describes as "de-extremification" efforts to combat terrorism, authorities have created an exclusion zone of state surveillance, arbitrary mass internment, brainwashing, and torture that covers an area more than four times the size of Germany and includes a population almost as big as Australia's. According to the United States State Department, between 800,000 and 2 million people, or up to 15 percent of Xinjiang's Muslim population, have been incarcerated in a growing network of more than 1,000 concentration camps.

You couldn't see any of that from our perch at the border. Everything looked peaceful. To our left, a shepherd's path ascended into white-capped mountains where herdsmen grazed sheep and cattle in summer, far above the fields of corn and sunflowers. To our right, beyond the ridge, the high-modernist future of international commerce was springing up out of the ground. You could squint and imagine you were looking at a time-lapse photo of the entire history of collective human activity, from the first wandering goat-herder all the way to the present.

China has never released any official map of Belt and Road routes nor any list of approved projects, and it provides no exact count of participating nations or even guidelines on what it means to be a participant. But this fuzziness may be one of its defining advantages. Rather than a list of megaprojects and bilateral deals, some of which might stumble or fail, the BRI can be understood as a vaguely visible hand guiding all the interlocking developments in infrastructure, energy, and trade where China plays any kind of role.

It is also a framework through which China's leaders can present virtually any component of its foreign policy, from a soda-ash plant in Turkey to China's first foreign military base, in Djibouti, as part of a nonthreatening vision of what party representatives like to call "win-win" global development. In recent years, China has floated several expansions of President Xi Jinping's initial Belt and Road vision that make its scope seem all but limitless: the "Digital Silk Road" into the frontiers of the virtual, the "Pacific Silk Road" to South America, and the Arctic-crossing "Silk Road on Ice." Xi himself has meanwhile extolled the merits of globalization at Davos and worked to brand his "project of the century" as a natural extension of the spontaneous trade routes that once laced across the Eurasian continent.

Critics have described the BRI as a new kind of colonialism or even part of a strategy of "debt-trap diplomacy," seducing cash-poor countries with infrastructure projects that are unlikely to generate enough revenue to cover the interest on the loans that funded them. That is the unhappy situation at the China-funded Port of Hambantota in Sri Lanka, which the China Harbour Engineering Company took over after Sri Lanka fell behind on debt service. The Center for Global Development lists eight countries that face high risk of "debt distress" from BRI projects that they can't afford.

Kazakhstan is poised to play a literally central role in China's plan. The BRI was first announced in Astana, at a 2013 ceremony attended by Xi and Kazakhstan's longtime president, Nursultan A. Nazarbayev. At the same event, Xi and Nazarbayev also celebrated the opening of a joint gas pipeline and signed $30 billion worth of trade and investment agreements. Although in the past Kazakhstan's economy has tended to orbit Russia's, in 2007 China edged out Russia as Kazakhstan's top importer, and some critics fear that the BRI is leading the country deeper into economic vassalage. "Some people think that China is too big," Nygmet Ibadildin, an assistant professor of international relations at Kimep University, in Almaty, told me. "Kazakh people want a win-win with the BRI, but in these situations China wins more often."

Even in a country with few meaningful democratic rights, there are risks to courting foreign investment. In 2016 a proposed law that would have permitted parcels of farmland to be leased to Chinese companies sparked nationwide protests, leading Nazarbayev to table the measure.

The human rights crisis in Xinjiang has not helped China's standing in Kazakhstan, either, although the Kazakh government has been careful not to make any public statements that might alienate an important economic partner. While diplomats may be negotiating on behalf of ethnic Kazakhs in Xinjiang behind closed doors—in January, the Kazakh foreign ministry announced that China would allow 2,000 ethnic Kazakhs to give up their citizenship and cross the border into Kazakhstan—the government is not letting the presence of a prison state across the border interfere with its collaboration with China.

That may be largely thanks to the immediate economic concerns of both states, not to mention a shared penchant for autocracy, but it may also owe something to the unprecedented nature of the BRI. In many participating countries, the project's very novelty seems to lend itself to gauzy optimism. In September the Chinese state-run media group People's Daily commemorated the fifth anniversary of the BRI with a music video modeled after Coca-Cola's famous 1971 "I'd Like to Buy the World a Coke" TV spot. The new video featured altered lyrics like "I'd like to build the world a road / And furnish it with love," sung by smiling representatives of dozens of participant nations, decked out in *ruquns,* hijabs, and dashikis. Rather than defining the initiative in any concrete way, the video slyly co-opts Coke's ability to serve as empty cipher, meaning anything to anyone. Whatever it is, the BRI is "what the world needs today / It's the real thing."

Khorgos Gateway rises out of the flat desert basin, a pale yellow moon base of cranes and storage silos into which, every so often, a freight train slowly rolls. A trio of rail-mounted gantry cranes loomed 50 feet overhead as I arrived on a damp, overcast morning. Khorgos Gateway may be the most advanced port in Central Asia, but it retains some of eastern Kazakhstan's rustic atmosphere. When I walked into the lobby of the dry port's main offices, a security guard was handing out apples he had picked in his garden.

The chief executive of Khorgos Gateway, Zhaslan Khamzin, welcomed me into a tidy office overlooking the freight yard. "The future lies here," he said proudly. Khorgos was blessed by its position in the middle of Eurasia. "Look at a map, and you'll see China on one side, Europe on the other, Russia to the north, and the Caucasus and Iran to the east. Why am I pointing this out? Precisely because ninety percent of cargo traffic to these countries is currently made by sea."

Since the dry port's inaugural train passed through in 2015, Khamzin said, companies who manufacture goods in China have begun to recognize the advantages of a modernized overland trade route across Asia. The dry port has transferred John Deere combines to Azerbaijan, he claimed, and Hewlett-Packard parts to western Europe. He added that it may be much cheaper to ship containers by sea, but it can take more than three times as long, and air transit is the most expensive by far. By contrast, a container passing through Khorgos can travel from a Chinese point of origin to Europe in about 14 days, faster than the sea and cheaper than the air. "We're going to be a central distribution point," he concluded. If all goes well, according to company forecasts, in a few years Khorgos Gateway will be the largest dry port in the world.

Out in the shipping yard, wild dogs sniffed at stacked containers. It started to rain. A train had just pulled into port, and workers in yellow slickers were jogging out to meet it. Friendship between nations notwithstanding, Chinese border authorities are tight-lipped about freight schedules. The port sometimes learns about an impending arrival only an hour before it appears on the horizon, whereupon a swift ballet of machine and human movement begins. A siren blared as a gantry crane began to creep toward me through the mist. The three 41-ton cranes straddled six rail lines—three are the wide-gauge rails that stretch across the post-Soviet world from Helsinki to Ulaanbaatar; three are the standard gauge used in both China and Europe—and from my perspective they appeared to tower impossibly over the mountains around us. From a dangling control booth, a crane operator lowered containers onto their beds with dull-eyed expertise.

The national railway company of Kazakhstan owns 51 percent of Khorgos Gateway. The remaining 49 percent is split between two Chinese state-owned companies. Khamzin viewed China's participation not as economic imperialism but as proof of the port's likelihood of success. The Chinese, he explained, "are the kind of people that if they saw no commercial opportunity, they wouldn't invest here."

Such arrangements are less one-sided in Kazakhstan than in some of the more debt-strapped BRI countries, so it's very unlikely that what happened in Sri Lanka will happen here. But Chinese investments have in all likelihood muffled Kazakhstan's response to the crackdown in Xinjiang.

Each train that arrives at Khorgos has to pass through the Chinese region, which is home to 24 million people, including more

than 12 million Uighurs and about 1.5 million Kazakhs. Although
political unrest has troubled the region for decades, including, in
recent years, a spate of knife attacks and bombings by Uighur separatists, authorities in Xinjiang have responded with brutal asym-
metry, rounding up hundreds of thousands of Uighurs alongside
thousands of ethnic Kazakh and Kyrgyz residents in a sweeping
internment drive the scope of which rivals Mao's Cultural Revolution. Their "offenses" range from open displays of religious belief
—wearing a beard, praying in public, owning a Quran, or refusing
to smoke or eat pork—to simply traveling with or even speaking to
relatives abroad. For those not yet detained, Xinjiang has become
a dystopian zone of extralegal checkpoints, patrols, GPS tracking,
and random home inspections.

Some experts say the camps and other security measures are
partly in reaction to the increased freight traffic across Xinjiang,
much of which now comes through Khorgos Gateway. "The role
of Xinjiang has changed greatly with the BRI," Adrian Zenz, an
academic expert on China's minority policy, told me. China's BRI
ambitions have transformed Xinjiang from a fringe territory into
what party leaders call a "core region" of development. That's why
awareness of the camps among people in places like Kazakhstan
was such an issue, Zenz said. "It has significant potential to cast a
very negative light on the Belt and Road."

After my tour of the dry port, I headed a mile down the road
to Nurkent, a newly built town of low bungalows and apartment
blocks. For all its symbolic importance, Khorgos Gateway is still
a modest operation; if it were a United States seaport, its 2018
throughput would place it somewhere around the 26th-largest in
the country, beneath the ports of Mobile, Alabama; Boston; and
Gulfport, Mississippi. There are just 190 employees, which Khamzin
said was close to capacity, and most of them live in Nurkent, alongside railroad workers, police officers, border guards, customs officials, and other agents of the new frontier. Except for the caw-
ing of crows nesting within an apartment building's crumbling
gables, the town was silent. During a visit to the region in 2016,
Nazarbayev predicted the population would grow and merge with
Zharkent to form a large city, but this was hard to visualize. The
site of a planned expansion was marked by a roundabout with a
tiered silver gateway—the "2001" obelisk as imagined by Frank

Gehry—through whose arch I could see only an untended field of scrubland.

As I stood looking at the archway, a car pulled up. A man in straw hat and sandals hoisted himself out of the passenger side. "I guard this place," he said. He uncoiled a hose on the ground and began watering the grass around the gate. "This is the double door to the future of Nurkent, where the city will rise up."

Khorgos's other major landmark is a boomtown of open borders known as the International Center for Boundary Cooperation, or ICBC, which China and Kazakhstan established in 2011 about six miles from the dry port. Here it is not only the goods that move freely back and forth but also the people. In this duty- and visa-free zone, Kazakh citizens willing to brave the hourlong wait at customs control are permitted to enter a walled section of the Chinese side of Khorgos across the border to buy cheap linens and electronics, and Chinese tourists may enter a walled leisure area inside Kazakhstan to buy souvenirs and eat Kazakh delicacies like *shashlik* and *laghman*.

A United Nations human rights panel describes the entirety of Xinjiang as a "massive internment camp," but that didn't stop workers I met at the dry port from suggesting I cross into China by way of the ICBC. Khorgos Gateway and the ICBC are the products of special economic-development zones set up in coordination with China: industrial and commercial arenas designed to foster jobs and investments. There are dozens of such zones within China—the first, Shenzhen, is now a megacity of more than 12 million people—but Khorgos is the first to exist partly outside China's own borders. That will soon change. Chinese officials have announced plans to build 50 more international zones in countries from Algeria to Vietnam.

At Khorgos, the ICBC seems intended to complement the dry port's vision of frictionless trade with an equivalent vision of borderless commerce, even if most Kazakhs understand the project as a wholesale depot for cheaply made Chinese goods. A popular hustle among shopkeepers from Almaty is to hire one of the locals who wait outside the ICBC, and who are euphemistically called "carriers," to help circumvent the weight limits on imports. By all accounts, customs officials tend to look the other way.

My state-assigned guide picked me up at my hotel in Zharkent in a sleek Mercedes sedan that he drove as if we had just robbed a bank. "Are you nervous?" he asked, laughing, as we careered around a watermelon truck. His name was Marat Abaiuly. If the ICBC was the most important of China's outposts in Kazakhstan, Abaiuly was its ambassador, the handsome liaison to opinion makers and potential investors. He made his power known by blowing through checkpoints with a friendly honk or, if necessary, by leaping out of the car to grip the soldier on duty by the forearm.

It was 10:00 in the morning, and a line of wholesalers and hopeful carriers had formed beyond a fence topped with concertina wire. Bus drivers reclined inside their open cargo holds, chain-smoking and preparing to nap through the day. Inside the customs-control building, a construction worker was destroying the tile floor with a jackhammer. Improvised lines formed around the rubble.

China is said to be spending billions of dollars building up its side of Khorgos. By contrast, Kazakhstan's share of the ICBC is mostly a dream of the future. Projects like a constellation of luxury hotels, a sports complex, and a Disneyland-style theme park called Happy Land Khorgos have languished for lack of funding. Fields of rubble and stalled construction projects are scattered among the few small retail buildings and the yurt-shaped gift shops that are the Kazakh side's most distinctive feature.

In recent years, the name "Khorgos" has instead become synonymous among Kazakhs with smuggling rings and high-profile corruption cases. In 2011 authorities arrested the head of customs at Khorgos as part of a larger takedown of a $130 billion smuggling ring. In 2016 the former head of the ICBC was caught on tape accepting a $1 million bribe for a construction bid. Locals do not tend to figure in these public scandals, but based on the crowds I saw in front of the border checkpoint, informal gray-market carrying at Khorgos seems to have replaced animal husbandry as the region's main line of work. "Most locals work at the ICBC carrying cargo," the chief executive of an Almaty-based truck transport company later told me, describing the work as a kind of pseudolegal smuggling. "That's how they make money."

Abaiuly arranged for an ICBC van to drive us across the open border into China, where the main attractions for visiting Kazakhs are four large, windowless malls. The malls are honeycombed with shops where women of all ages and a few older men sell under-wear, electronics, and an array of other inexpensive products un-der fluorescent lights. One mall was dedicated entirely to fur coats, a gift of ritual significance in Kazakhstan, particularly between in-laws at weddings. It was early, and there were no customers any-where. Floor after floor of identical shops stood empty, their racks of odorless pelts doubled and tripled by wall-length mirrors.

Some workers I met were Chinese citizens from Xinjiang. I had heard that, in some towns, even talking to a journalist is considered grounds for detention, so I didn't say much, and I was relieved to come across an outspoken furrier from Kazakhstan, Zhannur Erkenkyzy, who had worked at the border for six months. She got the job because she could speak Chinese, Russian, Uighur, and Kazakh. She was also the store's model, she said, and she showed me her Instagram page, on which she appeared nestled inside the furs of minks, foxes, and beavers, although at the moment she was wearing no fur at all, just a black cocktail dress that reflected no light.

Erkenkyzy said she worked seven days a week unless she hap-pened to ask for a day off. The time involved in crossing the un-predictable border meant that the job occupied most of her wak-ing life, of which one highlight was catching thieves. "When we see a shoplifter, we put on red armbands and beat them with sticks," she said excitedly. Abaiuly interrupted, whispering in low, snappy Russian: "Why are you saying such nasty stuff about us to the re-porter?"

Back on the Kazakh side, we wandered the yurts, which were staffed by Chinese clerks who spoke no Russian or Kazakh. Tour-ists were milling about inside one of them, browsing rows of instant coffee, jade eggs, and taxidermic hawks and antelopes. Outside, a row of golf carts and one stretch limousine waited to take the tour-ists back. I watched a group of women in ankle-length skirts cross a moonscape of rocks, heading toward China and dragging uselessly wheeled luggage behind them. When I asked Abaiuly about the prevalence of the carriers, he smiled. "On that subject I cannot speak," he said.

At an outdoor restaurant, I met a *shashlik* cook who lived inside one of the yurts where Chinese tourists ate. He left and reentered the ICBC once a week to stay out of legal trouble, and said it was cheaper than living anywhere else.

\*

One way to read the history of Central Asia is as a record of inter-actions between the mounted nomads who were long the primary occupants of the Eurasian Steppe and the sedentary populations who lived among them. As late as the 1930s, the dominant activity on the steppe was pastoral: herding sheep, goats, and other livestock. Herders roamed in large, shifting clans on either side of the Tian Shan and Altai ranges, traveling on horseback and occasionally fragmenting or forming political alliances. These nomadic hordes proved unconquerable until the late 18th century, when they began to fall to Chinese conquest and, in what is now Kazakhstan, to Russian—later Soviet—rule.

In 1929 the leaders of the Soviet Union determined that Kazakhstan's pastoral workforce would go to work on farms. This forced collectivization was framed as a civilizing mission to modernize a population whom many Russians had long viewed as primitive barbarians. Land formerly devoted to grazing was irrigated and turned over to wheat production, with the immediate result that around 90 percent of the country's livestock died. The subsequent famine caused the deaths of one-quarter of the population of Kazakhstan and anywhere from one-quarter to one-half of all ethnic Kazakhs, a human-made catastrophe that ended nomadism as it had been practiced in the region for thousands of years. Kazakhs became a minority in the nation the Soviets had founded in their name.

Nomadic pastoralism remains central to Kazakh mythology —Nazarbayev describes himself as "the son, grandson, and great-grandson of herders"—but as a practice it has retreated to the periphery of the country's economy. Most of the surviving herders in this part of Kazakhstan practice a form of seminomadism known as transhumance, alternating between winters in a low-altitude village and summers in a pasture, or *zhailau*, in the mountains. I wondered how those in the mountains above Khorgos were reacting to the economic foment that had emerged around their winter homes. One morning I visited a village of herders in the Zhongar Alatau, a northern stretch of the Tian Shan named for the last nomadic khanate to rule over the steppes of western China.

It was Friday, and most of the men were at the village mosque. I asked the local damkeeper's son, who said his name was Turar, to take me farther into the mountains where families graze their herds throughout the summer. I got into Turar's old Lada four-wheel drive, and we rattled and bounced up the edge of a steep bank that commanded a wide prospect of sand dunes and crumpled foothills. Hawks gyred overhead. I thought to myself that the beauty of Kazakhstan defied description, but Turar, who had lived here all his life, managed to capture its pristine emptiness. "It's like a screen," he said cryptically. Then, to clarify: "Like a computer. Like the Windows screen."

To reach the *zhailau,* we left Turar's car at the dam where his family controls the flow of snowmelt and mountain spring through a Soviet-era irrigation canal. Before long, we arrived at an emerald slope where a single yurt sat embosomed in alpine lushness. Turar said this area was called the Black Gorge.

A friend of Turar's emerged from the yurt, blinking at the sun. His name was Arsen Akhatay, and he'd been napping. Every spring, he helped drive the family livestock, a few hundred sheep and 50 cows and horses, up to the *zhailau* and tended them. He returned to the village when school started in the fall, leaving his parents to drive the animals back down. In between, there was a lot of free time. Sometimes he passed it playing *kokpar,* a popular Central Asian sport in which players fight over a headless goat carcass while on horseback. Akhatay was the attacker on his local team and was meant to be at training camp this week for nationals, but he'd fallen sick instead. He surveyed his sheep without enthusiasm. Each was labeled in resin with a large "5" marking it as a member of his family's flock. A solar panel staked into the ground near the doorway to the yurt powered a Chinese-made radio and a four-inch TV set. Turar gestured farther into the gorge, where Akhatay's family pastured their horses a mile or so in, and said that if you kept on in that direction, you'd hit China.

Akhatay was wearing a blue camouflage jacket, the kind worn by Kazakh police officers on field exercises. His cousin came out of the yurt wearing the same thing. During the school year they lived in a village near Zharkent called Turpan. Akhatay, who was about to start his senior year of high school, said he did not intend to look after sheep his whole life. I asked whether he wanted a job at Khorgos.

"Many people from the village work at the border as carriers," he said. "There are many official jobs but also many unofficial." All things being equal, he said, he wanted an official one. When he graduated, he planned to enroll at the military institute in Almaty to become a border guard.

On our drive down the mountain there was nothing to displease the eye, and before long we arrived at yet another small mountain village of white birches and potato gardens. Turar parked the car by a water pump and introduced me to a former classmate, a Kazakh named Zholaman Tashimkhan, who had come out to greet us.

We sat on the curb near the pump. Like Arsen, Tashimkhan spent most of the summer up in the mountains, but he was older and had already been drawn to the jobs at the border. He worked for a year for the railroad, a good job that is hard to come by through normal channels—"I used my connections," he said, and laughed—but then his sister's husband found him work as a carrier. "It's not an official job," he said. "Not a public job."

A few men from the village began to gather around the pump as we talked. Tashimkhan explained that he had worked for a wholesaler based in Zharkent, crossing into the ICBC four or five days a week to bring household products, mostly bedsheets and linens, back into Kazakhstan. He was paid according to how much he managed to get through customs. On an average day, he might earn $15 or $20—good money—and occasionally as much as $60. Customs enforcement was lax. "For us, you talk to the official working there, and you just bring things out," he said.

More villagers had come out to the road until they completed a circle around us. Tashimkhan changed the subject, then joked with a friend that he was starting to think he would regret talking to me. An older man who had been pacing the street squatted down beside us and began conspicuously sharpening a sickle a few inches from my head. Turar suggested it was time for us to continue down the mountain. We got into the Lada and drove off.

The great commonplace of our time also happens to be true: the world is more connected than ever before. But if it is more connected, the world is also more administered—its people more coerced and surveilled, more susceptible to the designs of authoritarian leaders and more dependent on the fortunes of mercurial international markets—than at any point in human history. If the first fact has made some parts of the world freer, the second has made the rest of it less so.

A continuing trial at the local courthouse in Zharkent underscored this inversion, which seemed to me to lie at the heart of the developments at Khorgos. The case concerned Sayragul Sauytbay, a Chinese-born Kazakh woman who had fled Xinjiang and was requesting political asylum in Kazakhstan. Before the crackdown in Xinjiang, ethnic Kazakhs freely crossed the border to visit friends and relatives. But in 2016, as crossings became increasingly fraught, Sauytbay's husband and two children decided to move permanently to Kazakhstan. Sauytbay, who was working in Xinjiang as a kindergarten director, remained in China with plans to join them; the rest of the family became Kazakh citizens in 2017. For more than a year, they met only in the free-trade zone at the ICBC.

On April 5, 2018, without telling anyone, Sauytbay entered the ICBC with forged identity papers, then slipped into Kazakhstan by posing as a member of a tour group. A few weeks later, she was arrested and charged with entering the country illegally, and then her story began to emerge. Not long after her family had left China, Sauytbay was assigned to work at one of Xinjiang's notorious detention camps. In her testimony, she described it as "a prison in the mountains," with high walls and barbed wire that kept in some 2,500 inmates. She said she was forced by authorities to accept a teaching job there, indoctrinating the inmates in state propaganda, and she was warned that the penalty for revealing any information about the camps was death. The authorities confiscated her passport.

At her trial, Sauytbay provided some of the earliest testimony about life in Xinjiang's camps. Her case made headlines in Kazakhstan's national newspapers. She was married to a Kazakh citizen and was herself a "returnee," a member of the diaspora of ethnic Kazakhs the government has been courting for years. But now prosecutors at Sauytbay's trial were arguing that she should be deported back to China, where she claimed she would be arrested or even killed for having made public her knowledge of the camps.

Most people I'd met in Almaty seemed to think she had little chance of receiving asylum, much less Kazakh citizenship. The acquittal rate in criminal trials in Kazakhstan is around 1 percent, and hasn't changed since the days of the Soviet Union. There was also the BRI to consider. Kazakhstan might decide Chinese investment was more important than any international agreements on refugees. It wouldn't be the first time a country was so swayed. In 2017 Greece vetoed a European Union statement criticizing China's human rights record at the United Nations, a decision that critics linked to China's controlling interest not just in Greece's largest port but also in its public power grid. In January, China hosted a Silk Road Celebrity China Tour, inviting journalists from six BRI partner countries—Egypt, Turkey, Pakistan, Afghanistan, Bangladesh, and Sri Lanka—on a highly choreographed tour of a "vocational center" in Kashgar, another famous stop on the ancient Silk Road. According to the state-run Xinhua news agency, the visitors uniformly "praised the development and stability" of Xinjiang. An editor from Bangladesh singled out the region's contributions "to the nonoccurrence of violence and terrorism."

My last day in town coincided with what turned out to be the last day of Sauytbay's trial. About 100 supporters had risen early and driven out from Almaty to the courthouse, which was opposite a park where marble busts of Soviet heroes watched over a playground. When the courtroom opened, the crowd crushed against the glass doors. I made it through with a handful of other reporters thanks to some strategic shoving by a few veteran activists; most of the crowd remained on the courthouse steps.

As the proceedings began, Sauytbay's lawyer introduced into evidence a copy of the asylum application that she had just filed. Both the judge and prosecutor interrogated Sauytbay, who from behind a clear protective wall related how, when she was arrested by the Kazakh police, an official told her that she would be sent back to China to die and her children would become orphans.

Sauytbay freely admitted she'd escaped China illegally. She was willing to serve a prison sentence. She just didn't want to be sent back. "There is no reason for me to live if I am not with my children," she told the judge. Her family sat across the room, near an open window through which we could hear the crowd murmuring outside.

The prosecution had previously rejected any kind of a plea deal. So what happened next was that rare thing: a dramatic courtroom reversal. In a closing statement, the prosecutor cited the outpouring of support the case had received across Kazakhstan. She requested that the judge allow Sauytbay to serve out a period of probation at her husband's house. "I ask you not to apply deportation," she said. "I ask you to set her free in the courtroom." Sauytbay's eyes went wide. Her lawyer, who seemed stunned, agreed. A few moments later, sounds of cheering rang out on the courthouse steps.

"I was surprised the law was kept," Rysbek Sarsenbay, a prominent opposition activist, told me later. He reasoned that the government must have weighed the consequences of deporting Sauytbay carefully against the risk of alienating China's leadership. "Even as a dictatorship," he said, "Kazakhstan must honor its international commitments."

Once the judge issued the expected ruling—prosecutors and judges in Kazakhstan rarely disagree—Sauytbay was ushered from the courthouse to the top of the steps, where she embraced her son and thanked President Nazarbayev for his beneficence. A poet took the stage to extemporize a victory verse in Kazakh. The crowd repaired to a restaurant a few miles outside Zharkent, where a spontaneous release party began with the singing of the national anthem. Waiters descended with plates of *beshbarmak,* a national dish of boiled noodles and horse meat in onion sauce. When Sauytbay arrived, holding her son in her arms, everyone stood up and clapped. She told me she hoped her testimony would "shine a light of hope" for her compatriots in China. "They know there is a country that will always protect them," she said.

The celebration may have been premature. As Sauytbay later told the *Globe and Mail* of Toronto, within a day of her release, her sister and two friends were arrested in Xinjiang—they have since disappeared into camps—and in October, Kazakhstan denied Sauytbay's asylum claim. For the time being, she is living at home with her family, but her legal status in Kazakhstan is uncertain.

Even if she manages to avoid deportation, Sauytbay is one of thousands of people with ties to Kazakhstan who have found themselves caught up in Xinjiang's detention centers. At the release party, I found myself sitting next to a Kazakh woman named Qarlyghash Ziparova, whose nephew, a former Xinjiang official named Askar Azatbek, had disappeared inside the ostensibly neutral free-trade zone of the ICBC. Azatbek, who had become a Kazakh citizen a few months earlier, entered the ICBC in 2017 with a friend, whereupon a group of men drove up in two cars and detained them. The friend was released, but Azatbek was hauled off. They hadn't even been on the Chinese side, the friend had said. Ziparova tried to complain to authorities in Kazakhstan, but without any luck. The ICBC told her there was no surveillance video, although she didn't believe it. She didn't understand how a Kazakh citizen could be taken away by China like that—without even a trial.

The ancient Silk Road was equal parts trade route and social network. The routes themselves were in constant flux and administered by no one, and they succeeded through incremental growth and local knowledge in response to changing needs—the exact opposite of the Ozymandian ambitions and sweeping autocratic statecraft that characterize the Belt and Road. For all its potential to create jobs and modernize infrastructures, the project has also created a halo of mass internment camps for the powerless and gray-market economies for the poor. While new official jobs in Khorgos are lifting a lucky few out of poverty, it is far more common to find farmers and herders moonlighting as taxi drivers, security guards, or smugglers, part of a precarious network of low-paid freelancers. Such work is susceptible by design to sudden changes in enforcement and depends on a constant influx of disposable workers. It seemed like a high cost for connecting the world.

I hired a taxi to drive me back to Almaty. We took a new highway that opened last year, part of a growing highway system affiliated with the BRI and known as the Western Europe–Western China International Transit Corridor. The highway cuts the travel time in half, from six hours to just over three hours, and driving atop it felt like riding an air-hockey puck. There were no rest stops or gas stations, and the few landmarks I could see stood at an unobtrusive distance. They included an old train station, a pumping house for a Chinese oil pipeline, and the alien forms of a half-built wind farm courtesy of SANY Group, the Chinese manufacturing behemoth. As the sun became a narrow red eye on the horizon, a dust storm descended the cliffs to our left and crossed the road into empty veld. There were no cars in sight. It was less a road than the idea of a road.

The driver didn't know anything about the trial whose outcome

I had just seen. He had never heard of Sayragul Sauytbay. He was happy to have such a fine new highway on which to drive his customers back and forth between Khorgos and Almaty. Kazakhstan, we agreed, was a beautiful country. He pointed to some fields he said would be full of cattle in the fall, then opened the sunroof and stuck his hand into the night air.

# My Father's Land

FROM *Stranger's Guide*

The sea is History.
  —Derek Walcott

WHEN I WAS eight years old, my father gave me three books: *The Selected Speeches of Malcolm X, Narrative of the Life of Frederick Douglass,* and *Selected Poems,* by Claude McKay. I tore through all three but was especially intrigued by McKay's slim volume of poetry. My father told me that he and McKay came from the same place: Jamaica.

My father was born in 1960 in the parish of Clarendon on the eve of Jamaican national independence. Twelve years later, my grandfather moved the entire family to South Bay, Florida, where he established himself as a mechanic working in the region's sugarcane fields. It was, my father recalled, a difficult transition.

"Yeah, man, we were Jamaican before it was cool to be Jamaican," he said. He told me that his African American classmates teased him and his siblings mercilessly, mocking their accents, calling them "Ju-bwoys" and claiming that West Indians ate rats. Eventually, though, they made friends with their classmates, and as more Jamaicans moved to the region to work in the cane fields, they slowly began to transform the cultural landscape of South Florida into a Caribbean outpost.

For most of my life, Jamaica was song and symbol to me, found in the funky-smelling dishes my father fed me and my brother: jerk chicken, curried goat, steamed red snapper (or as we call it, escoveitch), oxtail simmered in lima beans. We were baffled that none of our classmates had ever experienced the comfort of a freshly baked beef patty or cured a cold with a bitter cup of cerasee tea.

Jamaica was Marcus Garvey hanging from my father's rearview mirror. It was dancehall reggae and the sounds of Barrington Levy, Yellowman, and Gregory Isaacs playing in the garage as my father washed his car every Saturday. The Melodians singing "Rivers of Babylon":

> For the wicked carry us away to captivity require from us a song
> But how can we sing King Alpha's song in a strange land

Jamaica was 90-percent-proof white rum and Rastas named Smitty, whose regular visits to our working-class suburban home would turn my father from an Americanized, blue-collar immigrant chasing the good life into a patois-speaking yardie. I loved those Saturday nights in the garage, listening to this group of displaced yardies chatting and laughing and carrying on. I would practice my patois, rolling the accent around my tongue, wanting desperately to sound just like my father.

I encountered Jamaica for the first time in that garage with my father. For me, my father was Jamaica. But I also knew it was a real place, and I made a promise to myself that one day I would go there and learn to see it through my father's eyes.

## Montego Bay

### St. James Parish

On December 27, 1831, a fire broke out on the Kensington estate, a sugar plantation in St. James Parish, one of Jamaica's largest and most important sugar-producing regions. The fire signaled the beginning of the largest slave rebellion in the history of the British Caribbean. Such uprisings were not uncommon—they were a regular occurrence throughout the 18th century—but this one quickly grew into a massive rebellion, known as the Baptist War or the Christmas Rebellion, that swept the island's western parishes for 11 days. One British Baptist missionary, Henry Bleby, described the chaos in St. James in his abolition memoir, *Death Struggles of Slavery* (1853): "The horizon for miles was lighted up with a strong lurid glare by the burning estates." Throughout 1831 the question of emancipation loomed large on the island. As debates raged in

England, many enslaved people became increasingly convinced that emancipation was on its way, had perhaps already happened, and it was only the wickedness of the planter class that kept them from admitting this fact.

The Christmas Rebellion was led by Sam Sharpe, an enslaved Baptist preacher. Literate and charismatic, Sharpe became a leader among the native Baptists in Montego Bay, where he led religious meetings for his enslaved congregants. Sharpe used the Baptist meetings to organize a nonviolent work strike after the Christmas holidays in an attempt to force the planters to support abolition. But the strike leaders knew that the planter class would likely respond to the strike with violence, so they made plans to arm themselves to face this threat.

As the rebellion raged on, it spread from St. James to the neighboring parishes of Hanover, Westmoreland, St. Elizabeth, Trelawney, and Manchester. The rebels seized plantations, burned crops, and fought off the local militia until the colonial militia arrived to restore order. With the arrival of the military forces, the rebels were outmanned and outgunned, and the rebellion quickly fell apart. When the smoke cleared, an estimated 207 blacks and 14 whites were dead, with dozens more wounded. Although the rebellion was short-lived, its economic and social effects were devastating. The damage in St. James Parish alone amounted to approximately £600,000.

The crushing of the rebellion is vividly illustrated in the 1833 painting *Destruction of the Roehampton Estate, January 1832,* by the French printer and lithographer Adolphe Duperly, who established one of the first photography studios in Kingston. The work's focal point is the estate's sugar mill, which is enveloped by flames and black smoke. Rebels surround the estate, armed with machetes and wielding torches, their weapons hoisted defiantly in the air. In the background, rebels lay siege to the great house with torches. The slave quarters remain untouched. In the foreground, the rebels watch the chaotic scene unfold from a distant hilltop, pointing to the destruction. A young man blows into a conch shell, and a woman carries provisions in her arms and atop her head, her back turned toward the plantation as she leaves it behind. The rebels are tiny figures in this turbulent landscape, but their gestures of triumph are clear as they raise their arms and weapons, wave their hats, and begin their march toward Montego Bay.

The Roehampton estate was located roughly 15 miles from Montego Bay, near the border between St. James and Hanover parishes. The property was established in 1782 as a sugar and rum plantation. At the time of the uprising, Roehampton was owned by John Baillie, an absentee English planter, who purchased the estate in 1811. Baillie was, by all accounts, a highly successful planter, and by 1831 he owned 343 enslaved people as well as 37 heads of cattle. Baillie died in October 1832 while sailing to Jamaica—no doubt to see his ravaged plantation. The rebellion dealt a devastating blow to the plantation, from which it never fully recovered. Nevertheless, Baillie's descendants were not left empty-handed. When the British crown abolished slavery in 1835, Baillie's executors filed a reparations claim under the Compensation Act on his children's behalf. They received £5,745 for the emancipation of 322 enslaved Africans.

The vengeance of the planter class following the ill-fated uprising was swift and brutal. Regional militia forces raided and burned black villages on the rebel estates, indiscriminately rounding up and killing those suspected of participating in the uprising. Those rebels who avoided summary execution were arrested, then quickly tried and executed. In the end, more than 300 rebels were executed in the months following the uprising. Their bodies were dumped in a mass grave near the shoreline outside of town.

Sam Sharpe was the last of the rebels tried and executed on May 23, 1832. Bleby wrote that he attempted to remind Sharpe that "the Scriptures teach human beings to be content with the station allotted to them by Providence and that even slaves are required to patiently submit to their lot, til the Lord in his providence is pleased to change it." But Sharpe was unmoved: "If I have done wrong in that, I trust I shall be forgiven; for I cast myself upon the Atonement . . . I would rather die upon yonder gallows than to live in slavery."

Although the rebels were defeated, the 1831 uprising landed a decisive blow against the slave order. The British crown formally abolished slavery two years later, in 1833. Today, Sam Sharpe is considered a Jamaican national hero, and the square where he was executed with the other rebels was renamed in his honor in 1975. His likeness graces the Jamaican $50 bill, and schoolchildren learn about him alongside other revived national heroes, including Nanny of the Maroons and Marcus Garvey.

But this is not what brings 4.3 million tourists to Jamaica every year. Today, Montego Bay is more famous for its white sand beaches and turquoise waters that travelers from the United States, Canada, and Europe flock to each winter. Cruise ships dock in its natural deepwater harbor daily, and throngs of tourists pour out of the ships for carefully curated day trips where they experience a sanitized taste of Jamaica for a few hours. Tourists can go to the Hip Strip in the city center and return to their ships with their hair braided like Bo Derek, circa 1979, or they can complete their tourist look with the iconic red, gold, and green faux dreadlock caps or Bob Marley apparel that seem to be obligatory vacation wear. In Montego Bay, you can play a few rounds of golf at the White Witch Golf Course on the grounds of the Rose Hall estate, enjoy a meal of jerk chicken and rice and peas if you are feeling adventurous, or try something closer to home at the Sugar Mill restaurant. Unlike the capital city of Kingston, MoBay is widely considered safe for foreigners, a traveler's paradise that is the centerpiece of the island's tourist fantasy of sun, sand, and sex.

As a child, I knew very little about Sam Sharpe and the uprising that he led. But my connection to this struggle was deeper than I realized. My grandfather, Rennick Carlton Morris Sr., was born in Roehampton in 1928. I went to Roehampton for the first time in December 2015 with my father, my husband, and my mother. At the time, I knew nothing about the destruction of the Roehampton estate.

The morning after my parents arrived, we set out to find Roehampton. We rode in a route taxi headed west along the northern coastal highway for about seven miles. The road is one of the smoothest, most modern highways in the country, built to facilitate the comings and goings of tourists whose travels remain firmly on the beaten path of multinational big-chain resorts in MoBay, Ocho Rios, and Negril. When we turned south into the hills just beyond MoBay, we began to see the Jamaica that tourists don't visit. The tiny two-lane road winds along the edge of the hills as taxis and trucks careened around each curve so quickly that I was certain we would fly off the hill at any moment and end up in a gully so deep that no one would ever find us. The windows were down, and the wind whipped through the crowded route taxi as we climbed higher into the hills. I worried that the map might have been wrong or that the driver didn't know where he was going.

I leaned across my husband and shouted at my father, "Are you sure you know where you are going?" He looked at me and sucked his teeth—Jamaican for "Fool, please." He was already settling back into himself and the environment. "Nah worry, me know where it is." I was quiet, but doubtful. He hadn't been to Roehampton in more than 30 years. As usual, he proved me wrong; his memory is remarkable. We pulled into a quiet, working-class neighborhood and approached a small store. As we drove past the store, we saw a slight, elderly man wearing a straw fedora, a Bible in his hand as he walked to church. My father glanced back and banged on the roof of the taxi.

"Stop the car!"

Everyone in the taxi looked at him as though he were crazy.

"I think that's Unc," he said, and swung open the car door and dashed out of the taxi.

We sat uncomfortably for a few minutes and watched him talking to the elderly man. To our astonishment, the man's face broke into a wide grin as he threw his arms around my father. This was my great-uncle Ralford.

Uncle Ralford is my grandfather's youngest brother and one of the last surviving members of the Morris family on the island. He was tickled that after all this time, my father somehow recognized him. He couldn't stop patting his arm, calling my father "Colly," his childhood nickname. A committed bachelor, he has no children and lives in the same house that he and my grandfather were born in. We walked back up the hill to the house. It is a small cement structure with three bedrooms that sits on about an acre of land. Like his father before him, Ralford is a farmer who keeps goats and chickens on the property while maintaining a larger planting area a few miles from the house.

I asked him what he remembers about my grandfather. "He was a good man, you know," he says. "Anything him can do fi help you, if you need it, he will do it." I asked about his father, Ralbert, and his answer was warm but brief. "Him was a nice person, he mostly keep to himself." When I asked him how long the family has lived on the property, he shrugged. "Long time we been here. Mi fadda was born here and his fadda born here. Me no know exactly when them come here but them was here long time before I born." He didn't know anything about slavery or have any property records. I tried to hide my disappointment, but he could read it on my face.

"You want to see the tomb them?"

I perked up. "Tombs? Here? On the property?"

"Ya, mon, they right there up the hill." And with that he turned and began walking up the hill. When we reached the top, I spotted a cluster of three tombs. They were covered with vines, and an enormous tree trunk stretched across the newest one that bore a small headstone with my great-grandfather's name, Ralbert Morris. Uncle Ralford disappeared behind a tree and returned with three machetes. He silently handed them to my father and my husband, who removed their shirts and, without a word, began chopping away the brush on the tombstone. It was as though they were performing an ancient ritual. The sun rose high in the sky, and the three of them began to sweat but kept working. When they were done, we all sat quietly on the tree trunk on Grandpa Ralbert's tomb.

My father was the first to speak. "Alright, Grandpa," he said. "It's good to see you."

Ralbert was born in Roehampton in 1902 and, like both his son and his ancestors before him, worked the land his entire life. I was eight years old when he died in 1991, and I've only seen him in a three-by-five photograph that my father keeps tucked into the edge of a mirror on his dresser. In the photo, Ralbert stands in front of his house, leaning on a cane. He is slender, like all the Morris men, and his face is lined and weathered. He looks like a man who knows what it means to work with his hands. He isn't rich, but doesn't wear the look of defeat that I associate with poverty in the developed world. He appears comfortable and self-possessed, as though he has all that he needs in life.

The other tombs bore no headstones, and when I asked Uncle Ralford who was buried alongside his father, he said, sheepishly, "Me no know. I think me grandfather and me grandmother."

It's an experience that I have had many times. Black history in the Americas is fleeting and ephemeral. It slips through one's hands like water. The Europeans who colonized the New World left their imprint everywhere in semipermanent monuments that underscore their descendants' contemporary claims to dominate and shape the world in their own image. These monuments are everywhere—in the decrepit great houses that haunt the island, street signs, town names, the architecture. The descendants of the enslaved must look elsewhere—to the soil and the sea—to find our monuments, our martyrs, and the memory of our existence.

Having paid our respects, we made the march back downhill, and got ready to leave. On the way out, Uncle Ralford pressed grapefruits, rose apples, and fresh ackee into our hands. "You haffi wait until the ackee them drop pon the ground," he told me. "You cyaan eat them from the tree because them will poison you. But these one good." I thanked him and placed the deadly fruit into my purse, alongside my camera. We would eat them for breakfast the following day. I hugged my great-uncle and planted a kiss on his cheek. He patted my shoulder and blessed me. "Go good then."

And so we did.

## Rose Hall Great House

### Montego Bay

My work focuses on the question of memory—What do we remember and what do we forget? What stories survive, and what stories vanish into the sea of history? How does public memory shape our understanding of the places that we call home, and how does silence act on us in ways whose impacts are no less real because they remain illegible and invisible to us? What archives can tell the history of a people who are said to have no history worth speaking of ?

The following day, my parents, my husband, and I decided to visit the Rose Hall Great House, just east of Montego Bay. The greatest of the island's plantation great houses, it's an imposing white mansion built in the Caribbean Georgian style that defined colonial architecture in the 18th century. Framed by cotton trees and perched on a small hill, it appeared to rise up from the ground as though asserting its dominance over the landscape. Heading up the long driveway, I felt as though the house was watching me. As we approached the house, I thought of all the enslaved Africans who must have felt the same thing as they labored under the watchful eye of the estate's multiple owners.

Of all the island's great houses, none are as infamous as Rose Hall. The estate's notoriety is linked to the legend of its last and most famous occupant: Annie Palmer, known as the White Witch of Rose Hall. According to local lore, Palmer was born to British parents but grew up in Haiti. Her parents died when she was a child, and she was raised by her Haitian nurse, who taught her voodoo. When she turned 18, she moved to Jamaica, where she married the owner of Rose Hall, John Palmer. But the marriage was short-lived; John Palmer died shortly after the wedding, and it was widely believed that Annie Palmer used her knowledge of "dark magic" to kill her unwitting husband. She married two more times, and both of her subsequent spouses met similar fates.

Palmer was said to be a wicked woman who tortured her slaves and was in the habit of "taking male slaves as lovers and then murdering them when she tired of their service." According to legend, she met her own demise at the hands of a powerful obeah man named Takoo, who strangled Palmer in her bedchamber after she attempted to curse his daughter. After recounting this story, our tour guide paused dramatically and lowered her voice into a stage whisper. "It is said that the spirit of Annie Palmer haunts Rose Hall," she said. "At night, you can hear Annie wailing."

She led us through the formal dining room and the drawing rooms on the ground floor. As we ascended the staircase, we passed by an oil painting of Annie Palmer surrounded by a group of small children. She was petite, her face childlike. "Some visitors say that if you look at the portrait, you can see Annie's eyes watching you," the guides said. I stared at the portrait for a moment and felt nothing. We followed our guide upstairs, where she showed us Palmer's bedchamber. "This is where she was killed," she said. From Palmer's bedroom, we visited the bedrooms where her husbands met their own deaths.

We returned downstairs and headed to the basement down a stone staircase. We passed through an iron gate, and the temperature suddenly dropped, the air cold on my skin. The tour guide told us that this was the dungeon where Palmer held and tortured her slaves. A narrow mahogany table held half a dozen menacing-looking iron tools, including one that looked like an enormous bear trap held together by a red ribbon. When I asked what it was for, the tour guide explained that it was used as a punishment for runaway slaves. Shocked, all I could do was stare at this evil power object. The guide broke the silence: "The owners have converted the basement into a bar that you can visit during the Haunted House Night Tour." She lifted her eyebrows ominously and said,

"You might even see Annie Palmer walking the grounds." I looked at my father, who simply shook his head.

The legend of the White Witch has become its own cultural industry. There have been dozens of novels, plays, and poems written about Annie Palmer. Even Johnny Cash, who owned a vacation home in Montego Bay, wrote a song, "The Ballad of Annie Palmer," about the White Witch of Rose Hall. In fact, the Palmers lost their home in the 1820s after falling into debt and were forced to abandon the property. Annie Palmer died of natural causes in 1846. The estate fell into disrepair and was uninhabited for 130 years until it was purchased in 1977 by former Miss USA Michele Rollins and her husband, John Rollins, former lieutenant governor of Delaware. The legend of the White Witch of Rose Hall has become its own tourist attraction, bringing thousands of visitors to the estate each year.

We emerged from the dark basement, and the tour guide led us to Annie Palmer's tomb, which sits in a circle of stones. Our guide told us that Palmer's grave has become something of a destination spot for tourists interested in the occult and the supernatural. She spoke of a group of North American witches who traveled to Rose Hall years ago to perform a ritual that would allow her tortured soul to finally rest. After the ritual, she said without irony, they triumphantly announced that Palmer's soul was finally at peace. What of the enslaved Africans who were her property? Did this coven of witches pray for their troubled souls, too?

I asked the guide if there were any records about enslaved Africans who were held there, or any information about what life was like for them. She appeared troubled by the question. "There isn't much information about the slaves," she said. More accurately, there is *no* information about the slaves—no records, no plaques, no tombs or monuments to the enslaved Africans who built this plantation. No foreigners have traveled here to pray for their souls or bless their burial grounds. The tour guide said she doesn't know where their burial grounds are, but believes they are located somewhere south of the great house. No one knows their names.

I turned to look at my mother, her mouth pressed into a thin line and her arms folded across her chest. As she spoke, her voice quivered with rage. "I mean, I just find it incredible that there is all this information about this wicked woman and not a single word about the slaves who lived here and died here. I don't under-

stand what's so great about some woman who tortured her slaves
and killed her husbands and died because she was so awful," she
said. The guide said we had a point, but unfortunately that is the
way the tour is organized. Our anger was so strong that we barely
noticed that a group of German tourists had clustered around us.
They seem startled, asking their Jamaican guide to translate the
exchange.

The translator was annoyed—not with the tour guide, but with
us. "Americans always come here and want to make things personal," she said. "Slavery finished a long time ago; there is no point
in crying about the past. Nobody want to talk about that anymore."
But my mother wasn't finished. "I have a right to my opinion,"
she said. "And I don't agree with you. Slavery still matters. They
find time to get the furniture right and know everything about
this wicked woman, but don't know the name of a single slave who
worked this plantation." The translator is nonplussed: "Cry about
the past if you want. We have better things to do." She turned her
back to us and continued her translation.

The guide clapped her hands and smiled at the group, careful
to avoid our eyes. "That concludes our tour of Rose Hall," she said.
"You are welcome to visit the gift shop on your way out." We all
lifted our eyebrows in disbelief. The Germans headed to the gift
shop. We walked down the long driveway and back to the highway
to flag a taxi. We remained silent on the ride back.

## Good Hope Estate

### Trelawney Parish

Slavery produced a void in black social memory. Slavery is the reason it took me 33 years to learn the names of my great-great-grand-
father. Slavery is the reason nobody knows who is buried on the
Roehampton property. Africans held enormous value as property
for the people who owned them, but after slavery, their lives were
considered meaningless, beyond the purview of history, not worth
archiving or remembering. Slavery is the reason their lives can be
forgotten or overlooked in plantation tours and no one bats an
eye. Slavery is the reason that our history lives at the bottom of
the sea.

In January 2019 I dragged my father and husband to yet another great house. We traveled to the neighboring parish of Tre-lawney to visit the Good Hope estate. Once the largest plantation on the island, today Good Hope has become a popular tourist at-traction that is run by Chukka Adventure Tours, a multinational corporation that provides short- and long-term excursions for trav-elers in exotic locales.

Our tour guide was named Crystal. She is what black folks in the United States call "thick," curvy, with smooth, dark skin, a wide glossy smile, and a pleasant demeanor. She led us up the front stairs into the gallery, a long corridor that stretches across the length of the house linking the formal and informal drawing rooms. She pointed out the original wild-orange hardwood floors; the cloudy 18th-century mirror hanging on the wall opposite the entrance; the mahogany planter's chairs on either side of the mir-ror, which she told us were measured to fit their original owners; the exquisitely carved side tables. She pointed out the cedar shin-gles in the formal drawing room that contract to allow the breeze to pass through the room during dry weather and expand to keep out rain.

Crystal led us from the formal living room to estate owner John Tharpe's bedroom and his wife's private quarters. She made much of the mahogany bed frame, the authentic 18th-century traveling valises stacked at the foot of the bed, and the picturesque views of the valley below. We followed her into Tharpe's bedroom and personal bathroom. She claimed that Tharpe built the first jacuzzi in the 1790s to deal with his arthritis and gout, a common malady of the planter class who led pampered lives eating rich food, drink-ing rum and wine, and hosting enormous parties that lasted for weeks on end. Unfortunately, Crystal told us, Tharpe's jacuzzi was lined with lead, and after several years of soaking in this artisanal hot tub, Tharpe died unwittingly at his own hand.

We exited Tharpe's bedroom and stepped out onto the veranda, where a group of tourists was sitting down to an "authentic" Eng-lish tea offered to visitors. Everyone seated was white. Everyone serving them was black. As we passed them, their conversations turned suddenly quiet, and several guests shifted uncomfortably in their seats. I was preoccupied with my camera, and it took me a second to notice the subtle shift. When I looked up, I felt as though everyone was staring at me. I glanced at my father, who responded silently with a knowing, exasperated look on his face.

We sighed, turning our attention a few feet away to an imposing, elevated, one-story limestone structure with a wide staircase
surrounded by towering palm trees: the Counting House. According to our tour guide, John Tharpe was many things—a philan-
thropist, an inventor, a successful businessman, and, apparently,
deeply superstitious. Our guide told us that despite his success as
a planter, Tharpe was supposedly uneasy having made his fortune
on the backs of slaves. He did not like having his money counted
in his home, so he built the Counting House as an office for his
bookkeeper and never talked money or business inside his home.

During his lifetime, Tharpe enjoyed a reputation as a humanitarian who provided charitable aid to the poor and the enslaved.
Crystal told us that Good Hope was the only plantation in the area
that was not burned down during the 1831 rebellions, a reflection
of the slaves' regard for John Tharpe as a fair master. While the
rebels burned down other plantations, she said that the slaves at
Good Hope not only did not participate in the rebellion but continued working throughout the uprising.

Tharpe built a slave hospital with approximately 300 beds. It
was later converted into a birthing center, and after emancipation,
it was repurposed as a school. Today it is an aviary. Crystal told us
that Good Hope was the only plantation on the island that provided these services to slaves. She said Tharpe built the only slave
hospital on the island because he "cared about his slaves."

"I guess you could say he was a good slave master," she said.

"Ain't no such thing," I retorted. She laughed, and I couldn't
tell whether she was nervous or if this was simply part of the tour
guide script, or if she actually believed that Tharpe was a good
slave owner in need of defending. "Even a farmer," my father mut-
tered, "take care of his animals."

We continued the tour into the informal drawing room. Crystal
wanted to talk about the many dinner parties and social affairs that
were held at Good Hope. I wanted to talk about slavery. After she
finished, I asked if there are any records on site about the enslaved
men and women who may have been held at Good Hope. I know
that this information exists because several years ago, the British
government released the records detailing the reparations that the
planters received following the abolition of slavery in 1834 as well
as the annual Slave Reports that the planters completed each year
providing an account of their slave and property holdings to the

British government. Crystal was pleasant but firm: "No, we don't have anything like that here."

As we rode down the driveway, I looked at the rolling green hills that surround the house. They were covered in rocks and trees. I thought about the extraordinary amount of work it must have taken—with no heavy machinery, no electricity, just raw human energy—to clear this land and make it produce sugar. I had hoped that Good Hope would be different. That someone, finally, might be willing to tell the whole story.

After the shuttle dropped us off, we stopped so my father could take a cigarette break. As we sat under a pair of ceiba trees, I complained about the lack of attention paid to the people who built Good Hope from the ground up. "Why is there never any information about the slaves?" He exhaled and barked out a short, bitter laugh. "The slaves don't matter, Courtney. The sooner you get that through your skull, the sooner you understand that, then you will understand everything."

The sun climbed high, and the heat beat down on our shoulders. We needed food and water before we could talk about this any further. We headed to a restaurant on the main grounds to scare up some lunch, passing a group of tourists on ATVs getting ready to hit the obstacle course. My father sucked his teeth. I asked a staffer where the restaurant was, and she directed us toward the water park. We walked past a multiracial group of tourists getting ready to ride down to the park on a zip line, then descended a wide, winding staircase bordered by thick wooden rails. "They did a nice job," my father said. He's not wrong. An artificial waterfall thundered next to us, emptying into a pool that fed a slow-moving river. At the bottom, we approached a round bar covered in a thatched roof where we ordered a meal and took a seat in the Sugar House restaurant.

We ate a delicious, wildly overpriced meal of jerk pork and chicken, rice and peas, callaloo and festival, Jamaica's version of fry bread. The old Sugar House has high ceilings, and the breeze flowed through wide arcades that afforded a full view of the swimming pool. Dozens of white and a handful of Asian and Latino tourists sauntered through the corridors of the Sugar House in their bathing suits, sipping on rum punch and enjoying the warm weather. All I could think about were the people who worked this sugar house as slaves.

Suddenly I feel nauseous. I felt like a damn fool. I kept going back to these great houses as though I would discover something. I didn't know what I was looking for, but I could not stop returning to these sites that consistently break my heart. I shared this with my father. He was quiet for a moment. But when he spoke, his voice was heavy, deliberate.

"All these places, they just tell one side of the story. I don't want to see everything from the master's point of view. Slaves built all of this," he said, gesturing at the surroundings. "It just seems like an injustice."

We talked about the awkward encounter with the tourists having tea, how the logic of the plantation repeats itself across time and is embedded in the country's tourist economy. The tourism industry promises tourists a fantasy, the ability to travel back in time, to live like a planter even if just for an afternoon, without having to answer for or confront the past or acknowledge the people whose labor made that colonial fantasy possible. Tourists want to come to Jamaica to live like modern-day planters. But they don't want to talk about or think about or be reminded of slavery.

My father shook his head and picked at his food. "This is my island," he said. "But we don't own none of it. Still."

ALEJANDRA OLIVA

# At the Border, No One Can Know Your Name

FROM *ZORA*

I SPENT THE SECOND week of 2019 in Tijuana, Baja California. Or rather, I spent the nights of that week in San Diego, and every morning—as the sun rose over parking lots and outlet malls and border fences—I'd walk across the footbridge at PedWest, 7-Eleven coffee in hand, flash my passport at a Mexican border guard who, by the third day, recognized me and waved me through without even looking, and put my backpack through the X-ray machine. Just after climbing down a maze of concrete ramps that looked like a diagram of Dante's hell, past a security guard with an AK-47 strapped to his front who spent his mornings texting, I'd exit the turnstile and into a plaza with waiting taxis and 10-foot-high letters that said: MEXICO TIJUANA.

I was in Tijuana as part of a response caravan, coming from all over the country, to help meet the needs of the group of Central Americans who had walked northward from Honduras, Guatemala, and El Salvador in the thousands. By then, the midterms were over: the caravan was no longer in the news every day, anchors were no longer bloviating about the possibility of Muslims, or rapists, being smuggled in alongside pregnant mothers with small children in tow. I thought I'd be going there to help people prepare for their Credible Fear Interviews (CFIs), which determine whether someone will be allowed to apply for asylum, or be immediately deported, or to help people on the other side do actual asylum applications.

In both cases, you have a goal: a sheet of paper, a series of questions that you have to get through together. The application, the interview, provide a container for whatever is about to happen, a form for the interaction. The form, the interview, also provide a tangible measure of some kind of good. I can count the number of applications I've filled out, how many folks I've CFI-prepped, and how many people I've helped stay safe. Because that's honestly the messy truth of it: I went to Tijuana for myself. I went because I wanted to see what was happening *for myself*, because *I* wanted to be the kind of person who had gone to help. To some extent, I wanted to be able to say, "I helped this number of people, this number of people have a place to stay, some measure of freedom and safety, because of work I did."

Instead, what I ended up doing, where the need was, was in accompaniment, which means, roughly, just being there. Being there to play with kids, to hand out tamales and Styrofoam cups of coffee. Being there to hear someone's story, without a form between us, but just because they needed to tell someone, anyone, about their experiences as they cross the border. Being there to see scars, to see tears, to see immigration officials shouting, to be a warm hand on the back, or a tissue held out quietly, or a body between a person and someone else with a clipboard. Being there to gossip about other volunteers, to make jokes about eyebrow maintenance, or to commiserate about the cold or the rain. Being there to answer questions, or scan documents, or lend a telephone, to write names and numbers on arms in permanent marker. It meant being there in the plaza every morning, to be present for the calling of the numbers and the names.

El Chaparral, as the crossing is known on the Mexican side, is the central hub for most of the border-crossing activity in Tijuana. Every morning, a canopy tent is set up, surrounded by traffic cones and caution tape, and a beat-up notebook gets pulled out. This is *la lista*, a list with the names of every migrant who has declared that they want to cross the border "the right way"—that is to say, to cross, to get detained for an indefinite period of time, and during that detention, ask for, demand, insist on a "Credible Fear Interview," which is the first step in claiming asylum and their right under international law. Each name on the list is assigned a number, 10 names to a number, and every morning, a certain amount of these numbers, and the names beneath them, are called out. No one quite knows how or who manages the list—it's purportedly self-organized by the migrants, but they're closely guarded by orange-jacketed members of Grupos Beta, a semimilitary, semi-aid organization run by the Mexican government, and there are whispers of more shadowy collusions still—drug cartels, the US government.

The quantity of numbers called day by day varies—some days they barely get through 2, on other days they run through 60 in quick succession. When someone's number is called, they have a few minutes to run up to the tent and present a form of identification. Their names then get crossed off the list, and they are told when to come back. When you saw pictures on the news of children with their sleeves pulled up to show numbers scrawled on their forearms in Sharpie, those numbers were the numbers of *la lista*.

If they miss their name being called—maybe they were sick and stayed back at El Barretal, the concert venue repurposed into a shelter some 45 minutes' drive away, or didn't think they'd get to their number that day so stayed home to save the bus fare—then too bad. They have to get back in line, get another number, wait another month or two. At any given time, there are at least a few hundred people waiting, and they take across 20 to 40 individuals. When the situation is changing rapidly, day by day, and both the United States and Mexico regularly appear to be one's number on *la lista*, it has a huge impact on one's fate. It doesn't really matter when you get there; what matters is what your number is. A difference of two weeks—or a few dozen numbers—can mean crossing when the US government is shut down, and no one gives enough of a damn to put you into the system so friends and family can find you, or that Trump's wait-in-Mexico policy has been implemented, and you are released right back over the El Chaparral footbridge to a brigade of waiting reporters, dazed, and unsure of what comes next.

So in the mornings, we all gathered there: volunteers in hiking backpacks and sensible shoes, holding clipboards, people sprawled near suitcases, sipping food-stand coffee, keeping an eye on kids running shrieking through the maze of legs, and waiting for their numbers to be called. Volunteers from the United States and Mexico, migrants from El Salvador and Honduras and Guatemala and Cameroon and Haiti and Eritrea and Russia and Georgia, all trying to cross the border into the promise of California. Every morning it starts off just looking like a busy day in this particular plaza. Vendors sell tacos and smoothies, people are spread across the whole space, chatting, volunteers circling between family groups, explaining the *manita* of things you need to ace for your Credible Fear Interview, one for each finger. "Tu asilo está en tus manos," it says, and reminds people that in their CFI, they must say *what* happened, *who* did it, *why* they think it happened, whether they went to the *police,* and whether they had tried just moving *somewhere else.* Your asylum is in your hands, indeed. But as soon as the megaphone comes out, everyone clusters toward the tent, strains, leans in close.

They always start with the number, then read out the names underneath them. The crowd self-organizes into concentric rings, those with that number closest to the center, documents in hand, tense-faced, while farther out are people who know they won't be called until tomorrow or even next week—some people start showing up early, just to be sure. I usually hang back, make small talk with people who won't be crossing for a while. I sometimes get mistaken for a caravan member: volunteers stop to ask me if I know my rights in heavily accented Spanish, migrants ask me how long I've been here, what my number is, and on one occasion, the most aggressive member of Grupos Beta tells me to get my kids in order and get back in line.

And sometimes, with the magnetic power a name has, I mistake myself for a name on the list. I'll be chatting to someone, explaining the mechanics of the asylum-seeking process, or passing along a helpful phone number, and suddenly, out of the megaphone's crackly static, I'll hear my own first name. It pulls me up out of the conversational stream, turns my head, makes me pause, only to dissolve into a stranger's middle and last names, sometimes accompanied by a sudden upstretched hand, clutching papers, moving toward the tent. In this way, I hear my own name, both first and last, my mother's name, my father's and brother's name, my sister's name. My whole family is accounted for over the week I'm there, and every time, the sound catches me up.

My name, Alejandra, is an old name, a traveling name. It comes from the Greek, originally—*alexo,* "I defend," and *andros,* "man."

Its most famous carrier is Alexander the Great, who probably saw himself as a defender of men, and colonized half a continent to that end. My name is the Spanish version of it—none of the sharpness of the Greek, which came into English nearly untouched, nor the sibilance of the Italian Alessandra. Instead, it comes with the connotation and cognate of *alejar*—to move away from, to make distant.

My last name also carries this history with it. The Olivas were a family of cartographers in medieval Catalunya, among the first to chart the eastern coast of the Americas across an ocean. Funny, given where my branch of the family wound up.

What my last name *means*, though, is the hundred-year-old gnarled branches of olive trees reaching toward the sky, farmers keeping watch over their groves for generations. In other words, a symbol of an attachment to a land, to a home, and further, to watch over and guard peace where it grows. And if you lay my first and last names next to each other, like tarot cards you need to build a future from, you get a little of both. There's protection, which implies fighting, and there's the olive branch of my last name, peace and homebuilding.

This is also just my name: one my parents gave me because it "sounded strong" and another that means I'm my parents'. It's particular to me, my own minidestiny and how I've chosen to interpret it. I've never done it myself, but I have to imagine that naming a child involves some kind of imagining toward the future, a best attempt at casting a protective spell or articulating a hope.

Waiting in the plaza, I hear the names of poets, of singers, of apostles, and saints. I hear children's names that echo those of the parents, and names that have been left behind in favor of better ones everywhere but on identification documents. I hear names that have always been traveling names, and names that are only recently become it. Names in Spanish and French and Haitian Creole and Arabic and Russian and Portuguese. Names that are calling and casting forward some kind of future, names being asked to carry someone forward into survival.

After a name is called, and identification papers are checked, people are lined up against a fence surrounding a parking lot. Volunteers are allowed to be here for this part also, so we stand by them, playing tiring games with little kids to make their next few hours a little easier on their mothers, or lending out phones to make last-minute calls, or giving out phone numbers. The atmosphere is always at once tense and expectant, so much expectation and work and money and time and just sheer bodily effort has been expended to get people to this point. Some people waiting in line know what's coming next, others don't. One of the mornings, a man has a panic attack, and a volunteer stands close by him, murmuring reminders to soak up the sun and the warmth now for later, when he's in the *hielera*, asking him what cheers him up, reminding him that he can always sing a song to himself if it gets very bad.

Couples get married in this line, kiss each other goodbye in this line, cry. Mothers Sharpie phone numbers onto their children's skin—the separations have supposedly stopped at this point, but nobody wants to take any chances. Sometimes there is a priest or a pastor among the volunteers, and they'll stop and ask for prayers. Sometimes I translate, a huddle of us holding hands, the electric current of prayer running from the pastor's hand through mine and to those receiving the blessing. There are little moments of comfort: a woman passes a huge jar of Vicks VapoRub to a single man waiting in line next to her so he can use it to cover over scrapes and bumps on his legs; volunteers run to an office to get a folding chair for a man balancing on crutches and one leg.

And then the guy from Grupos Beta will start calling out names again, checking things off on a clipboard, sending people around the concrete bars that make up the fence, and onto waiting vans with metal grates across the windows. Up until this point, everything has felt ad hoc, informal, loose, but with that clipboard, and that line, there's an order put in place, the knowledge of some kind of an authority standing over it all, a knowledge that disobedience comes with consequences.

Sometimes, especially when there are mothers with young children, a volunteer or two are allowed to cross behind the fence, helping them carry their suitcases and bags and bundles, or holding hands of children to make sure they don't wander off. We try to linger as much as possible, shaking hands and hugging as they're divided into separate vans. If we aren't allowed to cross into the parking lot, we'll stand and reach our hands through the fence, sometimes squeezing fingers if we're able, waving madly through the bars if we're not. Every morning, we watch people get on the vans, watch as every last one of them gets on board, puts their luggage in the back, watch as the man with the mustache closes the door in front of them, and the grates close over. Then, as the vans slowly pull out of the lot, we stand there yelling: *Vaya con Dios! Adiós! Adiós! Buena suerte!* You can barely see their hands waving back out of the windows, faces peering back out of the glass.

Watching those vans disappear down the street always feels like watching them fall off the edge of the world. The weeks I was in Tijuana were the same weeks of the government shutdown, so after someone went into the system, they wouldn't appear in the ICE locator until days or weeks later, when a volunteer got a call that someone was stuck at a Greyhound station in San Diego without money or their things and with a fever.

San Diego is the Spanish name for Saint James, himself named after the apostle James, whose remains are rumored to lie at the Cathedral of Santiago de Compostela in Galicia, Spain. The pilgrimage to that cathedral has remained in continuous usage from the early Middle Ages to the present day. Pilgrims along the route travel for penance, for grace, for quiet and peace, for exercise, for the challenge of it, on the off chance that every step brings them closer to God. What they are literally approaching is the Cathedral of Santiago de Compostela, and a Pilgrim's Mass it celebrates twice a day, every day, where those with aching feet receive their blessing and recognition for their travels.

After leaving the Mass, many of the pilgrims keep going, another two days' walk all the way to Finisterre, Latin for "the ends of the earth." There, the land drops into the sea, and the pilgrim's path fans out into an ocean of possibilities, although the one most taken is to turn around and walk home.

There's also a spot at the edge of the American continent where the border wall plunges into the Pacific Ocean. The border wall between San Diego and Tijuana extends a good 50 feet out, far enough that you can see that if you tried to walk to its end, you'd end up past your depth. This portion of the wall has been there since the 1980s. If you drive east along it, farther into Tijuana proper, you'll start seeing portions of the wall that have only been there since October and are already beginning to rust in the sea air. On a foggy January afternoon, it looks like it could be the end of the world, but instead it's the beginning of empire, the point where someone has gone so far as to fight the sea for it.

It's also a place where God comes down: there's a church service here every Sunday, largely attended by volunteers and locals. We sing songs, take Communion, listen to a testimony from a deported veteran. We lay hands on the border wall, pray for healing, for forgiveness, to forgive—although it is hard to say if our hands on the wall are meant to heal that rift or to push the wall over.

As far as I can tell, other than the few faith leaders that come down every week from New York to work with New Sanctuary, no one is holding church gatherings for the migrant caravan. No one is blessing their journey, is washing their feet, is blessing their futures, as they prepare to walk toward San Diego, and toward the ends of the earth.

The vans with the boarded windows were headed, as best we could tell, to the San Ysidro border crossing, some 10 minutes down the road, where the people inside them would be processed and usually taken to another detention center or released after a few days sitting in an overcrowded conference room repurposed into an ad hoc facility.

The San Ysidro border crossing is named after Saint Isidro the Laborer, a Spanish saint who, in life, was a field-worker. His story is usually used to extol the virtues of a simple life of hard work, of keeping your head down and working hard, even through deplorable conditions, usually not for yourself. Miracles attributed to him are the rapid plowing of a field thanks to angelic help, and being able to redouble the amount of food from his meager allowance to feed his brothers in work. He's also the patron saint of La Ceiba, Honduras, which is where a large number of asylum seekers come from.

San Ysidro is the largest land border crossing in the world: it is estimated that 90,000 people cross it daily, both on foot and on cars, to work in the United States. It's at once as familiar and mundane a part of a daily commute as a subway turnstile, and also the final goal of people's international migration attempts.

For a week, at least, I was like a commuter, pulling my passport out of my backpack twice daily, always a few hours earlier or later than I might have liked, fighting off exhaustion, and trading small talk with border patrol agents. All of the border crossing is meant to make you feel like you're being surveilled, like you're lucky to be making it out as fast as you are: visible cameras, locked doors labeled menacingly, waiting rooms behind barely frosted glass where you can see people waiting, slumped into the poses of those held for hours without updates. While there's a brass line embedded in the sidewalk at some point in the 15-minute walk across, the whole area feels like one continuous line, one long area separate from either the outlet malls and highways on one side or the food stands and *mercaditos* for tourists on the other and given over entirely instead to the idea of government or country or surveillance or military.

I wonder how much your average person, crossing over at San Ysidro for cheap margaritas or Viagra or dental work in Tijuana is aware of these back rooms, how ominously they feel the hand of the government there, pressing down on the space, making all of it feel like the clean and law-abiding and gently menacing prelude to a prison.

Our place names mean something: who we glorify, who we want to set up on a pedestal as a matter of success, who we want to raise up as a model. San Ysidro matters, a subliminal message slung across the largest gates to our country, telling the people who walk through them to work hard and keep their heads down.

The Credible Fear Interview is seeded with trick questions. One of these is: "Do you intend to work while you are in the United States?" The only thing, the natural thing, is to say yes, of course, I need to support my family, I want to eat, I want to earn a place in a country that has made it clear they do not want freeloaders. If asylum seekers answer yes to this question, though, they may be placed in the category of "economic migrant," regardless of how credible any of the other fears they talk about. Economic migrants are not eligible to apply for asylum. If asylum seekers answer no, it not only ignores the realities of staying alive in a capitalist system, but also—although this is supposedly, on paper, fine, to any judge working in today's political realities—they will look like a freeloader, like someone just waiting for the United States' generous support net to catch them and attend to their needs, someone who won't pay taxes but will want social security. The only correct answer to the question is to answer the question standing behind it: "What I want is to be safe, I will only work just as much as I need to so I can feed my family, myself, I won't take anyone else's job. I will work as hard as San Isidro himself, and do twice the work with half the rations, will take as my patron saint the one who did not organize a movement but suffered in holy silence."

Once an asylum seeker passes their Credible Fear Interview, they are stripped of their names and instead assigned an "Alien Number." The A-number is an eight- or nine-digit number and is meant to follow a migrant throughout every step of their asylum-seeking process. This, more than any person's name, is what actually matters, how they're identified. The number is called out in court, entered into the ICE hotline to determine court dates and next steps, placed on files, petitions, and applications over and above an applicant's name. For the second time, at least, in their journey, they are stripped of their name, reduced to a number, a case file, a passport photo.

After my week in Tijuana, being home was strange. I went to classes, made dinner, walked my dog, read books, kept doing all of the usual things that make up my life. This was interrupted, sporadically, by remembering something suddenly. One morning, I cried in a coffee shop, holding hands with a friend, because he had asked me a question about how it was, had mentioned the LGBTQ caravan, and excited, I had told him how I had seen some of the last of that group cross.

And then, all of a sudden, I remembered the folks that had made family on the road and now were there at the wall, both jutting chins and rainbow flags and tear-stained goodbyes and shaky cigarettes, all of them being separated to head into their unknown new lives, remembered the long hugs, or the trans girl carefully folding her wig into her backpack and wiping her lipstick off with the back of her hand. It wasn't that I had forgotten, it was more that I hadn't spent time with it, and now, suddenly, I was.

I asked a friend about it, a friend who was much more used to accompaniment work, who was training to be a chaplain. "We're given all these things," she said, "and then we have nowhere to put them, so all we can do is archive it, put it away somewhere safe."

Part of the point of archives is to build them so others can delve. Historians often speak of the joy of the archive, finding the perfect, unexpected thing. The letters, the papers, the ephemera of the dead stay together as if by doing so, they might provide some answer, some silhouetted clue that would bring the person back to life. A close friend died a few years ago, a friend who loved books deeply, who lugged what I always pictured as steamer trunks full of them around the world, loved a good leather binding, a yellowed page. We got an email from her mother a few months later, letting us know that she was selling these steamer trunks of books to pay for a memorial video, and did we want to contribute. I kept thinking about these books, whose covers had been caressed, had been tucked under an arm I knew so well, in just such a way, being dispersed into strangers' hands, hands that wouldn't quite know how to hold them in the same way, and it felt like a separate kind of loss, or a second one. Archives prove a life, somehow.

I don't know how to become the kind of archive I want to be, don't know how to keep the details together so that no one gets lost, don't know how to tell any of it so that I can convince anyone, keep anyone safe. I'm struggling with my own "I," and where it belongs, how it's been both irrevocably altered by bearing witness and still somehow untouched and safe from suffering. I also know it's important to be an archive, to be able to surface a story that will move people into action, that might change a mind, or turn it to contemplation, at least. Here's an attempt not to put things down, but to elude the boundaries so I'm not the only one carrying them.

Here's the thing: In these pages, I have told you my name. I have told you who I am, where I come from, the things that matter to me, what I want. I have given you the outlines of a situation, I have told you the names of places, of saints. I cannot tell you the names of the people I volunteered with, the people I met waiting in line, cannot tell you their stories. At a time when the US government is detaining volunteers, lawyers, and journalists who cross the border too often, when it is treating asylum seekers more like criminals than ever, the only person I can put in danger is myself. When people are seeking asylum because someone is hunting for them by name, their name becomes not a blessing or a promise or a magic spell but a threat held against their necks. Because of this, in an essay on the importance of names, the things we name, I cannot name them.

# The Shape of Water

FROM *Outside*

THE NEW MOON is invisible, and the night is black. My sister, Jen, is paddling in the stern. Her shivering wobbles the bow where I'm sitting. Canoeing in 45-degree weather at midnight dressed in T-shirts and underwear is not our normal behavior while camping in northern Minnesota's Boundary Waters Canoe Area Wilderness in September. But an enormous black bear is on its hind legs, 10 feet away, aggressively swiping at the food pack dangling from a low tree branch at our campsite. By the sound of its grunts, it's hungry.

In our panic, we failed to forage for layers. Jen scooped up her sleeping bag and white Labrador, Sunny, I grabbed my knife and headlamp, and we tripped over ourselves to get to the water's edge, where we launched the canoe.

"Can you see it?" Jen asks while Sunny barks in docile intervals. The dog's genes have been so greatly diluted that she doesn't seem to be aware that we're facing a wild animal that can run at speeds up to 30 miles per hour and swim long distances.

"I think it's right under the pack," I say. The bear blends so well into the night that it's impossible to see, until my headlamp catches the glow of its eyes staring us down. It's dipping a clawed toe into the lake, as if testing the water to determine whether it's too cold to swim after us. There's something about its crystalline gaze that makes it look ruthless, like the grizzly that mauled Leonardo DiCaprio's character in *The Revenant*.

"Maybe we should have put the food pack on the island across from our campsite," I say, calculating how long the Clif Bar I stashed in my fanny pack will last two humans and a dog.

Combined, my sister and I have spanned almost a century paddling in the Boundary Waters, a 1.1-million-acre roadless wilderness rich with 1,100 lakes, some so massive that they take days to cross, others so small that you can swim to the other side, most filled with water so fresh that diehard paddlers don't bother to filter it. In total there are 1,200 miles of canoe routes lined by over 2,000 campsites. Jen and I visited the Boundary Waters first as tagalongs with our father, a Lutheran pastor, on his youth-group canoe trips, then on our own family's trips. Later we returned as college-age guides for Wilderness Canoe Base, a camp on Seagull Lake, at the northeastern edge of the Boundary Waters, and finally on annual trips as often as we can escape adulthood, which isn't too hard for me, but my sister is a married physician with three kids.

In college, Jen and I spent entire summers on trail, camping for weeks at a time in this wilderness, mostly guiding urban teens. I've evacuated a kid with a deep cut a day's paddle from help. I've been caught in the middle of the lake with my hair rising straight in salute to an incoming electrical storm. I've carried a canoe eight miles over the Grand Portage, a rugged historical superhighway once used by Ojibwe hunters and French voyageurs to reach Lake Superior. And I've cooked countless soggy meals over an open fire in the rain for hungry, nearly hypothermic campers.

That the bear is now destroying our pack is a result of a lack of vigilance and perfect weather. This morning was one of those rare, glorious late-summer days, with temperatures hovering around 80 and a cloudless blue sky from which the sun shone down on the water to create shimmering diamonds in the ripples. The effect was so mesmerizing that it made us lazy.

Entry points to this wilderness are tightly regulated, and some require a reservation a year in advance. Surprisingly, I found a last-minute permit to put in our canoe at a lake 18 miles northeast of Ely, a former iron-ore mining town turned tourist destination of 3,400 year-round residents that sits near the terminus of Minnesota Highway 169, almost a stone's throw from Canada. We planned to paddle quickly through two small lakes, then portage, with Jen carrying the canoe and me carrying the packs over a rocky, half-mile-long trail into the placid Kawishiwi River and beyond. Our goal was to spend a luxurious five days in the woods, veering off into remote lakes that neither of us have seen.

On our first day, we lined the canoe through riffly, benign rapids and plopped down on a granite rock for an hourlong lunch break, picking all the M&M's out of the trail mix to eat first. From there we paddled and portaged through five more lakes, passing an area deeply scarred by a 2011 forest fire where new spruce were starting their climb toward the sun. By late afternoon, we'd paddled into a small, isolated lake and found a campsite with a sprawling granite slab sloping into the water, lined by pillowy white pines and graced with a flat tent pad. The only missing element was an easily accessible tree branch strong and high enough to hang our food pack. It had been more than 20 years since either of us encountered a bear in the Boundary Waters, so we nonchalantly hung the pack on a branch precariously near our tent. We were impatient to toast the luxurious weather and reminisce away our grief over our father's recent death.

"Do you remember the time Dad hung two fishing lures in a tree and shined a flashlight to make them glow like a bear's eyes?" Jen laughed. "He scared the bejesus out of us."

"My earliest memory of the Boundary Waters is being ridiculed by my older siblings," I said.

"You probably *were* ridiculed, especially when you were six years old and came out of the tent in a frilly flannel nightgown on Lake Gabimichigami," Jen said. "Dad forgot to check what you had packed."

Jen and I laughed until tears streamed down our faces, remembering misadventures led by our father, a blond-haired, blue-eyed Scandinavian prankster and the man who ebulliently introduced his five kids to the Boundary Waters when Jen was seven and I was three. Since our parents already owned a canoe and a tent, it was by far the least expensive way for them to share the raw joy of the wilderness with us. In November 2017, Dad died of melanoma. As we watched the setting sun sparkle on the water, we had no idea that our existential loss would soon be overshadowed by the very acute loss of our food.

"The good news is that our pack will be a lot less heavy with no food in it," I say, shivering in the canoe after what seems like hours. Once the bear, tiring of its piñata game, had retreated into the woods long enough for us to feel safe about returning to the tent, we grabbed my sleeping bag and our pads and paddled to a rocky islet a quarter-mile out from our campsite.

"Now, this is living," Jen laughs as she lies down atop a cliff ten feet above the water. She falls instantly asleep, with Sunny curled at her side.

I stare up at the Milky Way. If I had been in a tent, I wouldn't have seen this mysterious blaze of billions of stars. I stay awake all night, talking to my dad in my mind, wondering if the bear is his last big cosmic joke on his daughters.

At daybreak, when Jen and I return to the campsite, the food pack is still hanging in the tree, albeit with a ragged hole in one corner. All six chocolate bars, the gorp, the cheese, the cashews, and the dried mango are gone. Baby carrots are scattered everywhere, along with four packets of oatmeal and a bag of coffee, which has a claw hole slashed through its center. The coffee filters are missing, so we find a clean pair of quick-drying underwear in our tent and use the fabric.

"It was our own damn fault," Jen says as we warm up in the sun, sipping coffee and consulting our maps to retrace yesterday's route back to the car. "This will teach us to never get too complacent."

Complacency, change, and loss are three factors that weigh heavily on me these days. As a kid, I assumed that these lakes and woods would remain pristine forever. Now, like the much fought-over Arctic National Wildlife Refuge, this wilderness, too, is in danger. The issue in northeastern Minnesota is a decades-long battle over mining.

Designated in 1964, the Boundary Waters is the most visited wilderness area in the United States, averaging 155,000 people per year—mainly anglers here to fish for walleye and paddlers who travel among bald eagles, wolves, coyotes, deer, lynx, moose, and, yes, black bears, while moving under their own power past dense pine forests and granite cliffs. When the sun goes down in late summer through winter, the northern lights often dance across the sky.

For centuries paddlers have plied these waters, starting with the Anishinabek and, later, the French voyageurs, pushing westward in search of beaver pelts and a passage to the Pacific Ocean. Because of its harsh climate and rugged landscape, northern Minnesota has also bred explorers like Will Steger and Paul Schurke, the co-leaders of the first unsupported dogsled journey to the North

Pole, in 1986. Both men still live near Ely and use this wilderness as a jumping-off point for exploration.

"I see the Boundary Waters as the first strip of wilderness leading to the Arctic," Steger told me when I visited him at his homestead outside Ely. In 1985 he traveled 5,000 miles from here to Barrow, Alaska, with a dogsled team. "It's probably as dangerous north of here as any other place I've seen," he said. "These are big lakes. If you capsize in cold water, you're not going to live."

Schurke, who owns Wintergreen Dogsled Lodge near the Boundary Waters and has led many expeditions in the Arctic and the Amazon, said, "The great thing about the Boundary Waters is that it's wilderness on a human scale. You're up close and personal every step of the way with the boreal forest, the pristine waters, the exquisite flora and fauna, and the endless shades of blue, green, and brown. It's wilderness that's accessible physically and emotionally to people of all ages."

In September 2015 adventurers Amy and Dave Freeman embarked on a yearlong paddling, dogsledding, and camping expedition in the Boundary Waters as a way to advocate for the wilderness. "One of the best parts about the Boundary Waters is that you can plop a toddler in a canoe and take them out for a sunny July camping trip," Dave told me. "But this place has moods. In spring and fall, the lakes are freezing and you're totally isolated. You can challenge yourself in ways that would be like navigating the far reaches of Canada or the heart of the Amazon. There's constantly challenging conditions, especially in the winter, when it's forty below zero and exposed skin starts to freeze in seconds."

Mining has long been a part of this region, too. South and west of the Boundary Waters, iron ore and its derivative, taconite, have been heavily extracted for more than a century. Between 1888 and 1967 Ely's five mines produced more than 86 million tons of iron ore. The amount of iron ore mined in northern Minnesota between 1892 and 2018 exceeded 5.1 billion tons, more than three-quarters of the country's total production.

The irony isn't lost on me that in 1883, my great-grandfather, Peter Pearson, left Sweden to start a new life in the mining and logging boomtown of Tower, 20 miles west of Ely. Peter logged until 1909, when he could afford to move his wife, Josephine, also a Swedish immigrant, and their growing family onto a homestead 10 miles from town.

My grandfather William spent his rare free time fishing and swimming with his eight siblings in Lake Vermilion, a 62-square-mile body of water that sits adjacent to what is now the Boundary Waters. My dad grew up two hours south in Duluth, and in 1963 he honeymooned with my mom on the same Lake Vermilion island where his parents took him on vacation as a boy. Mom and Dad returned from that trip the proud owners of a one-acre piece of shoreline property shaded by towering Norway pines. They built a single-room cabin that eventually grew into their year-round home. Every summer of my childhood I ran around that island, building forts, taking saunas, fishing for walleye, and learning how to flip Swedish pancakes over our outdoor stone fireplace. From our cabin, we could paddle and portage straight into the Boundary Waters. We took the abundance of fresh, clean water for granted. That line of thinking, I have come to realize, is dangerously naive.

Traditional iron-ore mines are almost depleted in northern Minnesota. But the Duluth Complex, an eyelid-shaped mineral deposit that begins southwest of Duluth and arcs 150 miles northeast through Superior National Forest and portions of the Boundary Waters, reportedly holds four billion tons of copper, nickel, platinum, palladium, silver, and gold that could be worth more than $1 trillion.

In 1978 the Boundary Waters Canoe Area Wilderness Act banned mining within the wilderness and established a 222,000-acre protected zone along entry corridors that would further shield fish and wildlife and ensure the highest water-quality standards throughout the entire Rainy River Drainage Basin, which also encompasses nearby Voyageurs National Park. But in 1966, preceding the ban, the Bureau of Land Management had issued two 20-year federal mineral leases on 4,800 acres of Forest Service land, one directly adjacent to the Boundary Waters and the other within five miles. Twin Metals Minnesota, a subsidiary of the Chilean conglomerate Antofagasta, eventually acquired them. The leases are within the 1854 Treaty Area, lands that the Chippewa ceded to the federal government in exchange for payments and provisions, in addition to reserving the right to hunt, fish, and gather in perpetuity.

The leases have been renewed twice, in 10-year increments. Since 2005, Twin Metals has drilled more than 1.4 million feet of core samples from 700 holes in preparation for an estimated $1.6 billion underground copper, nickel, and precious-metals mine located approximately nine miles southeast of Ely. Twin Metals' efforts stalled out during the Obama administration, after the BLM denied a third lease-renewal request in 2016, citing environmental risks. But in May 2018, the Interior Department under the Trump administration reinstated the two leases. And in December 2018, the BLM proposed to renew the leases for 10 more years, pending the completion of the agency's process, which includes reviewing 39,000 public comments in response to its environmental-assessment report. On May 15 of this year, the BLM renewed the leases.

What has many concerned about mining in this area is that the Duluth Complex metals are contained in sulfide ore, which would require a vastly different extraction process than the one used by the region's traditional iron-ore mines. When sulfide ore and its waste tailings are exposed to air and moisture, sulfuric acid is created. Water is the vehicle through which sulfuric-acid compounds can leach from mine sites and create acidic drainage, which can contaminate lakes, rivers, groundwater, and everything living in them.

"The primary difference is that the iron ore mined in Minnesota and the rest of the world is basically a sulfide mineral that has already been oxidized," says David Chambers, a geophysicist and president of the Montana-based Center for Science in Public Participation. "When you mine nonoxidized ore for copper, nickel, lead, and zinc, the waste contains sulfide minerals, which are the primary threat for acid drainage. And that's typically toxic to aquatic species at relatively low levels."

Twin Metals has not yet released the plan of operation for its proposed mine. But spokesman David Ulrich says the company is creating underground mining techniques and other design considerations that will meet or exceed local, state, and federal regulations to minimize and avoid environmental impacts. Ulrich also cites that "twenty-first-century technology allows us to do our work with remarkable precision and safety."

While sulfide-ore mining techniques vary and continue to evolve, in the past some safety records have caused concern. A 2012 study by the nonprofit Earthworks reviewed 14 US sulfide-ore copper mines—predominately open-pit—which produced 89 percent of the country's copper in 2010, the most recent data available from the US Geological Survey. All the mines experienced pipeline spills or other accidental releases. Tailings spills occurred at 9 operations, and at 13 of the 14 mines, the study says, "water collection and treatment systems have failed to control contaminated mine seepage, resulting in significant water-quality impacts."

That risk is more worrisome in Minnesota, where 6 percent of the surface area is water—more than any other state in the country. The three-million-acre Superior National Forest, which contains the Boundary Waters, holds 20 percent of the fresh water in the US National Forest System. It also borders Lake Superior, the largest and least polluted of the Great Lakes, which holds 10 percent of the world's fresh surface water. The Kawishiwi River, which my sister and I paddled, is under such threat from the potential mine that the nonprofit advocacy group American Rivers designated it the third-most-endangered river of 2018.

Now that the federal mineral leases have been renewed, Twin Metals will submit its formal plan of operation to the BLM. According to Ulrich, it expects to do that "in the near future." Once the plan is submitted, it will undergo a complex environmental review, involving multiple state and federal agencies and including time for public commentary, in order for the BLM to create a final environmental-impact statement. If the plan is approved, Twin Metals must obtain permits from various regulatory agencies. The entire process can take years. (But approval can happen. In March, after more than a decade-long environmental-review process, the company PolyMet was granted its final permit by the Army Corps of Engineers for a separate sulfide-ore copper-nickel mining project 52 miles southwest of Ely. PolyMet hasn't announced a timeline for the mining to begin.)

Last June, after the federal mineral leases were reinstated, nine northeastern Minnesota businesses and one environmental group joined forces to sue the Interior Department, seeking to overturn the decision. That lawsuit is pending. Meanwhile, Congress has requested the government documents and scientific and economic reports that administration officials used to justify the lease reinstatements.

"The Boundary Waters is being challenged by forces unlike anything we've seen in decades, if not a century," Ely native Becky Rom, a former corporate lawyer and the national chairwoman of the six-year-old Campaign to Save the Boundary Waters, recently told a group of supporters.

For people who enter the Boundary Waters from the west, the gateway is Ely, a town of hipster tourist cafés, dark taverns, trinket shops, and canoes stacked five high on outfitter lawns. Adventurers, miners, artists, and environmentalists live side by side yet are sharply divided about how to use and protect the surrounding woods and waters.

A study published in 2018 by Harvard University economist James H. Stock showed that over a 20-year period, an economy based on copper, nickel, and precious-metal mining would provide temporary growth in employment and income, but because of the boom-bust cycle of mining, it would ultimately underperform and potentially harm Ely's current economy, which is based on the outdoor-recreation industry and people moving to the area for its beauty and livability.

For its part, Twin Metals says that the mine project would create hundreds of jobs in the region. Joe Baltich, the owner of the Northwind Lodge and Red Rock Wilderness Store, is in favor of that. Baltich served as the mayor of Ely in 1985 and is the founder of the nonprofit Fight for Mining Minnesota. "The best path forward, I maintain, is solid employment through mineral resource use," he tells me over the phone. "We're sitting on a natural resource that is worth five hundred billion dollars. There's enough in that hole to make our taxes go away and still make money." And, he adds, "The anti-miners are anti-everything. When it comes down to it, they don't even want you to touch the Boundary Waters."

"It's a Chicken Little thing. 'The sky is falling, the sky is falling,'" says mining consultant Jay Mackie, who grew up in the middle of what is now the Boundary Waters Canoe Area Wilderness. (In 1965 the federal government moved his family off their land to create the BWCAW.) "Minnesota has the most stringent environmental rules in the nation," he says. "If the permits are issued according to those rules, then I have no problem with the mine going forward. I think it's for the strategic benefit of the United States, and it will benefit the area big-time. Tourism here does not pay a living wage to any multitude of people for twelve months."

If not yet outwardly hostile, the vibe in Ely is certainly tense. "Mining is of course the elephant in the town," says Steve Piragis, a lake ecologist and the owner of Ely canoe outfitter Piragis North-woods Company, one of the businesses suing the Interior Department. "The undercurrent is silent but deafening."

Mackie, who has lived in or near Ely his entire life, told me, "I'm seventy-six years old, and I have never seen the polarization like it is today. There's no reasoning, there's no communication, there's no nothing, and that's the sad part."

It's hard to live with that tension, Piragis tells me. But, he says, "Our business depends on the purity of the wilderness experience, and Ely's prosperity depends on it as well. With so few untrammeled wildlands still holding on, the Boundary Waters Canoe Area Wilderness is worth all we can do to help save it. This geographic wonder of eleven hundred lakes in a million acres exists nowhere else on the globe."

I've sent letters to politicians and participated in protests, but my only true antidote is to paddle these lakes as much as I can. Last August, a month before my sister and I set out, I rallied my boyfriend, Brian Hayden, to canoe a circuitous route bordering Canada that I frequently traveled with teen campers 30 years ago.

More of a cyclist than a paddler, Brian hasn't camped in the Boundary Waters for years. "It's exactly as I remember it," he says on the first night, as we watch a loon dive underwater while we swat mosquitoes at sundown. "The water is so crystal clear."

By day two of our four-day trip, we've paddled and portaged across six lakes into the fickle big water of 4,919-acre Knife Lake. We start early, paddling the length of it into South Arm Knife Lake, passing eight loons, a few soaring eagles, and a burn area that disorients me. In 2013 a forest fire charred nearly 200 acres, and instead of the towering pines and mountainous relief of my memories, the shoreline feels sparse and barren, like the Arctic tundra in summertime. But the water is still luxuriously cool and fresh, and the way it drizzles off my paddle with every stroke puts me in a trance I've known since I was three years old.

The beauty of a canoe trip is that when you're paddling, you have nothing else to do but take in the scenery, monitor the weather, talk, and think. I think about all the people nationwide who have stepped up in support of this wilderness. Since Becky Rom and other Ely business leaders organized the Campaign to Save the Boundary Waters in 2013, more than 340,000 Americans have publicly commented to the federal government in support of protecting it.

Last summer, 17-year-old Joseph Goldstein, a leukemia survivor from Springfield, Illinois, formed Kids for the Boundary Waters, an arm of the Northeastern Minnesotans for Wilderness organization "run by kids for kids who know and love the Boundary Waters."

"The Boundary Waters is like a gateway drug," Goldstein says in his promotional video. "It opens the doors for adventure."

Filmmaker and ski mountaineer Jimmy Chin grew up in southern Minnesota and still supports his home-state wilderness through the Campaign to Save the Boundary Waters. "It's true untouched wilderness, and its intrinsic value as such cannot be overstated," he wrote me in an e-mail. "But it's so much more. It's priceless habitat, its forests are critical for carbon capture, and it's one of the places left to offset the other wilderness areas we are destroying and giving up to mining interests."

By midafternoon, Brian and I paddle out of the burn and find a site with a rocky point that faces east toward tomorrow's sunrise. The lake is legendary for its walleye and trout, but Brian and I neglected to pack fishing rods. Instead, he jury-rigs a tarp over our cooking area while I gather water and scout a tree for the bear pack. When our chores are finished, we strip and splash into the calm, cool water, swimming laps around a small island sprouting six miniature white pines.

What strikes us both as we stretch out on the flat rock to dry off is the absence of noise—no call of a loon, gentle lap of waves, or wind whistling through the pines. Instead, we feel the eerie prestorm silence of the woods, before the sky turns pink, the clouds roll in, and all hell breaks loose in the heavens.

Until then, we lie in awed wonder.

"You don't hear silence like this anymore," Brian says, intermittently dozing off in the sun. Eventually, the rain comes in steady, gentle drops, and we suit up in raingear to explore the hill behind our campsite, where we find hundreds of plump, juicy blueberries.

"Let's leave some for the bears," Brian says, laughing at my blue teeth.

Done with our berries and a dinner of freeze-dried Thai noodles, we zip into the tent and fall asleep until the storm converges on us, the cracks of thunder and lightning flaring frighteningly close together.

The next morning breaks clear and smells clean. We dry out our gear, eat breakfast burritos, and load up to start the return paddle toward Ely via a string of six lakes that border Canada. The sun is bright, the wind is at our back, and we pass a half-dozen turtles sunning themselves on scattered rocks and a family of otters splashing along the shoreline. We don't say much, mostly because I'm struggling to feel the peace that, until now, this place has emanated. These lakes are where my great-grandfather, my grandfather, my father, my mother, my siblings and I, and countless others before and after us first felt the joy and freedom of the wilderness. If this million-acre universe of wild things and fresh, clean water is ever contaminated, I think, what else is there?

# Who Lives in Palermo Is Palermo

FROM *Airbnb Magazine*

EBOU'S HOME, FOR now, is a tall yellow building where a Catholic group houses a handful of immigrants his age. It smells of freshly washed shirts and cologne, the scent of young men striving. Ebou Mass is 18, a rangy soccer player with dark eyes and an ear-to-ear grin. He grew up in the small West African country of Gambia, and two years ago he arrived in Sicily, the mound of rock that, on a map, the Italian boot is kicking. His housemates are from Gambia, Guinea, Mali, and Senegal, and razz each other in Sicilian-inflected Italian. They trade off making dinner—Ebou takes Mondays and Thursdays—and play FIFA Soccer on PlayStation into the wee hours. They crave what they lacked in West Africa: stability, opportunity. Ebou tells me, "I don't want to become useless. I want to become something."

Four days a week, Ebou hops on his bike, which he saved 50 euros to buy, and races down Via Vittorio Emanuele. Seagulls caw, motorbikes grunt, laundry waves from balconies as if saying hello. He shoots past the markers of old Palermo, a port city that has been passed from conqueror to conqueror. The Palazzo dei Normanni, for instance, is an Arab fortress turned Norman palace turned home to the Sicilian Regional Assembly. Soon, he's in a labyrinth of alleyways in the old neighborhood of Albergheria, the center of a Palermo once again in metamorphosis.

He hurries into a restaurant named Moltivolti. It's run, in part, by an Italian native and his Zambia-born wife. Lasagna alla carne is on the menu, but so are moussaka and *mafé*, a West African peanut stew. Regulars include Sicilian attorneys but also a Ghanaian musician and his dog, Whiskey. The restaurant helps fund a suite of social justice groups. Peek into the kitchen: It's the world they're working to build. Ebou loads dishes. The head chef, who's from Afghanistan, dices tomatoes. It's Ramadan, and a cook from Morocco simmers eggs and onions for fellow Muslims breaking fast after sunset. I ask another cook, who's chopping carrots, where he's from. "Palermo!" he says, and everyone laughs.

Italy was once an exporter of people, so many that Americans think of spaghetti and pizza as our native cuisine. But in recent decades, the tides of migration reversed. The distance between Libya, a launch point for smugglers, and Lampedusa, Italy, is even shorter than the distance between Havana and Miami. In the past decade, close to 800,000 people braved passage across the central Mediterranean in rickety boats that felt more stable than the countries they'd fled. Many moved elsewhere in Europe, and the exodus to Italy has considerably slowed in the past year. Nevertheless, immigrants, only 4 percent of Italy's population in 2000, now make up about 10 percent.

Immigration has transformed the country's politics. The year after Ebou arrived, voters elevated the party of Matteo Salvini, a nationalist firebrand with a mastery of social media, to power. Until recently the interior minister, he's blocked migrants arriving by boat and made the lives of those here much harder. His party, the League, won more votes than any of its Italian counterparts in the recent European parliamentary elections, showing the resonance of his message "Italians first." Palermo, and in particular Albergheria, however, has become a center of resistance.

The Ballarò market in Albergheria awakens around 9:00 a.m. Around the corner from Moltivolti, wooden stalls and green and red canopies stretch for what feels like miles. Fishmongers arrange their wares as carefully as Gucci arranges its mannequins: mackerel fanned like playing cards; grouper fillets rolled like cigars; a swordfish head, bill skyward, as imposing as a palace guard. Tourists barter in broken Italian, cats sniff under stalls, a butcher lugs a dead pig over his shoulder, a *formaggiàio* stirs sheep's milk into cheese. One afternoon, I watched five men heave a tuna the size of a beer keg onto a table. It felt like street theater, there were so many people filming it.

Sicily has survived many conquerors: Romans, Arabs, Normans,

Spanish—and that's only a partial list. Instead of resisting their
overlords' ways, Sicilians usually absorbed them. Francesco Bellina, a Sicilian photographer, tells me one afternoon, "We don't
say, when we were invaded by Arabs or invaded by Spanish. We say,
when we were Arabs, when we were Spanish." The market, for example, is a remnant of Arab rule, the Italian version of a souk, or
bazaar. Merchants sing-shout to promote their wares, a technique
meriting its own name, *abbanniàta.* "Zucchina lunga, one euro!
Cantalupo, one thirty-nine!" A man near a wall of athletic T-shirts
joins in: "Adidas! Adidas!"

Palermo is the fifth-largest city in Italy, with nearly 700,000 people nestled between mountains and sapphire sea. Albergheria and
the bustling Ballarò market are part of its historic core. In Rome
and Florence, the historic centers can feel like outdoor museums
—impeccably preserved and quite expensive. Palermo has a similar rococo-ness, its churches, fountains, and town hall scalloped
like wedding cakes. But during World War II, the Allies bombed
Palermo, and some buildings remain a tremor away from becoming rubble.

For decades, the Mafia ruled the city, and the Cosa Nostra let
the historic core rot. Albergheria had few streetlights, sporadic
trash service; churches were dumps and alleys drug dens. Palermitans who could escape to the suburbs did. In the early 1990s,
however, voters rebelled against mob rule and elected anti-Mafia
crusader Leoluca Orlando as mayor. He later told a research team,
"I was born in Palermo. I had never been alone at night in the
historic city center. It wasn't possible. It was dark and dangerous."

Orlando's administration tried to reverse years of mob neglect
and diminish mob influence. He had help from a stream of immigrants: Bangladeshis, Sri Lankans, Ghanaians, Filipinos. Albergheria is the most integrated part of a city with more than 100
nationalities. The new arrivals were not bound by *omertà,* or the
Mafia code of silence: A few years back, immigrant shopkeepers,
fed up with mobsters demanding *pizzo,* or protection money, even
took the once unfathomable step of turning them in.

To be sure, this is a renaissance in progress. There are lights
in the neighborhood, but few street signs or tour buses. Sicily's
unemployment rate is among the country's highest, so it's hard
for newcomers to find even elder care or restaurant work. And the

Cosa Nostra lingers, running wee-hours illegal horse races (and sometimes discarding dead horses in the streets) and enlisting brutal Nigerian gangs in the drug trade.

But immigrants are Albergheria. Look up: A building-size mural of St. Benedict the Moor, one of Palermo's patron saints—and the rare black saint—presides over a soccer field in a monastic robe and cleats. Near the market, a poster for a meeting of Nigerian separatists, a flier for a club's Afro Euro Ladies Night ("Ladies B4 1:30 a.m. Are Free"). An African barber around the bend from a Sicilian barber; the African barber's line is longer. A dress shop named Imperial225, a nod to the Ivory Coast country telephone code. Most of its customers are tourists. I think of what Bellina, the photographer, said about Sicilian adaptability. "When we were African . . ."

When Ebou Mass left Gambia, at 14, he didn't know exactly where he'd end up—he just felt like, for his family's sake, he needed to go. A dictator had ruled his country since before he was born. One in three households scraped by on less than a dollar a day. Nearly 40 percent of young adults were jobless. So many Gambians had already fled that remittances made up an astonishing one-fifth of the country's economic activity. "I did not tell my sister or mother," he says. "I just left." Alone.

Ebou doesn't share much more about his odyssey; it's a specter that follows but does not subsume him. He's a devout Muslim, and he plays me a recording of his favorite prayer, the one that makes him feel safe: "In Africa, there are bad people who do bad things to people. So this is very important; it protects you from many things—from the evils." He got stuck for years in Libya, which, with no real government, is less a failed state than a circle of hell —migrants have been imprisoned, tortured, even sold into slavery. If you bring up Libya, his gaze drifts, and he steers the conversation elsewhere. I imagine he recited the prayer often.

Ebou's lawyer is a 28-year-old Sicilian named Alice Argento. For much of her adult life, dinghy after dinghy of Africans and Middle Easterners had washed up on Italian shores. To her, they were no less deserving of help than the Sicilians who carved out new lives in America decades before. "It's the same thing," she says. As a student, Alice volunteered at a center for immigrants. Then she helped start Sicily's first clinic for immigration law. She'd finished part of the Italian equivalent of the bar exam in 2017 when she was offered a job at a migrant camp.

She arrived at an airy seaside villa with a garden and 25 boys eyeing her suspiciously. Their journeys had taught them not to trust. Ebou was the youngest, and perhaps the wariest. "I approached him in Italian," she recalls. "He replied in English, asking me if I was insulting him." It took him weeks to thaw. Then he and Alice sat down to discuss his case, and, she says, "It was like he finally could unload."

Alice tried to explain the bureaucratic process that awaited the boys, something that baffles even adults. At one point, she asked them to draw a place where they felt protected—the way she believed Italy should make them feel. Many drew homes. Ebou drew a soccer game. ("I'm a good striker," he tells me.) When he learned that he couldn't start school right away because it was summer, he was crushed. "That was my dream," he says. "To go to school."

Most of Alice's clients are boys, ages 15 to 18. As we stroll through Albergheria one night, several run over with huge smiles. "Mi raccomando!" she half-teases them, an Italian maternal admonishment to not do anything stupid. A few years ago, the boys mainly came from Gambia, Senegal, Ivory Coast. More recently, they've come from Mali and Guinea. (The comparatively few girls are usually Nigerian and victims of sex trafficking.) If their country was at war, they asked for asylum status. If it was merely in shambles, they asked for a humanitarian protection permit, which lasted two years and could be renewed.

Back home, the boys' families often assume they're rich. They are gravely mistaken. The fall after Ebou arrived, the migrant camp where he met Alice closed. The next one ran out of food, and the boys panicked. "My father said, 'Stop, I won't hear it anymore, let's go to buy pizza,'" Alice says. That camp closed, too. By the winter, Ebou had moved six times. Back in Africa, his mother died (his father died years before). His older sister called to tell him. He says, "This was the saddest news I had ever had in my life." He didn't go back. He dreams instead of bringing his sister and her son to Europe. For now, Ebou relies on Alice and her parents for advice and reassurance; if she gets upset with him (because, say, he skipped school), he calls her mom instead.

I meet Ebou one day at a park in sight of the palace. Graffiti dances around the base of an obelisk marking the birth of the Italian state. The grass is parched, the bushes in need of trimming. Three kids shriek on a swing set. "Do you feel like a real Italian?" I ask. "No," he says. Ebou is having a rough day. He'd had a spat over chores with a staffer at his building. And though he'd been dishwashing at Moltivolti for months, he got the internship through a nonprofit, and his pay was delayed. He was so defeated, he ditched school again. Even so, his determination flickers. He says, "My mom told me this: I will never suffer in my life. And I believe it. And wherever I go, there will be a person who will try to take care of me and help me."

After the ascent of Salvini's party, in 2018, Italy rolled out new immigration rules. "Everything is different now," Alice says. "Everything." Fewer migrants have been granted asylum. Italy also largely stopped issuing new humanitarian permits. As tens of thousands of old ones expire, those who can't find work on the books or get other papers will become undocumented immigrants—or, as Italians call them, *clandestini*. Just before the changes, Ebou had his humanitarian permit hearing. The permits were issued to immigrants who didn't qualify as refugees but were deemed vulnerable in some other way. As an orphan who'd endured so much so young, Ebou had a strong case, but Alice knew that in immigration proceedings, there are no shoo-ins. Ebou learned the result at home; he called Alice, but he was too overwhelmed to speak and handed the phone to a staffer. She told Alice, who was driving: he got it.

My visit to Palermo coincides with one from Salvini. It's a big day for the town: the anniversary of the death of a judge named Giovanni Falcone. Falcone helped dismantle the Cosa Nostra, locking up more than 300 mafiosi during the famed Maxi Trial, so named because of its enormity. On May 23, 1992, as Falcone was traveling in a motorcade outside Palermo, Mafia hit men detonated a bomb and killed him, his wife, and three bodyguards. The way Sicilians mark the day reminds me of the Fourth of July—appropriate, since the cruelty of Falcone's death emboldened Sicilians to rise up against mob tyranny.

It's a bright afternoon, heat radiating off the pavement. I'm at a café on Via Luigi Pirandello, in a middle-class part of town. Almost out of nowhere, hundreds of people materialize—I hear them before I see them, chanting in Italian, "We hate indifference!" Children grip red, green, and white balloons; they wave signs that say MAFIA NO; they raise black-and-white photos of mob victims in silent tribute. As the procession nears, people in the six-story buildings flanking the street unfurl white sheets over their balconies, just as Palermitans did in protest after Falcone's death.

While 23 percent of voters in the south supported Salvini's party in the European parliamentary elections, on the eve of his visit I spot quite a few protest banners: WE ARE ALL PEOPLE and NO MAFIA, NO RACISM, NO NEOFASCISM. Near the port, a few dozen teenagers huddle outside their school, waving a giant white banner with red lettering: SALVINI, WE ARE HERE, WHAT DID YOU WANT TO TELL US?! Earlier in the month, education officials had suspended one of their teachers; her students, as part of a Holocaust remembrance event, had made a video comparing Salvini's immigration policies to those of Benito Mussolini.

Until recently, Salvini's party was called the Northern League, and it dreamed of seceding from Italy to create a republic in northern Italy called Padania. It demonized, in particular, the poorer, less educated southern Italians who journeyed north seeking work. They were *terroni*—ill-mannered farmers. Dirt people. When Salvini came to Palermo in 2015 to make amends, crowds greeted him by hurling tomatoes and eggs.

Salvini defends his crackdown as a way to keep Italians safe. "If I could reduce the number of these crimes and the presence of illegal immigrants, they can call me racist as much as they want," he told *Time* magazine last year. Like President Trump, he also frames the issue around economics. "Italians can't compete with illegal workers who are being exploited. So to restore dignity to work, we must control immigration."

The night before the Falcone remembrance, I stop by Mayor Orlando's office. He won reelection two years ago and has fashioned himself as a foil to Salvini. His aide tours me around the town hall, a pastiche of gold leaf and chandeliers. We pause at a sculpture of the Genius of Palermo, a city protector of sorts: a crowned, bearded man staring into the middle distance as a snake suckles his bare chest. "Palermo, the golden dell," an inscription reads in Latin, "devours hers and feeds the foreigners."

Orlando is an imposing presence; his hands act out his words. Palm fronds fan out behind his paper-strewn desk; to his left sits a framed letter from Pope Francis, applauding the mayor's advocacy. For example, he refused to carry out part of Salvini's signature immigration plan. Orlando joked, "The army did not arrive. If you see some soldiers, please call me." He smiles.

Orlando sees the new arrivals as integral to Sicily's economy and culture, part of, as he once told Al Jazeera, "our Mediterranean soul." He's even set up an advisory group of migrants to make sure they have a voice in city politics. Denying them residency only forces them into a life of illegality and exploitation, he says. "We have no migrants in Palermo. If you ask me how many migrants are in Palermo, I don't reply one hundred thousand, one hundred and twenty thousand. I reply, No one. Who lives in Palermo is Palermo."

Another evening, the sunset pinking the sky, I walk up the street from Moltivolti to a nearby Catholic-run community center. Local Muslims had gathered for iftar, the meal that ends the daily Ramadan fast, at the charity's invitation. Their imam was born in New York and moved to Sicily as a kid. The group nibbles on Italian pastries instead of dates, gulps water from plastic cups, drapes prayer rugs across the linoleum floor. Men slip off their shoes, and women scarf their hair. They pray. Once finished, they dig into boxes of pizza stacked high on a folding table, pink lettering beckoning BUON APPETITO.

Ebou hunches over the sink in the Moltivolti kitchen, wearing a red T-shirt with blue lettering that says NEW YORK and a thin gold chain. It's a tight space fragrant with olive oil; knives thwack-thwack, pots clang. This is Ebou's first job, and before he started, he worried he'd be treated like a dishrag—worn to tatters, then discarded. Many immigrants are. The head chef, Mohammed Shapoor Safari, recalls slaving under the table at another restaurant years ago. As vexing as the job was, it felt like proof that his trek—from Afghanistan to Pakistan to Iran to Turkey to Italy—had been worth it. When he was let go, "I just felt like I wanted to cry, because I missed my family. For three or four minutes, it was as if I couldn't remember my name."

Moltivolti opened five years ago. Safari knew the founders well enough to get work laying bricks and painting walls; he convinced them he belonged in the kitchen by whipping up ravioli and a meaty, oniony Afghan curry called *doppiaza* (which is still on the menu). Now, of 28 employees, half are immigrants. Their T-shirts say, in Italian, MY LAND IS WHERE MY FEET TOUCH. The menu is divided into Sicilian dishes ("North Africa," I hear someone joke) and African et al. ("South Sicily"). When Ebou smells the peanuty Senegalese *mafé*, he's home.

Ebou likes the job. He dabbles in prep cooking. When he goes on an herb run and forgets basil, no one yells. "They are so kind," he says. If Italy's immigration laws remain intact, when his permit expires, he will likely need full-time employment to remain a legal resident. This is so hard to find that, at an Albergheria construction site, I saw a sign warning hopefuls: NO JOBS. (And indeed, by the end of the summer, Ebou was no longer working at Moltivolti.)

During my visit, Ebou invites my translator, Giulia, and me to dinner. Because of Ramadan, it's late, and the streets near his building are so dark that I can barely make out an Air Italy billboard. We bring cannoli and a bottle of Coke, Ebou's favorite; beaming, he shows off a white ALWAYS COCA-COLA T-shirt that Alice gave him earlier that day.

In the kitchen, he's effortless, a musician tuning his instrument. He peels onions with one hand, knife flying like an extra thumb. He tastes his sauce, which tomatoes the air; sprinkles salt and pepper; waits as the flavors mature, thumbing through his phone, checking on friends scattered across continents. At last, he spoons out three plates, and we sit at a table in the living room. He'd made a dish called *chus:* fried chicken, basmati rice, and a tomato-and-onion sauce. It's his mom's recipe, and it's delicious.

*GIULIA ALAGNA CONTRIBUTED TO REPORTING.*

# Climate Signs

FROM *The New York Review of Books*

*For Mik*

OUR SON'S LOVE of trains was once so absolute I never foresaw it could be replaced. New York City is a marvelous place to live for train-obsessed boys. When he was three and four, we spent many a rainy day with no particular destination, riding the rails for the aimless pleasure of it, studying the branching multicolored lines of the subway map, which he'd memorized like a second alphabet. I'd hoist him up to watch the dimly lit tunnel unfurl through the grimy front window of the A train's first car as it plunged us jerkily along the seemingly endless and intersecting tracks. Some rainy mornings, our destination was 81st Street, where we exited the B or C with dripping umbrellas and his little sister in tow to enter the American Museum of Natural History.

There, at a special exhibition called *Nature's Fury,* our son's attention turned like a whiplash from trains to violent weather. Even before this show, the museum demanded a certain reckoning with the violence of the Anthropocene. What grown-up wouldn't feel a sense of profound regret confronting the diorama of the northern white rhinoceros in the Hall of African Mammals, or the Hall of Ocean Life's psychedelic display of the Andros Coral Reef as it looked in the Bahamas a century ago? Meandering the marble halls of the Natural History Museum is like reading an essay on losing the earth through human folly. Yet none of its taxonomies of threatened biodiversity, not even the big blue whale, moved my kindergartner like *Nature's Fury.*

The focus of the immersive exhibition was on the science of the worst natural disasters of the last 50 years—their awesome destructive power and their increasing frequency and force. Accompanied by a dramatic score of diminished chords and fast chromatic descents, the exhibit meant to show how people adapt and cope in the aftermath of these events, and how scientists are helping to plan responses and reduce hazards in preparation for disasters to come.

"Are they too young for this?" my husband questioned, too late. Our impulsive boy had darted ahead and cut the line to erupt a virtual volcano. I supposed it made him feel less doomed than like a small god that, in addition to making lava spout at the push of a button, the kid could manipulate the fault lines of a model earthquake, set off a tsunami, and stand in the eye of a raging tornado.

In the section on hurricanes at a table map of New York, the boy was also able to survey the sucker punch that Hurricane Sandy delivered to the five boroughs. This interactive cartography was a darker version of the subway map he'd memorized, detailing the floodplains along our city's 520 miles of coast. I can still see my boy there, his chin just clearing the table's touchscreen so that his face was eerily underlit by the glow of information while my girl crawled beneath. Seventeen percent of the city's landmass flooded, leaving 2 million people without power, 17,000 homes damaged, and 43 people dead. On the map, the water was rising to overtake the shorelines at Red Hook, Battery Park, Coney Island . . . All across the Big Apple, the lights were going out.

"Come away from there," one or the other of us called uneasily, because we weren't prepared to confront what climate change would mean for our children, to say nothing of our children's children. The boy was five at the time. The girl was three. In their lifetimes, according to a conservative estimate in a recent report by the New York City Panel on Climate Change, they could see the water surrounding Manhattan rise six feet. We pulled them away from that terrifying map of our habitat to go look at dinosaur bones—an easier mass extinction to consider because it lay in the distant past.

What strikes me now as irrational about our response isn't our ordinary parental instinct to protect our kids from scary stuff. It was our denial. Their father and I treated that display as a vision we could put off until later when it clearly conveyed what had already transpired. "We are now faced with the fact, my friends, that tomorrow is today. We are confronted with the fierce urgency of now," preached Martin Luther King Jr. in 1967 in one of his lesser-known sermons, "Beyond Vietnam: A Time to Break Silence." He may as well have been speaking on climate change. Sandy made landfall in 2012, the year after the boy was born, while I was pregnant with the girl. It gave a preview of what the city faces in the next century and beyond, as sea levels continue to rise with melting ice sheets. The storm exposed our weaknesses, and not just to flooding. I remember that when the bodegas in our hood ran out of food, some folks shared with their neighbors. But when the gas station started running out of fuel, some folks pulled out their guns.

As much as we may worry about our kids' future, it's already here.

Avoiding the map didn't annul its impact on our son. The subject of storms had gripped his consciousness as surely as his author-father's had been gripped by horror films. That part of the boy's brain that previously needed to know the relative speed of a Big Boy steam engine to a Shinkansen bullet train now needed to know what wind speed differentiated a category 4 hurricane from a category 5. Soon enough, and for months afterward, Mr. Wayne, the friendly librarian at the Fort Washington branch of the New York Public Library, would greet our boy with an apology. There were no more books in the children's section on the subject of violent weather than those he'd already consumed.

At bedtime, while his sister sucked her thumb to sleep, I offered my son reassurance that we weren't in a flood zone; that up in Washington Heights—as the name suggests—we live on higher ground. "You're safe," I told him.

"But the A was flooded during Sandy," he reminded me, matter-of-factly. "The trains stopped running and the mayor canceled Halloween." Then he'd go on rapturously about the disastrous confluence of the high tide and the full moon that created the surge, while I tried to sing him a lullaby.

Eventually, a different fixation overtook extreme weather, and another after that. Such is the pattern of categorical learners. It may have been sharks before the *Titanic,* or the other way around —I've forgotten. Two years have passed since we saw *Nature's Fury;* a year and a half since our president led the United States to withdraw from the Paris climate accords. The boy is 7 now, what Jesuits call "the age of reason." The girl is 5 and learning to read. If current trends continue, the world is projected to be 1.5 degrees Celsius warmer than preindustrial levels by the time they reach their late 20s. The scientific community has long held 2 degrees Celsius to be an irreversible tipping-point. Two degrees of global warming, according to the UN's Intergovernmental Panel on Climate Change (IPCC), marks climate catastrophe.

At 2 degrees, which is our best-case climate scenario if we make seismic global efforts to end carbon emissions, which we are not on course to do, melting ice sheets will still pass a point of no return, flooding New York City and dozens of other major world cities; annual heat waves and wildfires will scrub the planet; drought, flood, and fluctuations in temperature will shrink our food supply; water scarcity will hurt 400 million more people than it already does. Statistical analysis indicates only a 5 percent chance of limiting warming to less than 2 degrees. Two degrees has been described as "genocide."

In fact, we're on track for over 4 degrees of warming and an unfathomable scale of suffering by century's end. By that time, if they're lucky, our children will be old. It's pointless to question whether or not it was ethical to have them in the first place since, in any case, they are here. Their father writes about imaginary horrors. For my part, I'm only beginning to see that the question of how to prepare our kids for the real horrors to come is collateral to the problem of how to deal as adults with the damage we've stewarded them into.

What helped me to see this was a road sign. I came across it this fall in Harlem's St. Nicholas Park two weeks before the release of the UN's Climate Report that concluded we must reduce greenhouse gases to limit global warming to the 1.5-degree threshold. The sign was part of another exhibit, but I didn't know that when it stopped me in my tracks on my way to work. It was one of those LED billboards you normally spot on a highway, alerting drivers to icy conditions, lane closures, or other safety threats ahead. Oddly enough, the sign was parked in the grass two-thirds up the vertiginously steep slope to City College. How did that get there? I wondered. More surprising than the traffic sign's misplacement was its message:

CLIMATE DENIAL KILLS

St. Nicholas Park recently ranked among New York City's top five most violent parks, as measured by high rates of crime. I was assaulted there once by a girl in a gang who coldcocked me in the face. This sign hit me almost as hard. I felt like someone had punched through from another dimension to shock me awake. Was I seeing the sign correctly? Yes. It repeated its declaration in Spanish:

LA NEGACIÓN CLIMÁTICA MATA

Every couple seconds the sign refreshed, unspooling a disquieting, if strangely droll, string of warnings:

NO ICEBERGS AHEAD
50,000,000 CLIMATE REFUGEES
CAUTION
CLIMATE CHANGE AT WORK
ABOLISH COAL-ONIALISM

and so on.

The familiar equipment of the highway sign gave authority to the text. Because it was parked in the wrong place, the sign appeared hijacked—as in a prank. I understood myself to be the willing target of a public artwork but not who was behind it. The voice was creepily disembodied. I admired its combination of didacticism and whimsy. But even with its puns, the sign was more chilling than funny. The butt of the prank was our complacence, our lousy failure to think one generation ahead, let alone seven, as is the edict of the Iroquois' Great Law.

For several minutes, I paid humble attention to the sign, unsure how to react. The only practical guidance it offered was VOTE ECO-LOGICALLY—something achievable given the upcoming midterm elections. But what else was the sign telling us to do? My individual practice of composting and giving up plastic bags felt lame when the headlines were warning of genocide and civilization's end. I began to feel exposed, standing there, and briefly considered that I might be on *Candid Camera*.

I looked around the park for help, half-hoping the artist might pop out from behind a tree to explain him- or herself. I wanted to process the work's messaging with somebody else. It signaled the tip of a melting iceberg whose magnitude surpassed my cognition. How to move past the paralyzing fear that whatever we do is too little, too late? The trouble here was one of scale. Sadly enough, no one else in the park that morning seemed engaged by the sign at all. And so I snapped a picture of it with my iPhone and shared it on Twitter.

Almost immediately, a stranger with the handle @AwakeMik replied with a photo of an identical sign he'd just discovered in Sunset Park, Brooklyn, while walking his dog, Chester, named after Himes. VOTA ECO-LOGICALMENTE, it said. His wide-angle photo was better than my close-up shot because he'd framed the sign at dusk in the broader context of the cityscape.

I felt a sudden kinship with this man, Mik Awake, who'd noticed the same thing I had, from a broader perspective. The two signs were clearly of a piece. Intrigued, I did some internet sleuthing and discovered that they were part of a larger series by environmental artist Justin Guariglia, in partnership with the three-year-old Climate Museum and the Mayor's Office. All in all, there were 10 climate signs staged in public parks across the city's five boroughs—many of these in low-lying neighborhoods near the water, most vulnerable to flooding.

The Climate Museum's website described Guariglia's project as an effort to confront New Yorkers with how global warming affects our city now; to "break the climate silence and encourage thought, dialogue and action to address the greatest challenge of our time." To that end, the signs' messages were programmed with translations in languages spoken in the various neighborhoods in which they appeared: Spanish, French, Russian, and Chinese. Thus embedded in the diverse cultural landscape of New York City, the billboards projected a forecast of what we stand to lose with the rising sea. The Climate Museum's website also offered a city map indicating the locations of the 10 signs, with clear directions via public transportation to each. Finally, it introduced an adventure: anyone who could prove they'd visited all 10 signs would receive a prize.

I studied the map with a mix of obligation and gratitude. It reminded me of my earlier failure to process reality at the American Museum of Natural History. Here was an opportunity, perhaps, to do better—if not with my kids yet, then at least with another concerned citizen. I decided to take the artist's invitation to heart. On a lark, I asked Mik Awake if he'd be willing to navigate Guariglia's climate signs with me. Amazingly, given the time commitment, the soberness of the topic, the complicated semiotics, and the distance the pilgrimage would carry us, he said yes.

We had until midterm Election Day when the signs were scheduled to come down. By visiting one or two a week, between September and November of this unseasonably warm fall, we managed to witness them all. I've come to think of this period of my life — part scavenger hunt, part stations of the cross — as "Thursdays with Mik." By now we are no longer strangers, but friends. What follows is an account of our journey to grasp the effects of global warming on the place where we live.

The first sign Mik and I saw together sat at the end of Pier 84 in Hudson River Park, halfway between his neighborhood and mine in what was commonly known as Hell's Kitchen. Thanks to real estate development, it's now often referred to by the tonier names of Clinton and Midtown West. To get there, I took the downtown A to 42nd Street and pushed west through the crush of tourists gazing up at the digital billboards of Times Square, wondering if those poor suckers knew they were looking at the wrong signs.

Only someone not from New York City would describe Times Square as the heart of the metropolis. Most of us who are native to the city steer clear of it, especially on New Year's Eve. But today, it couldn't be avoided. Passing through the clogged commercial district on my mission, I recalled an unnerving image from the short film, *two°C* by French filmmaking duo Menilmonde. New York City is depicted in this movie as an Atlantis in the making, subsumed by the rising waters, with the Hudson and East Rivers converging to swallow a Times Square devoid of anyone to watch the blinking ads.

Is it possible to be haunted by the future as well as the past? The precise and intimate term for this feeling is "solastalgia," the desolation caused by an assault on the beloved place one resides; a feeling of dislocation one gets at home. I suppose one might feel this in the case of war, domestic abuse, or dementia, but the difference with environmental upheaval is the ingredient of guilt. I walked past the bright theater marquees and the slovenly Port Authority bus station, the brownstone on 43rd Street where my friend C. had thrown me a baby shower in her rent-controlled garden apartment, past the high-rise on 10th Avenue where I'd screwed my high school boyfriend on his parents' ratty foldout couch—past my former selves, and the ghosts of 20th-century peepshows and 19th-century slaughterhouses, to join my partner at the waterfront.

Here is Mikael Awake, a few weeks shy of his 37th birthday. He's the kind of guy who's at ease quoting Paul Éluard ("La terre est bleue comme une orange . . .") and whose friends ask him to officiate their weddings—a contemplative, caring, stylish man; the hardworking son of Ethiopian immigrants. Mik's last name is pronounced "ɑ-wə-kə," but its meaning in English fits his character. That is, the brother is politically "woke," stumping hard this election cycle for Stacey Abrams to become the nation's first black female governor down in Georgia, his home state. Mik grew up as one of few kids of color in the schools of Marietta. When I asked him what that was nearby, he joked, "Racism," before conceding, "Atlanta."

According to the logic of social media that has shrunk the planet, we're separated by only one degree, sharing several acquaintances and interests in common. Both of us are writers, and teach writing at CUNY—a vocation, we agree, that brings us closer to the city by putting us in touch with its strivers. We may eventually have crossed paths another way. He'd been following me on Twitter. But it was the climate signs that brought us together.

My instinct is to focus my lens on Mik, but, unwittingly, he's already taught me to take a step back. Still, the viewfinder can't capture it all. What I mean to show is too big. I settle for framing the tension between the human, the landscape, and the sign. This method will become our pattern.

To the right of the frame floats the former aircraft carrier USS *Intrepid;* to the left lies the Circle Line cruise ship departure site. The Hudson rolls by behind Mik. Beneath the river, the busy Lincoln Tunnel connects to New Jersey on the other side. Flooding of the tunnels into and out of Manhattan (along with flooding of the subway and energy infrastructure) have been identified as serious vulnerabilities in the *Climate Change and a Global City: Metropolitan East Coast Report,* a pre-Sandy document that examined climate-change impacts in New York.

Cyclists zip along the two-lane greenway in front of Mik. The bike path is but one perk of Hudson River Park, which was refurbished from the crumbling docks of a once grubby industrial waterfront as part of the city's renewal wherein, over the last generation, warehouse districts have steadily transformed into luxury housing. Sandy wreaked $19 billion in damage to the city, yet the rate of development along our coastlines has only increased since that superstorm. We have more residents living in high-risk flood zones than any other city in the country, including Miami. Local city-planning experts are rightly concerned about how we'll cope when the next great storm surge inevitably strikes.

After Sandy, Mayor Bloomberg declared that New Yorkers wouldn't abandon our waterfront. He, and de Blasio after him, have worked to revise codes to make new buildings more climate-resilient with flood-proofing measures such as placing mechanical equipment on higher floors, but each mayor has seen real estate interests in waterfront development as too precious a political constituency to suppress. In my picture, Mik faces 12th Avenue, across which, and slightly southeast, construction on the glassy towers of the huge Hudson Yards project is topping out, surrounded by a phalanx of cranes. Hudson Yards is one of many recent projects sited within the New York City climate change panel's projected floodplain for 2050, when sea level rise could reach 2.5 feet —meaning that all the tall buildings Mik and I behold cropping up at the waterline are shortsighted in that, gradually, they'll find their foundations inundated.

Investors tend to think in the short term, in the length of mortgages, according to the timelines of insurance policies. Even the newspaper headlines are guilty of this fallacy, tending to present Armageddon in the near future. Whether we frame it as 12 years away, or 30, or 50, or refer to ourselves as the last generation that can stop climate change, we seem to keep pushing back the clock, as if the countdown to the ball drop has only just begun. But when did the clock start ticking?

Over Mik's shoulder the sign flashes its warning. How well the city's personality coheres in the bustling elements that surround my new friend: defense, tourism, transport, development, expansion, confrontation, bullheadedness, and art. Yet my picture, like that short disaster film, is eerily pastoral, as if Mik were the sole survivor of nascent catastrophe.

His face registers concern. I won't venture a mutual diagnosis of eco-anxiety, the emerging condition described by the American Psychological Association as the dread that attends "watching the slow and seemingly irrevocable impacts of climate change unfold,

and worrying about the future for oneself, children, and later generations." I'm no clinician and such a prognosis pales in comparison to the plight of a person in Puerto Rico still without power
post-Maria, or a farmer in India driven to suicide by his perennially scorched crops. We're privileged not to have been directly hit
yet, as have so many in the Global South. It's our temporary luxury
to consider global warming intellectually rather than materially.
We have, as black Americans, each in our own way, more immediate threats to battle. Nevertheless, Mik confides in me that his
stress makes him compulsively pick at his face. I confess to habitually clenching my shoulders, and the nerve pain resulting from the
Atlas-like tilt in my neck. The stimuli are not exaggerated. The glaciers are melting. The water is rising. These are our body's signs.

The second and third signs we toured were located on Governor's
Island. Situated in New York Harbor between Lower Manhattan
and Brooklyn, the island was used from 1755 to 1996 as a military post by the US Army and Coast Guard. Dredged debris from
the harbor and landfill from subway excavation were used in the
early 1900s to more than double the island's size—an illustration
of the innovative if hubristic remaking of topography that's char-
acterized the city for centuries. In 2003 the city bought Governor's
Island from the federal government for a dollar. Since its transfer
to the people of New York, the island has been used as a public
park, accessible by ferry to day-tripping civilians like us.

There's a public school on this island. An organic farm. Artists'
studios. Playgrounds. A 57-foot slide. A "glamping" (glamorous
camping) retreat. There were even at one point a pair of friendly
goats named Rice and Beans, and a miniature golf course. Its elevated hills were designed with climate change in mind. The cin-
ematic view it offers of Lower Manhattan is glorious—the stuff of
a Gershwin score. I had never been to Governor's Island before,
though it's a place my children would fancy. The October day Mik
and I made our visit was warm enough for shorts.

To the left of my picture's frame stands the circular sandstone
fort, Castle Williams, built in 1811 to defend the rich Port of New
York against a naval assault that never came. Mik looks past the
climate sign toward the dense cluster of buildings of the Financial
District; at the ghost limbs of the Twin Towers and the arrogant

blue spike of the Freedom Tower sticking up like a middle finger. That precious spit of land beneath Mik's gaze seats a $500
billion business sector that influences the world's economy. Of
course, the Financial District wasn't the only part of Lower Manhattan devastated by Sandy. Within a 10-mile perimeter, 95,000
low-income, disabled, and elderly residents suffered because all of
downtown—like Governor's Island itself—lies in a flood plain. In
downtown Manhattan, as in other low-lying neighborhoods at the
water's edge, communication and transportation were cut off, infrastructure was damaged or wrecked, and thousands were without
running water and power. Mik and I contemplate the irony of the
prior use of Governor's Island for defense when the real threat of
attack to the city is the water surrounding it.

Also under Mik's gaze is a tidal gauge off the southern tip of
Manhattan. Measurements taken there indicate roughly a foot of
sea level rise in the last century. Climatologist Cynthia Rosenzweig,
who served on the IPCC, has compared sea level rise to a staircase. "The twelve-inch increase in NY Harbor over the last century
means we've already gone up one step. When a coastal storm occurs, the surge caused by the storm's winds already has a step up.
Continuing to climb the staircase of sea level rise means we'll see
[a] greater extent and frequency of coastal flooding from storms,
even if the storms don't get any stronger, which they are projected
to do," she said in a post-Sandy interview for Climate.gov.

So what are city planners doing to protect Lower Manhattan?
In Sandy's wake in 2013, the Department of Housing and Urban
Development's Rebuild by Design competition invited proposals
for climate-resilient flooding solutions to protect against future
storms. One of the seven finalists' designs, Bjarke Ingels's BIG U, a
vast 10-mile barrier system with a series of levees, is now underway,
with the first phase of construction planned to begin in the spring.

Naysayers argue that such barriers won't save Howard Beach
and other parts of southern Queens and Brooklyn; that a sea wall
enclosing the narrows of New York Harbor still leaves Long Island
in trouble, that these halting projects to save the city will take too
long, or fall short of the watermark, shifting the burden to stay
afloat onto our children. Meanwhile, students at the high school
on Governor's Island are gamely helping to restore the ecosystem
of the harbor with oysters, which, before they were killed off with

the dumping of toxic waste and raw sewage into their reefs, once served as the base that made this estuary one of the most dynamic, biologically productive, and diverse habitats on the planet. It occurs to me that this hopeful act contradicts the apparently anthropocentric sign, HUMAN AGENDA AHEAD, insofar as other forms of life are being taken into account.

"What do you think this sign means?" Mik asked me. It was the most enigmatic of Guariglia's messages. The signal seemed to suggest both itself and its opposite—accusing the emblem of capitalism in the background of a greedy agenda that's laid waste to the planet, while perhaps, at the same time, appealing to its beholder to be more humane, putting people before profit.

Later, I called the artist at his Brooklyn studio to ask about the climate signals, and to clarify this one in particular. "That one came out of the notion that we live in a corporatocracy," Justin Guariglia explained, quoting the bon mots that it's simpler to imagine the end of the world than the end of capitalism. "Corporations want this news hidden. Big business has had next to no incentives to care for the earth, though you'd think the preservation of the human race would be incentive enough." The project was meant to compel people to think ecologically, he told me, and was influenced by the object-oriented ontological writing of ecophilosopher Timothy Morton, as well as the text-based work of neoconceptual artist Jenny Holzer:

> We need to get more human-focused but not more anthropocentric. As a human, I'm on the same ontological playing field as garbage and galaxies—not above. As a visual artist, I'm trying to engage with a huge thing operating on several levels requiring several languages. This is an exceptionally urgent problem. It needs to get out into the broad public and raise consciousness. That's the responsibility of artists and writers. Not the corporations.

I know from a photograph that Guariglia's left arm is tattooed with a wavy line representing 400,000 years of carbon dioxide levels in the earth's atmosphere. It spikes at his pulse point and encircles his wrist like a handcuff. He embodies this stuff. Why the road signs? I asked.

"The medium of the highway sign is embedded with so much information," he said. "It's hyperaccessible, and a symbol of authority. People see roadwork signs and think 'Government.' They have a limbic response. I wanted to communicate on a broad public level and have people subconsciously absorb it."

I confessed to having difficulty absorbing the message, and to feeling very small in the shadow of the signs. The artist understood.

Because Guariglia recently traveled over Greenland with NASA to photograph quickly melting polar icecaps, he spoke on a more personal level about a particular pockmarked "galloping glacier" (so-called for the rapidity of its flow): "Could my brain really make sense of an object warehousing thirty-eight million Olympic-sized swimming pools of water? Or the scale of a one-hundred-thousand-year-old hunk of ice the size of California on the verge of calving from an ice sheet? No, but we have to talk about what happens when all this ice melts. *Where's it going?*"

Mik asked me at Yankee Pier on the other side of Governor's Island what I thought of the signs as art. I considered whether or not I liked them. It was as if, after a doctor diagnosed one of my kids with cancer, someone else in the waiting room of the ER asked my opinion of that doctor's beard. The signs didn't offer any solace. I hated what they suggested. I did like that they'd brought us to a place offering fresh angles on the city. Mainly, I liked the signs for connecting me with Mik. In my picture, the choppy Buttermilk Channel flows behind him, and off in the distance the elegant arc of the Verrazzano-Narrows Bridge connects Brooklyn to Staten Island.

When I asked him, in turn, whether he liked the signs, Mik answered that they made him feel less alone.

Before leaving the island, we stopped at the Climate Museum's temporary hub in the Admiral's House within a cluster of stately buildings that once served as officers' quarters. There, visitors were invited to simulate their own climate signs. These read like postcards from the brink, bumperstickers, or protest slogans:

SEE YOU ABOVE SEA LEVEL!

ISLAND NATION JUSTICE

MAKE AMERICA GREEN AGAIN

A pamphlet informed us that the earth's glaciers hold enough water to raise sea levels by roughly 230 feet. Mik wrote:

WATER IS THE IMMIGRANT THEY SHOULD FEAR

The Climate Museum is the nation's first museum dedicated to climate change. I later asked its director, Miranda Massie, to comment more elaborately about the organization's mission. Massie responded in an email about how art, even art with a dark message, can inspire us, "consciously or not," by reminding us of human creativity and potential:

> Museums have strengths including popularity and trust that make them essential to the cultural shift we need to see on climate. Art in particular has the power to move the needle on climate engagement and action for a couple of reasons. It reaches us physically, emotionally, and communally, where we really live. Climate change can seem abstract even in the middle of a hurricane. To fully confront the immense challenge posed by the crisis, we need a visceral sense of reality. We also need to be able to experience the full range of emotions art evokes — awe, grief, surprise, fury, tenderness . . . And perhaps most of all, we won't make progress without each other — and art builds community. It is a soft pathway into climate dialogue that lifts climate out of perceived polarization and stigma, allowing us to break the climate silence.

To talk about this subject seriously is to risk being called a doomsayer or a scold. Massie told me that 65 percent of people in the United States are worried about climate change, but only 5 percent of us speak about it with any regularity. (Since our correspondence, the number of Americans fearful of climate change has been identified by a Yale poll as surging to more than 7 in 10.) In truth, Mik and I talked less in the beginning about climate change than about our lives — his book in progress, our respective lesson plans, the imminent midterm elections, the costumes my children were planning for Halloween . . . But now I know we were also stumbling together on a path toward new language, led by the signs.

The following week, we ventured out to Flushing Meadows Corona Park in Queens to see the fourth sign. The park was empty that Thursday on account of a torrential downpour. We were feeling the sultry edges of Michael, a category 4 hurricane that made landfall in Florida the day before. The radial pathways leading to the

Unisphere were washed out. In the nearby isthmus neighborhood of Willets Point, where permanently flooded streets are bordered between Flushing Bay and the Flushing River, hundreds of small businesses are being torn down and relocated to make room for a multibillion-dollar megaproject. By the time we reached the sculpture, notwithstanding our umbrellas, Mik and I were both soaking wet. Visibility was so poor through the sheets of rain that we couldn't immediately spot the sign, and so we orbited the earth, like two lost satellites, until we found it by Africa, stuck on the word CAUTION.

On the new Google Earth plug-in, Surging Seas: Extreme Scenario 2100, created by Climate Central, which uses data from a report by the National Oceanic and Atmospheric Administration (NOAA) to make projections based on the country's greenhouse gas emissions, the future map of Queens shows that, unless the United States transitions to clean energy alternatives, Flushing Meadows Corona Park will be engulfed. So will JFK and LaGuardia airports, sections of North Astoria, College Point, and most of the Rockaways, while large swaths of Long Island City will be submerged in water. You can zoom in tight on the map. From an unscientific perspective, the flooding can appear biblical, like the wrath of a punishing god. For example, the site of the pizza joint in Howard Beach—where, in 1986, a mob of white thugs wielding baseball bats reportedly taunted 23-year-old Michael Griffith and his friends, "What are you doing in this neighborhood, niggers?" and then attacked and chased them toward the Belt Parkway where Griffith was killed by an oncoming car—will be mercilessly drowned.

Mik stands on a step, to avoid a puddle. The 350 tons of the steel Unisphere, which was the central icon of the 1964–1965 World's Fair, is more imposing in person than I had anticipated. Yet, in the context of the sign, and softened by a veil of mist, the earth it represents appears fragile, nearly delicate. The gauzy material of Mik's shirt echoes the fountain spray. Under his umbrella, and next to the lamppost dividing my picture, Mik looks like a version of Gene Kelly, too pensive to dance. The lamp at the top of the post marks South Sudan, just west of Ethiopia, whence Mik's parents fled Mengistu's Red Terror.

We discussed the comparative effects of climate change in the Horn of Africa and here on the Eastern Seaboard of the United

States. While that part of the world is drying out, leading to shriveled crop yields and water shortages that in turn contribute to conflict, famine, and forced migration, this part of the world is getting
more precipitation. Between 1958 and 2012, the Northeast saw a
more than 70 percent increase in the amount of rainfall measured
during heavy precipitation events, a greater increase than in any
other region in the nation, according to the EPA. That we're getting warmer and wetter here, however, doesn't mean we won't also
feel drought conditions in summer. We will.

All-time heat records were set all over the world last summer,
including in our global city. Some days were so hot I questioned
whether it was safe to send my kids to day camp. By 2050, New
York's average temperature is projected to rise between 4.1 and
6.6 degrees Fahrenheit, while annual precipitation is expected to
increase between 4 percent and 13 percent. The regional trend toward more rain has exacerbated localized flooding—not only during big storms, but also as a matter of course at high tide, since the
ocean is already brimming. Street floods are a regular nuisance in
some low-lying areas of Queens like Hamilton Beach. Residents
there have grown accustomed to swans and fish swimming in knee-
high water in the middle of the road when the moon is full.

Perhaps the most common place the average New Yorker experiences flooding is the subway. Even on dry days, the MTA is tasked
with flushing from its network some 13 million gallons of groundwater with overworked pumps. When flash floods from heavy rain
swamp the tunnels, those of us who commute are routinely delayed, spending more and more time griping underground.

Out in Queens, the 7 line is elevated. Mik and I didn't stay long,
not just because of the inclement weather but also because he was
scheduled that afternoon to sign on a townhouse he and his wife
were purchasing in Flatbush, Brooklyn. They made sure the property lay outside the floodplain before making their offer. Sloshing
our way back to the train near the Mets Citi Field ballpark, he
showed me the inscribed Montblanc pen he planned to sign the
contract with—a graduation gift from his brother. He looked the
part of a proud first-time homebuyer on the verge of the American
Dream.

Until they make the move to their new home, Mik, his wife, and
their dog, Chester, will still live in the low-lying waterfront neigh-

borhood of Sunset Park, where nearly a third of the residents live below the poverty line. I joined him there in the park of the same name to visit the fifth sign. Like other disadvantaged communities, this one bears the burden of environmental pollution and impacts of climate change. In addition to being susceptible to flooding, Sunset Park endures poor air quality because of passing traffic on the Gowanus Expressway and three nearby fossil fuel plants whose pollution, ironically, adds a pretty afterglow to the neighborhood's already remarkable sunsets.

Mik and I met hours before sunset, at high noon. In my picture, he stands squarely on his shadow, almost camouflaged with the trunk of the tree that appears to branch from his head. The dark blue water of the Upper Bay is just visible at the horizon line. What you can't see is the gang of tough old Chinese women doing tai chi behind me by the tennis courts, in the sudden cold. They belong to a large Chinese population in Sunset Park, which boasts New York City's largest Chinatown. Appropriately, the sign addresses that part of the neighborhood's demographic in Chinese. Autocorrect as Freudian slip: when I later asked Kimm, the Chinese midwife who delivered my children, to translate the sign, she texted, "It's weird—'Human Agenda for the Futility.'" And then, "Oops!—'Future'."

Donald Trump has accused climate change of being a fabrication on the part of "the Chinese in order to make US manufacturing non-competitive." He also appointed fossil-fuel advocates to lead the Environmental Protection Agency and Department of Energy. What makes this denial and disregard so egregious is that the United States is the second-largest contributor of $CO_2$ to our planet's atmosphere, though we're home to only 4.4 percent of its population. It would take four Earths to provide enough resources for all if everyone in the world consumed as much as we do in the United States.

Interestingly, Sunset Park is home to the city's first grassroots-led, bottom-up climate adaptation and resiliency planning project. Following Sandy, community members organized into a block-by-block, building-by-building plan for action called the Sunset Park Climate Justice Center. The organization's mission includes supporting local leaders "to coordinate allocation of community resources and mitigate the impacts of future severe weather, including the possible release of harmful chemicals."

Since many workers in Sunset Park are employed by natural gas and power plants that could be shut down or curtailed as new climate regulations take effect, activists have appealed to the governor to let communities like Sunset Park lead the development of a transition plan for workers in the fossil fuel industry to find good-paying new jobs in the regenerative-energy economy—in other words, to play an active role in their own adaptation. One example of climate adaptation underway in Sunset Park is a new initiative to shift to renewable energy on a cooperative ownership model. An 80,000-square-foot solar garden is under development nearby on the roof of the decommissioned Brooklyn Army Terminal. It will start to operate this year, open especially to low-income residents. Aiming to serve some 200 families as well as businesses, the solar array will be one of the country's first models of a cooperatively owned urban power supply, cutting energy costs and emissions for subscribers.

It's inspiring to uncover local action taking place despite federal inaction. It's a drop in an ocean-sized bucket of hypoxic tepid water, but it's inspiring. Mik told me that he and his wife were looking into applying for a solar rebate initiative and exploring how to green the roof of their new house. I thought it would be impertinent to ask if they planned on having kids, though I believe he'd make a great dad. We discussed their plans for renovation while Chester chased his tail in widening circles.

The sixth sign stood way out in Far Rockaway, Queens. I could have traveled there on the A train, but I chose to go by water. As usual, I was running late. I rushed through Battery Park's tight warren of streets over the African Burial Ground in time to catch the ferry at Wall St./Pier 11. The Freedom Tower jutted above, like the blade of a sundial. I ran past jackhammering workmen in orange vests and hardhats, the stock exchange, a discount store that used to be an outpost of the Strand, and on tiny Maiden Lane, the ghost of myself aged 25, disoriented and breathing dust, having walked over the Brooklyn Bridge on Rosh Hashanah to stumble upon Ground Zero a week after the World Trade Center attack. I jumped at the blare of a horn: a Moishe's moving truck rolled through a red light, nearly mowing me down. I was struck by how quickly the city remakes itself. These narrow, cobbled streets were made for horses. I raced waterward down Stone Street, aware of the ticking clock. Flanking the terminal were the Brooklyn Bridge and a noisy helipad. Barges. Water taxis. Seagulls. At Slip A, one dockworker playfully grabbed another from behind: "Yo, you got documentation? This is ICE, assume the position." A ticket to Rockaway Beach cost $2.75, the same as a subway fare.

The ferry windows were grubby. Seeing out of them was like watching a dream sequence. The shapes at the edges of Brooklyn were hard to discern: construction cranes, IKEA, a windmill, rooftop water tanks like the hats of witches, shipping containers, men with fishing poles. Mik embarked at Sunset Park, somewhat shaken—the day before, a bomb had been delivered to the CNN building, close to his wife's workplace.

On the boat ride, Mik and I discussed living in a post–September 11 state of alert, often fearing for our loved ones' safety. Recently, my children were evacuated from their school, where they regularly practice soft lockdown drills for active-shooter incidents. This is something beyond the quotidian mental exhaustion that comes from urban living. Behavioral studies have found city-dwellers pay more attention to dangers and opportunities but less attention in general. In spite of our sensory overload, or because of it, the climate signs have demanded our attention.

As we were ferried over the water lapping at Brooklyn's coast, through Gravesend Bay, past the Wonder Wheel at Coney Island and Brighton Beach toward Broad Channel, Mik and I imagined the heightened state of alert that must attend living on the coast. And yet, we envied our neighbors on the coastline their view. When you live, as my family does, in a mid-rise apartment building with a foreshortened view of the building across an alleyway of battered trashcans, it's easy to forget you're near water. New York's master-builder Robert Moses made it harder for pedestrians to access the rivers, creeks, straits, lagoons, and bays surrounding New York City, by hemming in the city with so many expressways. It takes a mental leap to make the worthwhile plunge.

Neither Mik nor I had ventured to Rockaway Beach before; we'd become tourists at the outer reaches of our own city. The ferry took its time. The sky opened out. We felt the primal allure of water, the drag of the vessel upon it. Soon enough, our heart rates slowed. Melville writes, at the opening of *Moby-Dick*, about gravitating toward the sea: "It is a way I have of driving off the spleen."

A feeling of danger gave way to a feeling of opportunity. We disembarked at Rockaway Peninsula, an 11-mile strip of two-family homes and public housing projects. A dome of gold light hovered over it, cast by the double reflection of Jamaica Bay and the Atlantic Ocean on the other side. On the free shuttle bus that drove us closer to our destination, I wondered aloud if people who live and work on the water feel happier. A local man with a Russian accent answered yes. "Why do you think people come all the way out here with their wetsuits and surfboards on the subway?" he asked. "To relax!" Then, he kindly directed us to Beach 94. The beach was empty. Mik and I couldn't stop smiling—we felt like we were playing hooky. We surveyed the vast Atlantic, and breathed.

The portrait I made of Mik at the waterline captures that repose. But to my eye, it also looks uncannily like the Andrew Wyeth painting *Christina's World*. The resemblance lies in the nuance of shadows and light, the waving grass, my subject's backward-facing posture, and the property on the horizon line (in this case, a Mitchell-Lama housing complex rather than a farmhouse) that appears imperiled by a looming, unseen force.

The sign sits on the new $341 million concrete boardwalk, built to replace the wooden promenade wrecked by Sandy. CLIMATE CHANGE IN EFFECT, it warns, in Russian. The more resilient boardwalk has been built at a higher elevation, with sunken steel pilings above a retaining wall designed to keep sand from being pushed into the streets.

Rockaway was among the New York City communities hardest hit by Sandy. When the hurricane slammed into the unprotected peninsula, flooding it with a 15-foot storm surge, the old boardwalk was ripped from its moorings to smash into beachfront properties, a raging six-alarm fire took out some 100 homes in the area of Breezy Point, another blaze decimated a commercial block, and power was down for weeks. The nearby Rockaway Wastewater Treatment Plant was out for three days, during which hundreds of millions of gallons of raw sewage were released into the waterways —a gross example of why the city must retrofit its wastewater facilities for higher tide levels, to avoid drowning in its own shit.

Post-Sandy, the federal government replenished Rockaway Beach with enough sand to fill the Empire State building twice. An Army Corps of Engineers project has proposed to build 18-foot reinforced dunes and 13 new jetties along the peninsula to help stockpile more sand, which would mitigate the force of storm tides on the beachside, and on the bayside, a $3.6 billion system of levees, gates, and floodwalls to control the level of water. Some blue-collar residents along the Rockaway rail line across Jamaica Bay have used funds from the city's Build It Back program to raise their houses higher up on stilts. But the Rockaways were built on a sandbar that geologists have argued should never have been developed in the first place. A troubling amount of restocked sand on Rockaway Beach has already been eroded by the relentless action of the waves. Outside my picture's frame, the sun-dazzled ocean kisses up to the dunes at narrowed parts of the shore, caressing the beach up as far as the new boardwalk.

How to reconcile these twin feelings of pleasure in the city's enjoyments and terror of its threats? I have learned that the world is running out of sand; that every second we're adding four Hiroshima bomb's-worth of heat to the oceans. I think of an hourglass. I think of my kids. But for now, being hungry, Mik and I set out for lunch.

Visiting the seventh sign, Mik humored my kids by agreeing to wear a Halloween mask in St. Nicholas Park. The mask is from the production of an adaptation of *Macbeth* called *Sleep No More*. My kids were in costume, too. I brought them along on our errand to reckon with the climate sign after their school's Halloween parade. The boy was dressed as a killer scarecrow, and the girl, a ninja. I was their mama wolf.

After I shot Mik looking like a nightmare in the mask with no mouth, standing before the sign that originally caught my attention, he was sweet enough to borrow my iPhone to make a family portrait of us. The kids were oblivious of the sign, using the park for its highest purpose—play. They could not keep still. Outside of the frame, they collected acorns, poked sticks in the mud, and tumbled joyfully down the hill.

Not far from here in West Harlem is another park, where their father and I take the kids ice-skating in winter. It's spread alongside the Hudson River above the North River Wastewater Treatment Plant, where the pumps are receiving an upgrade as part of a renovation to improve climate resilience. From the skating rink, you can see the plant's exhaust stacks rising like a pack of tall white cigarettes. When the wind is strong, it smells of rotten eggs. Recent air samples from the site showed levels of formaldehyde that exceeded guidelines established by the city's Department of Environmental Conservation, raising the ire of environmental justice groups fed up with the chronic placement of toxic and hazardous waste sites in low-income black and brown neighborhoods.

Formaldehyde, which has been linked with cancer, can be created by incomplete combustion of methane gas produced during the process of wastewater treatment. Molecule for molecule, methane's a stronger greenhouse gas than $CO_2$, though it's less abundant in the atmosphere. Its main human-derived sources are agriculture, such as cattle-farming, waste (such as from landfills), and the fossil-fuel industry. "Really, the best thing you can do to save the planet is to kill yourself," joked a stand-up comedian I had seen at a club in SoHo with a girlfriend the night before. "The second best thing is to stop eating beef." The earth has as much as six times more methane concentration in the atmosphere than before *Homo sapiens* emerged. With the thawing of the permafrost regions of the Arctic, more methane is being released. My kids are at the age where they love fart jokes, but as funny as I found that comedian, there's not much to laugh at in this.

The sign stands high above Mik on the bluff toward Sugar Hill. Uptown, we're rolling in hills, some so prominent that they grant sweeping southern views of Manhattan, razed in the 19th century of its forests, farms, rocks, and slopes to create the rectangular grid. Back when my son was obsessed with violent weather and I told him we were safe in the Heights, he understood it was an evasion. We aren't disconnected from the other parts of the city, just as our country isn't disconnected from the other parts of the world.

In the silent white mask, Mik faces the entrance to the 135th Street subway at the bottom of the slope. The B stops here, and the C. The subways are the blood vessels of our body politic. Even at three, my boy understood this. It's hard to imagine what the city would be like without its trains should flooding disable the system altogether; what the spire of the Empire State building in Midtown would look like from the rump of Sugar Hill—a buoy? I can't help wondering what the city will look like to our kids when we're no longer here.

At night, when I tuck in the girl, we play a game. I ask if she knows how much I love her, and she replies in the following ways:

infinity hundred infinity, more than all the world's worlds, long after you're dead, and I'm dead, and the world is dead, too. To each reply, I answer, "More." Maybe motherlove is a hyperobject, but so, Guariglia has told me, is climate change. For all the ferocity of my love, I'm powerless to protect my kids from the mass extinction we're in the midst of that could eliminate 30–50 percent of all living species by the middle of the 21st century. Why is this not the core of the core curriculum? Why aren't we all speaking about this?

Mik told me that the first user-generated question that came up in his search for St. Mary's Park in the Mott Haven section of the Bronx was about safety. The sign on a hilltop across the dog run was defaced with graffiti. Two dicks spouting cum and the dictate *Eat my ass* competed with Guariglia's flashing warning signals: FOSSIL FUELING INEQUALITY, CLIMATE DENIAL KILLS.

*Fuck you!* someone had also scrawled on the sign's orange base, which was surrounded by trash. Maybe teenagers had done it, like the two girls passing behind Mik in my photo. I like to think they wouldn't have, had the art offered comfort or beauty, or had the sign been useful in a practical sense. But in the context of the Southeast Bronx, where failing infrastructure is a fact of life, the graffiti read to Mik and me like an act of protest against the hazard sign itself.

It would have taken me four trains to get here from Upper Manhattan, though it isn't far as the crow flies, except that the third train wasn't running to carry me to the fourth, and so I got off at Yankee Stadium and walked three miles to reach St. Mary's Park—past the Bronx County Courthouse, through the Melrose Projects, and behind a trans woman in fabulous leggings printed with silver skulls, who clutched at her toothache on her way to a storefront dental clinic, moaning, "Why is the demon bothering me, why?"

Last week, single-use plastics were banned by the European Parliament, while the news came that the sea is absorbing far more heat than we'd realized, and that it's too late to save the earth by planting trees. Even if we covered the planet with trees, it would be too late. It is already broken. Another sign appeared in my feed. This one taped in the window of a bookshop in Cornwall, England: PLEASE NOTE: THE POST-APOCALYPTICAL FICTION SECTION HAS BEEN MOVED TO CURRENT AFFAIRS.

The densely packed Bronx is the poorest of New York's boroughs, making it more vulnerable to heat of every kind. It isn't
easy for the people who live here to leave. What does it mean, in
a neighborhood where many forces choke possibility and freedom
of movement itself is restricted by transportation that fails on the
regular, to be told that climate denial kills? When we suffer an
untreated toothache, the pain is so immediate that we can think
of nothing else.

At Hunts Point, two stops closer to the waterfront on the 6 train,
Mik and I discovered after crossing beneath the busy Bruckner
Expressway, that the sign in Riverside Park was blank. Its solar battery had been jacked, the master lock popped, the orange encase-
ment flung open like the lid of a pilfered jewelry box. We were
impressed by the thief's enterprise in recognizing the battery's
value. When I shot Mik sitting beneath the black screen, I felt curiously relieved by the sign's defacement, its silence. By this time, at
the ninth site, I had memorized the looping messages of the hazard signs, and could focus instead on the graceful posture of my
friend, who'd opened his coat to enjoy the sun; the sludge of the
Bronx River behind him, and the projects on the opposite shore.

Riverside Park is a little park, covering just 1.4 acres, a Faulk-
nerian "postage stamp of native soil." Once a vacant lot and illegal
dumping site, it's the first of a planned string of parks to be linked
by a bike route as part of the developing South Bronx Greenway. Behind Mik is a fishing pier and canoe launch. I've been here
before with my kids to ride rowboats in the summer when folks in-
flate bouncy castles for the kids, hold all-day barbecues, and pump
'90s hip-hop from big sound systems. Although we're now deep
into the fall and the only ones here, today is freakishly warm at 67
degrees.

Extreme heat is a dangerous element of our changing climate.
It kills more Americans per year than any other weather-related
event. Cities are often 2–8 degrees Fahrenheit warmer than the areas that surround them because of the urban-heat-island effect. At
night, when our bodies need to recuperate from stress and heat,
the contrast in temperature is more extreme—ranging as much as
22 degrees. This is due to urban design—our tall buildings, black
rooftops, and dark pavement, which attract and absorb the sun's
rays.

A 2013 Berkeley study indicated that people of color are up to 52 percent more likely to live in urban heat islands than white people. We face more health risks during heat waves as a result. What's more, long histories of underinvestment in black and brown urban neighborhoods have made our communities heat up more and faster overall than the already hot cities we live in. Hunts Point has one of the city's highest rates of heat-related fatalities. Ninety-eight percent of its residents are people of color. The NYC Environmental Justice Alliance has made addressing the urban-heat-island effect its top priority for climate justice because, while hurricanes and storm surges may smack us every five or more years, we can count on extreme heat to clobber us every single summer.

According to a 2018 article in *Grist* by Justine Calma, New York City sees a yearly average of 450 heat-related visits to the ER and over 100 deaths attributed to extreme heat, but the Environmental Justice Alliance estimates the actual death toll to be a lot higher —depending on the variable criteria different researchers use to link deaths to heat waves, the annual number could be over 600. A recent Columbia University study projected that by 2080, up to 3,300 New Yorkers per year could die due to heat-related causes exacerbated by climate change. In fact, New York is one of the most vulnerable cities in the developed world to the threat of urban heat.

The Hunts Point Peninsula is an example of a hot spot within a heat island, Calma writes. It's a heavily industrial neighborhood where residents, who make, on average, $22,000 a year, often live in packed apartment buildings with more heat-trapping surfaces and fewer green spaces to help cool the neighborhood. Who can afford an air conditioner on $400 a week, let alone the higher electric bill to run it, when there is rent to be paid?

The New Yorkers most at risk of heat emergencies live in fenceline communities of color like this one, burdened by decades of polluting infrastructure as well as poverty. For a long time, Hunts Point had one of the lowest parks-to-people ratios in the city, but over the past decade, locals have lobbied for more green space along its riverfront, like this one. To the left of my frame is a salvage yard heaving with crushed cars and scrap metal. At my back, across some railroad tracks, an idling produce truck is unloading cartons of ripe pineapples and strawberries. Hunts Point works as both mouth and ass for the city, getting food in, taking waste out:

this neighborhood of 13,000 people has the world's largest whole-sale produce market and over a dozen waste-transfer stations. Along with the rest of the South Bronx, it handles nearly a third of the city's solid waste. Meaning, there are trucks everywhere, all the time, piping out hot exhaust, heightening the risk of asthma attacks, and further broiling the air.

The city's Office of Recovery and Resiliency recently launched a Cool Neighborhoods Plan, to partner with grassroots organizations in efforts to mitigate the health risks of extreme heat in vulnerable communities. Strategies include painting surfaces white, plant-ing trees, checking on older people who might be housebound in stifling apartments, greening roofs, and getting out the word about cooling centers—public air-conditioned facilities like librar-ies, community centers, and senior centers, where folks can cool off for free. City officials piloted the initiative in three neighbor-hoods last summer, including Hunts Point. Without whole-cloth citywide initiatives toward cleaner energy, hotspots like this could be feeling summer days that are 15 percent hotter than today by the 2080s. Can you even imagine a 120-degree day? In the cities of New Delhi, Baghdad, Khartoum, Mexicali, and Phoenix, they're already there.

The unspoken threat remains in the frame, as does the tension between the sign, the human, and the landscape, but all the same, it was another beautiful afternoon for walking the city. Later on, I took my children trick-or-treating without need of their jackets.

The following week, Mik and I visited the tenth and last sign. We rode the Staten Island Ferry to get us closer to Snug Harbor, where the sign was stationed. It was the day before midterm elections, and gently raining. The air held an elegiac mist with an electrical charge: leaning over the ferry's wet rail, it was impossible not to conjure Walt Whitman thinking about us "ever so many genera-tions hence."

"Whitman was one of my gateway drugs to literature, and these days I have such a hard time connecting to his voice, optimism and vision of America," Mik admitted. "How hard it is now to have faith that future generations will even exist." We regarded the Statue of Liberty in a shawl of fog, and Ellis Island.

Climate change has become an often-unspoken contributing factor driving recent waves of immigration, such as the Central

American migrant caravan used by the right-wing media to stir up ire as it neared the Mexican border. Mik grew quiet looking out at the white wake of passing ships. Patrol boats, skimmers, tugs, barges, the ghosts of whalers and steamers, and the ocean liner *Queen Mary* 2. I asked what he was thinking about.

"The wildfires in California," he said, and all those fleeing fire, "but also how many more of us will be climate refugees in our own lifetime, all because folk turned greed into an economic system a few hundred years ago."

Belying his justifiable pessimism was the fact that Mik had just returned from Georgia, where he'd volunteered to drive elders without transportation to the polls for early voting. Understandably, he was nervous about the direction our country would go. There was a larger national anxiety about the feasibility of a "blue wave"—a Democratic sweep to win back the House. "I don't believe it," President Trump said of his own administration's November report, which stated, "climate change is transforming where and how we live." In the Republican stronghold of Staten Island, a borough known for voting against its own environmental interests, it cheered us somewhat to observe Democratic congressional election signs staked in the front yards of North Shore houses on the bus route to Snug Harbor.

Snug Harbor has been referred to as Staten Island's "crown jewel." People get married and shoot films there. Once a retirement community for aged merchant sailors, it's now a National Historic Landmark District set inside an 83-acre park that runs along the Kill Van Kull tidal straight. Mik and I wandered among lush gardens freakishly still in bloom, a duck pond, a fountain memorial to local rescue workers who lost their lives on September 11, a farm, a surreal field of brightly colored lanterns including the giant head of a dragon, and several Greek Revival, Beaux Arts, and Italianate-style buildings—a chapel, a foundry, a theater hall, a hospital—remnants of the 19th-century seafaring community, repurposed for the arts.

Inside one of these stately buildings, now operating as a museum, we found Gus, a maintenance worker built like a fire hydrant, who bragged about Snug Harbor with charming civic pride. He was grateful to Jackie Onassis for her part in preserving the site and was glad to share its history with other New Yorkers—who, he admitted, tend not to visit the borough because it's difficult to access, and because of lingering bad PR over the Fresh Kills dump that grew, over the second half of the 20th century, into the biggest man-made structure in the world.

Mik asked if the maintenance crew was doing anything particular to protect the landmarked buildings from sea level rise. Not that he was aware of, Gus said. "Like most New Yorkers, we only think about that stuff when it's too late."

On the subway map, Staten Island looks small and somewhat neglected, an afterthought boxed in the lower left-hand corner like a leftover chicken nugget. In reality, it's huge—over two and a half times the landmass of Manhattan—nearly as sprawling as the borough of Brooklyn. Situated in the crook of the New York Bight, the island suffered more than half of the city's 43 deaths during Sandy, bearing the brunt of a storm tide that peaked here at 16 feet.

Gus talked about the southeast shore of Staten Island, specifically the wooden-bungalow community of Oakwood Beach hit by the superstorm's worst flooding in a funnel effect that left some clinging to their rooftops while others drowned in their basements, trying to fix their sump pumps. That part of Staten Island is now rewilding with grasses, flowers, insects, possum, deer—returning to a natural wetland state. Most of the homes there were demolished after property owners took buyouts from the state government, choosing to relocate rather than attempt to rebuild—one of few examples in the city of managed retreat. As our coastlines become increasingly unlivable, this kind of deliberate migration away from the water's edge may grow more commonplace. In the meantime, a breakwater project is underway around the south shore to protect those stalwarts who remain, seeding oyster beds to prevent coastal erosion and absorb wave energy while cleaning the water, while the Army Corps is planning a $580 million seawall that many scientists claim would ultimately fail.

"Humans are stupid," Gus shrugged. "We want what we want, even when it don't make sense." He urged us to return to Snug Harbor for the Winter Lantern Festival. He'd mistaken us for a couple. In a platonic sense, I guess we were. Ours was a marriage of inconvenient truth. I couldn't show a face of fear to my family, and so I showed it to Mik, who held my gaze without judgment, and looked right back. Even though I knew I'd see him again, I felt a little sad that our assignment was ending. I enjoyed his company, and our journey gave structure to my scattered thoughts. The rain was growing heavier and so we took cover under a gazebo.

In our final portrait, Mik takes his hair down and folds his arms protectively over his middle. He looks older to me than he did in September, when we met by the first sign. *La terre est bleue comme une orange* . . . The world is blue like an orange. Orange is a color that strikes you in the gut. I am struck by the orange dominating this picture, turning it nostalgic. The traffic cone, the fall leaves, the gazebo walls, the base of the road sign, the text, and even the undertone of Mik's skin appear orange beneath the thunderclouds. The warm orange of autumn integrated with the bright orange of hazard.

VOTE ECO-LOGICALLY, warns the sign, approaching its target.

The next day, a lot of us did just that. Bronx-born Alexandria Ocasio-Cortez, the democratic socialist who was voted to represent New York's 14th Congressional District, has just posed the Green New Deal, which aspires to cut US carbon emissions soon enough to attain the Paris Agreement's most ambitious goal: preventing the world from warming any more than 1.5 degrees Celsius by 2100. "This is going to be the New Deal, the Great Society, the moon shot, the civil rights movement of our generation," the young congresswoman said at a town hall meeting a month after the election, drawing on the cocky attitude of American exceptionalism. Who am I to say "too little, too late," when she's supplied me with the script to motivate my children with this rallying cry: "The only way we're going to get out of this situation is by choosing to be courageous."

I heard the same conviction in Justin Guariglia's voice when I interviewed him about his art. He described what it felt like to photograph the Arctic meltdown from the troposphere with a mixture of emotions: fragility, urgency, anxiety, awe—the simultaneous contraction and expansion of self that Whitman sang about. "You sense your own insignificance and the sublime," was how Guariglia put it.

My route with Mik across New York felt like a less glorious, though still noble, version of that crossing. I hold in my mind a new map of the city as a vulnerable and precious entity, both larger and smaller than I had understood, an appreciation of the water that binds us, gratitude for the prize of a friend I didn't have before (worth infinitely more than the tote bag bestowed by the

Climate Museum), and the sinking realization that, eventually, we may have to migrate. Finally, I learned an altered sense of time, which I'll describe by paraphrasing the philosopher whose work inspired the climate signs that led us down a soft pathway out of silence into speech: we must awaken from the dream that the world is about to end; action depends on our awakening. When did the countdown begin? Let us reconsider the clock. Morton theorizes that the world has already ended. The ball dropped in 1784, he writes, with the advent of the steam train and the resulting soot that indelibly marked our footprint on the earth's geology during our swift carriage into the Industrial Revolution.

I think of the romance of the train, the iron horse that collapsed time and distance even as it began to undo us. How well my boy once loved trains. That boy is no longer here. In his place is another. In Mik's picture, my son stands as tall as my shoulder. Fittingly, for a kid whose latest passion is monsters, his favorite holiday is Halloween. At first I begged him not to chew Mik's ear off about supervillains from the Marvel universe and the darker actions of Greek gods. Then I stopped myself, and thanked my boy for his morbid curiosity. He is teaching us to pay attention. The signs hint at violence. I like how he and his sister are dressed in the context of the sign's bad news. CAUTION. The boy wields a scythe. The girl wears a katana tucked in her belt. She is stealthy; he is fierce. They look strong and alert. Good. They will have to be brave for the roadwork ahead.

PAUL SALOPEK

# Walking with Migrants

FROM *National Geographic*

FOR NEARLY SEVEN years I have been walking with migrants.

In the winter of 2013 I set out from an ancient *Homo sapiens* fossil site called Herto Bouri, in the north of Ethiopia, and began retracing, on foot, the defining journey of humankind: our first colonization of the earth during the Stone Age.

My long walk is about storytelling. I report what I see at boot level along the pathways of our original discovery of the planet. From the start, I knew my route would be vague. Anthropologists suggest that our species first stepped out of Africa 600 centuries ago and eventually wandered, more or less aimlessly, to the tip of South America—the last unknown edge of the continents and my own journey's finish line. We were roving hunters and foragers. We lacked writing, the wheel, domesticated animals, and agriculture. Advancing along empty beaches, we sampled shellfish. We took our bearings off the rippling arrows of migrating cranes. Destinations had yet to be invented. I have trailed these forgotten adventurers for more than 10,000 miles so far. Today I am traversing India.

Our modern lives, housebound as they are, have changed almost beyond recognition since that golden age of footloose exploration.

Or have they?

The United Nations estimates that more than a billion people —one in seven humans alive today—are voting with their feet, migrating within their countries or across international borders. Millions are fleeing violence: war, persecution, criminality, political chaos. Many more, suffocated by poverty, are seeking economic relief beyond their horizons. The roots of this colossal new exodus include a globalized market system that tears apart social safety nets, a pollutant-warped climate, and human yearnings supercharged by instant media. In sheer numbers, this is the largest diaspora in the long history of our species.

I pace off the world at 15 miles a day. I mingle often among the uprooted.

In Djibouti I have sipped chai with migrants in bleak truck stops. I have slept alongside them in dusty UN refugee tents in Jordan. I have accepted their stories of pain. I have repaid their laughter. I am not one of them, of course: I am a privileged walker. I carry inside my rucksack an ATM card and a passport. But I have shared the misery of dysentery with them and have been detained many times by their nemesis—police. (Eritrea, Sudan, Iran, and Turkmenistan have denied me visas; Pakistan ejected me, then allowed me back in.)

What can be said about these exiled brothers and sisters? About the immense shadowlands they inhabit, paradoxically, in plain sight?

Hunger, ambition, fear, political defiance—the reasons for movement are not truly the question. More important is knowing how the journey itself shapes a different class of human being: people whose ideas of "home" now incorporate an open road—a vast and risky tangent of possibility that begins somewhere far away and ends at your doorsill. How you accept this tiding, with open arms or crouched behind high walls, isn't at issue either. Because however you react, with compassion or fear, humankind's reawakened mobility has changed you already.

The first migrants I encountered were dead. They lay under small piles of stones in the Great Rift Valley of Africa.

Who were these unfortunates?

It was difficult to know. The world's poorest people travel from many distant lands to perish in the Afar Triangle of Ethiopia, one of the hottest deserts on earth. They walk into these terrible barrens in order to reach the Gulf of Aden. There the sea is the doorway to a new (though not always better) life beyond Africa: slave-wage jobs in the cities and date plantations of the Arabian Peninsula. Some of the migrants' graves doubtless contained Somalis: war refugees. Others likely held deserters from Eritrea. Or drought-weakened Oromos from Ethiopia. All had hoped to sneak across the unmarked borders of Djibouti. They became lost. They collapsed under a molten sun. Sometimes they dropped from thirst within sight of the sea. The columns of exhausted travelers walking behind hastily buried the bodies.

How long have we been depositing our bones like this on the desolate trails of the African Horn? For a long time. From the very beginning. After all, this is the same corridor used by the first modern humans to exit Africa during the Pleistocene.

One day I stumbled across a group of scarecrows hiding in the scant shade of some boulders—15 lean Ethiopian men who seemed to pretend that if they didn't move a muscle, they would be invisible. Some were manual laborers. Most were farmers from the Ethiopian highlands. The annual rains, the farmers said, had become impossibly erratic. Sticking it out on their sun-cracked fields meant slow starvation. Better to chance the ocean of white light that is the Afar Triangle, even if you never returned. They were pioneers of sorts, new climate change refugees.

A recent World Bank study calculates that by 2050 more than 140 million people in sub-Saharan Africa, South Asia, and Latin America could be tumbled into motion by the catastrophic effects of climate change. Ten million climate refugees could swell the trails of East Africa alone. In Ethiopia the tide may reach 1.5 million people—more than 15 times the emigrants now straggling annually through the Afar Triangle to reach the Middle East.

Inching north up the Rift, I was forced to consider the urge to leave a familiar world that was falling apart, a home where the sky itself was against you. All around me snaked the invisible battle lines of an intensifying range war between the Afar and Issa pastoralists—two competing herder groups whose shallow wells were drying up, whose pastures were thinning from a relentless cycle of droughts. They shot at each other over the ownership of a papery blade of grass, over a cup of sandy water. In other words, over survival. Here was the source of our oldest travel story. Drastic climate change and murderous famines, experts say, likely helped drive the first pulses of humans out of Africa.

How strong is the push to leave? To abandon what you love? To walk into the unknown with all your possessions stuffed into a pocket? It is more powerful than fear of death.

In the Afar Triangle I stumbled across seven unburied bodies. They were women and men clustered together. They lay faceup, mummified atop a dark lava field. The heat was devastating. The little wild dogs of the desert, the jackals, had taken these travelers' hands and feet. My walking partner, Houssain Mohamed Houssain, shook his head in wonder, in disgust. He was an ethnic Afar, a descendant of camel herders, the old kings of the desert. His people called the recent waves of transients *hahai*—"people of the wind"—ghosts who blew across the land. He snapped a picture.

"You show them this," Houssain said angrily, "and they say, 'Oh, that won't happen to me!'"

One of the unlucky migrants had squeezed under a ledge. Doubtless he was crazed for shade. He had placed his shoes next to his naked body, just so, with one sock rolled carefully inside each shoe. He knew: his walking days were over.

Walking the continents teaches you to look down. You appreciate the importance of feet. You take an interest in footwear. This is natural.

Human character, of course, is mirrored in the face. The eyes reveal sincerity, lying, curiosity, love, hate. But one's choice of shoes (or even lack of it) speaks to personal geography: wealth or poverty, age, type of work, education, gender, urban versus rural. Among the world's legions of migrants, a certain pedal taxonomy holds. Economic migrants—the destitute millions with time to plan ahead—seem to favor the shoe of the 21st century's poor: the cheap, unisex, multipurpose Chinese sneaker. War refugees escaping violence, by contrast, must trudge their wretched roads in rubber flip-flops, dress loafers, dusty sandals, high-heeled pumps, booties improvised from rags, etc. They flee burning cities, abandon villages and farms. They pull on whatever shoes lie within reach at a moment's notice. I first began to see such eclectic piles of footwear appearing outside refugee tents in the highlands of Jordan.

"I wake up to these mountains," cried Zaeleh al Khaled al Hamdu, a Syrian grandmother shod in beaded house slippers. Tiny blue flowers were tattooed on her wrinkled chin and cheeks. She waved a bony hand at the alien peaks around her. "It feels like these mountains, I am carrying them on my back."

Heaviness. Weight. The crush of despair. The mountainous burden of helplessness.

This is the badge of the war refugee. Or so our televisions, news-papers, and mobile phones would inform us. The stock media photo of the war-displaced: columns of traumatized souls march-ing with heavy steps, with slumped shoulders, along a burning road. Or families jammed into leaky boats on the Mediterranean, their gazes sagging with anguish, sunk in vulnerability. But these snapshots of refugee life—seen through the lens of the rich world —are limited, misleading, even self-serving.

For weeks I walked from tent to dusty tent in Jordan. At least half a million Syrians languished there—just one aching shard of some 12 million civilians scattered by the bloodiest civil war in the Middle East. War steals your past and future. The Syrians could not go back to the contested rubble of their homes—to Idlib, Ha-mah, or Damascus. Nobody else wanted them. They were stuck. All they owned was their miserable present.

Many toiled illegally on farms.

They eked out another breath of life by picking tomatoes for $1.50 a day. When I plodded past, they waved me over. They jaun-tily fed me their employers' crops. (Residents of a poor nation, Jor-danians spared little affection for their even poorer Syrian guests.) They poured gallons of tea with wild thyme down my throat. They shook out their filthy blankets and bade me sit and rest.

"Here, we only dream of chicken," one man joked. He'd eaten grass to survive in Syria. In one tent a young woman stepped be-hind a hanging bedsheet and reemerged in her finest dress—pink with silver stripes. She was dazzlingly pregnant, and her beauty passed in a clean hush through my chest, into the moldering tent, before blowing unstoppably out into the desert.

What I'm trying to say is this: Whatever else refugees may be, they aren't powerless.

They aren't the infantilized victims usually featured in the po-litical left's suffering porn. They resemble even less the cartoon invaders feared by right-wing populists and bigots—the barbarian hordes coming to take jobs, housing, social services, racial iden-tity, religion, sex partners, and everything else vital and good in wealthy host countries. (Since Neolithic times, the earliest popu-lations of Europe have been overrun and utterly transformed by waves of immigrants from Central Asia and the eastern Mediterra-nean. Without such interbreeding, modern "Europeans" wouldn't exist.)

No. The refugees I have walked among are bearded pharmacists and girl goatherds. Shopkeepers and intellectuals. That is, supremely ordinary beings grappling with meager options. Remembering their dead, they cup their hands to their faces and weep. But often they are incredibly strong. And generous.

"Please come, mister," a Syrian teacher whispered in Turkey, guiding me from a refugee-camp classroom out into the open air. Her students had been drawing decapitations and hangings as part of their art therapy. She noticed I had fallen silent. She was worried about *my* emotions.

A thousand walked miles to the east, in the Caucasus, a family of ethnic Armenian refugees from Syria hollered, "Don't come in please!"—making me wait outside their dilapidated home while they hastily set a table they couldn't afford. They recently moved into a house that once belonged to ethnic Azerbaijanis, a local population ejected during the decades-old Nagorno-Karabakh conflict. I found the Azerbaijanis 120 miles later. They refused my money in a refugee-camp café.

"We have been waiting for peace so long," Nemat Huseynov, the café owner, said. He had owned many sheep when the conflict began in 1988. It goes on, despite a cease-fire in 1994.

Huseynov stared at his big, work-swollen shepherd's hands splayed palm down on the worn tablecloth.

Home.

You cannot always choose your shoes on a long walk.

The world's refugees and migrants don't demand our pity. They just ask for our attention. Me they pitied because I walked on.


"May I practice my English?"

It was the teenage boys and girls of Punjab. Last year. Mile 7,000 of my slow journey. The scalding back roads of India's breadbasket.

Five, ten, twenty youngsters a day emerged from their houses, jogging to catch up after I slogged past. Sweating, puffing, unused to exercise, they unlimbered their English vocabulary and syntax for a few hundred yards before peeling off. They were studying for the International English Language Testing System exams. High scores were essential to meet the English-proficiency standards required for visas to New Zealand, Australia, the United Kingdom, Canada, and the United States. There was nothing lighthearted about these exchanges that were as old as the Stone Age—"Who are you?" "Where do you come from?" "Where are you going?" —because it was homework.

Faridkot was a town marooned in a sea of wheatgrass. About 100 private English-language schools there were preparing tens of thousands of young Indians to abandon their homeland. The fields of Punjab were already taken. There was little future in farming. Successful students aimed to join the 150 million migrant laborers who vault frontiers to find work. Punjab was undergoing an evacuation.

"The only ones who stay behind are those who can't afford it," said language-school owner Gulabi Singh, looking startled at his own information. The average cost of emigration: $14,000, or 23 times the annual median income in India.

I had just arrived from Central Asia. A walking partner in Uzbekistan slipped regularly into Kazakhstan to work without papers at construction sites. He carried scars from police encounters. In Kyrgyzstan and Tajikistan, I met migrants who flew to Moscow to punch cash registers or inhale poisons at nightmare chemical plants. The Afghans along my route were eyeing every continent to flee the war. And so on.

Yet here is the secret of this epic of human restlessness: It is probably the people who stay behind who will change the world.

Internal migrations—rural-to-urban stampedes—sweep up 139 million citizens within India. In China the figure approaches a quarter billion. In Brazil, Indonesia, Nigeria, Mexico, everywhere, the trend is the same. Three-quarters of the humans now stumbling across the planet are circulating within their own borders. New middle classes are being born. Old political dynasties are tottering. Megacities are exploding—and imploding. Stunning innovations collide with colossal disappointments. Entire systems of knowledge (traditional farming), accumulated over millennia, are being jettisoned. Urbanization is cracking apart old gender and religious norms. Environmental resources are in free fall. Chaos, longing, violence, hope, tearing down, building up, experimentation, astonishing successes and defeats. Nothing can stand in the way of this unprecedented force of yearning. By comparison, the hysteria in the Global North over international migrants seems a pale sideshow.

Walking India, I joined human torrents streaming along roads.

I saw them jamming bus stands. Packed atop trains. The hard-working poor ceaselessly coming and going. Sooner than later, the world must learn to harness the extraordinary energy behind such mass aspiration.

The migrant steering the course of our species' destiny this century saw me coming from afar. People always do. She couldn't have been 18. This was in a village of stray cows in Bihar, one of India's poorest states. I was bound for Myanmar. She strode up and boldly shook my hand.

"This place is very, very boring," the Bihari girl declared within a minute. "My teachers are boring. What do I do?"

I laughed.

Ambition and intelligence shone in her eyes. Soon enough she would be shouldering her way into one of India's metastasizing cities, testing her mettle against hundreds of millions of other dislocated villagers. There would be no wall high enough to contain her.

Where will she end up? Where will we? Nobody knows. The important thing on this road we share is to keep walking. And not be afraid. The way ahead may be uphill. I suggest doing your homework. Her shoes were sturdy.

# Lost in Summerland

FROM *The Atavist Magazine*

AS BEST WE can tell, the hauntings began after Andy's traumatic brain injury. On Christmas Eve 2005, outside a scuzzy bar on the east side of Milwaukee, a drunk man sucker-punched my elder brother, bashing his head against the wall of a brick alcove and leaving him splayed on the snow-confected sidewalk, unconscious with seven brain contusions. For several days, my family sat vigil around Andy's bed in the ICU, whispering prayers into clasped palms, wincing at the doctors' ambiguous status updates. At first the prognosis was fatal. So extensive was the bleeding, the hospital felt sure it was only a matter of time before Andy slipped irrevocably into a coma. But he woke fortuitously on the morning of the 30th, wide-eyed and cogent, requesting, of all things, a meal from Boston Market.

After a nine-month-long odyssey of dizzy spells and aphasic episodes, my brother, then 22, regained most of his memory and, as we liked to joke, the better parts of his personality. He bought his own apartment and finished a bachelor's degree, got married and took a corporate sales position. But something strange started to happen over the next couple of years. At night he heard creaky footsteps in the hallway and stray voices in the closet. Initially, we feared the worst and believed the head injury had jostled his brain into psychosis—a grim but not altogether unreasonable conclusion. Eventually, my dad flew out from Milwaukee to visit Andy at his new home in Houston, and when he arrived, he found my brother sitting meditatively cross-legged on the kitchen floor, with the lights of the chandelier above him flickering of their own accord. Without even the most cursory acknowledgment of my father's arrival, Andy said, with a kind of holy calm, "There's someone in the room with us."

In time my brother began to insist that he could speak to the dead and receive dispatches from the spiritual realm. Whenever I visited him on the West Coast, where he had eventually taken a job in the tech industry, his friends would pull me aside at bars to confide that Andy had "summoned" their dead relatives, battering me with questions about what it was like to grow up with him. Most of my family grew convinced of his paranormal talents. (Bear in mind that up until that point my parents had been lapsed Catholics and flinty-eyed midwesterners, with little tolerance for the supernatural.) My father once gawked at water glasses that slid across the breakfast island—presumably the work of spirits—while Andy stood transfixed at the kitchen's threshold. When my grandmother passed away, my sister-in-law reported seeing a green orb floating over Andy's bedside, and upon shaking him awake, they both watched, dumbfounded, as the glinting emerald sphere drifted toward the ceiling and vanished. "Your brother," my mother once said to me, in a solemn whisper, "has powers." Things reached some sort of apogee when Andy said he was stopped for a traffic violation and, just as the cop began scribbling a ticket, he channeled the ghost of the officer's mother, who had recently died from congestive heart failure. The cop let Andy off with a warning.

Naturally, I tended to regard these stories with smirks and sidelong glances. Andy, who is three years older than me, has long had a weakness for showmanship—his coworkers nicknamed him the Bull for his ability to BS his way through corporate presentations—and to those who know him well, it wouldn't be inaccurate to suggest that he has coasted through life on the wind of his own charisma. I have seen him make barrooms come to life with karaoke renditions of "November Rain." I have seen him dicker with car salesmen, performing such adroit campaigns of ingratiation that he invariably rolls out of the lot in a vehicle for which he has paid several thousand dollars below sticker. I once joined, very briefly, a rave at a club in Milwaukee, a victim of my brother's coaxing. And so it was precisely this capacity for stagecraft and sweet talk that made me doubtful of—and amused by—his claims of paranormal élan.

But soon these "visitations," as Andy likes to call them, began happening with a fervor and frequency that made his wife scared. Whenever he went on business trips to places like Amsterdam or Beijing, she'd receive odd transcontinental phone calls during the wee hours, with Andy sounding rattled and nonplussed, muttering darkly about spirits in the bathroom or unattributed thudding on the hotel room walls. Hoping to leaven the issue when I learned of it, I waggishly ventured that perhaps the noises were merely the clamor of some netherworldly tryst, lost souls reuniting in the honeymoon suite. But he dodged my attempt at humor and said, with absolutely zero irony, "You know, you might be right about that."

I worry my tone will seem to gainsay what I mentioned before about maintaining a dose of utmost skepticism. But if you could only hear the earnestness of my brother's testimony, then you too might entertain a squirm of doubt. You too might suspend your disbelief. Could it be that my brother, by fluke of grievous brain injury, had somehow become a maître d' to the underworld, summoning wraiths to ease suffering and evade misdemeanor tickets? Was he some kind of a modern-day Charon, straddling the river between the living and the dead?

In the spring of 2018, he called out of the blue and asked whether I'd ever heard of a place called Lily Dale, a quaint hamlet an hour south of Buffalo, New York. It is home to about 275 residents, many of them registered psychics and mediums. Each summer, some 22,000 tourists descend upon the town for séances and drum circles, hoping to reunite with departed loved ones. "Imagine *Wet Hot American Summer*," Andy said. "But with dead people."

Initially, I begged off, claiming a busy summer of yard work and university teaching. "Oh, come on. It could be a bros' trip," he said. "Plus, you could watch me do my thing. By the end of the week, I guarantee you won't think I'm full of shit."

"I don't think you're full of shit," I said.

A silence came over the line. Truth be told, I sensed that his bluster was Andy's cover, that perhaps he was trekking to Lily Dale because he'd grown frightened by what was happening to him and was now desperate for an explanation.

Cursory groundwork on the internet would later yield several reports of marquee figures who'd be heading to the camp that summer. There was the feral-eyed Michelle Whitedove, a 50-something "angelic channeler" and "forensic medium" with a mane of autumn-colored hair, a woman who had been named America's

Number One Psychic by a reality TV show in 2007. On YouTube, I found a clip of the show, called *America's Psychic Challenge,* in which Whitedove roams a 10-acre swath of desert and divines the exact location of a man buried six feet underground with a small tank of oxygen. Also in attendance would be Reverend Anne Gehman, a pearl-wearing, lid-fluttering medium who taught classes on bending spoons and whose clairvoyant abilities had allegedly helped investigators catch the serial killer Ted Bundy.

"Well, what do you think?" Andy said. "Do you want to come with me?"

Over the next few months, whenever I mentioned my impending trip to "Silly Dale," as online wags have rechristened it, colleagues at various universities would barrage me with paranormal tales. In the interest of leaving their reputations unbesmirched, I will refrain from uttering their names in print, but rest assured: these were highly credentialed members of their fields. In hushed tones, they told of dalliances with clairvoyance, about sourceless bumps in the night. One colleague, a poetry professor, regularly consulted psychics and mediums; another put her faith in the portents of tarot card readings. All this seemed of a piece with the broader resurgence of heterodox traditions, for in the days leading up to our trip, it seemed like I couldn't hop on the internet without stumbling across stories about millennials turning to astrology, or CEOs embracing eastern religions, or covens of young witches casting spells in New York City. Even the renewed interest in psychedelics —see Michael Pollan's *How to Change Your Mind* or Tao Lin's *Trip* —felt like a quest to open up the doors of perception.

It's telling that Spiritualism, the creed of Lily Dale, was born in the middle of the 19th century, a time when many Americans were suffering, in real ways, from a welter of epistemological disruptions—the Civil War and Darwinian theory, the death of God and the birth of capitalism. Spiritualism's nativity scene took place in upstate New York in the 1840s, when a trio of adolescent sisters—Leah, Kate, and Margaret Fox—reportedly heard mysterious rappings on the walls of their parents' house. Once news spread of their ethereal activities, the Fox sisters launched a whirlwind tour of New England and the Midwest, holding séances in town halls and hotel parlors, drawing audiences of all classes and backgrounds. What emerged over the next four years was a national craze for paranormal communication, with spirit circles—clubs for channeling the dead—forming in almost every city that the girls had visited. One newspaperman in Cincinnati claimed that some 1,200 local mediums came out of the woodwork in the wake of the Fox sisters' performance.

The notion that spirits could intervene in worldly affairs was, of course, not new, but there had never been a formal religion based exclusively on the premise that humans could receive communiqués from the dead, particularly their dead loved ones. While the movement's various sects quibbled over doctrinal differences, Spiritualists were united in the belief that a brigade of so-called spirit guides helped each individual find their way toward Summerland, a term that eventually became the religion's sobriquet for heaven. And while we might expect modern science to have rinsed such thinking from the American imagination, the movement remained surprisingly durable, as evidenced by the political tumult of the 1960s—another period of narrative breakdown —when many people turned to New Ageism for balmy existential comfort.

Once again the center was not holding. By 2018, the country lacked a workable epistemology, and even our most cherished pieties were wobbling or already lay in smithereens. I'm not sure how many examples I should provide. Need I mention that the *New York Times* was running page-one stories about the existence of UFOs? Would it suffice to say that scientists were alleging, in peer-reviewed journals, that octopuses were aliens, that reality was nothing more than a pixelated shell game? Meanwhile, our nuclear codes were in the hands of a buffoonish real estate mogul, and millions of Americans had fallen under the sway of fake news and conspiracy theories. Perhaps this was why members of the commentariat began sounding the death knell, contending that, with the 2016 election, America had at last fulfilled John Adams's 1814 disclaimer about the fate of any democracy. "It soon wastes, exhausts, and murders itself," he wrote in a letter. "There never was a democracy yet, that did not commit suicide."

It seemed that we had passed on to some bleak, dusky afterlife, a mist-swarmed purgatory of facts and alternative facts out of which emerged such fearsome ghouls as InfoWars, Stephen Miller, and Space Force. Given that our lives had essentially become post-humous, could you really blame me for wondering if my brother could summon ghosts?

The route to Lily Dale wended through a swath of upstate New York that once served as the fertile crescent of American utopian thinking—John Humphrey Noyes's Oneida Community, Frederick Douglass's abolitionist newspaper—and yet the scenery itself was hardly so auspicious. Much of this area was waylaid by the 2008 recession, and husks of mills and factories still dotted the wearisome landscape. As Andy and I drove, we glimpsed remnants of the old Bethlehem Steel plant, and the Concord grape vineyards south of Buffalo looked like a postapocalyptic Napa Valley. So godforsaken was this neck of the country that Donald Trump, in the waning days of the 2016 election, had condemned it, not unfairly, as "a death zone."

Hunched at the wheel, I snuck glances at my brother, whose face was sallow and draggy with fatigue. Most days he resembles a bald and musclebound Elijah Wood, but his flight the previous night was delayed by several hours, so both of us were running on no sleep and looked a bit like revenants.

"Here are just a few of the workshops on deck this summer," Andy said, thumbing his smartphone and scanning the agenda from the Lily Dale website. "There's Fairyology: Finding Fairies 101. There's Orb Phenom—Orbs Are Among Us! Or we could check out Getting to Know Your Spirit Guides. Plus, there's a drum circle on Friday, and a séance tomorrow night."

"You sure you're up for this?" I asked.

"Yeah, man," he said. "Let's get weird."

Mercifully, things brightened as we veered toward our destination. A sign read LILY DALE 1 MILE AHEAD. We flew past three lakes rimmed with cottages, and when the clouds parted, the sky unleashed a bucolic, life-affirming blue. Nevertheless, I felt a burgeoning unease about our whole larkish adventure. Not only was this the first trip I'd ever taken with my brother, but I also wasn't sure if I was prepared—emotionally, spiritually—for the week ahead. What if our cavortings with mediums caused Andy to have a psychotic break and I had to commit him to some remote upstate hospital? There were historical precedents for such crack-ups. In 1852 some 90 individuals from around the country were said to lose their minds and enter asylums after partaking in spirit rappings. Or what if I discovered that Andy had been lying about his abilities and this effected some irrevocable schism in our relationship, sundering our bond for all time? Then there was the possibility that he'd prove himself a bona fide medium, which would mean what, exactly, I had no idea. Yet for reasons I struggle to explain, I secretly hoped that my brother was the real deal, that he'd prove me wrong by the end of our voyage. Something lodged deep in our past—a moment long banished and left unspoken —seemed crucially to depend on it.

At the end of a secluded road, Lily Dale came into view.

"Look at my forearms," Andy said. His skin was brailled with goosebumps. "The energy here is ridiculous."

Threading through a warren of elm-studded streets lined with pastel Victorians, we saw a battalion of stone angels guarding the porch of one Gothic-looking home, and a couple of blocks later, a bay window had been plastered campily with a decal of a cartoon ghost. Was it possible that I heard, from somewhere far off, a group of people singing Bob Dylan's "Blowin' in the Wind"? Soon we passed a hillock near the main auditorium where a scrum of aging tourists was performing the languorous waltz of tai chi. Near the pet cemetery, we made a wrong turn and had to swerve past an open field, which was already filling up with tents and RVs. My first thought was that Lily Dale looked like an old-fashioned summer camp, except that instead of trust falls and archery class, there were astrology walks and confabs with ghosts.

When it was our turn at the parking gate, the attendant met our eyes, then pressed his fingers to his temples, as though receiving a radio dispatch via dental fillings. "Welcome, welcome," he said with an impish grin. "We've been expecting you two."

Our first day on the grounds was a derby of occult activities. After meditating in something called the Healing Temple, we met a septuagenarian Reiki instructor named Pilar who had tufts of peacock feathers superglued to her spectacles. She called them her "eyeglashes" and explained that she was slowly transforming into a blackbird. On the patio of a coffee shop, Andy befriended an affable blond man named Jayson, who professed to be a medium in training from Brooklyn and whose first coup as a psychic came when he divined the future spouse for one of his clients. (The couple's subsequent gratitude was noted in the Vows section of the *New York Times*.) He and Andy hit it off by making fun of my skepticism — *God, he's so emotionally closed off, isn't he?* — at which point Jayson scrolled through his phone, showing me grainy nocturnal photos of Lily Dale's enchanted Leolyn Woods, an apparent hot spot for nymphs and orbs.

"OK, so these you could argue are bugs or whatever. But this," he said, pointing to the relevant photo, in which a cricket was frozen wing-spread in the flash of a smartphone camera. "I mean, come on. That's a fucking fairy."

Throughout the day, people kept sharing their photos. A gray-haired pilgrim named Susan accosted us on a veranda. "Can I show you guys something?" she asked. Before we could answer, she riffled through her purse and unearthed a dozen photos, each of which she laid on the surface of a wicker end table. "I have a lot of activity in my house," she said. One image showed a mishmash of Scrabble letters in which I slowly perceived the relevant message. MOTHER LOVES SUSAN, it said, WHO IS MY DAUGHTER.

Automatic Drawing with Miss Bonnie took place in the Octagon Building, not far from the Lily Dale Museum. After a short prayer and some guided breathing, we were paired off and asked to close our eyes before "surrendering to spirit." From across the room, I watched Andy blindly sketch a tableau of what looked, frankly, like a thicket of penises, which I was worried would offend his partner, a medium in training from Pennsylvania. When time was up, Andy relayed his message. "I know it's strange," he said, "but I keep seeing the name 'Tom' among all these phallic symbols."

The woman gasped. "Tom is my husband's name," she said. "And that's just his issue. I'm going through menopause right now, so let's just say that he's been frustrated with certain aspects of our marriage." I watched as she and Andy erupted with guffaws, whereupon Andy turned to me and raised his eyebrows, simpering triumphantly. Yet it was hard for me to take this as ironclad evidence. Show anyone a hodgepodge of random images, and if they've thrown off the tethers of logic and good judgment, doubtless they'll be able to conjure associations to their own interpersonal dilemmas. Still, that Andy had intuited the husband's name did leave me somewhat dazzled.

Things on my side of the classroom were hardly so jovial. I was partnered with a rawboned blond woman named Ashley who looked to be in her late 30s and who had come to Lily Dale with her parents. Gravel-voiced and sullen, she worked full-time in a Walgreens warehouse, and while there was an Amazon distribution center down the road, it was hard to land a gig there. So far at Lily Dale, the messages she'd received "from spirit" had been spot-on and uplifting—exhortations to stop stressing. I asked what sorts of things she fretted about.

"Sometimes I wish I had gone to college and actually done something with my life," Ashley said. "The problem was, I didn't know what I wanted to do. So I never ended up doing anything."

In the face of her weary candor, I couldn't seem to muster the journalistic moxie needed to ask a follow-up question. But what I would discover in the coming days was that Ashley's story chimed with many testimonies of the Lily Dale pilgrims. Hailing from beleaguered rural towns across New England and the Midwest, they were suffering from all manner of emotional or financial disaster and were desperate for a more hopeful story—that their lives were being guided by cadres of benevolent spirits, that though present circumstances were bleak, they shouldn't give up the ghost.

That evening at the Maplewood Hotel, I unpacked my suitcase while Andy lounged on his bed, swiping languidly at his smartphone. Between responding to what appeared to be a deluge of work emails, he told me, with a baffling nonchalance, that he'd been having a recurring vision of a kidnapped midwestern girl whose face had colonized network news that summer. He was vague about what exactly these visions entailed, though the images he disclosed were not especially promising (cornfield, head injury). Then, without prompting, he said, "Whenever you travel, it's always important to unpack. That's what makes it feel like home."

I wasn't quite sure how to respond to any of this—the visions, the unsolicited travel advice—and so our conversation was full of awkward lapses and long moments of silence.

Not since childhood had Andy and I shared such close quarters, and even then, the propinquity usually resulted in a verbal skirmish or an all-out fracas. I suppose our relationship in those days could be best described as Cain and Abel-ish. This was owing, more than anything else, to our wildly divergent temperaments. Whereas he spent most nights hunkered in the basement and pummeling a Stratocaster, I would toil under the glow of a desk lamp, trying to make honor roll for another semester. Whereas he wore earrings and a leather jacket, I jogged across town in ankle weights, hoping to make varsity as a freshman. Our mother often explained the variance in our personalities this way: "Aren't genes amazing?"

Still, as adults, we somehow managed to construct a passable relationship as brothers, even if, at times, it could feel performative and falsely nostalgic. For instance, whenever our family got together for birthdays or Christmas celebrations, a preening one-upmanship tended to infuse our interactions such that, within minutes of him picking me up from the airport, we'd be quoting lines from old movies, doing our bad Al Pacino impressions, or making fun of each other's hairlines, all of it delivered with the snappy banter of brothers on a network sitcom. Rarely did we spend much time alone, however. And while we had joked over the years about his psychic abilities, we had never once hazarded an earnest discussion about them.

Which was why it was so unsettling to find ourselves inside the cramped precinct of our hotel room, brushing our teeth or changing clothes only a few feet away from each other. Almost by reflex, I found myself curious about his habits of being—his shaving techniques, his pre-bed calisthenics—rather the same way I would creep into his room as a child to marvel at his possessions. I'd flip through his CDs—Nine Inch Nails, Spiritualized—or try on his flannels, occasionally summoning the courage to pluck out a few notes on his Fender. And so, even though I was a man in his 30s —a husband, a university professor—I somehow found myself becoming again my brother's little brother.

Perhaps this was why I found it so gratifying that the merry denizens of Lily Dale kept referring to us as a unit. As we shuffled from one psychic appointment to another, or traversed campus on our way to a séance, they'd bellow at us from across the road, "Hey, hey, it's the brothers!" One medium traipsed over while Andy and I were eating dinner at a picnic table and said, "Well, are we making any progress with this guy?" I assumed he was referring to my glacial incredulity, and I was curious to hear what my brother might say. "I think he's weakening," Andy said. "But I'm not sure he buys it."

"Bah," the medium said, waving his hand at me, like a Dickens character. Then he slapped Andy's back with affectionate gusto and stomped off toward the Healing Temple. We chewed for some time in silence. Then Andy gave me a styptic look. "I know you think this place is nutty," he said.

I reminded him that we'd just seen a man barf up jewels that he claimed were relics from the spirit world. This was at a demonstration of something called "apportations," in which a medium will brusquely produce supernatural objects through a transdimensional portico (in this case, his mouth).

"It's just, I was really hoping to get some answers here," Andy said. He explained that his wife had become increasingly worried about him. Before he left for Lily Dale, there'd been a scene. They feuded in the car outside the airport, with finger-pointing and furrowed brows. Perhaps she doubted him, called him crazy, something like that. His prognostications had grown darker over the years, more unsettling, and she didn't want to believe what he had to say.

"Things have gotten pretty grim, so I know that she wants me to get it under control," he said.

In the mid-19th century, Spiritualism's earliest practitioners were inclined to believe that technological advances like electrical wires could be divine portals to the spiritual realm. It was for this reason that Benjamin Franklin became the movement's patron saint and that its flagship periodical was dubbed the *Spiritual Telegraph*. One early adherent believed that electricity was "the vehicle of divine mentality," which could be harnessed to communicate with "all parts and particles of the universe." At a distance of two centuries, it's easy to malign these Americans for their naiveté, but we must remember that, within the span of two decades, they'd gone from waiting months to get a letter in the mail to somehow receiving a cross-country dispatch by telegraph within minutes. From there it was only a short leap of logic before supposing you could commune with ghosts.

Part of me wondered whether my brother's job in the tech industry had made him susceptible to precisely this delusion. An evangelist for cloud software, he had decked out his house over the years with a whole flotilla of smart technologies: thermostats that respond to voice commands, a refrigerator that alerts him whenever the eggs are running low. Even Amazon's Alexa had become a frequent interlocutor at family dinners, telling knock-

knock jokes to his children or dispensing *Jeopardy*-grade trivia to him and his wife. To be ensconced in such an environment—one so seamlessly attuned to your whims and predilections—perhaps it was only a matter of time before you regarded yourself as similarly omniscient.

The reigning consensus at Lily Dale, however, suggested otherwise, because virtually all the mediums to whom I spoke insisted that my brother's premonitions were likely caused by a cerebral hemorrhage. "That or a high fever can trigger it," said fifth-generation Spiritualist Gretchen Clark. Lauren Thibodeau, a Lily Dale medium with a PhD in psychology, explained that it's not uncommon with near-death experiences. "Depending on the study," she said, "you find that between three-quarters to one hundred percent of people who almost died will tell you that they became psychic, they became healers, they became mediumistic."

This supposition is more or less in keeping with the findings of Diane Hennacy Powell, a neuroscientist trained at the Johns Hopkins School of Medicine. Powell has written a book called *The ESP Enigma: The Scientific Case for Psychic Phenomena*, which I brought with me to Lily Dale and had been reading surreptitiously whenever Andy went on jogs or bedded down for the evening. Though derided by critics as wholesale bunkum, the book is interesting in places, particularly when it conjectures a direct correlation between brain trauma and clairvoyant prowess. While some mediums are genetically predisposed to their gifts, Powell has said, "There are also cases where people haven't had psychic abilities until they've suffered head traumas. What's common is that these people who've had this head trauma, the structure and function of their brain has changed."

Ordinarily, I would not be willing to lend these theories much credence. After all, as a dutiful child of poststructuralism, I'm well aware that science suffers from a dastardly case of confirmation bias, and one needn't wander far to locate rigged experiments or cherry-picked data. But it turns out that modern researchers *can* replicate the results of parapsychological studies—those that supposedly prove the existence of clairvoyance and telepathy. Shortly before our trip to Lily Dale, I had dredged up an article from *American Psychologist* by Lund University professor Etzel Cardeña, who suggests that the most cogent and persuasive explanations for these phenomena involve fringe physics and quantum entanglement, which conceive of objects not as isolated and entropic but threaded together in a vast tapestry, where every movement is connected via gorgeously reticulated spindles, even across time and space. It gets weirder. Calling upon the research of Princeton physics philosopher Hans Halvorson, Cardeña has suggested that this "superentanglement" explains why an individual can sense, even across great distances, the abrupt death of a loved one. It was this theory, in particular, that I kept returning to in the days and weeks that followed. Was it possible that family members could be quantumly entangled?

About a year before our trip to Lily Dale, in the midst of an unremitting depression, I began to contemplate suicide. I will resist the sentimentality of describing the causes. Enough to say that I had been plagued by a neurochemical glitch since childhood, and some periods of my life were worse than others. I had tried everything: Prozac and CrossFit, yoga and therapy. Routine occurrences prickled my thoughts like wind against a burn scar, and most days were less endured than climbed. For the first time in two decades, I found myself down on my knees, my hands threaded in unstudied prayer, whispering pleas and apologies to the God-shaped hole in my mind. I told no one—not even my wife—of my plans, that the escape offered by leather belts and ceiling beams had begun to strike me as inordinately appealing.

Then I awoke one morning to a voice mail from my mom, telling me to call as soon as I got up. Naturally, I worried that someone had died, that our family had been visited by yet another disaster. But it turned out that Andy had called her in the middle of the night, terrified and inconsolable. There were tears in his voice. Out on the West Coast, he'd been barhopping with friends when he got the most unnerving presentiment.

"What did he say?" I asked.

"He—" my mom started, her voice wounded with concern. "Oh," she said. "He just drank too much. I'll tell him you're fine, honey."

On our second afternoon at Lily Dale, Andy and I wandered to the Forest Temple for one of two daily "message" services. It featured a round-robin of seven or eight mediums standing at the front of an outdoor amphitheater and haphazardly beckoning spirits. We sat below a sun-dappled canopy of hemlock and elm, amid roughly

200 other tourists, and watched as, one by one, the mediums did their thing.

Like all niche communities, the Spiritualists at Lily Dale have evolved their own extensive lingua franca, rife with daffy euphemisms for the brute facts of life, the most representative of which are their various phrases for death. These include "passing over," "in spirit," "going from the earth plane," and "departing for Summerland." So much of the ethereal argot is gooey and granola crunching, but at times its poetics attain a distinctly erotic mood, especially when a medium approaches a member of the audience and asks, "May I come to you?" Other idiomatic expressions amplify the carnal entendres with shades of penetration. "May I step into your vibrations?" or "May I touch in with you, my friend?"

This consent seeking seems proper. After all, the communiqués can get fairly intense. Toward the end of the service we attended, one of the mediums brought forth a message for a shaggy-haired 20-something named Bobby, who was sitting in the back pews with his friends, a cluster of raffish-looking bohemians. The medium described the spirit of a gaunt, pallid man who'd been pacing across his apartment in the moments before he died and over whom "a river of tears had been shed." After the service, Andy caught up with Bobby and asked whether the medium's description had meant something to him.

"Yeah, man, that's my cousin, who OD'd on heroin," Bobby said. "The last couple days, he's been following me around."

That evening we met up with Bobby and his friends under the gazebo of Lily Dale's dock, which jutted into the moon-glazed shallows of Cassadaga Lake and offered us shelter from a pinprick drizzle. Soon cans of Budweiser were slugged and packs of American Spirits were torn open. There were seven friends altogether, gregarious and in their early 20s, wearing hemp fibers and various configurations of tie-dye. One got the sense that their Birkenstocks had treaded the grounds of many outdoor music festivals. Each introduced themselves with a fun fact and their astrological sign, as was their special custom whenever meeting new people. Bobby was a Taurus who was slogging through a master's degree, penning a thesis on agricultural-reform movements in postcolonial West Africa. His girlfriend, Erica, was a grad student with a pixie haircut whose fun fact was that she was a rabid fan of the Red Hot Chili Peppers. But the obvious ringleader of the group was Mekenna, a big-eyed, fast-talking hairstylist with a Harry Potter tattoo. A Pisces, naturally, she said, and everyone laughed.

It turned out that Mekenna and her cousin Meredith came from seven generations of Spiritualists, and their distant ancestors helped found Lily Dale at the crack of the 20th century. They grew up coming here every summer, studying the Fox sisters and playing tag among the crystal-clutching tourists who thronged the streets from June to August. Mekenna's grandmother is a longtime Lily Dale resident, and her mom is a practicing medium in Milwaukee. For a moment, I tried to imagine a childhood where your parents routinely nattered with spirits—where nightly prayers might involve the ectoplasmic manifestation of your dead grandpa. Reckoning with such phenomena as a digital native must have been a trip. Consider the impulse to post about family séances as a sullen, irascible teen: *FML, Mom is channeling grandpa again. He says I'm too boy-crazy for my age. LOLZ.* But growing up, Mekenna and Meredith tried to keep the theology under wraps. Turned out their peers weren't exactly accepting. Often recess featured a hail of vicious schoolyard epithets: *Demon! Satanist!*

Of course, now that nearly every strain of American occultism had experienced a sudden renascence, the group didn't much witness this kind of opprobrium anymore. If anything, they said, there'd been a growing consumer market for all things esoteric: jade stones for Kegel exercises, crystals for off-kilter chakras. Even a mainstream lifestyle brand like Goop could get rich by peddling New Age curios. It was enough for me to wonder why occultism had come into vogue again.

"Look at what's going on in the planetary alignment," Meredith said. "That would help explain things. The outer planets are generational, so when we think about big movements or certain decades as having unique characteristics, it's probably because Pluto was in Libra then." Pluto in Libra turns out to be a quintessential astrological formation among stargazers, who believe it to be responsible for the upswell of divorce throughout the 1970s.

Despite whatever coldhearted materialism I professed to endorse before our trip, I nevertheless found myself enthralled by a worldview that could so neatly explain massive social disruptions. Part of me worried that the group would think I was baiting them, but I asked anyway: "So why is Trump happening?"

The gazebo resounded with their collective groans. But Meredith had an answer at the ready: "So, last year's solar eclipse lined up with his chart exactly, in countless ways."

"But astrology is not determinist, so it didn't make Trump happen," Bobby cut in. "There's plenty of sociopolitical underpinnings to our societal problems." Unlike Meredith, who had been raised in the cradle of Spiritualism, Bobby became interested in this theology as an adult, and I got the sense that he was worried I might see them as witless yahoos, clutching maladaptively to backward explanations.

Again Meredith countered, looking toward the stars. "You can do charts of countries or events—anything that has a time and place—and the birth chart of America is, like, very, *very* Cancer," she said. "So why is the United States so concerned about defense? Why are we about protecting the homeland?"

"Well," Bobby said, "whomever we elect is a symptom of a larger disease—that being our economic system of capitalistic exploitation. Obama was a symptom of this larger disease as well. He came at his particular time and his particular place. And we didn't get a whole lot different from Obama." He quickly sketched the last decade of geopolitical woes—Syria, Libya, Turkey—before eventually concluding with syllogistic finality: "So all of this is part of a larger disease that exists in the United States."

"But that's been going on way before Obama," Meredith said.

"Oh yeah," he said. "That's how we've been operating since this country's inception."

"Obama's a Leo," Mekenna said, "in case anybody's curious."

As the evening unraveled and the lake boiled with rain, our talk shifted, and the group became curious about the origins of my brother's mediumship. "I would hear stuff," Andy said. "And I would be like, I'm going fucking insane. I'm losing my mind." A few years ago, when his wife's uncle died, freakish things started happening in their house. Furniture would move. They were lying in bed one night when a picture frame skated across the dresser. "Every time we fought, something would intervene," Andy said. "We would walk into a room screaming at each other—two Scorpios, right?—and the lights would start flickering, or the volume on the TV would go wildly up and down." One night he woke up and saw the apparition of his wife's uncle loitering in the bedroom's corner.

"I didn't understand any of it. I didn't know what the fuck was going on," he said. "But eventually I got to a point where I was like: *I get it.* And I could start hearing the messages. I would pray, and I would actually hear responses."

I had heard bits and pieces of this story before, but always in the elusive, half-joking manner in which Andy tended to relay them. To hear him speak so earnestly now was a little unnerving, and I glanced at the kids to see whether they might roll their eyes or snicker at him. But they never did.

He started transmitting dispatches from his wife's dead relatives, which was difficult, he said, because they were Dutch and only spoke broken English. (At this point, my skepticism flared — *what, they can break through the time-space continuum but have no access to Google Translate?*) He began doing readings for his wife, predicting that certain events would happen on a given timeline, and to her astonishment, they consistently panned out. Soon she was dragging friends home on girls' night— "when they were all hammered at two o'clock in the morning"—so he could do readings for them, too. Sometimes he'd find himself wandering out of the house and driving to the grocery store for no apparent reason. It wasn't until he saw a particular shopper that he'd realize why he was there: "I'd be walking the aisles and find myself saying, 'Is your name Mandy?' And I'd be like, 'Uh, your mom's here.'"

"That's some *Long Island Medium* shit," Mekenna said.

Andy turned to me and, seeming to register my skepticism, remarked, "Barrett thinks I'm full of shit, because he's never seen it before."

"Analytical Aquarius," a girl named Fargus said, rather wearily.

"All weekend, I think he's been googling 'How to test your psychic brother,'" Andy said.

I felt, for the first time, somewhat ashamed of my hidebound incredulity, perhaps because I was newly aware of how desperately my brother needed this story—an Iliad in which his injury wasn't random misfortune but a godsend that endowed him with spiritual purpose. Perhaps this was related to the wider cultural appeal of a worldview like astrology. After all, at least some of these millennials were professing to read our worldly turmoil by the stars, which offered the tantalizing prospect that if I could understand such celestial oscillations, then maybe I could rest assured in knowing that Saturn would soon be in retrograde, that Trump would be ousted, that words like "truth" and "facts" might one day mean something again. Given the grief we've endured at the hands of this administration, to say nothing of the head-swiveling instability caused by our most recent recession, one could be forgiven for pursuing such a totalizing narrative, with the reassuring plot twists of conflict, climax, and feel-good denouement. What united my brother and these kids was that they were looking for a benign, large-hearted way of being in the world, a story that could cleanly explain what was happening and why, and I couldn't help admiring the sheer blamelessness of that.

As the rain slowed to a drizzle, we headed back to the encampment, where the air was flavored with bonfires and lights were still glowing in the Maplewood Hotel. Perhaps a séance or two was yet underway? Our farewell was full of hugs and promises to hang out tomorrow. Maybe it was owing to the day's marathon of activities, but I found myself weirdly enamored of these Spiritualist kids, who were now somewhat adorably counseling my brother on finding a New Age community. Mekenna offered to put Andy in touch with her mom. Fargus and Meredith were confident that there were Spiritualist churches in California. But Andy confessed that he was scared to come out publicly as a medium. "The energy here is really safe," he said. "But back home I'm just a freak at two a.m. for drunk friends who want to talk to dead relatives."

The next morning, I woke at dawn to tunnels of sunshine blaring through the window. Songbirds chirped metallically in the trees. My sleep had been scanty and thin, not only because of Andy's prodigious snoring, which resembled the flatulent-sounding horn of a sea freighter, but also because our accommodations were decidedly rustic. Our narrow room boasted two twin beds, each monastically appointed with scratchy blankets and crick-inducing pillows. Indeed, the bedding seemed to have been last updated during the Reagan administration.

Likely, part of my sleeplessness could be attributed to our upcoming class with Reverend Mychael Shane, a medium who offered an eight-hour(!) workshop on enhancing your mediumistic skills. If ever there were a test that could prove my brother's claims, this would be it, which was why I hurried us across campus, admonishing Andy, who was still dripping from a brisk shower, as we veered toward the Assembly Hall.

Soon we made our way toward the rostrum, over which a large

stained-glass window read CHURCH OF THE LIVING SPIRIT. There sat Reverend Shane, a beefy heap of a man with wisps of silver hair and soft, bearish eyes, wearing a lavender polo and ecru slacks. Sitting in a horseshoe of folding chairs around him were our fellow classmates. There were Mark and Allen, a couple from a Spiritualist church in Florida; Karen, a local medium who served in the Healing Temple; Reverend Jane, an "international medium" with feathered bangs and disco-era makeup; and Margaret, a self-avowed "Mychael Shane groupie." Over the subsequent eight hours, we were offered a whirlwind tour of physical mediumship, including things like apportations and "trance channelings."

During introductions, Andy told the group the story about his brain injury, at which point Shane launched into a personalized sermon.

"You know, there's nothing wrong with you," he said.

Andy laughed. "Can I get that in writing, please?"

"I'm really trying to be serious here, OK?" Shane said, noticeably peeved. "There's really nothing wrong with you. Who has a right to say even that there is? Who can say that you have a problem or something's not working right? Maybe you're thinking, Why did these things happen to me? Only you are gonna find out the answer. Luckily, you have the support of your family. I mean, your brother is sitting right there."

Andy looked at me. The rest of the group looked at me. I gave a little sheepish wave. Suddenly, I felt like some scurrilous gate-crasher, here only to poke fun at some downtrodden individuals, my own brother among them. Soon I had a memory of Andy splayed on his hospital cot, his forehead gashed and bleeding, a nest of IV tubes snarling up his arms.

Then, almost as an afterthought, Shane advised Andy to invest in PepsiCo and Aflac.

My brother turned to me, his eyes throttle-popped and spooked. Later he would tell me that he'd just closed deals with both of those companies.

"You're always going to appear off to others," Shane continued. "That's never going to change, but that's OK. Because you are a divine, beautiful entity that has purpose and is necessary and needed in this world."

The next segment of class involved billet readings. Shane explained that, one by one, each of us would come to the front and have silver dollars duct-taped over our eyes, which would then be covered by an eye mask and a bandanna. Everyone else in the room would jot a question on a note card, and on the other side we'd scribble a number. "Could be eleven, could be ten thousand forty-three. Doesn't matter," Shane said. Everyone's note cards would be placed in a wicker basket, which would then be handed to the blindfolded medium, who in turn would "read" both sides of the cards. Feats like these, Shane told us, can be "the worm on the hook to get people interested in this stuff."

The early results were pitiful. Reverend Jane went zero for six. Mark and Allen batted about .300. I got two of the numbers right and felt momentarily cocky—do psychic abilities perhaps run in the family?—but then flubbed every subsequent card.

"Can you see through there?" Shane asked Andy after I'd blindfolded him. There was something ceremonial, if not eerily religious, about this tableau, with Andy sitting before me, eyes closed, humble as a monk, waiting to be tested.

"No," Andy said. "I wish I could. I actually have a fair amount of anxiety in claustrophobic spaces. Ever since my injury, I don't do well with tight spots."

I returned to my seat and watched as Andy began shrugging in a jerky, vaguely Tourettic way, and when he reached for the first card, his hand quavered noticeably, reminding me of the spasms he'd suffered from cerebral edema during those long, anguished nights in the ICU. For a moment, I wanted to call this whole thing off, but then he placed the first note card against his forehead and inhaled deeply, audibly. "Nine," he said. "And uh, I'm not sure if it's my claustrophobia or something I'm picking up, but the number nine and a question about space."

He handed the card to Reverend Shane. "The number is a nine. And the question is: 'What is a sacred space for me to go to?'"

"Good job," said Karen, the healer.

"Not bad," Shane said. "Well, my job is done. See you all later." Everyone laughed.

Andy rummaged through the basket before extracting the next card. "I see a one and a seven, so maybe seventy-one, but I'm not getting the question." He passed the card to Shane. "Seventeen," the reverend said. "So that's what's called spiritual dyslexia. The question is: 'Where are my shoes from?'"

For the next card, my brother said, "I don't know if it's the answer to the question or the number, but there's only 'one.'"

"There is a circle with a one in it," Shane said. "Not bad. OK, a couple more."

Even with the blindfold, I could tell my brother was distressed. His cheeks were flushed, a paddled crimson, and his forehead was a geyser of sweat. Shane's assistant, Cynthia, noticed this, too. "You're almost there," she said. He bungled the next one, which was my card, but I didn't reveal this. Then, unbidden, he said, "Well, that was my brother's card."

I shook my head, happily perplexed, but before I could unleash a cynical rejoinder, he was plucking another card from the basket. "I see the number 2019. And I see my tattoo"—inked on his left arm was the symbol for infinity.

"Your tattoo is on there," Shane said. "And the question is, 'What will be the big news story for 2019?'"

At this point, people in the room were shaking their heads, their eyes mirthful and guileless, astonished in a childlike way. I turned around to gauge the reactions of two Lily Dale facilitators, who had been hovering in the back throughout the proceedings and who now gave Shane a covert thumbs-up, as if to certify that my brother was the real deal, the genuine article. The next afternoon, one of these women would suggest that Andy give readings at the 4:00 p.m. message service. Another would urge him to get certified by the Lily Dale board. Even Reverend Shane would offer to be Andy's mentor at the end of the night.

Andy couldn't read the last card, but even with a couple of blunders, the room was still full of swift converts to his cause. Karen the healer said, "Could you tell me your last name again, so that when you're rich and famous I can say I met you?"

"That made me *really* uncomfortable," Andy said.

"You got every number right," Mark said. (And most of the questions, too, I think.)

"That's one for the records," Allen said.

By the time the workshop had ended, it was midnight, and a big moon loomed overhead, washing the campus lawns with a thin ethereal light. Somewhat predictably, our walk back to the hotel was punctuated by sprees of unmitigated fraternal boasting ("So, bro, how do you like *them* apples?"—that sort of thing), and I was worried that my brother's laughter, as it ricocheted across the courtyard, would rouse some angry spirits or perhaps a few pilgrims trying to catch some post-séance shut-eye.

I asked Andy what he felt as he was blindfolded, how he was able to identify so many cards.

"I could feel these different energies approaching me," he said. "So I just asked them to make it go fast."

A silence fell between us as we shuffled under a vault of wind-hissed elm trees, and without really thinking it over, I found myself asking the question that had been grating at me all week and that, I realize now, was the whole reason we came.

"A year ago, Mom called me in the middle of the night and said you were worried about me. Do you remember that?"

"Yeah," he said.

"Do you remember why you were worried?" I asked.

As soon as I posed the question, I regretted it. The truth was, I didn't know what to make of what I'd witnessed that night, and suddenly, I was leery of what he might say.

"I kept seeing visions of you killing yourself."

I stopped and looked at my brother, who kept walking and peering around. Even in the twilight, I could see that his eyes were darkened with stress and little sleep, the oncoming erosion of middle age, and on the other side of the continent, there was a whole other life waiting for him. It was a minor cruelty to remember that this week wouldn't last, that somehow we had become men in our mid-30s, duty-bound to jobs and the burdens of our own families. The next day, we'd drive back to Buffalo, and at some point that night, he'd vanish without a trace, taking an Uber to the airport, leaving me to wake alone in the pre-dawn stillness of a sullen July morning.

But right then, in the dark of the Spiritualist campus, I was ready to believe my brother knew something that I simply could not fathom. If he intuited my past struggles—if he could divine the place in my life where the narrative began to break down, where the plot took a swerve—then maybe he could also foresee the future, which had come to seem ever more uncertain, a monstrous void of flux and foreboding. Given what I'd just seen him do, I wanted to believe my brother knew the ending to this story. I wanted to believe that I would listen. But all I could manage was a blithering acknowledgment, a little-brother's sheepish confession.

"That was a really lonely time for me," I said.

He was quiet for a moment. Then he shrugged. "Well, you weren't alone," he said.

The next morning, pilgrims were queuing up at the doors of the Healing Temple. There were elderly people inching toward the entrance with the help of metal walkers, plus a posse of young women with slovenly topknots, their tote bags emblazoned with FEMINIST WITCHES. A maroon-haired woman from Cleveland rapped with me about LeBron James's recent move to the Lakers, then offered to balance my chakras with the swings of her pendulum necklace. The line moved slowly. And eventually, the early parishioners who were already inside the temple emerged from its heavy oaken doors—their faces were radiant and changed.

Next to the temple's walkway was Lily Dale's gnarled and stunted prayer tree, whose crown of spired branches had been tessellated with thousands of ribbons in every possible shade of teal and magenta, orange and pink. On them, lonesome Americans had scribbled abridged prayers, hopeful bulletins, little valentines to the dead. *Mom, I miss you every day. Enjoy Heaven!* and *Love + Light to Those in Need* and *Unify My Family.*

Back home this effusion of wishful thinking would've struck me as saccharine and pathetic. But here, under gentle wind chimes and blue sky, I found myself shorn of cynicism, earnestly moved by these barefaced gestures of pathos and heartache. When future historians try to understand how we reckoned with our cultural and political disasters, they'll need only to comb through these variegated streamers to see how desperate and mournful we'd become. I thought of Susan, waiting for more Scrabble-letter dispatches from her mom. I thought of Ashley, back home in Connecticut, stocking product for Walgreens. And I thought of those bright-eyed millennials, our spirit guides—Erica and Mekenna, Kate and Fargus, Meredith and Bobby. Six of the colored tassels I affixed to the prayer tree were for them. Then my mind turned to my own mom and dad, to the rest of my family, all of whom were worried about me and Andy, hoping against hope that, despite everything, we'd be OK.

Inside the temple, nine healers stood at the altar. They wore bright white smocks, like special envoys from heaven. Seated before each of them, in a wooden chair, was a congregant with upturned palms and shuttered eyes. The healers waved their hands over each congregant's body, their movements mime-like and untouching, a silent legerdemain. A tall man with a gray ponytail stood at the back of the room and played a wooden flute whose soulful, dirgy tones were both solacing and elegiac. Piquant incense perfumed the air, and eventually, the temple commandant pointed me toward the altar. I took a seat in front of a soft-voiced, bespectacled man who directed me to close my eyes. Put at the front of your mind, he told me, all your dead, all those who've passed into spirit. "We believe in everlasting life," he said, "so know that those people are with you right now."

You'll think I'm exaggerating, but something started happening to me. As the man performed his arcane ministrations, some trapdoor on the left side of my brow flew open, and ages of stratified blackness were leaking out. Soon there were tears running from my eyes.

Somehow I was transported to a moment from 20 years ago, when I was standing at the edge of a river in the midst of my first adult-grade depression. Twelve years old, with a dark, spinning brain, I had wandered away from our family's camp and was peering into the depths of a river, watching the brunette water froth and churn over a herd of jagged stones. I cannot tell you what came over me next, but in a moment I was there, disappearing into the violence of a brown crystalline burst.

The current was alive, a man's hands, and almost immediately I was regretting my decision. But when I managed to breach the river's surface, I could see my brother appear on shore, a blur of dark jeans and red T-shirt, entering the water just as soon as I went under. Somehow I was being tillered toward a raft of downed branches, where my brother had pulled us to refuge, where I had a moment to calm down and wipe the water from my eyes. I found that I was crying, still terrified, still boyishly confused about what I had done and what I still might do. How near that story of total obliteration had been, of following my dead to the other side of the river, of wanting so desperately a final and irrevocable exit.

My brother said nothing. His face was full of a terrible understanding. Always, even across time and distance, his face has been full of this terrible understanding. Then he was telling me it was time to go, and with our heads barely above the surface, he reached out to me, and I held on to him, and he ferried me back across the water.

SHANNA B. TIAYON

# Vacation Memories Marred by the Indelible Stain of Racism

FROM *Longreads*

As I LOOKED out the bus window I was awestruck by the magnificence and vastness of the canyon that stretched farther than my eyes could see. I stared at the brown hues with hints of red, orange, and blue, and the rock textures that were still visible even from a distance. The Grand Canyon was breathtaking and I was taking it all in for the last time as the bus drove by.

A loud voice disturbed the peace of my window gazing.

"There's no eating on the bus," it said. "The kid—she dropped the paper and there's no eating on the bus."

My eyes never left the window. When the disruption passed, I turned my thoughts to our trip. It was March 2018. Hailing from the DC Metro area, this was the first trip we took as a family after I completed my PhD program in May 2017.

My husband and I, with our four kids ranging in age from 2 to 20, had just finished the arduous but magnificent hike of the canyon's Cedar Ridge Trail. The hike was challenging, but we made it. As I sat on the bus returning to the visitor center, I could already feel my muscles starting to tense up from navigating the trail's 6,120-foot elevation gain.

"The paper," the voice interrupted again, "somebody needs to pick that paper up."

This time I turned my head toward the front of the bus, realizing that the person spoiling my daydreaming was the bus driver. The National Park Service bus driver glared at us through the rearview mirror, gesturing toward a Kind bar wrapper my two-year-old had accidentally dropped on the floor. We weren't the only ones eating on the bus, but we were the only ones being admonished for it. Also, we were the only black family on the bus. In fact our family represented six out of the total eight black people on the trail at all that day, among dozens of white visitors.

I bent down to pick up the paper just as we arrived at the second stop. The bus driver pressed the brake. Still partially out of my seat, my body lunged forward with the momentum of the bus. When it came to a complete stop, my back jolted to the back of the seat. I looked up and the bus driver was now out of her seat, coming toward us with her hands flailing. She was a thin-framed, older white woman, I guess in her early 60s, with long, straight, bleach-blonde hair hanging down her back. Wide-framed, tinted glasses sat on her face. She had on dark jeans and a red puff vest, and she reeked of cigarette smoke.

She stopped within a foot of my family. "I need you all to get up and move to the back," she said. "I need those seats so the passengers can board."

We'd been the last ones to board the bus at the South Kaibab Trailhead, adjacent to the Cedar Ridge Trail. By the time our family of six got on the bus, the only seats left were those reserved for the elderly and the disabled at the front of the bus. We looked around and there were no elderly or disabled people in need of the seats, so we sat down, as we'd seen so many other able-bodied individuals do during our two-day stay at the canyon. We occupied five of the eight reserved seats (we held our two-year-old), and we were fully prepared to relinquish a seat if necessary.

The bus driver started to make shooing motions at my 12-year-old son, telling him to "Move, go!"

I slowly turned my head to look out the window at the bus stop, expecting to see a senior citizens' group waiting to board. Instead I saw one elderly white woman with a walker, a middle-aged white woman, and a younger-looking white man.

I turned my head and counted the seats still available at the front of the bus—one, two, three. I turned my head back to the bus stop and counted the passengers, only one of whom had any rightful claim to the reserved seating—one, two, three.

The bus driver stood there, refusing to continue the trip until we got up. The silence on the full bus was palpable.

My husband yelled out, "This is ridiculous," as he got up in frustration. We relented and vacated our five seats. The passengers boarded, took the seats in the front, and the bus driver went back to her seat. As the bus pulled away from the bus stop to continue to the visitor center, it was like a scene from the 1950s. My black family stood in the aisle, while five seats at the front of the bus remained empty. I heard my 18-year-old daughter say, "What the . . .", stopping short of the natural profanity that should close that phrase, and my 12-year-old son looked at me, confused.

I had no answers for my son, as I was still processing everything myself, so I turned around and looked at the other, predominantly white, passengers on the bus, many of whom had high-fived us and cheered us on along the trail, only to meet averted gazes and choked throats. No one wanted to confirm what I knew my family was experiencing, no one wanted to risk demonstrating any active expression of empathy. Until, shortly after we pulled away from the bus stop, one white woman rubbed my hand, looked at me remorsefully, and got out of her seat, gesturing for my oldest daughter to sit down with the two-year-old.

Her gesture meant that we were not invisible. This was not a figment of our imaginations.

In the only act of defiance he could think of, my husband grabbed my hand and said, "Come on, we're sitting in those seats," pulling me toward the remaining seats at the front of the bus. I sat down in a fog, leaned on my husband, and completed my daughter's poignant observation in my head: What the hell!

Racism is insidious. Even with a lifetime of lived racist experiences, I'm still caught off guard every time it happens to me. Moments before the bus scene, my family and I were trotting down the Cedar Ridge Trail, a three-mile out-and-back trail in the Grand Canyon trail system, carrying our two-year-old daughter in a blue hiking backpack we borrowed from a friend. I carried all 30 pounds of her down the trail, perched on my back like the Queen of Sheba. I received great accolades of supermomdom from others on the trail that day, mostly whites, some foreign, most not. My husband, God bless him, carried her back up the trail, bypassing others along the way. He was met with casual chitchat on the way up, and was applauded for his athleticism.

We got back to the top of the trail as a family, proud and grateful for the opportunity to see one of the seven natural wonders of the world. Little did we know at the time of the racism that awaited us on the bus—racism that our elated spirits weren't prepared to receive, yet our subconscious minds feared could be a possibility. Racism that would intrude upon our experience, seeping into the cracks of our joy and tainting the memory of our family vacation.

For most of the assault on the bus, we would stand alone, literally and figuratively. A mother, father, and four kids, cloaked in their invisible middle-class status, high level of education, and accomplished children, none of which would be enough to save us from being viewed as other. With our visible similarities too disparate and the assault to my family perhaps not egregious enough, our humanity would be overlooked on the bus that day by all except one woman who dared to acknowledge our humanity and give up her seat; who chose to be an ally.

We would encounter two more allies when we got off the bus.

When we arrived at the visitor center, my husband and I immediately disembarked the bus with our kids, and instinctively huddled together to discuss what had happened. During that time the driver got off to go to the restroom. In the midst of our deliberations, another family who was on the bus, consisting of a white woman, two kids, and a Hispanic man, walked over to us. Unsure of their intentions as they approached, by that time on the defensive, we were poised to quickly retort if necessary.

I felt my shoulders tense as they came closer. They introduced themselves and started to express how sorry they were for what had just happened to us. My shoulders came down a bit. They apologized again and went on to acknowledge how we were obviously targeted. They assured us they would file a formal complaint with the National Parks Service about the bus incident.

They lingered a bit to chat with us, but out of the corner of my eye I spotted the driver leaving the restroom and heading back to the bus. I walked toward her and called out, "Excuse me." My husband turned in my direction to monitor the conversation. The couple departed to catch their next bus, but kept their eyes on me as if to bear witness to what was happening.

As I approached the bus driver I was thankful that this other family would file a formal complaint, and that they continued to watch my interaction. Many a cell phone camera, camcorder, or observant onlooker has been the single thing that made all the difference in public displays of racism toward minorities. We would have witnesses, who unfortunately, because they weren't black like us, would likely be believed as telling the truth, instead of presumed to just be acting in solidarity with us.

The bus driver and I approached each other. By that time all the negative feelings of the experience bubbled to the surface; it was visceral. I could feel my heart pounding in response to how angry I felt.

When we were close enough to speak without yelling, with the limited composure I could muster, I asked, "Help me to understand why my entire family had to get up for one senior citizen to board?" I raised my index finger to place emphasis on the number "1."

"I was just trying to ensure that the senior citizen could board with her walker," the driver cooed in the most patronizing tone, while trying to pat my arm as if to console me.

I jerked my arm away from her.

"It's illogical to vacate eight seats to accommodate one person," I countered.

She had no response.

"Your actions smack of discrimination," I continued.

At the mention of the word "discrimination," she sucked her teeth, turned on her heels, and started to walk away.

"I'm going to file a complaint," I yelled, as I tried to throw the words at her back like a dagger.

"Sure you will," she responded in a condescending tone.

Surviving as a minority in the United States is a bit of a math game, based on estimations and calculations. You estimate the risks and possible benefits of entering certain spaces before making a decision. I'd been reluctant to plan a trip for my family to Arizona or the Grand Canyon. There are countless anecdotes about racism in the National Park System, and Arizona has a history of racist legislation. For example, Senate Bill 1070, which at the time of its passing in 2010 was ostensibly touted as the strictest anti-illegal-immigration bill in the United States, but instead was really a legalized vehicle for racial profiling by police. Or Arizona House Bill 2281, outlawing the teaching of ethnic courses in schools, devised to attempt to shut down a school district's Mexican American stud-

ies program. Despite all of these harbingers, the allure of showing our children the Grand Canyon prevailed—estimations and
calculations.

In exchange for our bravery traveling to an environment where
we knew there was the strong possibility we would be unwelcome,
we were rewarded with spectacular views of the Grand Canyon, the
feeling of accomplishment from walking the Cedar Ridge Trail,
some magical time together as a family—and an all too familiar
dose of discrimination and condescension. The bus driver's "Sure
you will" continued to prick at me long after my confrontation
with her. Oh, the internal conflict and insidiousness of racism. It
enters the most joyful of experiences, frays the edges, and lingers
long after the offense is over.

That night, while eating at a Mexican restaurant in Tusayan, a
small town near the Grand Canyon, we talked to our kids about
racism. We used our last night in Arizona to explain to them what
happened to us, why it was wrong, and what they should do about
it, should they experience something similar in the future.

As we walked back to our hotel, the couple who said they were
going to file a complaint drove by. They stopped the car to say
hello and assure us that they filed the complaint. They expressed
their hope that the experience didn't completely spoil our trip.
We managed a half smile in response to their hopefulness, and
thanked them for their active empathy, for seeing us and being
allies.

By the time we filed our own complaint with the National Parks
Service and Paul Revere Transportation, LLC, the company that
manages the National Park Service's bus drivers, they were already
aware of our case from the other family's complaint. As a result, instead of having to enter a lengthy explanatory process about what
happened and convince others it was wrong, both the bus management company and the superintendent of the Grand Canyon were
poised to offer an apology, and evoked the word "discrimination"
without provocation.

It's been more than a year since our trip and the bus experience
is still the dark undertone behind our memories of our vacation.
But the small actions of three people amid a bus of choke-throated
others made a difference.

Contributors' Notes
Notable Travel Writing of 2019

# Contributors' Notes

**Sam Anderson** is a staff writer for the *New York Times Magazine,* where he has written portraits of writers (Haruki Murakami, Anne Carson, John McPhee) and athletes (Russell Westbrook, Bill Walton, Phil Jackson) and odd places all over the world, including Mount Rushmore and a Charles Dickens theme park. His work has won a National Magazine Award for Essays and Criticism, as well as the National Book Critics Circle's Nona Balakian Citation for Excellence in Reviewing. Anderson is the author of the book *Boom Town: The Fantastical Saga of Oklahoma City, Its Chaotic Founding, Its Apocalyptic Weather, Its Purloined Basketball Team, and the Dream of Becoming a World-Class Metropolis.*

**Fred Bahnson** teaches at Wake Forest University School of Divinity, where he directs the Food, Health, and Ecological Well-Being Program. He is the author of *Soil and Sacrament,* and his essays have appeared in *Harper's Magazine, The Sun, Orion,* and *The Best American Spiritual Writing.* He is a recipient of the W. K. Kellogg Food and Community Fellowship, the North Carolina Artist Fellowship, and the Terry Tempest Williams Fellowship for Land and Justice at the Mesa Refuge. He lives in North Carolina with his wife and three sons.

**Molly McCully Brown** is the author of the poetry collection *The Virginia State Colony for Epileptics and Feebleminded* (2017), which won the 2016 Lexi Rudnitsky First Book Prize and was named a *New York Times* Critics' Top Book of 2017, and the essay collection *Places I've Taken My Body.* (2020). With Susannah Nevison, she is also the coauthor of the poetry collection *In the Field Between Us* (2020). Her poems and essays have appeared in the *Paris Review, Tin House,* the *New York Times, Virginia Quarterly Review,* and elsewhere. She lives in Gambier, Ohio, and teaches at Kenyon College, where she is the Kenyon Review Fellow in Poetry.

**Jackie Bryant** is a New York–born, San Diego–based writer who covers food, cannabis, travel, cocktails, wine, arts and culture (more widely known as all the fun stuff in life). She has written for *Afar, New York,* the *San Diego Union-Tribune, Eater, Harper's Bazaar,* and many more. She is at work on a book about cannabis culture. Her work can be found at jackiebryant writing.com.

**Ken Budd**'s work has appeared in the *Washington Post, National Geographic Traveler,* NationalGeographic.com, *Smithsonian,* the *New York Times, AARP The Magazine,* Departures.com, *CityLab,* and many more. He is the author of the award-winning memoir *The Voluntourist* and the host of 650,000 Hours, a podcast and digital series on travel, giving back, and maximizing your 650,000 hours of life. Ken also writes a monthly newsletter: you can sign up at 650000Hours.com.

**Kyle Chayka** is the author of *The Longing for Less: Living with Minimalism,* and a freelance contributor to publications including the *New York Times Magazine,* the *New Republic,* and *Vox.*

A native of Iran, **Mojgan Ghazirad** graduated from Tehran University of Medical Sciences with a medical degree. She studied pediatrics at Inova Children's Hospital and received her neonatal medicine specialty from George Washington University. She currently works as an assistant professor of pediatrics at George Washington University NICU in Washington, DC. She has published three collections of short stories in Farsi: *A Lover in White Jacket* (2012) in Iran, *Turquoise Dream* (2014) in Germany, and *In the Solitude of Suitcases* (2016) in the UK. Her English essays have appeared in *Michigan Quarterly Review,* the *Idaho Review, Longreads,* and *The Common,* among others. She holds an MFA in creative writing from Southern New Hampshire University. Her memoir, *The House on Sun Street,* depicts her memories of growing up in Tehran during the Islamic Revolution in 1979 and eight years of war between Iran and Iraq after the Revolution. She lives with her family in Great Falls, Virginia.

**Emmanuel Iduma** is the author of *A Stranger's Pose,* a book of travel stories, which was long-listed for the 2019 Ondaatje Prize, and *The Sound of Things to Come,* a novel. His stories and essays have been published widely, including in *The Millions, LitHub, Aperture, British Journal of Photography, Off Assignment, Art in America, Guernica,* and the *New York Review of Books.* He was awarded an arts writing grant from the Creative Capital/Andy Warhol Foundation, for his essays on Nigerian artists, and the AICA-USA inaugural Irving Sandler Award for New Voices in Art Criticism. He teaches at the School of Visual Arts, New York, and divides his time between Lagos and New York.

**Lacy M. Johnson** is a Houston-based professor, curator, and activist, and author of the essay collection *The Reckonings*, the memoir *The Other Side*—both National Book Critics Circle Award finalists—and the memoir *Trespasses*. Her writing has appeared in *The New Yorker*, the *New York Times*, the *Los Angeles Times*, the *Paris Review*, *Virginia Quarterly Review*, *Tin House*, *Guernica*, and elsewhere. She teaches creative nonfiction at Rice University and is the founding director of the Houston Flood Museum.

**Chloé Cooper Jones** is a philosophy professor, writer, and journalist. Her first book, *Easy Beauty*, will be published in spring 2021. She lives in Brooklyn, New York.

**Heidi Julavits** is the author of four critically acclaimed novels (*The Vanishers*, *The Uses of Enchantment*, *The Effect of Living Backwards*, and *The Mineral Palace*) and a memoir, *The Folded Clock: A Diary*, as well as coeditor, with Sheila Heti and Leanne Shapton, of the *New York Times* bestseller *Women in Clothes*. Her fiction has appeared in *Harper's Magazine*, *McSweeney's*, and *The Best American Short Stories*, among other places. She's a founding editor of *The Believer* magazine and the recipient of a Guggenheim Fellowship. She lives in Manhattan, where she teaches at Columbia University. She was born and raised in Portland, Maine.

**James Lasdun** has written books of fiction, nonfiction, and poetry, as well as two screenplays, including *Sunday*, which won Best Feature and Best Screenplay awards at the Sundance Film Festival. His short story "The Siege" was adapted by Bernardo Bertolucci for his film *Besieged*. His first novel, *The Horned Man*, was a *New York Times* Notable Book. His second, *Seven Lies*, was long-listed for the Man Booker Prize. His latest, *Afternoon of a Faun*, was described in the Guardian as "an instant masterpiece that brings the taut psychological precision of a Chekhov story to a hypermodern, post-#MeToo setting." His essays have appeared in *The New Yorker*, *Harper's Magazine*, *Granta*, and the *London Review of Books*.

**Yiyun Li** is the author of four novels, two collections of stories, and a memoir, including her most recent novel, *Must I Go*. She has won numerous awards, including a MacArthur Fellow, a PEN/Hemingway Award, a PEN/Jean Stein Award, and many others. Her work has appeared in *The New*

*Yorker, A Public Space, The Best American Short Stories, The Best American Essays, The O. Henry Prize Stories,* and other places. She teaches at Princeton University.

**Jeff MacGregor** is the writer-at-large for *Smithsonian.* He has written often for the *New York Times, Sports Illustrated, Esquire, ESPN,* and many others. He is the author of the critically acclaimed book *Sunday Money.* This is his second appearance in *The Best American Travel Writing.*

**Ben Mauk** is a journalist and writer. His first book, an account of a journey among nomads, hunter-gatherers, refugees, and other groups living in the shadow of the state, is forthcoming. He was born in Maryland and lives in Berlin.

**Courtney Desiree Morris** is a photographer and a performance and conceptual artist. She is currently an assistant professor of gender and women's studies at the University of California, Berkeley. Her writing has been published in *Stranger's Guide; Feminisms in Motion: Voices for Justice, Liberation, and Transformation;* and *Asterix.* She has shown her photography at the Ashara Ekundayo Gallery, the National Gallery of Jamaica, and the Photographic Center Northwest. For more about her work visit www.courtneydesireemorris.com.

**Alejandra Oliva** is an essayist, embroiderer, and translator. She has a master's degree in theological studies from Harvard Divinity School. She is an Aspen Words Emerging Writers Fellow for 2019, and her essay "Walking into the River" was nominated for a 2020 Pushcart Award. She has published writing in *Electric Lit, Human x Nature, Bookforum,* and more.

**Stephanie Pearson** is a contributing editor to *Outside.* Her stories have appeared in *National Geographic Traveler, Wired,* the *New York Times Magazine, Bicycling,* and other publications. She splits her time between the lakes of northern Minnesota and the high desert of the Southwest.

**Ashley Powers** has written for *The New Yorker,* the *New York Times,* and the *California Sunday Magazine.* Previously, she was a national correspondent for the *Los Angeles Times.* She is a co-director of Princeton University's Summer Journalism Program, an annual journalism and college admissions initiative for low-income high school students. She lives in Brooklyn.

**Emily Raboteau** is a professor of creative writing at the City College of New York, in Harlem. Her books are *The Professor's Daughter* and *Searching for Zion: The Quest for Home in the African Diaspora,* winner of a 2014 American Book Award. Her shorter works have appeared in *The Best American Short Stories, The Best American Mystery Stories, The Best American Nonrequired Reading, Best African American Fiction, Best African American Essays,* and elsewhere. She was born when $CO_2$ levels were at 330.06 parts per million in the atmosphere. Since the publication of "Climate Signs," when atmospheric $CO_2$ levels were almost 80 ppm higher, she has been writing exclusively about the climate crisis.

Born in California in 1962, **Paul Salopek** was raised in central Mexico. As a writer and journalist, he has traveled to more than 50 countries and earned most of America's top print media awards, including Pulitzers for his reporting on human genetics and the civil war in Congo. In his past lives, Paul worked as a commercial fisherman in the Atlantic and Pacific Oceans, mined gold in Australia, and managed a ranch in Mexico.

**Barrett Swanson** was the 2016–2017 Halls Emerging Artist Fellow at the Wisconsin Institute for Creative Writing, and he was the recipient of a 2015 Pushcart Prize. His short fiction and essays have appeared in many places, including *Harper's Magazine, The New Yorker,* the *Paris Review,* the *New York Times Magazine, The Believer, American Short Fiction, The Atavist Magazine,* and *The Best American Travel Writing 2018.* His essay collection, *Lost in Summerland,* will be published in May 2021.

**Shanna B. Tiayon** is a sociologist with a specialization in social psychology and the owner of Wellbeing Works, LLC. She writes, speaks, and conducts trainings on topics of well-being. Her writing focuses on well-being and the ways in which we may infringe upon the well-being of others. To maintain her personal well-being she homesteads with her family in the greater DC Metro area.

# Notable Travel Writing of 2019

SELECTED BY JASON WILSON

DAVID FARLEY
    The Lost Cheeses of Georgia. *Saveur,* March 27.
IAN FRAZIER
    Never Going to Italy. *The New Yorker,* March 11.
ALEXANDRA FULLER
    Globe-Trotter's Lament. *Departures,* September.

PETER HESSLER
    My House in Cairo. *The New Yorker,* May 7.

PICO IYER
    In the Realm of the Gods. *T: The New York Times Style Magazine,* May 19.

BROOKE JARVIS
    American Sphinx. *The New Yorker,* September 23.
LESLIE JAMISON
    Baggage Claims. *Harper's Magazine,* September.

ADAM KARLIN
    Welcome to the Land. *The Statesider,* October 17.
ALICIA KENNEDY
    The Year in Martinis. *Hazlitt,* December 2.
PAUL KVINTA
    In the Land of Vanishing Giants. *Outside,* December.

NINA LI COOMES
    Notes on Citizenship. *Longreads,* April 17.
BRITTA LOKTING
    Hitting the Road. *Curbed,* March 6.

MEG HOUSTON MAKER
    Barefoot in the Douro. *Terroir Review,* February 22.
LIGAYA MISHAN
    A Vanishing Feast. *T: The New York Times Style Magazine,* May 19.
JON MOOALLEM
    The Senseless Logic of the Wild. *New York Times Magazine,* March 24.
MICHAEL J. MOONEY
    On the Magic of a Hotel Bar. *Texas Highways,* September.
JASON MOTLAGH
    Among Mountains and Martyrs, *Outside,* January/February.
MICHAEL MOUNT
    My Year on a Shrinking Island. *Longreads,* October 25.
SARAH MOSS
    Happy Where the Grass Was Green. *Travel + Leisure,* December.